The Plain Rhetoric

Second Edition

The Plain Rhetoric

Second Edition

S. LEONARD RUBINSTEIN

ROBERT G. WEAVER

The Pennsylvania State University

ALLYN AND BACON, INC.
BOSTON

FOREWORD TO
A NEW EDITION

Writing is the act of understanding. It is the discovery of form. It is a rescue from chaos. It is a necessary act, full of profit and danger.

The new edition of *The Plain Rhetoric* places special emphasis on the relation of form to chaos. Man fears chaos, with reason. Man is the abstractor of systems, the maker of forms. But chaos is, in truth, the source of detail and energy. A man armed with proper intention can face chaos boldly and make it yield profit. Proper intention for the writer means respect for chaos, respect for form, respect for himself.

The Plain Rhetoric, entering a new edition, asks again and anew that the danger in the act of writing be recognized and converted to profit. Each writer's material begins in chaos. Each writer must make form. Each writer needs to know established forms to create the unique form his material demands. Material badly presented remains chaos. A writer must not stop work until rhetoric has realized substance, until rhetoric and substance are one.

PREFACE

All writing shares a basic nature. That basic nature is capable of many variations. A student who does not recognize the basic nature tends to think that the many variations are independent, unrelated, and perhaps contradictory elements. He is confused. Emphasis in *The Plain Rhetoric* is on that basic nature.

A composition unites logic of structure with integrity of writer. From logic of structure comes clarity of thought. From integrity of writer comes freshness of language.

The logic of structure stresses the relationship of parts to the whole. Each part must be identified and its contribution to the whole established. Whether one is explaining a process or judging a situation, whether discussing gears or evidence, the relationship of the part to the whole determines validity.

Stale and dull writing results from language that is approximate rather than exact. Phrases are used because they are immediately accessible; they are accessible because they are familiar; they are familiar because they have been used and used and used. The reader is in an echo chamber. The writer's thought is distorted by language exact perhaps to someone else's original purpose but only approximate to his own. A writer must recognize that his own vision is unique, and his language must be faithful to that uniqueness. His honesty to his own perception is integrity. From fidelity to his perception come precision—and freshness.

A good composition is individual and valid. The writer should be self-absorbed, rather than self-conscious. He should discover form in the material, rather than impose form on the material. He should invent appropriate phrases, rather than apply borrowed phrases.

The intent of *The Plain Rhetoric* is to establish what makes writing clear, responsible, and graceful. The three qualities are perhaps one. *The Plain Rhetoric* aspires to be practical.

CONTENTS

The Whole Composition

The Paragraph

The Sentence

The Word

Punctuation: Outline of Uses

Grammar

Manuscript Mechanics

Spelling

Glossary of Errors

Appendix

The Plain Rhetoric

Second Edition

THE WHOLE COMPOSITION

1 / Writing: Chaos, Experience, Form

1a / Chaos

Writers understand form and chaos; that is, the relation of fixed form to the flux of chaos. To write, we must recognize chaos. We must nourish ourselves on chaos. It is on chaos that form burgeons, and it is form that makes chaos profitable. We must gain the utility of form without losing the vitality of chaos.

A writer must know that language is not an oracle; to regard language as a divine well of truth is madness. We search among words for absolute understanding; in truth, there is nothing among words except what we have put there. That is the limitation of language. We must make language more able, even as language makes us more able.

Language enables us to name what we see. But every thing is at least more than its name describes, and may be other than its name describes. Our language sees the world as nouns and verbs—

as things and deeds—as actors and actions. But in reality a thing may be an act. All things may be states of activity.

A table is, like all other things, from the instant of its completion, already in a progressive state of decay. That is evident. It is also true, if not evident, that what we call a table is a collection of molecules in constant and rapid motion. We must define situations, but we must not be trapped by static definitions. The world is in flux; we must fix instants of that flux; we must not, however, mistake these fixed instants for the constant flux.

A noun is a lie if all phenomena change. If there are no *things* in the universe, only constantly changing states, then a noun, which freezes an instant in the change and gives it a name, is an anachronism the next instant.

We must not make the universe resemble our language; we must make our language resemble the universe. Nouns are necessary, but they are not necessarily right. We must be clear without being certain. We must not confuse the product with the process. We must not place our faith in anything terminal; we must be continuing.

Writing enables judgments. The writer makes judgments— and makes judgments possible. Judgments must be based upon evidence. The writer must provide evidence: the particulars of knowledge and experience. A writer must continually alter his judgment to accommodate the continuing arrival of evidence. He must continually enable readers to judge his judgments. Writing is a process which must not stop.

1b/   Experience

We do not understand another man's condition unless we share that condition. We must undergo his experience. Explanation attempts to convert what experience suggests into what can be stated. The full meaning, however, is the experience itself. All writers know that they must provide not only explanation of experience, but experience as explanation.

All writers know they must instruct both the intellect and the flesh. All writers know that information must obey *a schedule of arrival*. If any information arrives too soon, conceptually or emotionally, it has not generated full force; too late, it has lost full force.

All good writers know drama: juxtaposition, tension of opposites, shifts of rhythm, the inexorable progress toward climax, the use of silence.

The miracle of experience is that, however unbelievable it may be, it is undeniable. Writing convinces when the reader participates. Mass slaughter is one thing; a naked mother tickling a naked baby in her arms to keep the child from sensing what the machine-gunner is about to do is another.

Experience is responses to stimuli. All men respond to stimuli. The writer, however, goes on: having responded, he examines his responses; having examined, he identifies the stimuli; having identified, he deploys the stimuli; having deployed, he causes the reader to respond.

A writer respects silence. He uses silence. He causes responses. He does not obscure the causes by reporting his own reponses. Who knows what to say knows what not to say.

1c/ Form

Ideas of form are many. But ideas are a view of reality, not reality itself. Reality is always more complex than any idea. Ideas enable us to recognize aspects of reality. We speak of forms of discourse: *narration, description, exposition, argument.* We speak of forms of exposition: *definition, analysis, interpretation, evaluation.* The form, however, of any given piece of writing is a complex of forms. A piece of writing is itself, not a term.

Categorical forms are helpful: they suggest general natures which will become unique identities in response to the needs of specific situations. The student must be given a reservoir of forms. He will create new forms from old forms.

Epilogue

Writing requires knowledge. Of what? Grammar? Punctuation? Rhetoric? These are essential to but not sufficient for an essay.

Desire to write is needed.

Proper intention is needed.

Who really confesses to himself why he is writing? Does he write to please the teacher? To impress somebody? To hide not understanding? To confuse somebody? To hide being confused? To deceive somebody?

These are often real intentions. They produce imitation essays.

What are proper intentions? To understand something? To explore something? To clarify something? To share something? To be true in reporting and discovering what and how to see? To gather and join together?

Can an essay exist without these intentions? Can these intentions be faked? Can any essay reward the writer without these intentions?

The following essays, written impromptu on the last day of a writing course, addressed these problems:

I Have Come to Learn*

I have come to learn that I cannot write when I don't know who the audience is. But I only stop to worry about the audience when I am unsure of myself and/or the material. The three are never separable.

When I write a personal letter, there is no problem. I know who the audience is; the material and my relationship to both are clear cut. I find myself writing as though I were talking to the person. And I feel the subject is something of interest to both of us. Grade school letter writing exercises left me cold because my role, the material, and the audience were vague and/or artificial. These same feelings carried over to most classroom writing assignments.

I entered this course in an apprehensive state. I was unsure of myself, mistrustful of the course, and afraid I'd find out I "couldn't write," for writing was already an excruciating experience for me. I have not had time to assimilate all I've learned in the past ten weeks, but I feel I have so much raw material now that given time, a powerful assimilation will result.

I have learned to begin with myself—to look inward and get to know me. Before I can write I must get hold of my whirling thought processes and channel them into clear-cut purposes. Intent to clarify has given new meaning to writing, for I had never associated them in one phrase and then applied that to writing. But with that, I have learned that a large part of clarifying entails sorting out the irrelevancies in my thought processes. For me a new intent has taken shape. I had been doing it unconsciously in personal letters, but now that it is known to me, I feel a compulsion to make it a conscious part of my future writing—that is, putting myself on the paper. I felt this so keenly with Sartre and Stein. They were animated and their ideas flowed and blended. They were there before me, talking spontaneously in a state of constant

* Reprinted by permission of the author.

process, therefore very much alive. I could see sparkling eyes reflecting a mind that was always one step ahead of itself. The animation prevented the essay from having the artificiality that paper and print usually have.

This animation doesn't come from the writer's ability to express himself in living words alone, but also from his enthusiasm about his material. Learning to never write without this was a big gain for me. This, in combination with muddled thinking, had been the downfall of my previous writing experiences.

Given clear thought processes, enthusiasm about material, both of which result in intent to clarify, audience becomes a minimal problem. It is only a problem when concern is put at a superficial level such as "How will they react to me?" "Will they like me?" The concern should be "Are my thinking, enthusiasm, and intention sufficient to get my material to them, or will I have to do more to reach them?" The concern should be extraverted, not intraverted.

Probably most important, though, that encompasses all of these, is knowing myself. I must constantly remind myself that I have no limitations beyond those which I place on myself, that I am constantly growing and changing. And I am what I make of myself out of the infinite possibilities afforded by growth and change.

SUSAN BOHANNON

Trying to Say Something
by Writing*

When trying to say something by writing, a writer finds himself faced with responsibilities peculiar to writing and ones which he must honestly confront before he can ever hope to say anything. If these responsibilities are not recognized before the writing begins, they inevitably are *discovered* by the very act of writing itself. The writer discovers that the *material* demands a great deal of knowledge; he discovers that before he can say anything he must thoroughly understand his *audience* and write to them; he finally, and most importantly, discovers who *he* is.

When this man, David McConkey, sometimes writer, sits down to write something, he does so with an audience in mind. Whether it is my father to whom I write a letter or a teacher and class to whom I write a paper, I know something about my audience. Throughout the process of writing, however, I constantly discover how little or how much I really know about them. Can they understand this reference to Plato? Have they read Plato? Will they object to my use of the word "goddamn"? If so, is it important that I offend them? If not, am I using it to befriend them—by drawing them into my personal world of foul language? Who am I, using this word?

The writer, without consciously recognizing it, is often faced with

* Reprinted by permission of the author.

the question of "Who am I?" because of his audience and because of
his material. When I sit down to write about conscientious objection or
Sartre's rhetoric, I don't know what I think about either. I do know
that my reaction to the term "conscientious objection" is one of trust:
"The individual should have a right to object to anything." But what
the hell does that mean? What do I really think about a man's objection
to traffic laws? Or another's rejection of conscription? What is conscription? I know that Sartre's writing was appealing and informative and
exciting, but why? The process of writing becomes a continual reaction
of the writer with his material, with what he knows about his audience,
with the result of showing himself what he is.

This problem of getting to know who you are by writing (which
I am not sure I fully understand, but which is being clarified somewhat
by this writing exercise) is indeed a complex one. It appears to me
that if one is truly to get out of writing all that the process of writing
offers he must be an existentialist. That is, he must be willing to admit
that he is responsible for every word he puts on the paper. If he does
not accept this theory his writing will be doomed to dishonesty. He will
be writing what he wants people to hear; he will never be able to engage
in the process of discovery—in allowing himself to react to both audience
and material and then discover what he honestly believes—and then
write that.

It seems to me also that the relationship of existentialism to writing
can be reversed. That is, by writing the individual discovers existentialism.
If, in fact, I begin to write with an audience in mind—with a subject in
mind—and then try to honestly examine my reactions to both audience
and subject and attempt to discover what I think and ultimately who
I am—I discover that this writing is such an awful responsibility; I discover despair.

Perhaps I have confused in my own mind honesty and existentialism;
perhaps, though they are identical. When writing I discover that the
concept of God is irrelevant; He is not here pounding out these words,
reacting to an audience, reacting to my material. I alone have to face
this blank piece of paper. I alone am responsible for the words that are
written here. And when I recognize that I am recognizing existentialism;
and when I recognize that, my writing will be honest.

DAVID MCCONKEY

2 / The College Theme

Every human being sees the world uniquely. No man should take
for granted that the way he sees the world is the way everyone sees

the world. If a man recognizes that his vision can enlarge everyone else's vision, he realizes that he has a contribution to make, and that the contribution lies in being honest to his own vision.

The first necessity, then, in writing is: respect yourself.

The rest of writing lies in making that vision responsible; in supporting every opinion with facts; in providing particulars to clarify the general; in citing concretes to justify the abstract. The writer separates his subject into parts, defines each part, establishes the relationship of each part to the whole. The writer recognizes not only his reaction, but what he is reacting to.

A man who respects himself and can say what he wants to say is more effective in his trade or profession, whatever his trade or profession. The writing of college essays intends to help a man learn how to say what he wants to say.

2a / What is a college theme?

A theme is a short essay, a writing exercise common to freshman English classes. Its purpose is to prepare the student for the arbitrary writing assignments of the world. A college theme often requires about five-hundred to one-thousand words. It is usually limited to one central idea that can be stated in a one-sentence summary. Sometimes the topic is assigned; frequently, the student chooses his own topic. The theme is written to meet a deadline, and it is evaluated by an instructor and awarded a grade. To succeed, the theme must say something worthwhile in well-developed paragraphs applying the accepted standards of English usage and mechanics.

2b / What are the characteristics of a good theme?

What you have to say when you write deserves to be made clear and graceful. The principles that serve grace and clarity are discussed individually in later chapters. These principles can be simplified into fourteen characteristics. A good theme must have:

1. A topic limited enough to allow a thorough investigation.
2. A specific aim. What do you want your theme to do for the reader? Can you state that aim in a sentence?

3. An idea which can be summarized in one sentence. What is the point your essay is written to make?
4. A controlling attitude to govern the tone of your writing. Will you treat the subject humorously, reverently, seriously, objectively?
5. Adherence to the principles of order; that is, an organization that seems reasonable and logical.
6. Discussion paragraphs that develop some aspect of the theme statement, and that have a topic sentence expressed or clearly implied.
7. Support of the topic sentence of each paragraph: details, enumerations, definitions, analogies, evidence, logical structures as needed to support your general statements.
8. Consistency in person, tense, voice, number, and tone.
9. Words that say precisely, not approximately, what you mean.
10. Clear sentences employing the accepted standards of punctuation and grammar.
11. A variety of sentence structures.
12. A title which suggests or states the point the essay was written to make.
13. Capital letters, italics, syllabication, hyphens, and other manuscript mechanics as needed.
14. Neat manuscript in prescribed format.

Keep this checklist before you as you prepare your rough draft. Refer to it again as you proofread your manuscript.

3 / Choosing and Limiting Your Topic

Although an instructor may sometimes give his students free choice, usually he makes specific writing assignments. He may make them because he has found that students given a free choice are paralyzed by a surfeit of alternatives. Perhaps he may want to check the students' ability to handle arbitrary assignments, or he may want the writing to be based on reading. These selections may be simple exercises.

More likely, the instructor's assignment will be more challenging. It may call for a personality profile, a summary, a description of a process or a device, a definition, a narrative sketch, or an evaluation by fixed standards.

3a/ Where do you get information?

If your instructor gives you a free choice of topics, you will find three sources of information. They are personal experience, imagination, and research.

□ PERSONAL EXPERIENCE. You are a unique person. Things have happened to you that have not happened to anybody else, at least not in the same way. Because of this unique experience, you see the world in a special way. As John Ciardi has said, "Anything significantly looked at *is* significant." If you can relate your world honestly to a reader, he will be interested.

□ IMAGINATION. Some kinds of writing can be enriched by the writer's imagination. Some writers have written convincingly about dying. Some of the best war stories were written by people who have never been in battle. How many science-fiction writers have traveled to distant planets? Although imagination may not provide you with facts, it may give you some insight into your subject; it may lead you to understanding and may suggest ways to communicate your view of reality.

□ RESEARCH. Getting information from areas outside your memory and your imagination is research. If you ask somebody what time it is, this would hardly be called research; but if you read a book, consult an encyclopedia, interview a person, observe a situation for the purpose of writing a theme—this is research. It is probably the most extensive, though not necessarily the best, source available to you.

3b/ Possible topics

Your experiences and your interests fall into general categories. Since it is unlikely that you will find an adequately limited topic immediately, look over some general categories. Such an examination will remind you of buried interests and forgotten incidents. After you have found a general area of interest, narrow it down. The list on pages 14–15 should help you get started.

3c/   How do you limit a topic?

The beginning writer often has trouble realizing the importance of limiting a topic. He works through a list of general topics until he finds an item of interest—"Family Camping." He feels that he has a topic about which he can write easily. He sits down to prepare his rough draft, and he finds that all he is able to say are a few generalizations about how much fun camping is, how healthful it is, and how inexpensive it is. He scratches his head and stares at the wall. He finally decides that he has picked too narrow a topic. He tries to remedy the situation by enlarging his topic to something like "Summer Vacations." Now he feels sure that he can get at least 500 words by writing a paragraph or two about camping, a paragraph or two about seashore resorts, and a paragraph or two about mountain lodges.

He is doing precisely what he should *not* be doing. His feeling that he had nothing worth saying about family camping came not because the subject was too limited but because the subject was too broad. First, he should have broken the general subject down into categories such as the following: Campsites, Camping Equipment, Foods for Camping, Best Months for Camping, Unusual Camping Experiences, Interesting Campers I Have Met. The list could be extended indefinitely. A writer who is stymied by a general topic, "Family Camping," should be able to write fluently on the topic entitled "The Night the Tent Blew Down." For the general topic, he has nothing but vague impressions, hazy memories. For the specific topic, his memory will furnish sights, sounds, and smells; details, causes, and effects; enumerations that will enable him to make the experience live for his reader—all because he has properly limited his topic. If you have trouble limiting a theme topic, here are a few suggestions:

1. Can this topic be further limited by number? For example, you have limited your camping topic to "Camp Sites." But

you can not write adequately about thousands of camp sites. You settle for a working title—"Three Good Camp Sites: a Comparison." You have limited your topic by number.

2. Can you limit your topic according to kind? If you want to discuss tents, what kind: umbrella tents? pop-up tents? pup tents? wall tents? mountain tents?

3. Can you limit your topic according to part or aspect? One aspect of camping is campfire cooking. You may know something about wrapping whole meals in aluminum foil and burying the package in hot coals while you go for a swim. Ask yourself the question, "What aspect or part of the topic do I understand best?"

4. Can your topic be limited by time? A theme entitled "Winter Camping" would be a limitation by time on the general subject. Even "Winter Camping," though somewhat limited, may still be too broad a topic. "Christmas Eve in a Sleeping Bag" might suggest a personal experience that is drastically limited in time.

5. Can your topic be limited according to some human element? A subject, "Interesting People I Have Met on Camping Trips," already limited to a human element, may still be too broad. Some further limitation, such as "Mike McGill, the Camper's Friend," lets you write about a man who helps other campers.

6. Can your topic be limited by place? "Seashore Camping," a limitation by place, can be further limited to "Camping at Cape Hatteras."

7. Can your topic be limited by motive or cause? "For Better Health—Go Camping." "What Causes the Camping Craze?"

Please remember that, within reason, the more you limit your topic the more you will be forced to develop your theme with specific detail and the more likely you will be to succeed. A theme entitled "The Disadvantages of the Umbrella Tent in Early Fall Camping at Cape Hatteras" is a severely limited topic. It is limited according to place, according to time, according to kind, according to part or aspect. There is no room here for vague generalizations constantly repeated.

3d / Seeing, stating, and solving a problem

If you have nothing to say, don't write. Because if you write when you have nothing to say, you're going to fail anyway. Save your energy.

The first thing, therefore, is to have something to say. The second thing is to have a method by which to say it. The opposite of method is panic.

Some papers submit a single paragraph as an essay. Some papers simply make a summary of class discussion. Some make vague general claims, unclarified by particulars, unsupported by evidence. Many make no effort at all to assemble statements and incidents into a pattern of meaning. Since the reader is given no opportunity to examine evidence, he can neither agree nor disagree with the writer. Such essays profit no one.

Writing an essay should be a process of discovery for the writer. It makes an examination and records the results of that examination. Both writer and reader should learn from the examination.

An assumption that will enable you to write is:

"The solution to a problem is the full statement of the problem."

Problems are usually the result of insufficient knowledge. The more fully a problem is recognized, the more obvious the solution becomes. A problem is a matter of choosing among many alternatives. Increase of knowledge narrows the choice of alternatives. When alternatives are narrowed to one, it is no longer an alternative; it is the solution. Did you have a problem of which college to attend? How did you solve it? Examining how you solved a problem in real life will suggest how to solve the problem in writing a theme.

At first, a question is only a startled bleat:

1. Which college should I attend?

    If there are 3,000 colleges in the country, you now have 3,000 alternatives. But your problem is only partially stated.

2. Which college should I, having $2,500 a year available, attend?

This increased statement of the problem eliminates costlier colleges, and reduces the number of alternatives to perhaps 1,700. But your problem is only partially stated.

3. Which college should I, having $2,500 a year available and wanting a co-ed campus, attend?

Now the number of alternatives may be reduced to 900.

4. Which college should I, having $2,500 a year available, wanting a co-ed campus, needing to come home weekends, attend?

Now only the colleges within 200 miles of home are eligible, and alternatives reduce to 30.

5. Which college should I, having $2,500 a year available, wanting a co-ed campus, needing to come home weekends, eager to get a substantial education in electrical engineering, attend?

Now alternatives reduce to three.

When your problem becomes fully stated, alternatives reduce to one: the solution.

A function of an essay is to recognize the problem; separate it into its crucial questions; discover, organize, and present the information to which the questions direct you. This procedure will steadily reduce alternatives.

The first question, then, is "What problem will my essay state?" A law of inversion obtains. The larger the problem, the less fully an essay can state it.

The problem must be large enough to be meaningful, and small enough to be stated. The fuller the statement, the greater the profit.

3x/ Exercises

1. From the following list, select five general topics. From each of these draw five specific topics. Can a topic be too limited? Explain your answer.

Accidents
Advertising
Agriculture
Ambitions
Ambulances
Anesthetics
Animals
Architecture
Armed Forces
Art
Astronomy
Auctioneers
Authors
Automation
Automobiles
Aviation
Bands
Banking
Baton twirling
Baseball
Beliefs
Beverages
Bibles
Bicycles
Birds
Blind
Books
Bosses
Boy Scouts
Bridge
Buildings
Burglars
Business
Caddies
Camping
Candy
Celebration
Celebrities
Cemeteries
Child care
Childhood

Children
Choir
Christmas
Church
Circus
Classified ads
Clocks
Clothes
Clubs
Coffee
Coins
College
Communications
Concerts
Conservation
Contests
Conventions
Corporations
Cotton
Courts
Crafts
Creativity
Credit
Crime
Crops
Customs
Dancing
Dates
Dogs
Do-it-yourself
Dreams
Driving
Eating
Education
Electricity
Employment
Engineers
Evangelists
Fairs
Families
Farming

Fathers
Feet
Fine art
Fireplaces
Fire prevention
Fishing
Flowers
Folk songs
Folklore
Food
Football
Forest fires
Fraternities
Freaks
Fruit
Funerals
Games
Ghost towns
Girl Scouts
Girls
Gossip
Grades
Guns
Health
Hobbies
Hoboes
Hotels
Human relations
Hunting
Industry
Juvenile delinquency
Left-handedness
Libraries
Marriage
Medicine
Men
Milk
Morals
Music
Movies
Newsboys

Nicknames	Safety	Travel
Occupations	Sailing	Truck drivers
Opportunity	Salesmen	Uniforms
Outdoor life	Schools	Universities
Painting	Science	Vacations
Parties	Sleep	War
Pets	Smoking	Water
Picnics	Sports	Weather
Premonitions	Teachers	Weddings
Proverbs	Teenagers	Window shopping
Radio	Telephones	Women
Railroads	Television	Wonder drugs
Rats	Tombstone	Worry
Restaurants	Traffic	Zoos

This list can be enlarged at almost any point in the alphabet. For additional ideas, see the Subject File or the Vertical File Subject Catalog in your college library.

2. Examine the following problem: An ocean liner, enroute from Singapore to San Francisco, is totally destroyed by an explosion.

Only eleven people have managed to reach a lifeboat thrown clear in the explosion. The boat is but a temporary escape, for it too has been seriously damaged and is leaking badly. In spite of feverish bailing and extensive efforts to repair the craft, it is obvious that in a matter of hours it will crack up. Aboard the boat is a small, inflatable rubber raft, so small that it will take but four persons. It represents the only chance for escape.

Which four of the eleven passengers would you select for salvation? Explain fully why you would give each of these four a chance at life.

A listing of passengers in the lifeboat, together with pertinent facts about each, follows:

John Phillips—aged 18. Only child of missionaries who have been working in Africa for a number of years. Extraordinarily fine mind. Person of high integrity. Very personable. Is on the way to the U.S. to accept a scholarship at M.I.T.

William Kent, Commander, USMM—aged 52. Navigator of ship. Competent at job. No outstanding qualities otherwise. Wife and four children.

John Ober (Doctor)—aged 61. Long, selfless career in medicine, specializing in treatment of cancer. Is on the verge of arriving at a definitive explanation and cure of that dread disease.

George Ober—aged 11. Grandson of Doctor Ober.

Howard Lacey—aged 41. Graduate of Taft, Princeton, Harvard Law. Brilliant career. Now on leave of absence from State Department and assigned to U.N. Security Council staff. Is returning from Japan with important information on Far-Eastern relations.

Igor Krales—aged 33. Son of immigrant parents. One of the most brilliant violinists of our day. Is returning from an entertainment tour of armed forces.

Arthur Cole—aged 29. Boilerman aboard the ship. Little or no schooling. Only support of mother, a chronic invalid. Lost three brothers in previous war.

Emil Muelk—aged 72. Born in Russia, but moved to Germany while very young. After outstanding achievements at various schools and universities, entered field of nuclear physics. Left Germany in 1933. Went to England, thence to U.S. Employed at Oak Ridge following work on Manhattan Project. He is considered by leading scientists as one of the two or three really great experts on atomic energy. Recently has been working on counter-radiation project, a means of dissipating and minimizing the effects of atomic explosions.

Warner Lamb—aged 43. Vice-president of American National Bank. Extensive civic work in his hometown, New Rochelle, New York. Community Chest, Council of Churches, Boys Clubs, Civil Defense, Better Government League, etc.

Betty Lamb—aged 34. Warner Lamb's wife. She is pregnant.

Harold Arnold—aged 49. Unknown to his fellow passengers, is a Captain, U.S.N., attached to Central Intelligence Agency. Returning from what has apparently been a casual vacation. Actually has uncovered vitally important information about Russia's aims in the Far East.

4/ Getting and Controlling Ideas

4a/ What do you want your essay to do for the reader?

What is the *specific aim* of your essay? What do you want to do for the reader? You know what you are going to say, but *why* are you going to say it? Do you want your reader to vote for a certain political party? Do you want him to learn how to operate a specific machine? Do you want him to know the situation of a factory worker?

You've got a point to make—*why* should you make it? *Why* should your reader know this particular point? The answers to these questions establish your specific aim, your purpose for writing the essay.

4b/ What point is your essay written to make?

If you want your reader to understand the situation of a factory worker, that's why you write the essay. But now *what* is the point that the reader should know? Is it that a factory worker should use leisure time for thinking and creating to develop a self-respect threatened by a repetitive, mechanical job? Is that the point that the rest of the essay will make clear and valid? Then that point is the *thesis statement.*

The profit of your essay derives from that statement. You get it in answer to a question:

> "What, in a single sentence, is the point your essay is written to make?"

Every word, every sentence, every paragraph in your essay can be tested by your answer. You ask of each part, "What contribution does it make to the point?" If it makes none, throw the part out. It doesn't belong.

Your essay is an explanation of the sentence which states your theme. The essay demonstrates, dramatizes, discusses the theme.

The essay defines and illustrates every significant word of that sentence. The essay develops the logic of that sentence. Every word in the essay intends to make that single sentence understood. Theoretically, once the examples, the particulars, the illustrations have made that sentence understood, the reader can discard them. They disappear when they have served their purpose: to make the reader understand the point. Your thesis sentence should be a statement of the point your essay will amplify. Your thesis sentence should not be an announcement of your general intention.

Not this:
1. Tell about Plato's background, where he lived and who he was.

But this:
1. Plato, a Greek who lived about 400 B.C., developed a philosophy which has helped to form the nature of the western world.
    Now: What is that philosophy? What is the nature of the western world? What is the relationship between the two? The essay amplifies the sentence.

In short, your point should be wrapped up in a single sentence that the reader can take away as his profit. All else in the essay should be demonstration, dramatization, discussion of that point.

Your essay may not have the explicit statement present. But if the statement is not present, it must be so strongly implied that the reader can formulate it.

4c/   What is your attitude toward your material?

Tone conveys the author's attitude toward his material. It must be consistent. If a writer now parodies, now respects the same material, the essay cracks and shatters. No one trusts a mirror which shifts at random from reflection to distortion. Such a writer has lost personal clarity and reader confidence. Wreckage is left. Tone must unify and sustain an essay.

Tone is closely related to *Appropriateness*, discussed on page 101. Tone helps to bring into harmony the writer's attitude toward the subject, his personality, and his attitude toward the audience he has chosen. He must use language consistent with all three: his subject, his personality, his audience.

What do you think about your material? Do you think it's funny? Do you think it's serious? Do you think it's both? Which aspect is more important? What do you want your reader to think about the material?

What is your attitude—ironic, cynical, dispassionate, reserved, romantic, humorous, scientific, Olympian?

Recognize your attitude before you write. Be honest to it. Don't let cleverness destroy that honesty.

Honesty to that attitude will determine your choice of incident, of detail, of language. Tone unifies an essay.

4d/ Where do you get your raw material?

We have talked about *specific aim, thesis statement,* and *tone,* as if these were a sequence. Now we are going to talk about piling up ideas. We recognize, of course, that these elements are in reality so involved with each other that they are simultaneous. But we can talk about them only one at a time. When you write, you have to work back and forth among them. There is no other way.

You have a topic. You've limited your topic. Now what is there to say about the topic?

Invite ideas. But don't judge them; not yet. Go crazy; write down anything the topic suggests to you: associations, inventions, memories, speculations, observations, puns; *anything.* Whatever occurs, write it down. Get it all out of your system. Because out of that sludge you can pick the solid pieces.

Now you can exercise judgment. Now you can select. Before you can accept or reject material, you must have the indiscriminate heap, the raw ideas. What you reject helps you to form your essay as much as what you accept does. Nothing is wasted. The larger your pile, the clearer and richer you can make your final essay.

Don't forget what enables you to select: your thesis statement, against which you test every item in your heap. Of course, you may not get your thesis statement until you've examined the heap.

4e/ How do you refine your raw material?

The pile of rough ideas is before you. Your thesis statement is before you. Now what ideas in that list converge on the thesis statement? Write them down. What ideas are irrelevant to the thesis statement? Throw them out. Good. You have a thesis statement, and ideas to support that thesis statement. What you don't yet have is order. Thesis statement plus supporting ideas plus order ought to accomplish the specific aim. We will, therefore, discuss order in the next chapter.

4x/ Exercises

1. What does the word *circus* suggest to you? Write it all down.

2. What point would you want to make about a circus? Write it down.

3. What would you like your reader to know, feel, or do about a circus? Write it down.

4. What attitude toward a circus would your essay establish? Write it down.

5. Which of the previous questions deals with *specific aim?* Which with the *thesis statement?* Which with the *tone?*

6. How do *specific aim, thesis statement,* and *tone* affect each other in an essay?

5/ Putting Your Ideas into Acceptable Order

5a/ Principles of order

Thought must be ordered. Different orders can be described. They are here isolated as if they were separate from each other. But in use they are never separate; they exist always in some combination peculiar to the need of the essay. The writer's intention determines the combination. If what you write makes sense, you are using a pattern of order; there is no alternative. The descriptions below are only to help you do better what you have always done anyway.

□ TIME.   The chronological order tells what happened next. It keeps answering the question, "And then what happened?" It is an order easy to follow. If used well, it evokes and satisfies curiosity. But it is an order that must be correlated with some other order, else there is no profit. Else the reader will say, "So what?"

A simple time sequence would be: "Betty and Oliver met. They became engaged. They were married and had two children. They argued. They were divorced. Betty kept the children."

So what? What are we supposed to learn from that? Are we supposed to recognize that one thing is the cause of another? That one is the result of another? That incidents rise in intensity to a climax? Does the story of Betty and Oliver have meaning? What order will select and arrange the details within the time order to reveal the meaning?

The time order makes things clear, but not meaningful. The help of other orders is needed.

□ SPACE.   The spatial order tells what is in a place. We must see not only the things, but their physical relationship to each other. We cannot describe them helter-skelter or they will fly all over the place. We must have system.

We must establish a point from where the things are seen. Now all things described are related to that point. It may be fixed or moving. If the point is fixed, things are placed by their distance and direction from that point. If the point is moving, things are placed by the direction of the point's movement.

Things exist in space all at once. But writing can tell only about one thing after another. Time is always involved: we are making the simultaneous sequential.

He pushed through the revolving door. His glasses steamed in the heat of the building. He walked through the aisles, past tables piled with plastic-wrapped shirts, racks of neckties, boxes of coiled belts, to the escalator. Carried upward by the steel grate underfoot, he looked down at shoppers moving from table to table, holding material up to the light, waiting by cashiers, carrying packages. Suddenly, the steel grate slid his shoes gently onto the second floor.

Here *time* and *space* are both serving order. It makes no difference what we call it, so long as the presentation accomplishes the writer's intention. Most important of all is that the writer *have* an intention.

□ PARTICULAR TO GENERAL. Add detail to detail until they spring together into a single picture—that's *induction*. Give example after example until they reveal something in common—that's *induction*. Parts lead to the whole. Every man learns by pulling details together. Make your reader a detective. He will work with you. Induction is a clear method—and a convincing one. The essay moves toward a general statement:

> Scum floated on the water. The glass sat on a sodden paper napkin. Heavy and sweet in the air was the smell of hot, stale fat. Flies pulled wildly at a brown strip spiralling from the overhead light. The waitress threw silverware on the table, pushing aside the crusted bottle of catsup. A tine on the fork was scabbed with yellow. Changing brilliant lights squirmed in the plastic casing of the juke box. Music blared and rebounded. The waitress pulled a pencil from her hair and stood, waiting. The restaurant was unpleasant.

How necessary is the last sentence? How inevitable is the general statement? The more inevitable it is in the reader's mind, the less necessary it is in the essay.

How is *time* used here? How is *space* used? The primary emphasis is, of course, on particulars.

□ GENERAL TO PARTICULAR. This book discusses an essay as a whole before separating it into components. Biological classification establishes a large category which includes smaller categories into which, finally, specific animals or plants are placed. If the writer is concerned with transmitting information rather than creating effect, movement from general to particular is swift and practical. The purpose of a textbook is primarily to transmit information. The preceding passage about the restaurant could be changed into a general-to-particular order by placing the last sentence first.

◻ SIMPLE TO COMPLEX. To write, you need to know many things all at the same time. Your needs are simultaneous, not sequential. The frustration rises from the fact that while you are discussing one thing, you are not discussing another. There is only one thing to do: Isolate one idea, clarify it; reach into the tangled mess and isolate another idea, clarify it, and relate it to the first—for ever and ever, time without end, Amen.

What idea first?

If you can find it: the simplest idea, the one that has to be understood first. The movement is from the simple to the complex. A complex idea is composed of simple ideas in interrelationships. The process is demonstrated in the discipline of analysis.

If we analyze an automobile engine, we must know what makes an engine possible. We must know first its underlying principle. We must know the fundamental law the device was constructed to employ. Once we know this, we can understand why the device has its size and its shape, and we can understand how each part intends to use that law.

For an automobile engine, we must know:

Gas, when heated, expands. The engine is a device for using the expansive power of heated gas. Now we can being to understand the engine:

1. What makes the gas?
   Feed lines mix liquid fuel and oxygen.
2. What heats the gas?
   The mixture is drawn into a chamber and compressed by a piston and ignited by a spark plug. Rapid expansion of gas takes form of an explosion.
3. How is explosion of gas used?
   Force of explosion depresses cylinder.

If we were analyzing the entire automobile, then engine leads to transmission, drive shaft, differential, then to chassis and body in the logical development of the use of a natural law. All of this emphasizes, again, the basic method of logic: to explain by going from the simple to the complex.

□ FAMILIAR TO UNFAMILIAR. Man learns about the unknown in terms of the known. Similes, metaphors, analogies are based on this principle. Whoever described a man from Mars to us would have to relate the Martian's appearance to things we know: surface like an alligator's hide; locomotor extremities like an ostrich's legs; sound utterances like a boot being pulled out of mud. Start with what is familiar; it is both comfortable and meaningful to the reader. He has solid ground from which to launch himself.

An analogy (see 7i, p. 58) helps us to understand a phenomenon:

> Nuclear fission is a chain reaction. It resembles what happens when you place set rat traps on the floor of a wire cage, put a ping-pong ball on each set spring, and drop one ping-pong ball through the top of the wire cage. The ball springs a trap which sends another ball into the air to fall on another trap to send other balls up to hit and bounce and spring other balls up to hit and bounce and spring other balls. . . .

Use an analogy to clarify a situation or to suggest a relationship but not to *prove* a point. Analogies break down if pushed too far.

5b / An essay plan

Words are the flesh of an essay. If words are the flesh, the plan of organization is the skeleton. The essay has a shape. The three parts of an essay join together as gracefully and naturally as the head, torso, and limbs of the human body. The shape of the essay is formed by the *introduction,* the *discussion,* and the *conclusion.*

Introduce your subject. Include your thesis statement in your introduction. Your thoughts will pivot about this statement. The discussion will be drawn from this statement. The conclusion is derived from this statement.

A usable plan has a sentence for the introduction; a sentence for each point of discussion; a sentence for the conclusion, which states the accomplishment of the discussion.

Each sentence of the plan will become full grown in the essay.

Each sentence will become a paragraph. The plan will look approximately like this:

1. Introductory sentence
2. Discussion sentence
3. Discussion sentence
4. Discussion sentence
5. Concluding sentence

After the introduction, paragraphs of discussion follow. Each thought will contribute naturally to the next thought. Each will have a paragraph. Each paragraph will begin with a thread picked up from the preceding paragraph. These thoughts will arrive at a stage where the conclusion will be obvious and will need only to be stated. This statement of the points made clear by the discussion will be the reader's profit. Since the conclusion often contains a concise summation of the essay, it is sometimes the essay in miniature.

As the writing progresses, changing and improving, growing larger and more mature, the creation of your thought assumes the natural and graceful shape of the essay. Its personality is yours. The parts join together into a living whole. *No part is finished until the whole is finished; your introductory paragraph cannot be complete until your conclusion has been written, and you have checked each part against the whole.*

The following essay chart is a device to make visible a principle which is not visible. When you understand the principle, discard the device. It is a distortion to serve a purpose. Remember the principle; forget the chart.

This chart is not a form for you to fill out. You have a personality. This chart does not. It is a device to simplify and dramatize the logic of an essay. Take liberties with the outline—invent different ways of satisfying the elements of introduction, discussion, and conclusion. Perhaps two or three paragraphs of discussion will result from one sentence in the introductory paragraph. Perhaps a point is omitted in the introduction to allow its arrival as a surprise in later discussion. Know the liberties you are taking and be prepared to justify them in terms of surprise, emotional impact, or suspense. Know what you are doing, and why.

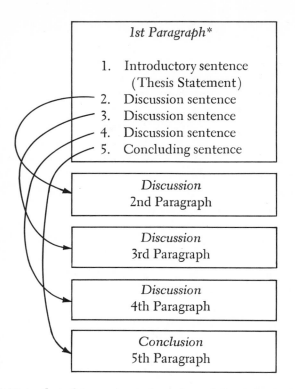

1st Paragraph*

1. Introductory sentence
   (Thesis Statement)
2. Discussion sentence
3. Discussion sentence
4. Discussion sentence
5. Concluding sentence

Discussion
2nd Paragraph

Discussion
3rd Paragraph

Discussion
4th Paragraph

Conclusion
5th Paragraph

* Note that this mechanical version of the introductory paragraph recapitulates the rough plan for the essay.

Let us examine the following student essay. Its simple structure makes visible the presence or absence of the principles discussed.

Here are the title and introductory paragraph:

The Advantages of Freshman Customs

The term "customs" is used at Central State University to refer to the various rules and regulations imposed upon new freshmen by the Freshman Customs Board. These regulations develop a freshman socially and academically and stir in him a feeling of respect and loyalty for his college. I am strongly in favor of having freshman customs at the Central State University; and since I am a freshman and have just been through customs, I feel qualified to express a definite opinion on the benefits derived from them.

The author has a limited subject: *The Advantages of Freshman Customs.* He has indicated, in a theme statement, what point his essay is written to make: "These regulations [freshman customs] develop a freshman socially and academically, and stir in him a feeling of respect and loyalty for his college." We discover later that from the theme statement four discussion sentences will derive:

1. Freshman customs develop class unity.
2. Freshman customs enable freshman girls to get dates.
3. Freshman customs provide procedures of conduct and study in a new environment.
4. Freshman customs help the student to identify with the university.

The writer did not state these points explicitly in the opening paragraph, because in such a short essay the effect would have been mechanical.

We see that in ordering his essay the writer moves from the general to the particular.

First Discussion Sentence: Freshman Customs develop unity.

Customs instill in freshmen a feeling of class unity and help to develop good class spirit. Because all freshmen have many things in common—their little blue beanies, name cards, and blank expressions—they feel a certain togetherness, a certain closeness that comes from knowing that they are all in the same situation. The name cards help freshmen to become acquainted with the names of the members of their class and to learn a few facts about them, such as their hometowns, curriculums and, in some cases, phone numbers. If they were not required to wear these signs, freshmen would spend months instead of weeks learning to associate names with faces.

Second Discussion Sentence: Freshman Customs enable freshman girls to get dates.

Customs may also benefit freshmen socially, especially freshman women. When upper classmen see girls wearing beanies and name signs they have a good excuse to stop the freshmen and learn more about them. This may be a great opportunity for a freshman girl to get a date with an upperclassman. Even though a freshman may not be stopped, she may receive a call later on from an upper classman who saw her name and looked up her number. As a result of customs, freshmen have many chances to make unlimited contacts that could help to make their college days the most enjoyable ones of their lives.

Third Discussion Sentence: Freshman Customs provide procedures of conduct and study in a new environment.

Although most freshmen are young adults when they enter college, they may still need a little guidance to get them settled down to studying and to orient them in conduct becoming a Central State student. To help start them off on the right foot, the Customs Board sets up regulations to make their adjustment as easy as possible. For example, freshman women are required to be in their dormitories by nine thirty in the evenings during the orientation period so that they get used to coming in early to study. Although there are no direct restrictions placed upon freshman men, they can usually be controlled indirectly by restricting freshman women. If these regulations were not made, many irresponsible students would not settle down and would probably fail to pass their courses. Therefore, customs helps prevent failures by teaching freshmen good habits when they are first beginning. Rules of conduct, such as forbidding freshmen to smoke outside of their dormitories, to place their hands in their pockets when walking, are enforced to get them accustomed to good practices and to improve the general appearance of the campus.

Fourth Discussion Sentence: Freshman Customs help the student to identify with the university.

One of the greatest benefits that freshmen receive from customs is the feeling of being part of their university. To help them learn about their university as quickly as possible, the customs board requires freshmen to learn the college songs and cheers, the names and locations of buildings and outstanding sites on the campus, and the names of the administrators in their particular colleges. Learning this information is important for several reasons: first, knowing the words to songs and cheers is not only enjoyable but also essential if the student wants to show his support for his team at athletic events. He will use them throughout his college years and probably remember them long after he has been graduated. Second, a student should be familiar with all parts of the campus so that he knows the locations of places and can find them easily and quickly. And third, learning the names of administrators is necessary if the student has a problem and wants to consult a person who may be able to help them. It is also a gesture of courtesy and respect. Most students, if they were not forced to learn this information as soon as they arrived, would have gradually learned bits of knowledge that were necessary to get along; but they would not have a general, all-around knowledge of the university or its campus.

Conclusion:

To sum up my ideas regarding the desirability of freshman customs, I feel that they do a lot to help freshmen become generally well-adjusted to their new lives as students at Central State University. They encourage friendliness and strengthen the student's sense of security and well-being.

We can make certain statements about weaknesses in parts of this essay. The concluding paragraph, for instance, is weak because:

1. It is self-conscious. (Don't announce what you are going to do; do it.) If announcement is necessary, it should be as brief as possible.
2. It wastes words ("To sum up my ideas regarding the desirability of freshmen customs, I feel that . . .") What do all these words contribute to the paragraph? If they do not contribute, they detract from the paragraph.
3. The summation should be more than mere repetition; it should be repetition with profit. For instance, if the wasted words were removed and a final strong sentence, such as "Freshman customs quickly make a stranger feel at home," were added, the final paragraph would climax the discussion. The end is a position of great emphasis and must be respected.

But there is a more serious weakness, a weakness of the whole. It is clear *what* the essay says. We recognize the thesis statement. It is not clear *why* the essay makes the statement. It is not clear what the author wanted his essay to do for his reader. What is his *specific aim?* For whom did he write his essay? For other college students who share this experience? Why? To reminisce? Is the essay addressed to a student body about to vote on whether to retain Freshman Customs or not? Or is the essay intended for high school seniors who may have fears or misconceptions about the coming college events? Does the author want to correct their misconceptions, or allay their fears? A decision by the author on what he wanted the essay to do for his readers would have given this essay greater purpose and force.

The writer could have early established for whom the essay was intended. He could have introduced and reinforced such a sentence as: "Entering freshmen, if they recognized the consequences of Freshman Customs, would welcome them wholeheartedly"; or, "I think it the responsibility of every student attending this college to protect and maintain the tradition of Freshman Customs."

The author's tone—his attitude toward his material—is pleasant. He is not belligerent or defensive. He finds humor in his material— ". . . all freshmen have many things in common . . . blank expressions"—and conveys it.

The two student essays that follow are more sophisticated and more personal than the preceding essay. In these essays, which have to do with the process of becoming mature, each student is exploring his own vision, his own experience. The result, in each case, is an essay only that particular person could have written.

The Bus Ride

Childhood is like a blanket that covers one from head to foot. Most children try to throw off this warm, comfortable blanket woven of love, security, understanding and perhaps a few threads of overprotectiveness. One of the first steps I took toward the removal of this blanket was an eight-mile bus ride.

Riding on a bus is an easy process—now. But when I was five or six years old, it seemed like a very exciting and complicated thing. When we went from our home in the suburbs for a day of shopping in the city, Mother always went along. I had often seen the "big" girls going downtown alone. How I envied them! I longed for the day when I could go downtown without Mother. I wanted to pay my fare instead of creeping under the turnstile, to sit beside a stranger, to pull the buzzer and to get off at the right stop—*alone*. Since this bus riding was such an intricate process I had fears like: How would I know when to pull the buzzer for my stop? How would I be sure of getting off at the proper corner? Even more disturbing than these questions was getting home again—would I get to the bus stop on time? Would I get on the bus which said *Reifton* so that I would, at the end of the ride, find myself home again?

Occasionally, Mother and I would pretend we were strangers riding on the same bus. She would sit in the front and I would pick a seat near the rear of the bus. As the time approached for us to get off, Mommy would pull the buzer, get up and I would follow her—never saying a word. This game was fun because I never had to worry about getting out at the proper time and place. Mommy was there, she would do everything just on time.

When I was eight the big day arrived. I was going to make a bus trip in town and back—alone. The trip was familiar. I had been making it since the age of four. I was going for my monthly appointment at the hairdresser's for a trim (Daddy hated long hair!). I was excited and scared. Of course, I did not reveal my fear to anyone. While I was putting on my yellow pinafore, Mommy gave me last-minute instructions. "Don't forget to pay the driver." "Don't forget to get off at Sixth Street near Whitners." "Watch the policeman when you cross Penn Street." We went downstairs and Mommy waited on the lawn until I rounded the corner. As I rounded that corner, I was faced with two strong emotions, fear and pride. My fear told me to turn around and run home to Mommy, to ask her to please come along. Pride outweighed fear. I was just like the "big" girls now. So I waited at the bus stop alone.

The bus finally came. I got on and paid Bill, the driver who always had the one o'clock Reifton route. He asked where my mother was. Very loudly, so that all of the passengers could hear, I announced, "She is busy and couldn't come along." Without another word, I pranced to my seat by an open window and proceeded to watch the other people riding with me.

I remember seeing the older men and women smile. Now I know that they were smiling at this little girl in a yellow dress with black patent leather shoes and white gloves not because I was "a cute little girl" but because perhaps they were remembering their first trip alone.

The first few miles of the ride were fun; but as we neared Reading, I was frightened. I almost missed my stop but in probably the only lucid minute out of the preceding five I remembered that Whitner's was my stop. I pulled the buzzer and rose with shaking knees. The bus stopped, I stepped down. There I was, I had made my first single ride. The excitement I felt quickly erased all previous fears, and I could hardly wait to tell my parents and playmates what fun it had all been.

Getting home after my haircut was no problem. I had the confidence which I lacked in the beginning. I knew that I could be at the proper place at the right time for the next bus home. I met the bus, rode to Reifton and got off just around the corner from my house. As I rounded the corner for the second time that day, I was different. I did not look different, perhaps a little mussed and shorn, but I felt older. I realized I was capable of relying on myself. My self-confidence was given a boost. From that summer day until this spring day, I have been walking around more and more corners, often wanting to run home and have Mommy or Daddy come along. Somehow I have never turned around—something irresistible, the thought of a new adventure, has drawn me forward.

An Incident Which Caused My Departure from Innocence

When is it that one's state of mind is transposed from that of a child to that of an adult? Is it a slow process beginning with birth and ending with death? Are we not all a child in one form or another, regardless of age? Or is it rather a lightning-swift change caused by a single incident? A child witnesses death. The unexpected, crushing death of a parent is followed by an entirely different method of viewing life. Is it safer to assume that innocence is gradually lost? Slowly one's trust slips away in small matters. A toy is stolen or a puppy poisoned. The customary, tiny kiss a child places on his father's cheek is not returned. Complete faith ebbs to doubt. The process of growing begins.

Certainly, in a few cases, an outstanding incident occurs which completely changes the child's perspective. In most people's lives it is a series of small incidents which make the difference. At the age of six I listened to a story told to me by a nun. This same story had been retold for two thousand years. Yet, I had never been exposed to it until first grade. It is the story of the death of Christ. This placed my abstract idea of cruelty in a tangible position.

Children are highly impressionable. I was no exception. As a child, little incidents molded me. This particular incident occurred my first weeks in school. We were assigned a home room and nun to teach us. Sister Francella made a striking appearance. She was tall and extremely pale. The black habit of the Sisters of Charity marked her as a nun in the service of God. She may have been beautiful as a girl, for her black eyebrows betrayed beneath them a pair of lively dark eyes, and at forty, her chisled features were only slightly lined. Sister Francella spoke softly in a refined, low pitched voice. Only several years later did I learn that she left the home of her wealthy father, who was president of a Pittsburgh corporation, to enter the convent. Because of the constant, nervous little movements of her hands, I was never at ease in her presence. This was the woman who related to me the first and only horror story to move me to tears.

Sister Francella had been telling the class things most of us had never heard before. I had a vague notion of Christ dying. A crucifix hung above my crib. I said my evening prayers beneath it. I knew Jesus had been crucified. But what was crucifixion? How did it happen? Why was Jesus outstretched above my head? I had never asked aloud "Why?" Simplicity is a part of childhood.

She began with the Agony in the Garden. Vividly she interspersed the story with a slow Scripture's reading. Jesus sweat blood on the rocks. He threw himself to the ground crying, "Father, if it be so, let this chalice pass from me. But not my will but thine be done." Forty children listened spellbound. Judas appeared, as much a badman as any Western villain. Jesus was led before the Sanhedrin to be mocked and scourged at the pillar. Scourging? "What was scourging?" a little voice ventured to ask. The two nervous hands grasped a yardstick. The crack which followed stunned me. Sister broke the yardstick over her desk. "Now picture a long heavy rope, knotted at the end, used to beat a man for hours." There may have been a bit of Hollywood in her presentation. It affected me as nothing ever has since.

She spared no details. When flesh was ripped, it was ripped gruesomely. The crown of thorns was not just placed on Christ's head. It was ground through his flesh. It cut above his eyebrows. The blood matted in his hair. I shivered. Cold-blooded torture to a man no older than my daddy was something I found hard to grasp. Innocence disappeared. Cruelty became tangible for me. When Sister Francella spoke the words of the crowd, she mocked the hatred of Christ's own people. Dignity left her voice. She was screaming, "Crucify Him, Crucify Him." And every step under the cross to Golgotha became real. The soldier's whips lashed our Lord's back. The women along the road wept with compassion. Christ suffered humiliation as he was stripped of his garments. I cried. Very softly, I cried for him. I cried when the impact of hatred reached beyond my innocence. And there was no returning. Something left my life that day.

"My Father, forgive them, for they know not what they do." With one last gasp of breath,. Jesus commended His soul into His Father's kingdom. I looked up at Sister Francella. A serene beauty encompassed that nun. Her hands hung quite still at her sides. They did not quiver. I lowered my eyes.

5x/ Exercises

1. Assemble details about a teacher. Limit details to matters of fact. What general statement do these details make clear? Do you have to make the general statement, or has the assembly of facts (particulars) made the opinion (general statement) inescapable?

2. Into what aspects would you divide your facts about the teacher? How much space would you give to each aspect? What does each aspect contribute to your general statement? Make an essay outline based on your answers.

3. Your reader has never met the teacher. Does the teacher resemble persons with whom your reader is familiar? What are the resemblances?

4. Do you want to report to your reader your opinion of the teacher—
   or do you want the reader to form an opinion that corresponds
   to yours? What is the distinction between these two questions?

5. Write an essay about the teacher which fulfills your intention.

THE PARAGRAPH

6/ From Plan to Paragraph

The themes you write will be developed in paragraphs. But what is a paragraph? Perhaps all you know for sure is that it is a block of writing between indentations. Writers of business letters, newspaper stories, popular magazine articles use the paragraph primarily to do one thing: Let daylight into the copy. But your paragraph has other—and more important—jobs.

You must learn to see the major ideas of your plan as paragraphs. You must understand the importance of a "topic sentence" and its relationship to the controlling idea of the theme, and you must learn the several standard ways of developing a paragraph. After you understand these concepts, you can do as the experienced writers do—forget the forms, the rules, the categories, and just do your best to express yourself clearly, precisely, and economically.

6a/ The "developing" paragraph

A developing paragraph is one that elaborates, proves, or demonstrates one aspect of your thesis. The freshman theme is often able to complete its idea in four to six developing paragraphs, each containing three to eight sentences and fifty to two-hundred words. There will be a topic sentence, expressed or implied, in each developing paragraph. The whole purpose of the other sentences within the paragraph is to make the topic sentence "come true."

6b/ Seeing your major ideas as paragraphs

Paragraphs grow out of topic sentences. Topic sentences derive from an outline, from a plan. That plan comes from your examining your list of raw ideas to find the items that are worth developing into paragraphs. Look at the essay on freshman customs, page 26. The thesis is clear: *freshman customs benefit the student*. The introductory paragraph of the essay establishes the writer's qualifications for writing on that topic, and defines the key words. The succeeding paragraphs develop four major ideas of the outline:

1. Freshman customs develop class unity.
2. Freshman customs enable freshman girls to get dates.
3. Freshman customs provide procedures of conduct and study in a new environment.
4. Freshman customs enable the student to identify with the university.

These four points support the thesis that freshman customs benefit the student. The writer's ability to see major ideas as paragraphs ensured a developed essay.

6c/ The topic sentence, the controlling idea, major and minor support

A developing paragraph must deal with one major idea—and *only* one. Look at each paragraph of your theme. Be certain you see the major idea it treats. If it treats more than one, something is wrong. The topic sentence expresses that major idea in a complete sentence.

Diamonds are a girl's best friend. Any sentence that doesn't have something to do with the kindly way girls take to diamonds would be out of place in a paragraph intending to develop that idea.

War is hell. The key word here is *hell.* This must become the controlling idea of the paragraph. Sentences showing the camaraderie of soldiers would destroy the unity of the paragraph. This controlling idea calls for words like *blood, terror, noise, confusion* and the other components of hell.

Test your supporting sentences against your topic sentence. Consider the following example:

The same lack of sophistication which led the colonists to quacks and faith-healers kept them forever tinkering with their own bodies [*topic sentence*]. Remedies were passed from house to house and accepted with benign confidence. [*Doesn't this supporting sentence suggest self-diagnosis and self-treatment of ills?*] Itinerant beggars made a living by bartering prescriptions for meals. [*Doesn't this suggest lack of sophistication? Doesn't it have something to do with tinkering?*] Every section of the countryside had one or two laymen who were adept at bleeding and cupping. People dropped in to be "let" with the same casual air with which they pick up the aspirin bottle today. [*This last sentence doesn't quite support the key words, "forever tinkering with their own bodies," but it comes close. Perhaps a change in the topic sentence to "kept them forever experimenting with home remedies and lay doctors" would keep the paragraph honest. Analysis of this kind will show possible weaknesses in your paragraphs.*]

6d / Introductory paragraphs

A good introductory paragraph usually gives in miniature the development of the essay (see p. 25).

More than a million Americans—a record number—will be going abroad this year, according to the United States Passport Agency. Last year 906,900 passports or renewals were issued, a 5.7 per cent gain over the 857,961 issued in 1961. My own, totally unconfirmed statistics show that there will be further increases this year, as follows: tourists doing the wrong things, 19.9 per cent; tourists going to the right places at the wrong time or to the wrong places at the right time, 23.7 per cent; tourists who have no idea whatsoever why they are going in the first place, 31.6 per cent. The loss to the individual is incalculable, and so is the drain on our country's precious gold reserves.

JOSEPH WECHSBURG

Probably the most confusing and least understood term in the securities business is *over-the-counter*. Actually, the over-the-counter market is simply a method of buying and selling securities without a centralized market place. Securities dealers all over the country do business with one another over a network of telephones instead of meeting in one place and bargaining face to face, as they do on stock-exchange floors.

In each case the introductory paragraph gives the reader the essay in capsule form. The rest of each essay is an elaboration of the main point stated or implied in the introduction.

If you examine magazine essays you will notice that the first paragraph is not always the introductory paragraph in the sense defined here. Sometimes a short attention-getting paragraph using an anecdote, a pun, or a command is used as an opening just before the true introductory matter.

When Mississippi Negroes gather to discuss their struggle for equality, as they frequently do, one story they tell concerns a plantation field hand named John. Seized by civil rights fever, he pays a visit to the big house to proclaim the new order.

"Mister Charlie," he says to the white planter, "all these years you and Miss Ann has called me 'John.' That's all right. But things is changed. There ain't gonna be no more 'Mister Charlie' and 'Miss Ann.' It's just 'Ann' and 'Charlie' now. And, Charlie, one other thing: Ain't gonna be no more Mississippi, either. From now on, it's just 'Sippi.'"

CLAUDE SITTON

This opening anecdote, although it is appropriate to author Claude Sitton's thesis, does not give in miniature, the development of the essay. That function is performed by the second paragraph.

Mississippi whites see little humor in the story. Mister Charlie and Miss Ann quickly lose the graciousness and warmth with which they are rightfully credited if one suggests that racial customs must be modified. They know that change is inevitable. But the mind boggles at the thought—and sometimes slips its moorings to reality.

This is a device that must be used with caution. It can work well in a long essay, but is less likely to be successful in a short essay.

6e/ Transition paragraphs

In a sense every paragraph is a transitional paragraph in that it is part of a movement from thought to thought. However, there are certain brief paragraphs that nakedly and bluntly do only one thing: change the subject. Such paragraphs are invariably brief. They should be used sparingly in long papers and never in short papers.

The function of a transition paragraph is to lead the reader from Item A, which has been developed at some length, to Item B.

Examples:

Item A—a discussion of Berlin.
Transition paragraph: Thus France is the main factor in the future of Germany and you turn, for further enlightenment, to Paris.
Item B—a discussion of Paris.

Item A—a discussion of man's plundering the resources of nature.
Transition paragraph: Now that we have seen some of the terrible results of our waste, greed, mismanagement and carelessness, let's turn our attention to a possible program of reconstruction.
Item B—a plan to allow nature a chance to restore her beauty and balance.

Sometimes the transitional matter is grafted to the end of Item A or to the beginning of Item B and not set off as a separate paragraph.

Caution: Beware of phrases which attempt to make previous paragraphs part of the present paragraph. Readers often feel insult at phrases such as "see above," or "discussed above." The writer seems to believe either that the reader is stupid and cannot remember, or that the material must be re-established and it is too much work to do it.

A greater danger may reside in such phrases. A sentence like "If the reprisal policy, as noted above, is carried out, the coalition will disintegrate" stops the flow and jolts the reader. If an essay is successful, reader, writer, and argument are one: the argument. Why shatter that unity, that greater identity, and suddenly return the reader to the recognition that this is an essay, that someone else is the writer, and that he is the reader?

6f / Concluding paragraphs

Your conclusion to a short essay should be short. The conclusion may be a sentence or two of the last developing paragraph: more often, the conclusion is itself an entire paragraph.

Your conclusion should indicate strongly the accomplishment of the entire discussion; and convey a satisfying sense of completeness. If the reader turns the page to see whether or not something follows, the conclusion is weak.

Let us hear the conclusion of the whole matter: Fear God and keep His commandments: for this is the whole duty of man. For God shall bring every work into judgment, with every secret thing, whether it be good, or whether it be evil.

Ecclesiastes

The foregoing is a harsh criticism and may be thought illiberal. But as Mr. Gifford assumes a right to say what he pleases of others— They may be allowed to speak the truth of him.

WILLIAM HAZLITT. "Mr. Gifford"

Such are some of the lineaments of the ethical character, which the cultivated intellect will form, apart from religious principle. They are seen within the pale of The Church and without it, in holy men, and in profligates; they form the beau-ideal of the world. They partly assist and partly distort the development of the Catholic. They must subserve the education of a St. Frances de Sales or a Cardinal Pole; they may be the limits of the contemplation of a Shaftsbury or a Gibbon. Basil and Julian were fellow-students at the schools of Athens; and one became the Saint and Doctor of the Church, and the other her scoffing and relentless foe.

NEWMAN. Conclusion of "Knowledge
Viewed in Relation to Religious Duty"

That was five years ago. Since his death, his fame in America has grown greater with every year. The laurel wreath that should have crowned his brow is exchanged for the garland laid upon his grave. And the time is coming, let us hope, when the whole English-speaking world will recognize in O. Henry one of the great masters of modern literature.

From "The Amazing Genius of
O. Henry," by STEPHEN LEACOCK

6g/ Paragraph coherence

A sentence is fixed yet flowing. The separate words are joined into a unit by meaning. Through the words an idea flows to completion.

As a sentence is a unit of words, so is the paragraph a unit of sentences, and so is the essay a unit of paragraphs.

What makes words unite into sentences, sentences into paragraphs, paragraphs into essays?

□ COHERENCE.   In each unit, an idea is brought to completion. The larger the unit, the more complexly developed the idea.

What is coherence?

Coherence is a pattern of thought in which:

(a)   The central idea is established;
(b)   The relevance of every other idea to the central idea is clear; and
(c)   The sequence presents each idea at the point where it becomes crucial to the reader's understanding.

To achieve coherence, then, a writer must know the relationship of the ideas he means to express; develop an order that will best reveal that relationship; choose the words, structures, and rhythms that will form and complete the pattern of thought.

The best instrument to make a paragraph cohere is logic. The relationship of ideas to each other must be strongly established. Ideas contribute to each other. What idea is important only because it contributes to another idea? Put that relationship into an equivalent physical structure. Subordinate the less important idea to the more important one. Logic makes coherence.

Specific words make many relationships clear. Ideas of equal importance are connected by coordinate conjunctions: *and, but, or, nor, for.* Relationships among unequal ideas are identified by subordinating conjunctions: *because, when, if, although,* and others. Conjunctive adverbs—*moreover, nevertheless, then, so, yet;* transitional adverbs—*likewise, first, second, finally, similarly;* transitional phrases—*on the other hand, in addition, some time later*—all these can help achieve coherence, if logic demands them.

But, essentially, coherence is not a matter of artifices; it is a tension created by the precise unfolding of logical thought.

6x / Exercises

1. Write for each of the following theme statements three or four sentences, each to serve as a topic sentence for a paragraph developing a different aspect of the central idea.
   a. Ball point pens are superior to fountain pens.
   b. An attic is an enchanted storehouse of sentiment and family lore.
   c. The curriculum of this college includes too many (or not enough) practical courses.
   d. The world is too much with us.
   e. He that increaseth knowledge increaseth sorrow. —Ecclesiastes I, 18.
   f. There are some things about which a wise man might wish to remain ignorant.
   g. A true university is a collection of books.

2. Write a paragraph developing each of the following topic sentences.
   a. Misery loves company.
   b. Taste is the only morality.
   c. Some people should marry early (late, never marry).

3. Examine paragraphs from collateral reading. Identify topic sentences, transitional devices; comment on the unity, coherence, and general effectiveness of each paragraph.

4. Study paragraph division in any copy of *The Reader's Digest*, *Time*, a newspaper, any essay by a nineteenth-century author— Coleridge, Lamb, Hazlitt, Carlyle, etc. Identify, in each case, the principles which determine the nature of the paragraph.

5. How effective is the paragraphing of the following student themes?

   a.   *How Can a Man Accept Communism?*

   How can a man who loves humanity, accept communism? This question puzzles many non-Communists because they can see the dangers in the premises upon which most of the men who, thinking they love humanity, have based their acceptance. But the man who believes the Communist doctrine does not know the inherent dangers, he only knows, or assumes as true, the premises which appear logically sound but are really fallacies.

He believes the ultimate goal of present life is the future happiness of mankind and peace. The individual man is not important; it is mankind which is. Since mankind can never be happy or live in peace while there is conflict between classes arising from class distinction instead of quality, and while minority groups—industrialists, merchants, politicians —rule instead of the people in general, the masses, ruling themselves, class distinction must be abolished; minor groups must be eradicated. The masses, however, must be guided and directed toward participation in establishing equality; they must be educated to understand the structure and function of such a social body. To educate, or, in the case of the old generation, re-educate, and to guide the proletariat a group of leaders is necessary. When the masses have learned to live cooperatively, each producing to his capacity and each receiving according to his need, without private property and different social positions, the leaders will become obsolete, the proletariat, as such, will cease to exist, and the state, organ of class rule, will have withered away.

With this education, time and knowledge produce technical development as class rule begins to wither. But technical developments in turn produce new factors, new combinations, new structures of the social body which the masses cannot penetrate, comprehend, or handle for a time. During this time the rulers are still necessary to help people's minds grasp the new ideas and changed state of affairs. This adaptation of the masses to changed circumstances is not a simple one; it is complex and slow moving, instead of decades it takes centuries. However, this time and training necessary for adaptation produces more new factors and continues the cycle. The proletariat leaders never become obsolete and the state never deteriorates in its necessity.

Another premise is that to assure peace, security, and certain salvation for the whole of mankind, a world of one faith and one leadership must be created. History has indicated, through its evolutions, that if the world contains one faith and if one force rules it, without conflicting doctrines or minority forces interfering, peace will be the consequence. To this future happiness the present generation and the rights of individuals must be sacrificed for mankind is far more important than a single man. If terror and brutal treatment will establish one faith and one leadership faster, its use is justified. No one knows, however, if sacrificing man today to create this rule will assure social justice and perpetual peace tomorrow; this assumption is only based on a scientific prediction. Man is a tangible object, mankind itself is not. Who knows what history books will say about these times and how the words will affect future men.

The assumption also that private property must be abolished for equality and freedom because nature created all men free and equal and because its original state of nature knew no private property is also a fallacy. The reasoning might be logical but there is danger in assuming nature is materialistic and created man. Neither can man rightly assume or say man was originally free and equal. The idea is only one which sounds correct and beautiful to people oppressed by class difference; it is most appealing to sympathy and feelings which are the worst enemies of logical thinking.

Upon close examination of these premises man discovers that they are all based on one main assumption that the end justifies the means, and on a minor one that history repeats itself.

b.   *Night Sounds*

Anyone who has ever visited the Maine woods during the summer months needs no explanation as to the wonder of their beauty. They already know the breath-taking illusion created by the sun beaming down on the huge pine, oak, and fir trees, as the wind slowly permeates the branches and causes the leaves to softly rustle in the breeze. They already know the sound of motorboats churning up the peaceful waters of the nearby lake; the sound of fish jumping in the water; and the sound of the waves gently lapping the shoreline. However, as any experienced woodsman or any summer visitor can relate, all these familiar daytime sounds and noises change drastically at night. Like many others before me, I too was surprised and delighted when I discovered this.

Every summer my family and I spend a month at a small community of cabins in Maine. Almost all these cabins face a small lake which separates "our" Maine from the other side—New Hampshire. Although I was well aware of the beauty of the surrounding nature during the day, I never noticed it at night until once when I had to walk home alone at midnight. Even though the moon was shining brightly enough through the trees to light the path I was following, I was still nervous and jittery. I had never before walked to our cabin alone at such a late hour, and I was unused to the quietness that surrounded me. Only suddenly I noticed that the woods were not quiet at all. Every little sound echoed louder than usual, and this only served to scare me more. Finally, the sudden realization that the sounds of nature in the woods at night were different from those in the daytime struck me, and I stood still for a minute just to listen to this strange phenomenon.

I could hear the frogs jumping through the underbrush, and every now and then I could even spy one as it hopped across the path in front of me. The bullfrogs were croaking love songs in their vibrating bass voices, and their fair ladies were answering in a slightly higher and more feminine croak. I could hear the crickets chirping as the cool summer breeze swept through the leaves and created a soft sound like crinkling paper. If I listened very carefully above all these other noises, I could detect the occasional splash of a few active fish as they frolicked together in the lake. Even the soft tone of the water hitting the shore was evident in the still night air. As I began to walk on, I noticed also the noise of my feet crunching down on the dead leaves and pine needles. The rest of the way home, all these sounds kept echoing in my mind, like a broken record repeating itself over and over again. Now, looking back on that night, I know I shall never forget that wonderful first experience of discovering those unique and absorbing night sounds.

c.   *Free Thought*

In the world beyond our world, in the Brave New World, mass production demanded a shift in the emphases given to knowledge and to truth. Knowledge could no more be considered the highest good, and truth could no longer be the most supreme value. These ideas must be debased so that "universal happiness" can be attained.

Today, in our own world we seem to be doing much the same thing. We, as a people, have also been forced to succumb to standards that others have set for us. We are not conditioned to accept these standards in the same manner as the members of the Brave New World, but it is safe to say that we in the United States are also conditioned to think along specific lines; our freedom of thought is checked.

The comparison of the attitudes of both societies toward a subject such as "clothes" will serve as a good illustration in proving that our freedom of thought is discouraged.

Here in our world, in the world of Modern America we strive to keep up with the styles. We all try to raise our social status. The well-dressed woman of today would never dream of wearing a "sack dress" this year because people just aren't wearing "sack dresses" this year. "Vogue" tells her to buy something new. All of our lives are motivated toward consumption. We are, as are the members of the Brave New World, conditioned to believe this is right and almost necessary. Mustapha Mond, of the Brave New World, can be quoted as saying, "We haven't any use for old things. . . . We don't want people to be attracted by old things. We want them to like the new ones." The Brave New World used hypnopoedia as a method of conditioning. Hypnopoedia tells these "civilized" people that . . . ending is better than mending. The more stitches, the less riches . . ." Our conditioning tells us the same things, only our methods differ. American psychologists use hidden suggestions in all types of magazine articles, advertisements, and other written material as their method of conditioning.

Our thinking is also guided in other ways. We are more or less forced to accept certain beliefs and values. For example, our society has a specific set of morals. We are conditioned, by the rules set up by this society, to believe them. If our own ideas deviate from the accepted ones, we become individuals ostracized from our group. In most cases the individual will remember what he has been taught (or conditioned to believe) and will follow those teachings simply because he has little other choice. This same factor also holds true for the members of the Brave New World. Again I will quote Mustapha Mond, "People can't help doing what they ought to do . . . one believes things because one has been conditioned to believe them."

I could go on and on citing different examples that would further prove my thesis; however, I really don't think it necessary. I doubt our world will ever reach the extremes attained in *Brave New World* but I do feel that in many respects we are already very similar.

7 / Developing a Paragraph

7a / Providing detail

The value of details comes not from their number but from how they fit together. And they won't fit together by accident. Every idea or situation consists of parts held in tension. Separate the situation into its parts, identify each part, establish the relationship of each part to the whole. These particulars either lead to a general statement or support a general statement.

But any situation consists of an infinity of details. Should we list details until we get tired? What details should we use? What details should we reject?

Let us re-examine a paragraph used earlier:

Scum floated on the water. The glass sat on a sodden paper napkin. Heavy and sweet in the air was the smell of hot, stale fat. Flies pulled wildly at a brown strip spiralling from the overhead light. The waitress threw silverware on the table, pushing aside the crusted bottle of catsup. A tine on the fork was scabbed with yellow. Changing brilliant lights squirmed in the plastic casing of the juke box. Music blared and rebounded. The waitress pulled a pencil from her hair and stood, waiting. The restaurant was unpleasant.

Why don't we add to the paragraph a sentence such as "A wet rag hung over a chair back"? Because we already have a detail to represent that category of details: "The glass sat on a sodden paper napkin."

Why don't we add the sentence, "A roach scurried along the base of the wall"? Because we already have a representative from that category of effects: "Flies pulled wildly at a brown strip spiralling from an overhead light."

Why not add the sentence, "Lipstick stained a cup rim"? Because we already have "A tine on the fork was scabbed with yellow."

We want in a paragraph to do the most we can in the time and space we have. We choose each detail to represent a whole category of details. To repeat a category is to waste opportunity. Each added detail should bring with it a whole new category of associations and meanings.

We must use details to represent as much of the situation as possible. We must select. We must discard. We must use details to anticipate or to affirm a general idea. A verdict requires evidence. An opinion requires facts. An abstraction requires concretes. The general requires particulars. Whatever the terms, the principle is the same.

7b/ Giving examples and illustrations

We understand an idea best by seeing it in action. The mind needs testimony from the senses. What you want the mind to accept, you must present for the senses to report. This means something for the eye to see, the nose to smell, the ear to hear, the fingers to touch, the tongue to taste. The abstract informs the mind; the concrete informs the senses. Full understanding requires that both be informed. A general statement requires specific instances. Show the idea in action. Give examples.

The first paragraph of the following passage gives examples of the discipline afforded United States soldiers during the Mexican War; the second paragraph, of the conditions in which those soldiers lived:

To make them good soldiers took doing, but both the old-line officers and the West Pointers knew how. Always keep soldiers busy cleaning rifles and equipment, drilling in the dust or mud, or on parade, or mounting guard, or policing the grounds. Put them to tending horses, repairing roads, painting, building, gardening. Tie offenders across wooden horses. Hang signs around their necks and stand them on barrels for everybody to see. Run them behind wagons, tied to the tailgates and carrying weights. Slip poles crosswise between elbows and knees tied close to their chests, and stuff gags in their mouths. Brand them, shave their heads, drum them out of camp. Slap them in guardhouses and threaten the worst with the rope or the firing squad.

Johnston's kind of private lived hard. He ate his share of tainted and moldy food, and drank plenty of bad water. He came down with smallpox, yellow fever, malaria, typhoid, diarrhea, consumption, dropsy, and apoplexy. To shore up his health or forget he was sick he usually got drunk. Liquor was about the only medicine he knew, and his doctors often agreed. In the end, if he survived and behaved, he might make a good soldier.

From *Zach Taylor's Little Army*
by EDWARD J. NICHOLS

In the next excerpt, the author has an idea to make clear; he cites a particular case to illustrate the idea:

. . . if we misuse [tradition], and take it as a collection of cut-and-dried statements, to be accepted without further inquiry, we are not only injuring ourselves here, but by refusing to do our part towards the building up of the fabric which shall be inherited by our children, we are tending to cut off ourselves and our race from the human line.

Let us first take care to distinguish a kind of tradition which especially requires to be examined and called in question, because it especially shrinks from inquiry. Suppose that a medicine-man . . . tells his tribe that a certain powerful medicine in his tent will be propitiated if they kill their cattle; and that the tribe believe him. Whether the medicine was propitiated or not, there are no means of verifying, but the cattle are gone. Still the belief may be kept up in the tribe that propitiation has been effected in this way; and in a later generation it will be all the easier for another medicine-man to persuade them to a similar act. Here the only reason for belief is that everybody has believed the thing for so long that it must be true. And yet the belief was founded on fraud, and has been propagated by credulity. That man will undoubtedly do right, and be a friend of men, who shall call it in question and see that there is no evidence for it, help his neighbors to see as he does, and even, if need be, go into the holy tent and break the medicine.

The rule which should guide us in such cases is simple and obvious enough; that the aggregate testimony of our neighbors is subject to the same conditions as the testimony of any one of them. Namely, we have no right to believe a thing true because everybody says so, unless there are good grounds for believing that some one person at least has the means of knowing what is true, and is speaking the truth so far as he knows it.

From "The Ethics of Belief,"
by W. K. CLIFFORD

7c/ Comparing and contrasting

Both comparison and contrast place things which are similar beside each other. Comparison points out how they are alike. Contrast points out how they are different. The two methods are often used together. If you point out only how two things are alike, you seem to imply only that they are identical. In some cases, you must also point out how the two similar things are different. Comparison allows us to understand one thing by a similar thing. Contrast allows us to distinguish one thing from a similar thing.

These two principles combine in the process of definition. We place the word into a family of similar meanings. This is the principle of comparison. Then we distinguish the word from the meanings it resembles. This is the principle of contrast. All methods of developing thought are forms of definition, and definition is primarily comparison and contrast.

Three forms of comparison are the simile, the metaphor, and the analogy. The *simile* is a comparison made explicit by such words as *like, as:* "He was swift as a hare"; "Her smile was like a snarl"; "A hatchet is like an axe, except that an axe is larger." The *metaphor* is a comparison which imputes to one thing a quality of another thing; resemblance is implied: "the raging sea"—the sea does not possess anger or any other emotion, yet the action of the water suggests a violence produced by emotion. The *analogy* is a comparison which points out how two essentially unlike things have aspects that resemble each other. It is usually a comparison sustained at some length. The example given previously of a mouse trap, set with a ping-pong ball, being sprung to toss up the ball to spring other traps to toss up other balls represents an analogy by which the fission of atoms can be better understood. Ping-pong balls and atoms do not belong to the same class of subjects; they are not akin to each other;

they are not obvious comparables. Much of the power of Biblical language comes from comparison:

> Yet man is born unto trouble, as the sparks fly upward. (V 7)

> . . . Remember, I beseech thee, that thou has made me as the clay; and wilt thou bring me into dust again? (X 9, 10)

> Hast thou not poured me out as milk, and curdled me like cheese?

> He cometh forth like a flower, and is cut down; he fleeth also as a shadow, and continueth not. (XIV 2)

> From The Book of Job

The following selection illuminates the character of a gentleman and the character of a scholar by showing how they are alike.

There is a character of a gentleman; so there is a character of a scholar, which is no less easily recognized. The one has an air of books about him, as the other has of good breeding. The one wears his thoughts as the other does his clothes, gracefully; and even if they are a little old-fashioned, they are not ridiculous: they have had their day. The gentleman shows, by his manner, that he has been used to respect from others; the scholar that he lays claim to self-respect and to a certain independence of opinion. The one has been accustomed to the best company; the other has passed his time in cultivating an intimacy with the best authors. There is nothing forward or vulgar in the behavior of the one; nothing shrewd or petulant in the observations of the other, as if he should astonish the bystanders, or was astonished himself at his own discoveries. Good taste and good sense, like common politeness, are, or are supposed to be, matters of course. One is distinguished by an appearance of marked attention to every one present; the other manifests an habitual air of abstraction and absence of mind. The one is not an upstart, with all the self-important airs of the founder of his own fortune; nor the other a self-taught man, with the repulsive self-suffi-ciency which arises from an ignorance of what hundreds have known before him. We must excuse perhaps a little conscious family pride in the one, and a little harmless pedantry in the other.

> From "On the Conversation of Authors,"
> by WILLIAM HAZLITT

The following excerpt clarifies its point through contrast. It was written when suffrage for women was still seriously debated.

When nature gave concentration to the setting hen it was to ensure the hatching of eggs. Likewise has she endowed woman with a narrow and intense interest in life, and for much the same reason. Man is a mixer. From the first tribal war-dance down to the Stock Exchange man has worked with man for common ends, and that is the essence of government. Woman is passionately loyal to her own. She is unmoved by abstract justice and the common good when they conflict with her personal interests. He who governs must seek the common advantage or he will fail. Man has proven capable for the task, while woman's very nature unfits her for it.

From "Competition or Co-operation," by JULIA D. HENRY, 1913

7d / Examining causes and effects

If a man had a full head of thick curly hair before the atom bomb was exploded and became bald ten years afterward, it is dangerous to assume that because baldness resulted *after* the bomb was exploded it resulted *because* the bomb was exploded. Don't confuse succession with cause. Such a confusion is an error known as *post hoc, ergo propter hoc,* Latin for "after this, therefore because of this."

Yet important to our understanding anything and to our making anything clear is establishing why something happened. *Why* is the cause. *What happened* is the effect. We must be careful and responsible in relating one to the other.

If a teacher doesn't like a student and the student gets failing grades in the course, is it evident which is the cause? Is it evident which is the effect? Is it even evident that the two are related? Perhaps the teacher doesn't like the student because he chews gum noisily. Perhaps the student gets failing grades because he gives wrong answers.

When you examine an effect to discover its causes, test your findings. Does B *always* result when A is present? Is A alone enough to produce B? Must A always be in combination with something else to produce B? Is A the cause of B, or does A produce something else which causes B? Your answers will enable you confidently to claim causes, or tentatively to suggest causes. Your discussion will be a responsible one.

William Hazlitt, the British essayist, discussed the causes of laughter. Examine the following paragraph:

The essence of the laughable then is the incongruous, the discon-
necting one idea from another, or the jostling of one feeling against another. The first and most obvious cause of laughter is to be found in the
simple succession of events, as in the sudden shifting of a disguise, or
some unlooked-for accident, without any absurdity of character or situation. The accidental contradiction between our expectations and the
event can hardly be said, however, to amount to the ludicrous; it is
merely laughable. The ludicrous is where there is the same contradiction
between the object and our expectations, heightened by some deformity
or inconvenience, that is, by its being contrary to what is customary or
desirable; as the ridiculous, which is the highest degree of the laughable,
is that which is contrary not only to custom but to sense and reason, or
is a voluntary departure from what we have a right to expect from
those who are conscious of absurdity and propriety in words, looks, and
actions.

From "A Lecture on the Comic,"
WILLIAM HAZLITT, 1819

The essayist suggests that we laugh when what happens is not
what we expect. But we know that, although the upsetting of our
expectations is necessary to laughter, it will not invariably make us
laugh. It sometimes makes us cry. Upset expectations then are a
necessary but not sufficient condition to cause laughter.

What else must be present? We are applying our tests. Does
laughter *always* result when anticipations are tumbled? Are tumbled
anticipations alone enough to produce laughter? Must tumbled anticipations be found with something else to produce laughter? Do
tumbled anticipations cause laughter, or do they produce something
else which causes laughter? We can examine cause and effect; we
can discuss them responsibly.

Mr. Hazlitt is establishing cause here; he is also defining. He distinguishes among three levels of laughter: the merely laughable;
the ludicrous; the ridiculous. Methods of developing thought are
used naturally, and almost invariably, in combination. Our separation is simply to make the uses clear, not to encourage separation.

7e/ Defining

It is bad for people not to understand each other. It is worse
for people to *mis*understand each other. Words are made by men.

Meanings are given to words by men. A definition is a social contract whereby persons agree on the area of meaning occupied by a word.

You often have to draw up that contract for your reader—else what you hope is a discussion will be, in reality, a burlesque. Discussion is impossible unless words are limited in meaning to an area upon which participants agree, and unless words remain constant in their meanings during the discussion. Violate these requirements and words waver and dissolve. Meanings shift. Talk becomes babble.

How is that contract drawn up?
By definition.
What is definition?
Definition is the process of limiting the meaning of words.
How is the meaning of a word limited?
Definition is the process of placing a word (or *term*) into a family (or *genus*) and then separating the word from the other members of the family by showing the difference (or *differentia*). For instance, a *desk* (term: word to be defined) is a table (genus: family to which the term belongs) equipped with drawers and used for writing or reading (differentia: differences between the term and the rest of the genus).

Most people do not need the word *desk* defined. This book, however, says, "Writing is a discipline." The reader knows that when a child is disciplined, the child is punished. Does this book mean, "Writing is a punishment"? For this book to be clear, it must clarify its use of *discipline*. It must limit. It must define.

Writing is a discipline. It is a system. It arranges ideas into clear and effective order. It establishes relationships. It uses specific methods to explain and demonstrate and unify ideas. Writing requires the knowledge and the exercise of certain principles and techniques.

In the following excerpt, an author defines a thing by separating it into parts, each of which he then in turn defines:

. . . I shall use the term zoology as denoting the whole doctrine of animal life, in contradistinction to botany, which signifies the whole doctrine of vegetable life.

Employed in this sense, zoology, like botany, is divisible into three great but subordinate sciences, morphology, physiology, and distribution, each of which may, to a very great extent, be studied independently of the other.

Zoological morphology is the doctrine of animal form or structure. Anatomy is one of its branches; development is another; while classification is the expression of the relations which different animals bear to one another, in respect of their anatomy and their development.

Zoological distribution is the study of animals in relation to the terrestrial conditions which obtain now, or have obtained at any previous epoch of the earth's history.

Zoological physiology, lastly, is the doctrine of the functions or actions of animals. It regards animal bodies as machines impelled by certain forces, and performing an amount of work which can be expressed in terms of the ordinary forces of nature. The final object of physiology is to deduce the facts of morphology, on the one hand, and those of distribution on the other, from the laws of molecular forces of matter.

Such is the scope of zoology. . . .

> From *Discourses—Biological and Geological*,
> THOMAS H. HUXLEY

John Henry Newman, in his *The Idea of a University*, profits us not only in how he defines, but in what he defines. At one point, he says, "I suppose the *prima-facie* view which the public at large would take of a University, considering it as a place of education, is nothing more or less than a place for acquiring a great deal of knowledge on a great many subjects." At another point, he defines his own views, using both figurative and literal terms:

A university is a place of concourse, whither students come, from every quarter for every kind of knowledge. You cannot have the best of every kind everywhere; you must go to some great city or emporium for it. There you have all the choices and productions of nature and art all together, which you find each in its separate place elsewhere. All the riches of the land, and of the earth, are carried up thither; there are the best markets, and there the best workmen. It is the centre of trade, the supreme court of fashion, the umpire of rival talents, and the standard of things rare and precious. It is the place for seeing galleries of first-rate pictures, and for hearing wonderful voices and performers of transcendent skill. It is the place for great preachers, great orators, great nobles, great statesmen. In the nature of things, greatness and unity go together; excellence implies a centre. And such, for the third or fourth time, is a university; I hope I do not weary out the reader by repeating it.

It is the place to which a thousand schools make contributions; in which the intellect may safely range and speculate, sure to find its equal in some antagonist activity, and its judge in the tribunal of truth. It is a place where inquiry is pushed forward, and discoveries verified and perfected, and rashness rendered innocuous, and error exposed, by the collision of mind with mind, and knowledge with knowledge. It is the place where the professor becomes eloquent, and is a missionary and a preacher, displaying his science in its most complete and most winning form, pouring it forth with the zeal of enthusiasm, and lighting up his own love of it in the breasts of his hearers. . . .

From *The Idea of a University*,
JOHN HENRY NEWMAN, 1873

7f / Listing cases to reach a rule, and using a rule to examine cases

We think in two ways. Either we apply a general rule to specific cases, or we examine specific cases to find a general rule. The first is deduction; the second, induction.

If a man says, "All red-heads are hot-tempered," he is giving a *general rule* (how true it is is another matter; if you don't think it *is* true, there is no use listening to what he's going to draw from that general rule). If he then says, "My wife is a red-head," he is giving *a specific case covered by the general rule.* He has now made the conclusion inevitable: The man is saying, finally, "My wife is hot-tempered." The sequence is *deductive.*

If a man says, "My wife, who is red-headed, has a hot temper," he is giving *a specific case,* which as yet has little general meaning for us. If he says, "That Titian-haired Rosa flares up at the slightest thing," it is another specific case, but of what we do not yet know. If he adds, "Lois has a temper just as fiery as her hair," we begin to suspect what the general significance is. All these specific cases cite women who share two qualities: they are all red-headed; they are all hot-tempered. The specific cases have led us to a general rule: "All red-heads are hot-tempered." Whether he has sufficient instances to justify the general rule is another matter; the procedure is *inductive.*

Usually, thought fuses induction and deduction. We apply generalizations to particulars and form new generalizations in the process. We separate the process in two so that we understand what we do.

7g / Classifying

We understand much by putting similar things together and by seeing how similar things differ. People who teach are teachers, a group or *classification*. In what ways do they differ? We isolate one way, apply that way to the group, and see what smaller groups result. We apply *subject*, a basis of classification, to *teachers*, a classification, and get *science teachers* and *humanities teachers*, categories that themselves can be further divided. Or we can apply *levels* to *teachers* and get *elementary teachers, secondary teachers, higher education teachers*. Students classify teachers constantly on different bases: *methods, personalities, grading practices, vulnerabilities, attitudes toward absences*. Both the bases and the resultant categories are often unexpected and revealing.

Classification is a process of collection and division, each providing information, each enabling the other. We know what a sentence is, we gather sentences together and see that there are different kinds of sentences. Why different kinds? We see differences in structure and get categories: simple, complex, compound. We see differences in function and get categories: declarative, imperative, interrogatory.

Many investigations begin by establishing differences among like things. Pascal, in *Pensées*, begins a section:

> There are only three sorts of people: those who serve God, having found him; those who put forth every effort to seek him, not having found him; those who live without seeking and without having found him. The first are reasonable and happy; the last are foolish and unhappy; the middle group are unhappy and reasonable.

He then explores these categories and defends the judgments made upon the categories. He has separated men with categories based upon men's attitudes toward God. Discussion has begun.

7h / Developing by elimination

We must be sure not only that we are understood, but that we are not misunderstood. We must be sure that our idea is freed from ideas that might be confused with it. The process of elimination points out what we do not mean. It removes a possible misunderstanding. For instance, in the following passages, we recognize that when John Henry Newman speaks of an educated man, he does *not* mean a man who can recite whole catalogues of information. He says, ". . . the end of a Liberal Education is not mere knowledge, or knowledge considered in its *matter* . . ." Now that the writer has told us what he does not mean, he has the obligation to tell what he *does* mean. And so, elimination consists of two parts:

a. The negative: a statement of what you *do not* mean.
b. The positive: a statement of what you *do* mean.

Cardinal Newman's sentence concludes with ". . . I shall best attain my object, by actually setting down some cases, which will be generally granted to be instances of the process of enlightenment or enlargement of mind, and others which are not, and thus, by the comparison, you will be able to judge for yourselves, Gentlemen, whether knowledge, that is, acquirement, is after all the real principle of the enlargement, or whether that principle is not rather something beyond it."

Cardinal Newman, in a later passage, explains further, using in great part the combination of negative and positive statements we call elimination:

. . . The enlargement consists, not merely in the passive reception into the mind of a number of ideas hitherto unknown to it, but in the mind's energetic and simultaneous action upon and towards and among those new ideas, which are rushing in upon it. It is the action of a formative power, reducing to order and meaning the matter of our acquirements; it is a making the objects of our knowledge subjectively our own, or, to use a familiar word, it is a digestion of what we receive, into the substance of our previous state of thought; and without this no enlargement is said to follow. There is no enlargement, unless there be a comparison of ideas one with another, as they come before the mind, and a systematizing of them. We feel our minds to be growing and expanding *then*, when we not only learn, but refer what we learn to what we know already. It is not the mere addition to our knowledge which is the illumination; but the locomotion, the movement onwards, of that mental centre, to which both what we know, and what we are

learning, the accumulating mass of our acquirements, gravitates. And
therefore a truly great intellect . . . possesses the knowledge, not only
of things, but also of their mutual and true relations; knowledge, not
merely considered as acquirement, but as philosophy.

From *The Idea of a University*,
JOHN HENRY NEWMAN, 1873

7i/ Giving an analogy

An analogy should be used to clarify or to suggest—but not to
prove. An analogy is a likeness between two things that are essentially unlike. The ancient Greeks helped man to understand his
condition by making an analogy between a life and thread. Three
powers worked on that thread: Clotho, the spinner, who made the
thread, (life); Lachesis, the disposer, who measured the thread, (des-
tiny); Atropos, the inexorable, who cut the thread, (death). This
analogy does not prove anything; it does not give evidence to support a verdict. It does, however, give us a vocabulary by which to
discuss an idea. It does make temporarily and roughly visible that
which in actuality is not visible. It does give us concrete equivalents
for an abstraction. It gives us things to represent an idea.

An analogy is often used to suggest possibilities. If two things
are alike in some respects, may they not be alike in other or all respects? Examining this possibility is profitable—if done cautiously.
The two things may run parallel for a space—but sooner or later
they must diverge. Pointing out where two things join is honest and
useful—if you also recognize where they separate.

Walter Hilton, a fourteenth-century Christian mystic, uses the
analogy of fire to clarify the nature of spiritual love. Yet he recognizes the danger of the analogy. Chapter 26, "On the Fire of
Love," consists of just one paragraph:

Those who speak of the fire of love do not always fully understand
what it is. Indeed, I cannot myself tell you what it is, but I can tell you
that it is not physical, nor is it a bodily sensation. A soul may experience
it during prayer and devotion, but although the soul dwells within the
body, it does not feel it through its bodily senses. For although it may
happen that the working of this fire in the soul may cause a sensation
of bodily heat, as though the body warmed in response to the exertions
of the spirit, nevertheless the fire of love is not a bodily sensation, for

it is caused by the spiritual desire of the soul. Nobody who experiences this devotion has any doubt on the matter, but simple people sometimes imagine that because it is called fire it must be hot like natural fire. And that is why I have mentioned this.

From *The Ladder of Perfection,*
by WALTER HILTON

Analogies can compare tangibles with tangibles, intangibles with intangibles, tangibles with intangibles. Analogies can range far and wide. But in comparing to clarify and to suggest, we must remember that, although different things may have similarities, they are different because they have differences. Never forget the differences: they are the limitation of analogy.

7j / Enumerating

Enumeration is a method that supports and clarifies a general thought by providing a list. The list may itemize parts, catalogue examples, record categories, specify stages, register a sequence. Enumeration establishes a series.

In the following excerpt, the general statement "To everything there is a season, and a time to every purpose under the heaven" is made vivid and dramatic by a list of specific times:

To everything there is a season,
And a time to every purpose under the heaven:
A time to be born, and a time to die;
A time to plant, and a time to pluck up that which is planted;
A time to kill, and a time to heal;
A time to break down, and a time to build up;
A time to weep, and a time to laugh;
A time to mourn, and a time to dance;
A time to cast away stones, and a time to gather stones together;
A time to embrace, and a time to refrain from embracing;
A time to seek, and a time to lose;
A time to keep, and a time to cast away;
A time to rend, and a time to sew;
A time to keep silence, and a time to speak;
A time to love, and a time to hate;
A time for war, and a time for peace.

Ecclesiastes

In the next excerpt, the intricacy and force, the marvel and wonder of a living thing are evoked by a series of questions followed by a list of acts:

> Hast thou given the horse his might?
> Hast thou clothed his neck with the quivering mane?
> Hast thou made him to leap as a locust?
> The glory of his snorting is terrible.
> He paweth in the valley, and rejoiceth in his strength:
> He goeth out to meet the armed men.
> He mocketh at fear, and is not dismayed;
> Neither turneth he back from the sword.
> The quiver rattleth against him,
> The flashing spear and the javelin.
> He swalloweth the ground with fierceness and rage:
> Neither believeth he that it is the voice of the trumpet.
> As oft as the trumpet soundeth he saith, "Aha!"
> And he smelleth the battle afar off,
> The thunder of the captains, and the shouting.
>
> The Book of Job

7k / Combining methods of development

A paragraph uses what is necessary to the intention of the writer. Most paragraphs combine the different methods to accomplish that intention.

In the following paragraph, the author uses whatever he needs to make his point:

> . . . In that great social organ, which, collectively, we call literature, there may be distinguished two separate offices, that may blend and often do so, but capable, severally, of a severe insulation, and naturally fitted for reciprocal repulsion. There is, first, the literature of *knowledge*, and secondly, the literature of *power*. The function of the first is to *teach*; the function of the second is to *move*; the first is a rudder, the second an oar or a sail. The first speaks to the mere discursive, understanding; the second speaks ultimately, it may happen, to the higher understanding or reason, but always through affections of pleasure and sympathy. Remotely, it may travel toward an object seated in what Lord Bacon calls "dry light"; but proximately it does and must operate —else it ceases to be a literature of power—on and through that *humid* light which clothes itself in the mists and glittering iris of human pas-

sions, desires, and genial emotions. Men have so little reflected on the higher functions of literature as to find it a paradox if one should describe it as a mean or subordinate purpose of books to give information. But this is a paradox only in the sense which makes it honourable to be paradoxical. Whenever we talk in ordinary language of seeking information or gaining knowledge, we understand the words as connected with something of absolute novelty. But it is the grandeur of all truth which can occupy a very high place in human interests that it is never absolutely novel to the meanest of minds; it exists eternally by way of germ or latent principle in the lowest as in the highest, needing to be developed, but never to be planted. To be capable of transplantation is the immediate criterion of a truth that ranges on a lower scale. Besides which, there is a rarer thing than truth—namely, *power*, or deep sympathy with truth. What is the effect, for instance, upon society of children? By the pity, by the tenderness, and by the peculiar modes of admiration which connect themselves with the helplessness, with the innocence, and with the simplicity of children, not only are the primal affections strengthened and continually renewed, but the qualities which are dearest in the sight of heaven—the frailty, for instance, which appeals to forbearance, the innocence which symbolizes the heavenly, and the simplicity which is most alien from the worldly—are kept up in personal remembrance, and their ideals are continually refreshed. A purpose of the same nature is answered by the higher literature, viz., the literature of power. What do you learn from *Paradise Lost?* Nothing at all. What do you learn from a cookery-book? Something new, something that you did not know before, in every paragraph. But would you therefore put the wretched cookery-book on a higher level of estimation than the divine poem? What you owe to Milton is not any knowledge, of which a million separate items are still but a million of advancing steps on the same earthly level; what you owe is *power*—that is, exercise and expansion to your own latent capacity of sympathy with the infinite, where every pulse and each separate influx is a step upwards, a step ascending as upon a Jacob's ladder from earth to mysterious altitudes above the earth. All the steps of knowledge, from first to last, carry you further on the same plane, but could never raise you one foot above your ancient level of earth; whereas the very first step in power is a flight—is an ascending movement into another element where earth is forgotten.

> From "Literature of Knowledge and Literature of Power" ("Alexander Pope" in *The North British Review*, 1848) by THOMAS DE QUINCEY.

Thomas de Quincey's paragraph exemplifies the method of development called *enumeration*. It is also a *definition* of two terms:

the literature of knowledge, and the literature of power. It uses *analogy*:

> The function of the first is to *teach*; the function of the second is to *move*; the first is a rudder, the second an oar or a sail.

Here Mr. de Quincey uses a thing, *rudder*, to clarify an idea, *teach*. He also uses *contrast* to distinguish two kinds of truth:

> But it is the grandeur of all truth which can occupy a very high place in human interests that it is never absolutely novel to the meanest of minds; it exists eternally by way of germ or latent principle in the lowest as in the highest, needing to be developed, but never to be planted. To be capable of transplantation is the immediate criterion of a truth that ranges on a lower scale.

The paragraph uses *details*; it separates a general statement into particulars:

> . . . The qualities which are dearest in the sight of heaven— the fraility, for instance, which appeals to forbearance; the innocence which symbolizes the heavenly, and the simplicity which is most alien from the worldly—are kept in perpetual remembrance, . . .

It uses *examples*:

> What do you learn from *Paradise Lost?*

It uses *comparison*:

> . . . each separate influx is a step upwards, a step ascending as upon a Jacob's ladder from earth. . . .

There are many other elements we can recognize in the anatomy of this paragraph. There is the sentence of transition on which the paragraph pivots from a discussion of the literature of knowledge to a discussion of the literature of power:

> Besides which, there is a rarer thing than truth—namely, *power*, or deep sympathy with truth.

There is the *rhetorical question,* in which a point is made by a question whose answer is so obvious it need not be stated:

> But would you therefore put the wretched cookery-book on a higher level of estimation than the divine poem?

The methods of development are not separable in practice or identity. We isolate them arbitrarily, we name them artificially simply as devices whereby we can discuss some of the things words can do. If we understand the functions, we can discard the devices.

7x / Exercises

1. Choose one of the following statements. Write four paragraphs, each developing that statement by use of a different appropriate method. Select the best effects from the four paragraphs and combine them gracefully into a fifth paragraph. Which paragraph seems to you the most interesting? Which the most meaningful? Are they different paragraphs? Are they the same paragraph? Why? Can you judge your paragraphs by de Quincey's discussion of the literature of knowledge and the literature of power?
   a. To do injustice is more disgraceful than to suffer it.—PLATO, *Gorgias.*
   b. Little learning is needed for a good mind.—SENECA.
   c. I judge a person by the way he talks.
   d. God offers to every mind its choice between truth and repose. Take which you please—you can never have both.—EMERSON, Essays: *Intellect.*
   e. College has made me less sure about what is right and what is wrong.
   f. My acts reveal my values.
   g. For doubting pleases me no less than knowing.—DANTE.
   h. I must enable my reader to judge my judgments.

2. In the following passage, what methods of development are emphasized? What is the contribution each method makes to the central point?

   A shipowner was about to send to sea an emigrant-ship. He knew that she was old, and not over-well built at the first; that she had seen many seas and climes, and often had needed repairs. Doubts had been suggested to him that probably she was not seaworthy. These doubts preyed upon his mind, and made him unhappy; he thought that perhaps he ought to have her thoroughly overhauled and refitted, even though this should put him to great expense. Before the ship sailed, however, he succeeded in overcoming these melancholy reflections. He said to himself that she had gone safely through so many voyages and weathered so many storms that it was idle to suppose she would not come safely home from this trip also. He would put his trust in Providence, which could hardly fail to protect all these unhappy families that were leaving their fatherland to seek for better times elsewhere. He would dismiss from his mind all ungenerous suspicions about the honesty of builders and contractors. In such ways he acquired a sincere and comfortable conviction that his vessel was thoroughly safe and seaworthy; he watched her departure with a light heart, and benevolent wishes for the success of the exiles in their strange new home that was to be; and he got his insurance-money when she went down in mid-ocean and told no tales.

What shall we say of him? Surely this, that he was verily guilty of the death of those men. It is admitted that he did sincerely believe in the soundness of his ship; but the sincerity of his conviction can in no wise help him, because *he had no right to believe on such evidence as was before him.* He had acquired his belief not by honestly earning it in patient investigation, but by stifling his doubts. And although in the end he may have felt so sure about it that he could not think otherwise, yet inasmuch as he had knowingly and willingly worked himself into that frame of mind, he must be held responsible for it.

Let us alter the case a little, and suppose that the ship was not unsound after all; that she made her voyage safely, and many others after it. Will that diminish the guilt of her owner? Not one jot. When an action is once done, it is right or wrong for ever; no accidental failure of its good or evil fruits can possibly alter that. The man would not have been innocent, he would only have been not found out. The question of right or wrong has to do with the origin of his belief, not the matter of it; not what it was, but how he got it; not whether it turned out to be true or false, but whether he had a right to believe on such evidence as was before him.

There was once an island in which some of the inhabitants professed a religion teaching neither the doctrine of original sin nor that of eternal punishment. A suspicion got abroad that the professors of this religion had made use of unfair means to get their doctrines taught to children. They were accused of wresting the laws of their country in such a way as to remove children from the care of their natural and legal guardians; and even of stealing them away and keeping them concealed from their friends and relations. A certain number of men formed themselves into a society for the purpose of agitating the public about this matter. They published grave accusations against individual citizens of the highest position and character, and did all in their power to injure these citizens in the exercise of their professions. So great was the noise they made, that a Commission was appointed to investigate the facts; but after the Commission had carefully inquired into all the evidence could be got, it appeared that the accused were innocent. Not only had they been accused on insufficient evidence, but the evidence of their innocence was such as the agitators might easily have obtained, if they had attempted a fair inquiry. After these disclosures the inhabitants of that country looked upon the members of the agitating society, not only as persons whose judgment was to be distrusted, but also as no longer to be counted honourable men. For although they had sincerely and conscientiously believed in the charges they had made, *yet they had no right to believe on such evidence as was before them.* Their sincere convictions, instead of being honestly earned by patient inquiring, were stolen by listening to the voice of prejudice and passion.

Let us vary this case also, and suppose, other things remaining as before, that a still more accurate investigation proved the accused to have been really guilty. Would this make any difference in the guilt of the accusers? Clearly not; the question is not whether their belief was true or false, but whether they entertained it on wrong grounds. They would no doubt say, "Now you see that we were right after all; next time perhaps you will believe us." And they might be believed, but they would not thereby become honourable men. They would not be innocent, they would only be not found out. Every one of them, if he chose to examine himself *in foro conscientiae*, would know that he had acquired and nourished a belief, when he had no right to believe on such evidence as was before him; and therein he would know that he had done a wrong thing.

It may be said, however, that in both of these supposed cases it is not the belief which is judged to be wrong, but the action following upon it. The shipowner might say, "I am perfectly certain that my ship is sound, but still I feel it my duty to have her examined, before trusting the lives of so many people to her." And it might be said to the agitator, "However convinced you were of the justice of your cause and the truth of your convictions, you ought not to have made a public attack upon any man's character until you had examined the evidence on both sides with the utmost patience and care."

In the first place, let us admit that, so far as it goes, this view of the case is right and necessary; right, because even when a man's belief is so fixed that he cannot think otherwise, he still has a choice in regard to the action suggested by it, and so cannot escape the duty of investigating on the ground of the strength of his convictions; and necessary, because those who are not yet capable of controlling their feelings and thoughts must have a plain rule dealing with overt acts.

But this being premised as necessary, it becomes clear that it is not sufficient, and that our previous judgment is required to supplement it. For it is not possible so to sever the belief from the action it suggests as to condemn the one without condemning the other. No man holding a strong belief on one side of a question, or even wishing to hold a belief on one side, can investigate it with such fairness and completeness as if he were really in doubt and unbiassed; so that the existence of a belief not founded on fair inquiry unfits a man for the performance of this necessary duty.

Nor is that truly a belief at all which has not some influence upon the actions of him who holds it. He who truly believes that which prompts him to an action has looked upon the action to lust after it, he has committed it already in his heart. If a belief is not realized immediately in open deeds, it is stored upon for the guidance of the future. It goes to make a part of that aggregate of beliefs which is the link between sensation and action at every moment of all our lives, and which is so organized and compacted together that no part of it can be isolated from the rest, but every new addition modifies the structure of the whole. No real belief, however trifling and fragmentary it may seem, is ever truly insignificant; it prepares us to receive more of its like, confirms those which resembled it before, and weakens others; and so gradually it lays a stealthy train in our inmost thoughts, which may some day explode into overt action, and leave its stamp upon our character for ever.

And no one's belief is in any case a private matter which concerns himself alone. Our lives are guided by that general conception of the course of things which has been created by society for social purposes. Our words, our phrases, our forms and processes and modes of thought, are common property, fashioned and perfected from age to age; an heirloom which every succeeding generation inherits as a precious deposit and a sacred trust to be handed on to the next one, not unchanged but enlarged and purified, with some clear marks of its proper handiwork. Into this, for good or ill, is woven every belief of every man who has speech of his fellows. An awful privilege, and an awful responsibility, that we should help to create the world in which posterity will live.

From "The Ethics of Belief,"
Lectures and Essays, W. K. CLIFFORD

THE SENTENCE

8 / The Logic of Sentence Structure

A sentence combines words to get meaning. Each part of speech, each mark of punctuation, each link of grammar serves a function. Each exists because it does something only it can do. It exists not by law, not by rule—but by logic of function. Don't learn a law. Don't learn a rule. Learn the function. Learn the function of each as you would learn the function of a hammer or a saw. Then you will be able to say what you want to say. Syntax is the logic of function.

The logic of sentence structure is simple. It uses words to give an idea form and weight. The relative importance of ideas is made visible by sentence structure. Ideas equal in importance are put into structures equal in importance. Less important ideas are put into less important structures. A sentence structure is the physical equivalent of a non-physical entity. It makes a thing of an idea. It gives meaning weight.

When you write, you may face two problems: What to say, and how to say it. One person may be unable to recognize ideas and to say anything clearly. Another person may recognize ideas, but say them clumsily and tastelessly. The two problems may be simply two degrees of the same problem. It may be that the more clearly you recognize an idea, the more clearly you say the idea.

When a person says, "I know what I mean, but I can't say it," he may be confusing two things. He may be confusing the *apprehension* of an idea with the *comprehension* of an idea. He may be aware that an idea is present, but he does not yet know the identity of the idea. He knows that an idea is in the vicinity, but he hasn't yet surrounded the idea. The moment he knows *what* the idea is, he knows *how* to say it. If he has an idea which can be stated and he cannot state it, he does not have the idea. The statement of the idea is the comprehension of the idea.

An essay always contains more than the reader carries away. It consists usually of the statement of an idea, and the demonstration and dramatization of the idea by examples, illustrations, comparisons, details, analyses. The idea is essential; it is the reader's profit. The demonstration and dramatization help the reader to understand the idea fully; he no longer needs them once they have served that function. The reader will retain the essential, and may discard the additional. The writer should know what is essential and what is merely additional.

Try naked writing. State ideas simply; relate them to each other strongly. Clarify your idea as directly as possible. Your presentation will be more graceful and forceful than it would have been had you tried for ornamentation and complexity. You cannot be complex until you have been simple. You should never be complex where you can be simple. Nakedness must be honest—and can be beautiful.

9/ A Fragment of a Sentence

All precepts in writing exist to enable you to carry out your intention. Any precept can be violated—*should* be violated—if your intention requires it. But the accomplishment must justify the violation. The gain must be greater than the sacrifice.

A sentence should be complete. It should possess a subject and a predicate. It should be self-sufficient and self-explanatory. Therefore, it is a precept that incomplete sentences—sentence fragments —should *not* be used.

Unless you have some special emphasis to make. Some special effect to accomplish. But if you use sentence fragments often or habitually, they become ordinary, weak, ridiculous. If you use them occasionally, they *are* special: they can shock and impress. You are right to use a sentence fragment if you know (1) when you are using one, and (2) why you are using it. Otherwise, you are probably wrong. Or worse: ineffective.

Sentence fragments violate conventional sentence structure. They are justified only as special effects. They are effective only when they come as a shock in the midst of conventional structures. If they are used consistently, they lose all surprise value, they are monotonous, and they are solely and wholly what outlawed them in the first place: awkward and unclear.

The following excerpt begins with a sentence fragment and ends with a sentence fragment. Posed against a sustained passage of complete sentence structures, they provide surprise and emphasis:

Mules—1900 of them. They carried up to 300 pounds each and Mexican *arrieros* were hired to pack and drive them. Grant's colonel tapped him to help the system work, but Taylor's $20 bargains put a strain on the lieutenant's rule against swearing. Mules bucked or ran off, scattering their loads, rolling on them, snapping tentpoles, throwing pots, kettles, mess pans, axes, picks, coffee mills, chests, and ammunition boxes. Captains Henry Giddings and Kenly, who were not involved, could enjoy the show. In the end the *arrieros* usually won. Sweating in tight leather jackets above flaring pants split to the knee, they outbrayed, outmanuevered, and outfought their animals in a daily storm of dust and flying hoofs. Something new and colorful in logistics.

From *Zach Taylor's Little Army*,
by EDWARD J. NICHOLS

10/ Sentence Variety

Sentences must have variety. They must have changes of structure. But variety is not imposed on thought. Variety is the nature of thought as it shifts and develops between simple and complex, suggestive and assertive, blunt and subtle. Follow the thought clearly; variety results.

A sentence must assume one of three forms. It may be a *simple sentence*; it has one idea to state; it has one subject and predicate.

> He types his papers.

Any number of modifiers may be added, but it still remains one idea, one subject and predicate.

> He types his papers with many errors, erasures, and smudges.

A *complex sentence* has at least two ideas, but one of them is there only because it serves the other. One idea is subordinate to the other. Two clauses, at least, are present. The servant idea is in the subordinate clause; the important idea is in the independent clause.

> When I have money, I eat steak.

The first clause is dependent, the idea cannot stand alone. The sentence form reflects two unequal ideas. The dependent clause is introduced by a subordinate conjunction such as *when, although, since, if*, and *because*.

A *compound sentence* consists of at least two ideas of equal importance. At least two independent clauses are present. These ideas of equal importance are in the same sentence; they are related to each other in some way. Sometimes the ideas are coordinated by some specific word of relationship: a coordinate conjunction, such as *and, but, nor, or*, and *for*, or a conjunctive adverb, such as *therefore, nevertheless, however, yet*, or *hence*. When the relationship is clear from juxtaposition, no explanatory word is needed.

> Man proposes, but God disposes.
> I am afraid to speak; nevertheless, I will speak.
> To act is brave; to hesitate is wise.

The three sentence structures—simple, complex, compound—are shapes that mark the developing thought. They play against each other in the paragraph. They prevent monotony. They relieve, surprise, refresh the ear and the eye.

11/ The Unity of a Sentence

Whenever you talk about one idea, you have to bring up other ideas. The others are important because they contribute to the first. But if your talk about the secondary ideas does not remain pertinent to the primary one, your ideas compete. The sentence becomes a mob, not an organization. There are essential ideas, additional ideas that clarify, and irrelevant ideas that confuse. Dismiss irrelevant ideas: They are in breach of order.

> My house, which is part of a community developed by Mr. Haskins, who is noted for his stamp collection, has a beautiful view of the mountains, part of the Cascade Range.

If you continue to make your point after you have already made your point, you will bury it.

> I am forced and compelled to do things against my will.

Forced and *compelled* and *against my will?* Does each of these terms add meaning to the other two? They ought to add meaning; else why are they there? But since the reader cannot see added meaning, is it possible that he doesn't understand the first meaning? The repetition makes the reader less sure, rather than more sure, of meaning.

12/ Subordination in a Sentence

12a/ False coordination

Secondary ideas serve a principal idea. They are present not to draw attention to themselves, but to contribute to the principal idea. They must show themselves servants; they must relate themselves strongly to the principal idea. If distinctions are not made between secondary ideas and principal ones, if all ideas are given the same emphasis, ideas blur. Clarity is lost.

Secondary ideas take shape in subordinate structures. If they take any other structure, they weaken, distort, confuse the writer's intention Let's examine the following version of a previous passage:

> Distinctions are not made between secondary ideas and principal ones. All ideas are given the same emphasis. Ideas blur.

Three independent sentences exist. All have the same emphasis. All seem to be equal in importance. But why three ideas? Are we making a collection of ideas? Or is there one idea the other two are serving? One idea the other two are making clear? Then which idea is the important one? Which ideas are the contributing ones? The passage fails because it gives two secondary ideas and one principal idea as if they were three equally important ideas, three coordinate ideas. This error is called *false coordination*. We show the relationship of the two lesser ideas to the principal idea by putting them in subordinate structures—clauses made dependent by the subordinate conjunction *if*:

> If distinctions are not made between secondary ideas and principal ones, if all ideas are given the same emphasis, ideas blur.

The servants have made their service clear.

12b/ Upside-down subordination

More confusing, even, than *false coordination* is *upside-down* subordination, in which the principal idea is put into a subordinate structure, and the secondary idea is put into a principal structure:

> When the car skidded across the road and toppled down the bank, the brakes failed.

12c/ Choppy sentences

Some passages attempt to avoid establishing relationships and emphases. They put one idea into one sentence, and one sentence after another. Everything is equally important—or equally unimportant. The result is *choppy sentences*. It can mean anything—or nothing. What the writer intends, the reader can only guess:

> I attended the lecture. The lecture was about music. I like music. The lecturer played some records. He played parts of a symphony. I wish he played all of the symphony. The lecture lasted two hours. I did not know that two hours had gone by. I learned about music. The lecturer talked about composing music. It must be very pleasant to compose music. The lecturer said it was hard work. The lecture was good. But I don't think I want to hear another one.

The passages is about as significant and entertaining as a leaking faucet.

13/ Coordination in a Sentence

13a/ Coordination

Coordination means joining two things equal in importance and similar in structure. The word *and* in the above sentence connects the phrase "equal in importance" to the phrase "similar in structure." The word *and* acts as a pivot allowing two things of equal weight to hang in equilibrium. The word *and* is called, therefore, *coordinate conjunction*. Similarity in structure of phrases indicates equality of importance.

13b/ Parallel structures

The basic words that join like elements—clause to clause, phrase to phrase, word to word—are the coordinate conjunctions *and, but, or, nor,* and *for*. They establish *parallel structures*. If similar ideas are not similar in form, the reader has to compensate the sentence to make the logical scale balance. He has to do the writer's work.

> Mountain climbing and to explore caves are his hobbies.

Either two gerund phrases—"mountain climbing and cave exploring" —or two infinitive phrases—"to climb mountains and to explore caves"—would correct this sentence. But mating a gerund to an infinitive is unnatural and ungraceful.

Items in a series should be parallel in form.

> The desk has three advantages: the large surface, it has six drawers, comfortable.

Lumped under one classification, *advantages,* are three different structures: a noun phrase, *the large surface;* an independent clause, *it has six drawers;* an adjective, *comfortable.* The reader has to cut and hammer to get them into the same class of meaning.

13c/ Repeated connectives

Phrases and clauses become clearly parallel when the connective is repeated. The connective may be a preposition, a relative pronoun, a subordinate conjunction:

> Men will fight for food, for self-respect, and for ideas.
> We pray that nations will lay down their swords, that men will love one another, that peace shall be everlasting.
> Because men have different values, because men have conflicting ambitions, because men distrust one another, history is a succession of wars.

13d/ Parallel forms after correlative conjunctions

Correlative conjunctions demand parallel forms. The scales must be balanced. *Either* this *or* that; *neither* this *nor* that; *not only* this, *but also* that; *both* this *and* that; *whether* this *or* that. The second conjunction of a correlative pair forces a counter-balance. If the weight is not equal, the sentence will tip:

> Either he is smart or lucky.

Either is followed by a clause; *or* by an adjective. One side of the sentence is heavy; the other side, almost weightless, hangs high in the air. The sentence should read: "He is either smart or lucky," or "Either he is smart or he is lucky." The correlatives are balanced; the forms are parallel.

> I not only dislike borrowing money, but also paying it back.

The verb present after *not only* is absent after *but also*. The scale tilts. The sentence should be "I dislike not only borrowing money, but also paying it back."

13e/ Coordinating relative clauses

A relative clause can be coordinated only with another relative clause. A clause beginning with *which* modifies some specific noun or pronoun; you can have an "and which" clause only if you are adding it to a previous "which" clause. Otherwise you are adding the clause to air—and nothing else:

> I saw a play about the Napoleonic wars, *and which* I enjoyed very much.

Perhaps this means, "I saw a play which was about the Napoleonic wars, and which I enjoyed very much." Of course, simpler would be better: "I enjoyed the play about the Napoleonic wars."

"And who" relative clauses are often connected only to air:

> He is a man scrupulously honest, and who always reports errors made in his favor.

> *Corrected:* He is a scrupulously honest man who always reports errors made in his favor.

Related to these is the "and that" noun clause which hangs unconnected:

> I was told to apply for the job and that I should enclose references.

> *Corrected:* I was told to apply for the job and to enclose references.

13f/ Parallel forms in comparisons

Comparisons examine like things. The like things require like structures. Like structures are parallel in form. In short, comparisons are parallel in form. But since the second form is often abbreviated and implied, comparisons are often illogically phrased:

> He is taller than me.

We recognize the intention; but the accomplishment is technically meaningless. Stated logically—and stiffly—the meaning is:

> He is taller than I am tall.

The graceful and correct rendition would be:

> He is taller than I.

Comparisons must always obey the logic of like things in like forms.

> Adding figures is more exhausting than a bricklayer.

Adding figures may be more exhausting than laying bricks, but a job is not comparable to a person.

> Bricklaying is more constructive than any skill.

Since bricklaying is a skill, it is more constructive than itself? Bricklaying can be compared only with *other* skills. The statement logically would be: "Bricklaying is more constructive than any *other* skill [is constructive]."

14/ Dangling Modifiers

14a/ Dangling participles, gerunds, infinitives

Modifiers dangle if there is no noun or pronoun to which they refer. Supply the noun or pronoun and you have corrected the error.

> *Dangling participle:* Walking down the street, a car splashed me. [Was the car walking down the street? That's what the sentence says: A car walking down the street splashed me.]
> *Improved:* As I was walking down the street, a car splashed me.

Dangling participle: Learning three languages, John's trip to Europe qualified him for an interpreter's job. [The trip didn't learn the languages; John did.]

Improved: Having learned three languages on his European trip, John was qualified for an interpreter's job.

Dangling gerund: Before taking a long trip, road maps must be obtained. [Are road maps going to take a trip?]

Improved: Before you take a long trip, get road maps.

Dangling gerund: Before reading 1984, some facts about George Orwell's life should be understood. [Can facts read "1984"]

Improved: Before reading 1984, you should know some facts about George Orwell's life.

Dangling infinitive: To become a skillful writer, dangling infinitives must be avoided.

Improved: To become a skillful writer, one must avoid dangling infinitives.

Dangling infinitive: A careful diet should be followed to avoid obesity.

Improved: To avoid obesity, one should follow a careful diet.

14b / Dangling elliptical clauses

Sometimes the subject and verb are left out of a dependent clause (*when reading* instead of *when one is reading*). Such a clause is called elliptical. If the subject of an elliptical clause is not made clear in the main clause, the elliptical clause will dangle.

Dangling elliptical clause: When reading, a good light should be used.

Improved: When one is reading, he should use a good light.

Better: Be sure to use a good light when you read.

Dangling elliptical clause: Although tired and hungry, a camp had to be made and fire started before the troops could eat and rest.

Improved: Although the troops were tired and hungry, they had to make camp and start a fire before they could eat and rest.

Note: Dangling elliptical clauses, dangling infinitives, and dangling gerunds frequently result from awkward use of the passive voice. Build your sentences around verbs in the active voice and you will eliminate many of these errors.

14c/ Acceptable conventions

Some expressions are acceptable even though technically they dangle:

> *Acceptable:* Generally speaking, the National League is stronger than the American League. [*The National League is not speaking generally, but it would be pedantic to insist on the logical noun or pronoun.*]
> *Acceptable:* In fly casting, the elbow should move very little.

Other acceptable introductory expressions include *taking everything into consideration, judging from past experience.*

> *Acceptable:* Taking everything into consideration, parachute jumping is not a dangerous sport.
> *Acceptable:* Judging from past experience, the cost of living index will probably go up five points between January and March.

15/ Misplaced Modifiers

15a/ Split infinitives

Splitting an infinitive—putting modifiers between the *to* and the verb form, *to better know*, etc.—generally produces an awkward construction. You should avoid split infinitives if possible but use them fearlessly *if* you can show that any other construction is weaker. A satisfactory defense can be made for splitting the infinitive in the following sentence: "He hopes to more than double his income next year."

15b/ Misplaced adverbs

In formal writing, limiting adverbs like *only, almost, nearly, merely, never, seldom, quite, scarcely* should be placed immediately before the words they modify. Notice the differences in meaning of the following sentences:

Only John Halsingford can hope to win the Ohio golf championship.

John Halsingford can only hope to win the Ohio golf championship.

John Halsingford can hope to win only the Ohio golf championship.

15c/ Misplaced clauses and phrases

Place phrases near the words they modify. Be sure that no ludicrous misreading is possible.

Misplaced modifier: One summer our fruit stand was closed because we had sold apples to customers that had worms.

Improved: One summer the authorities closed our fruit stand because we sold wormy apples.

Misplaced modifier: Beer must not be sold to a student containing more than 3.2% alcohol.

Improved: Beer containing more than 3.2% alcohol must not be sold to a student.

15d/ Squinting modifiers

Frequently, in hasty writing, you may produce a modifier that seems to have two referents in the sentence.

Squinting modifier: People who go to the beach often don't like to swim.

Comment: "Often," placed between "*people who go to the beach*" and "*don't like to swim,*" can refer either to what precedes it or to what follows it. Such ambiguity results sometimes in unintentional absurdity.

Correction: Often, people who go to the beach don't like to swim.

16/ Pronoun Reference

16a/ Two possible antecedents

Faulty: The Loyalists want to take the islands, and the Nationalists want to keep them. It will be too bad if they have their way.

Comment: The writer's intention is not clear. Does he mean it will be too bad if the Loyalists have their way or too bad if the Nationalists have their way?

Faulty: There is no reason why a mother and a daughter cannot get along well. If she is willing to cooperate and give up certain rights and privileges, there should be no problem.

Improved: There is no reason why a mother and a daughter cannot get along well. If "both" are willing to cooperate [or if the mother is willing to cooperate—or if the daughter is willing to cooperate] and give up certain rights and privileges, there should be no problem.

16b / Remote antecedents

If the pronoun is separated from the antecedent by so much material that the reader may miss the relationship, it is a good idea to repeat the antecedent or revise the sentence.

Remote: The fox was dropped at 2:30 P.M. At 3:15 the dogs were turned loose. The hunters on horseback followed them down through Stauffer's cornfield, across Black Creek. About 5:20 it hid in a stone fence near Silver Hill.

Improved: About 5:20 the fox hid in a stone fence near Silver Hill.

16c / Vague reference

Be sure your pronoun has a specific noun or pronoun reference. In some cases, a general reference is allowable, if the sense is clear.

Vague: The headmaster said in chapel that henceforth students would go directly from chapel to lunch rather than back to their rooms. This provoked a great deal of discussion.

Improved: This announcement [or this change in policy] provoked a great deal of discussion.

Implied antecedent: There is a baseball factory in Philadelphia that will re-cover them for one dollar.

Clearer: A factory in Philadelphia will re-cover baseballs for one dollar.

Faulty reference: Some people think there is more stealing in a university than in a city of similar size, which is a myth.

Improved: It is a myth that stealing is more prevalent in a university than in a city of similar size.

See also "They, you, and it" in Glossary of Errors in Diction, p. 207.

Allowable general reference: Hunting season usually begins the first Monday in November, but this has not always been the case.

16d/ Pronoun usage

Use the relative pronoun *who* to refer to persons.

Mr. Johnson is the one who painted that marvelous landscape.

Use *which* to refer to animals and inanimate objects.

The insect which causes the greatest economic loss in the South is the boll weevil.

That may be used to refer to animals or things; or to persons included in an antecedent also containing animals or things; or to persons alone when the pronoun introduces a restrictive clause.

Acceptable: It's the bears and the poison ivy that ruin camping for me.

Acceptable: It's mosquitoes, poison ivy, and litterbugs that spoil summer for me.

Acceptable: There's the man that started all the trouble.

17/ Unnecessary Shifts

Keep your point of view consistent in person, tense, voice, number, tone, and objectivity.

17a/ Shift in person

Unless an *athlete* is willing to watch his diet, get plenty of good food and sleep, and train his body in his chosen skill, *you* can never expect to make a varsity team.

Comment: Notice the change from third person [*athlete*] to second person [*you*].

Corrected: Unless an athlete is willing to watch his diet . . . , *he* can never expect to make a varsity team.

17b/   Shift in tense

The horse *gets* frightened by the fire, *runs* wildly around the field, *steps* in a chuck hole, and, unfortunately, *broke* his leg.

Comment: Here present tense shifts to past tense. The logic of time has been violated.

17c/   Shift in voice

John ate all the eggs, but the toast wasn't touched.

Comment: Why should our attention be shifted from John to the toast?

Consistent: John ate all the eggs, but he didn't touch the toast.

17d/   Shift in number

If anyone gives information leading to the arrest and conviction of the man who murdered John Appleby, they will receive a reward of $10,000.

Consistent: If anyone . . . *he* . . .

17e/   Shift in tone

Shift in tone: Stock prices change because of the law of supply and demand. If more people want to buy than sell, the price of a stock goes up. If more want to sell than buy, it *takes a nose dive.*

Consistent tone: Stock prices change because of the law of supply and demand. If more people want to buy than sell, the price of a stock goes up. If more want to sell than buy, *it goes down.*

17f/   Shift in objectivity

Consistent objectivity: On August 30, Michael Uritsky was slain by an SR assassin. That same evening Lenin was hit in the neck by two bullets fired by Fania Kaplan-Roid. Lenin was in the hospital for two weeks. The assailant was captured and executed.

The account so far is factual and unimpassioned. It seems to be consistently objective. The account goes on—

> Wreckers led by Trotsky, Bukharin and other riff-raff of the Left Communists must have known of and supported the attack. Hate mongers in the ruthless machinery of Allied diplomacy doubtless assisted.

This last part represents a shift in objectivity. The reader is suddenly fed hate-words and undocumented charges. Such shifts cause the reader to suspect the writer's purpose.

18/ Faulty Constructions and Comparisons

18a/ Mixed constructions

A writer has several choices of sentence construction for expressing an idea. He may use a subject-verb construction. He may begin with a prepositional phrase, a verbal phrase, an expletive, a subordinate clause, or even a coordinating conjunction. There will be advantages and disadvantages to any selection he makes. So long as the relationship of parts is consistent and clear, the reader will not object; but he will object if the parts put together do not belong together.

> *Mixed:* Any talented engineer the space age can use him.
> *Clear:* Any talented engineer can get a job in the space age.
> *Clear:* The space age has created a demand for talented engineers.

> *Mixed:* Sometimes it wouldn't be until suppertime before we stopped swimming.
> *Clear:* Sometimes we didn't stop swimming until suppertime.
> *Clear:* Sometimes we kept swimming until suppertime.
> *Clear:* Sometimes it was suppertime before we stopped swimming.

18b/ Incomplete Constructions

> *Incomplete:* My brother has and always will be an ardent baseball fan.

Complete: My brother has been and always will be an ardent baseball fan.

18c / Incomplete comparisons

Incomplete comparison: The group life insurance program at Winchester Widget Company is better than any other company.
Complete: The group life insurance program at Winchester Widget Company is better than the group life insurance program at any other company.

Ambiguous: John likes Anne better than George.
Clear: John likes Anne better than he likes George.
Clear: John likes Anne better than George does.

19 / Emphasis

The end of a sentence is the strongest position. The next strongest is the beginning. The weakest position in the sentence is the middle. It follows that you should place important ideas—ideas that must move your reader—in the strong positions. To the old saying, "It's not what you say, but how you say it," we must add a new variation: "It's *where* you say it that counts."
Compare the following sentences:

1.   I saw two cars crash head-on while I was vacationing in a little Kentucky town near the Tennessee border.
2.   While I was vacationing in a little Kentucky town near the Tennessee border, I saw two cars crash head-on.
3.   While I was vacationing, I saw two cars crash head-on in a little Kentucky town near the Tennessee border.

The important idea in these sentences is the crash. Sentence number two subordinates all other ideas, using the strong end-position to record the terrible fact. (Emphatic sentences of this kind are called *periodic sentences.*) Sentence number three is the least emphatic. The reader feels that the crash is a minor interlude in a summer afternoon. (Unemphatic sentences like number three are called *loose sentences.*) You must decide how much emphasis your ideas deserve and place them in sentences accordingly. The periodic sentence will serve you best in some cases; the loose sentence, in others. Don't build suspense to an anti-climax:

> In a lonely mountain cabin deep in enemy country, by the dim half-light of a candle stuck in an empty liquor bottle, Ralph and Bill ate lunch.

If such a sentence is worth writing at all, the writer must respect the relative importance of the elements it contains. Simply reversing the construction in this sentence (even without eliminating some of the melodramatic detail) would distribute the emphasis more justly.

> Ralph and Bill ate lunch in a lonely mountain cabin, deep in enemy country. . . .

Remember—in sentences, paragraphs, themes—position controls emphasis. The middle is least emphatic, the beginning is more, and the end is most.

20/ Sentences: Qualities, Things, Acts

20a/ Use adjectives and adverbs sparingly

Ideas involve qualities, things and acts. But we know qualities only as they invest things and acts. The closer our words adhere to the thing and the act, the more strongly our senses grasp them. Sentences of concrete nouns and active verbs have thrust and substance. Nouns and verbs name things and acts. Adjectives and adverbs name qualities found in things and acts. But adjectives and adverbs should be used sparely; frequent use robs the sentence of thrust and substance. The more adjectives and adverbs used, the less effect each has. Used sparely, they can surprise and strike the reader's sensibility. Used sparely, they deserve the reader's attention and trust.

Think in terms of things and acts. Let, wherever possible, the thing and the act reveal the quality. Use nouns and verbs to make an idea. Remember that adjectives and adverbs decorate the idea.

Save them; use them with frugality and discrimination; natural beauty requires only a touch of cosmetics.

20b/   Use active rather than passive voice

In general, the active verb is cleaner and sharper than the passive verb. Structures in the passive voice often inflate to massive size highly satisfying to the ego of the writer happily puffing. But they are like bubble-gum balloons: They contain only air.

> Citizens who are to be considered responsible should be motivated by a desire to have been an effective participant in the prior formulation of programs of social welfare undertaken by agencies of the national government.

The passage has verbs, but verbs robbed of action. It has nouns, but nouns in excess of the number needed. The passage may mean:

> Responsible citizens should want to help form federal programs of social welfare.

But the passage evades meaning. Words are wasted. Thrust is lost. Substance is evaporated Use active verbs: identify the act. Use nouns: name the actors. Let nouns and verbs suggest, wherever possible, the qualities: adverbs and adjectives. Make each word bear its full weight of meaning. Establish relationships strongly.

21/   Movement Is in the Verb

One way of looking at the universe sees all phenomena as forms of motion. Thus, for the Chinese, the green, leafy tree is not a static thing, but a manifestation of force. He does not say, "The tree is green"; he says, "The tree greens itself." It is effective to think in terms of verbs: verbs are meant to perform work. Thinking in verbs will prevent you from loading all the work on nouns, adding nouns to nouns, trying to conceal by excitement that all a noun can do is stand there. Movement is in the verb.

An inflated-noun sentence often attempts to give life to a sentence whose verb was rendered inactive:

> His success is the result of the highest level of persistence, combining an enthusiastic response to any competitive challenge with an intensely motivating desire to be victorious in every case.

When we replace the many nouns with a few verbs, the sentence reads:

> He succeeds because he won't quit until he wins.

The words are fewer; the force, clarity, and grace are greater.

8–21x/ Exercises

1. What is the effect of these sentence fragments? Is the violation of sentence wholeness justified? Re-write passage to improve sense, grace, and effectiveness.
   a. Alec fell. Causing him to break his ankle. We carried him to the office of Dr. Smith. Who is a good doctor. And does not charge high fees. Dr. Smith set the ankle and put it into a cast. And told Alec to rest. For two weeks.

2. How is meaning in these sentences diluted? Re-write. Discard irrelevancies and excesses.
   a. Because I ate too much cake, which we bought at the new bakery, a block and a half from our house, and ice cream, a delicacy that I have liked ever since I was a child and used to spend every cent I could get to buy chocolate, my favorite flavor, I became ill.
   b. Dr. Smith is a brilliant man, well-versed in his field, thoroughly educated, highly trained.

3. Are these ideas of equal importance? If not, re-write the sentences to establish relationship and importance of ideas.
   a. Shakespeare had a spade beard, and he wrote illuminating dramas about the human situation.

  b. I thought about the speech I was to deliver, and I drove off the road into a tree.
  c. Doctors are asked to many parties, but they are needed to help persons who are sick and injured.

4. Are these ideas given their correct importance? Re-write sentences to give each idea the importance it deserves.
   a. When the furnace exploded and set fire to the house, destroying it completely, we were watching television.
   b. As a child learns to speak more distinctly, he grows older.

5. Are these simple sentences marching single file going somewhere? Re-write to show their relationship and their destination.
   a. Men want what other men want. Men want to keep what they have. Men will fight for what they want. Men fight in wars. In wars men often lose what they want most. Men want most to live. In wars men kill each other.

   Do you approve of short, choppy sentences? Are they always effective? Are they ever effective? Should they be used only occasionally and only in brief passages? Explain your answers.

6. All of these sentences are unbalanced; some are ambiguous; a few, incoherent. Make each graceful and clear: give parallel ideas parallel forms.
   a. He is a pianist and plays trumpet, too.
   b. I like beer, to play cards, and singing.
   c. Edward did not know whether he should write the man a letter or to see him in person.
   d. He is neither selfish nor is he stupid.
   e. The guest was told to pack his bags and that he should leave immediately.
   f. The council voted that salaries be raised, to install three street lights, and have garbage collected twice a week.
   g. A politician realizes that the people can terminate his career at election time and he must earn their confidence.
   h. Because I was tired, I had no money, and I had a severe sunburn, I cut short my vacation.
   i. Jack accepted the position, not because he liked the work, but for the high salary.
   j. They have more resources at their command than us.
   k. The study of ethics teaches us integrity, responsibility, how to treat our fellow man, and self-respect.

7. Re-write the following sentences to eliminate any dangling constructions.
   a. Screaming with terror, the rope tightened around his neck.
   b. Swinging through the trees, we saw ten little monkeys.
   c. Situated on the coast of Maine, his chief occupation is fishing.
   d. After striking out three times, the coach benched the short-stop.
   e. After showing us to our seats, we thanked the hostess and she left.
   f. To be a professional writer, at least one thousand words must be turned out every day.

8. The following sentences have modifiers misplaced. Re-write the sentences to correct the errors.
   a. I hope that you will be able to sometime come up to see us.
   b. He says usually the climate is good in Colorado.
   c. The new recruits were ordered to immediately report to the medical examiner.
   d. The person who steals small things frequently will steal big things.
   e. They had a quick lunch off the tailgate of the station wagon which consisted of cold ham and cheese, corn muffins, and hot coffee.

9. Identify and correct the errors in the following sentences.
   a. The little boy told his father that he was wrong.
   b. If price supports for agricultural products are discontinued, they will have to do something special for the farmers of this county.
   c. A doctor doesn't have the hours of a shoe clerk, but it is still a good job.
   d. I don't think the Eagles could win unless Hawkins makes another long run.
   e. She washed the windows and then the curtains were hung.
   f. He tried to support a wife and a mistress and practice three different professions, which just can't be done.
   g. An M-9 transforms porous soil into impervious matter instantaneously. It halts cave-ins and underground seepages. It permits man to tunnel and excavate until he is blue in the face.
   h. If anyone is found around this chickenhouse at night, they will be found there the next morning.
   i. If one wants to succeed in business you better make good use of your years between thirty and forty.

j. Any job that paid good money he went after it.
k. There are several reasons why California has more people than any state in the Union.
l. The lawyer told him that he would be hanged by the neck until dead if the case came to court and the prosecution could convince the jury that he was guilty of the crime without a reasonable doubt.

THE WORD

22/ Word Choice

22a/ Levels of usage

People should be less concerned about labeling words *right* or *wrong* than about using them in the right time and place. A word or phrase may be unacceptable in a conversation with the Dean but be the best possible choice in a locker room argument. In this respect diction is like dress. Shorts and sandals are comfortable, attractive, and proper attire for a great many informal activities; but few people wear them to church. In matters of dress we take our cue to some extent from fashion magazines, shops, and books; but primarily we imitate the dress of the people we respect. In a similar way we form our habits of language. To some extent we are influenced by textbooks, teachers, and scholarly articles, but for the most part we try to talk and write like the people we respect on educational, social, and professional levels.

In other words, most of us want to control the language used by educated people—writers, public speakers, educators, political leaders. We want to use Standard English when the occasion demands it, but we want, also, to be familiar with Non-standard English because of its vigor, picturesqueness, or other special quality.

Levels of Standard English

The *formal level* is characterized by word choice more likely to be found in the written language than in the spoken language. Generally it is sparing in its use of first person pronouns. Sentences tend to be long and of complex construction. Language is distinguished by restraint; diction and syntax are conservative (see Section 22k and *Glossary of Errors in Diction*). Contractions are generally avoided. Good writers use formal English without sounding stuffy or pompous:

> That man, I think, has had a liberal education who has been so trained in youth that his body is the ready servant of his will, and does with ease and pleasure all the work that, as a mechanism, it is capable of; whose intellect is a clear, cold, logic engine, with all its parts of equal strength, and in smooth working order; ready, like a steam engine, to be turned to any kind of work, and spin the gossamers as well as forge the anchors of the mind; whose mind is stored with a knowledge of the great and fundamental truths of Nature and of the laws of her operations, one who, no stunted ascetic, is full of life and fire, but whose passions are trained to come to heel by a vigorous will, the servant of a tender conscience; who has learned to love all beauty, whether of Nature or of art, to hate all vileness, and to respect others as himself.
>
> From "A Liberal Education and Where to Find It,"
> by THOMAS HENRY HUXLEY

The *informal level* of Standard English is characterized by the rhythms of everyday talk. It's relaxed, unpretentious, direct, simple; yet in excellent taste, thoroughly respectable. Most newspaper columns, editorials, magazine articles, speeches are written at this level. Following is an example of good, clear, informal writing:

> Every time somebody sells on the New York Stock Exchange, somebody else buys.
> That's elementary, of course, but sometimes it's the elementary facts we lose sight of, particularly when prices move sharply up or down.

It's worth remembering that half the people don't agree with the trend of the market at any given time. They buy when the others sell, and they sell when others buy.

Another thing to remember: Price isn't always the complete measure of the value of a stock, particularly at a time when the market is strongly influenced either by pessimism or optimism about business prospects.

Whatever your opinion may be of any company's stock, may we suggest that you do everything you can to be sure such opinion is solidly based on facts—facts about the company's sales, earnings, dividends, outlook.—MERRILL LYNCH PIERCE FENNER & SMITH

The informal shades into the *colloquial. Colloquial* suggests an easy, relaxed use of the language—approaching breeziness (see Section 22m). The formal is meticulous; the informal, careful; the colloquial, relaxed about the finer points of grammar and usage:

> *Formal:* The mass of Americans were sanguine and self-confident, partly by temperament, but partly also by reason of ignorance; for they knew little of the difficulties which surrounded a complex culture.
>
> *Informal:* Most Americans were cheerful and sure of themselves, partly by nature and partly from ignorance, since they didn't know the troubles a complex society could have.
>
> *Colloquial:* Americans thought they could do anything, because they were built that way, and because they didn't know what they were getting into.

Non-standard English

Except for dialogue or illustration, you should avoid dialectal words, slang, and illiteracies.

Dialectal words—also called localisms or provincialisms—should be avoided because they belong more to an area than to the whole country.

Her hair is *strubbly.* This is a precise, expressive word in the Pennsylvania Dutch country. It means a combination of uncombed, unkempt (the two are really the same thing; Old English *cemban,* meaning comb), and disheveled. It's a very good word, but it's not in the standard language. When in doubt about the currency of a word, check the dictionary.

Slang constantly forms and disappears. It's created because we sometimes feel that our conventional words lack force and color. Usually new slang can expect a short life. Everybody uses the term for awhile; then it dies. How many people today use slang words like *spondulix, snakehips, kibosh, moniker, horsefeathers?* When a shapely girl walks down the street, do you ever hear anybody say, "Pipe those gams"? However, some slang expressions are successful social climbers. They begin as second-class substitutes and gradually work their way up to the varsity. *Varsity* is such a word. It once was a slang term for *university.*

Slang is sharp, vibrant, sparkling. Keep up with it. Use it only on the appropriate level.

The *illiterate* level includes all the terms in obvious bad taste— *ain't, he don't, bust (for burst), not hardly, have went.*

22b / Denotation and connotation

Denotation is the bare and objective fact represented by the term. It is the meaning as defined by impartial authority. It demarcates the area of meaning that all men agree a word occupies. Denotation is the meaning recorded by the dictionary: a specific, precise definition accessible to all.

If denotation is precise and objective, connotation is not. *Connotation* is the emotional and associative value represented by the term. It is the area of memory, evocation, suggestion that surrounds the precise meaning of a word. Sometimes the association with a word is so subjective that the connotation is wholly personal. Many connotations, however, are shared.

A man who as a child was locked by accident into a black, close mushroom cellar may break into a sweat when he hears the word *mushroom;* his reaction to the word depends upon a purely private connotation. But most people experience the same associations of *warmth, comfort, affection, food, concern* when they hear the word *mother.*

The connotation of a word is an important instrument for the writer. Connotation can establish or destroy the writer's tone. It can support or collapse his central idea. If a man were a concert performer, would you call him a *fiddler*—or a *violinist?* Would you call another concert performer a *pianist*—or a *piano-player?* What would determine your choice in each case?

Often, in describing situations, you must choose among alternative words. You choice is contingent on what you want the word to do to the reader, on what the connotation of the word is. If you describe a catsup bottle in a cheap cafe, what is the effect upon your reader of the statement, "The neck of the catsup bottle was caked"? How would the effect change if you used the word *crusted?* If you used the word *clotted?* If you used the word *coagulated?*

Use the word whose denotation *and* connotation serve your purpose, your tone, your idea.

22c/ Synonyms

Be sure you have picked the precise word demanded by the context of your sentence. One's *goal* in life may be the same as his *object* in life. In some contexts the words may be interchangeable. But you can't have your hockey player skate through the opposition and make an *object.*

In "Ode to a Nightingale," Keats says, "Now more than ever seems it *rich* to die." Why rich? Why not *good? Proper? Appropriate?* Suppose you are going to *pay* money to someone. Will you *compensate, remunerate, reimburse, indemnify,* or *recompense* him? Remember: Synonyms rarely have identical meanings.

22d/ Invented words

Our language is by no means word-poor. The word you need to express your thought exists. Don't feel that you must invent your own. An invented word, it is true, can often add spice to a sentence. If a cold shower is *invigorating,* why shouldn't a warm one be *laziating?* If recalcitrant children are *unruly,* why shouldn't docile ones be *ruly?* Why not say you were *underwhelmed* by a boring show? *Word-inventionitis* is a disease, that's why. Unless controlled, it casts a fevered flush over the writing. It seems to be the occupational disease of sports writers particularly. Basketball teams become *hoopsters;* a baseball player, a *swatsmith;* a boxer is *paralaxed* (presumably a combination of *paralyzed* and *pole-axed*). If you must invent words, do it in moderation, and use them at the rate of two a year.

22e / Foreign words

The English language is a great borrower of words from other languages. You should be aware of certain attitudes governing their use.

If it is necessary to use a foreign word in your writing, be sure to italicize it. But don't use the foreign word or expression if you can find a satisfactory English equivalent.

Often, useful foreign words gain, after a time, full citizenship papers:

protege	ex officio	a la carte
resume	melee	a la mode
prima donna	nuance	alter ego
exposé	wanderlust	vice versa

No longer foreign, such words are not italicized.

Some foreign terms are traditional identifications. Other foreign terms have no exact equivalents in English. Still others convey with economy ideas that would require involved or cumbersome structures in English:

ad hoc	*ad hominem*	*flagrante delicto*
de facto	*persona non grata*	*non sequitur*
de jure	*ibidem*	*sine qua non*
status quo	*ipso facto*	*deus ex machina*

These terms, less assimilated, are usually placed into italics. Sometimes, authorities differ about how much assimilation the foreign word has undergone. In such cases, italics are optional.

Habitual use of foreign words seems to some readers an affectation. Use foreign words sparely; reserve them for situations where they are more precise than any English alternative. Terms such as *hors de combat, esprit de corps, ne plus ultra,* used indiscriminately, become a mannerism rather than an instrument.

22f / Illiteracies and improprieties

An *illiteracy* is a word or expression in non-standard English— "I ain't got," "shouldn't a did," "haven't saw," "I seen," "he don't." Such expressions are universally avoided by educated people except for purposes of humor or rebellion. Even in these rare uses, the educated person gives the illiteracy an inflection sufficient to indicate that he really knows better.

An *impropriety* is the use of a word in a non-standard way, usually the use of a noun as a verb or adjective: "He *homicided* his neighbor." "Wilson *authored* a book on goat-raising." It may also be a word coinage—often unconscious—based on analogy with similar words: "As soon as I get *orientated* [for *oriented*] I *will call* you." "He spoke with *rightuous* indignation" [unconsciously combining *righteous* and *virtuous*]. "The *Reverent* [for *Reverend*] John Priest spoke for an hour." Other improprieties are advise (for *inform*), aggravate (for *irritate*), amount (for *number*), individual (for *person*), most (for *almost*).

22g / Idiomatic language

Much of our language can be explained by the principles of reason. The logic of grammar accounts for the relationships of words found in most constructions. There are certain crystallized forms of speech, however, that ignore grammatical rules: *Many a man has suffered that fate.* (*Many a man* seems plural; yet a singular verb is used.) The old industrial quip, "There's no reason for it; it's just company policy," can be restated to apply to language: "There's no reason for it, it's idiomatic." Why do we say *"in* the evening *by* the moonlight" instead of *"by* the evening *in* the moonlight"? The answer, which is really not an answer, is—"One's idiomatic; the other isn't."

If you've grown up speaking English, you can be sure that you are speaking idiomatically. In writing, however, you may make an occasional slip, usually in the use of prepositions. Some idiomatic uses of prepositions follow:

change *for* the better
change *from* one thing to another
change seats *with* a person
agree *in* principle
agree *on* rules
agree *to* a proposal
agree *with* a person

Note: Ending a sentence with a preposition is not bad—if the sentence gains economy or grace. But ". . . he is able to illustrate the tenets of his philosophy in terms which the average reader is familiar with" gains neither. Either "with" should immediately precede "which"—in which case the rhythm is natural (". . . terms *with which* the average reader is familiar")—or "which" should be omitted—in which case the economy has provided a new rhythm (". . . terms the average reader is familiar *with*").

22h/ Omnibus words

In certain card games players designate one or several "wild cards"; that is, the card so designated can be used as the equivalent of any card in the deck.

There is a tendency in speaking and writing to use certain words as "wild words," to let certain words do the work of any other. Words like *aspect, case, factor, field, important, nice, point, thing, type* seem to pop into our minds whenever we can't find the exact word we need.

There's another *aspect* of the *case* that may be an *important factor* in improving the whole *field*. This *type* of *thing* would make a very *nice point* with our customers, too.

As you can see, these words are most useful when you have nothing to say or when you have something to say but can't decide just what it is.

22i/ Figures of speech

Connotations make figurative language possible, indeed inescapable.

When we say, "He is a rat," we cannot mean it literally. He is not four-legged and fur-bearing. What we mean is that he is metaphorically a rat; that is, some connotations of the word *rat*—sly, beady-eyed, greedy, furtive, dirty, cunning—can be applied to him. When the poet says, "My love is like a red, red rose," he cannot mean it literally. He means that his love and a rose share certain qualities—youth, beauty, transitory loveliness. Robert Frost summed up the importance of figurative language in these words:

> The metaphor whose manage we are best taught in poetry—that is all there is of thinking. It may not seem far for the mind to go but it is the mind's furthest. The richest accumulation of the ages is the noble metaphors we have rolled up.

Figurative language is inevitable, but the ability to control it escapes us easily. Therefore, a few suggestions:

1. Don't use figurative language ostentatiously.
   "Then Romance reared its seductive head."
2. Avoid trite figures.
3. Don't mix figurative and literal statements incongruously.
   "She was a Phantom of Delight and about five feet three inches tall in her stocking feet."
4. Avoid inconsistent, absurd, or vulgar figures of speech.
   "He tried his hand at singing."
   ". . . an island on which the hand of man had never set foot."
   "The skunk that squealed on Louie the Clutch is the same rat that chickened out in the Memphis caper."
5. Don't mix figures of speech.
   "He shot a bolt that came home to roost like a boomerang."
   "Her orbit is as carefully chartered as that of the planet Jupiter, and she lives so much within a goldfish bowl that it is difficult to disassociate her private life from her public existence."

22j / Trite expressions

What you have to offer is your personal vision. The way you see is unique; nobody else occupies your world. Your value lies not in how you are like other men, but in how you are different. You do not repeat their vision; you enlarge their vision by yours. If all a writer has to tell us about a girl is that she is "pretty as a picture," who needs him? The use of clichés reveals something worse than that the writer is of no use to his readers: it reveals that he lives on borrowed vision. He sees only what others have told him to see.

Many clichés are comparisons that have gone stale: they no longer surprise, they no longer evoke. The reader has become immune. His nerves don't jump, his mind doesn't make images when he is given such phrases as:

> caught like a rat in a trap
> busy as a bee
> like a bolt from the blue
> fresh as a daisy
> white as a sheet
> cool as a cucumber

Some clichés are lines of literature that have been quoted so often that we know that anyone quoting them is quoting not the literature but somebody else who is quoting somebody else who (perhaps) read the original.

> Neither a borrower nor a lender be.
> Uneasy lies the head that wears a crown.
> To err is human, to forgive divine.
> Fools rush in where angels fear to tread.
> What fools these mortals be!
> Hope springs eternal in the human breast.
> Lo, the poor Indian!
> A little learning is a dangerous thing.
> All is not gold that glitters.
> All sorts and conditions of men.
> Consummation devoutly to be wished.
> Lean and hungry look.
> Method in his madness.

As usual, what is not Pope is Shakespeare. The Bible, too, has been so often quoted, or misquoted, that clichés result:

. . . money is the root of all evil [The Bible actually says, "The love of money is the root of all evil."]—*New Testament,* I Timothy, VI, 10
. . . filthy lucre—*New Testament,* I Timothy, III, 3

Indicating that you know that you are using a cliché won't rescue a cliché from being a cliché. You will seem self-conscious, apologetic, defensive. Quotation marks won't help.

I was "sober as a judge."

It's worse when you confess you know the term is hackneyed and use it anyhow. Guilt is increased.

It's trite but true: blood is thicker than water.

This cliché grows two heads where there was one. Don't use quotation marks for a cliché; don't apologize for a cliché; don't be coy about a cliché. Don't use a cliché. Unless you have an unusual reason—and hope for an extraordinary effect.

Say honestly what you have to say. Don't be a penny machine with stock phrases falling into the slot. Don't let a cliché "rear its ugly head." Don't be "tired but happy." Don't "stew in your own juice" "until the bitter end." See with your own eyes; speak with your own words. Remember: "to thine own self, be true"; and "variety is the spice of life."

22k / Appropriateness

Sometimes we suspect that all classifications are false; or if not false, slightly dishonest; or if not slightly dishonest, arbitrary. *Appropriateness* is listed as a separate category of diction, when in reality it is the total of all categories of diction. Yet this separation —while artificial—allows us to make an emphasis.

Plato, in the *Phaedrus,* indicates that we best persuade men, not when we intend to persuade men, but when we intend to uncover truth. Honesty, therefore, is more important than cleverness. Substance is more important than ornament. A speech, according to Plato, persuades only to the extent that it resembles the truth.

Speech, to be most effective, must attempt to discover truth. For this reason, Plato says, *dialectic*—conversation between men— is more effective than *rhetoric*—the art of presentation. A dialogue consists of statements offered, responses made, and responses to responses—therefore its growth is natural and organic, its findings are not known beforehand—it is a process by which truth is discovered. Rhetoric, however, consists of a conviction already possessed, of a calculated arrangement of statements leading to that anticipated conclusion—it is a process by which an assertion is imposed.

The paradox is that we best persuade when it is not our primary intent to persuade. We are most effective, then, when we adhere as closely as possible to the nature of dialogue, or dialectic. For this reason, writers attempt to retain the virtues of speech—the tentative statements, the examination of objections, the formulation of new statements, the examination of new objections—in an ever-continuing process of discovery. Writers try to achieve by printed devices the effects we get by inflections, intonations, gestures, winks, body movements, when we talk and respond to each other. This personality of the writer—sometimes called *voice*—is both a product of the writer's character and a response to the person to whom he is talking. We speak to a child with one aspect of our personality; to an elder with another; to our doctor with another. We have to write, then, in a way which is appropriate:

1. To the personality of the writer; and
2. To the personality of the reader

We have to choose the persons we address and that aspect of our personality which best responds to the persons we address.

Our words must fit not only the personality of the writer in response to the personality of the reader; they must fit also a third element: the nature of the subject, the material being shaped by the personalities of writer and reader. Our choice of words must indicate the ideas that reside in the subject; the importance of the subject; the general level of dignity the subject deserves.

Appropriateness in diction should bring three elements into harmony:

1. The aspect of the writer's character most responsive to
2. The personality of the reader with whom he will discuss
3. The nature of a particular subject.

All the instruments of diction we discuss, all the instruments we name, must work toward *appropriateness:* the ideal harmony.

221/ Directness

When you write, relax. Say what you think. Know that you have a thought only when you express it. Tell no one, "You know what I mean," because he doesn't—unless you tell him what you mean. Write and talk clean, clear, and sharp. Your words are your strength—with words you command respect, affection, and cooperation. Respect words, alone and combined.

Don't waste words. Wasted words dilute ideas and sometimes wash them away. Make each word bear its full weight of meaning. Relate ideas strongly to each other. Give particulars. Give more important ideas positions of greater importance: at the beginning, and at the end. Give most important ideas short sentences. They make ideas stark and strong.

You should get satisfaction from being forced to communicate. The enjoyment you get is from being forced to reduce and clarify ideas. Your essay is the place where you succeed or fail in communicating the ideas. If you succeed, you are sure of one thing: you understand the ideas you want your readers to understand. When you demonstrate to others that you understand, you demonstrate it to yourself. Understanding is a pleasure.

No one can be sure that the person who wrote the following sentence knows what he means:

In the career of a dentist a large and well-chosen vocabulary is needed to have an intelligent conversation with the patients he has.

What does he mean? How did he get so jumbled? Well, the passive voice, in many cases, is weak, vague, and flabby. When he says "In the career of a dentist, a large and well-chosen vocabulary *is needed* . . . ," does he mean, "A dentist needs a large, well-chosen vocabulary"? Let's hope so. We'll change the passive voice to active. Now: ". . . to have an intelligent conversation with the patients he has." We suppose that if a dentist talks to patients, he talks to his own patients, so we will omit the useless words *he has*. Now the sentence, revised, is "A dentist needs a large, well-chosen vocabulary to have an intelligent conversation with the patients." What does this mean? That certain patients patronize only dentists with large, well-chosen vocabularies? That makes little sense. Perhaps he means, "A dentist needs a large, well-chosen vocabulary to talk with all sorts of patients." But is this what *he* means, or only what we *think* he means? No one knows. In any case, it would cost this man a fortune to send a telegram. And then the recipient would have to telephone the sender to find out what the telegram meant.

If two words meant exactly the same thing, there wouldn't be two words. But often two words are enough alike to make the use of both in the same sentence wasteful and absurd. "His writing is trite and hackneyed." Hackneyed doesn't add to *trite* here; it doesn't intensify *trite*. Since no particulars distinguish the difference intended between *hackneyed* and *trite, hackneyed* dilutes *trite*. "I want to reiterate again my opposition to the plan." *Reiterate* means "say again." The sentence says, then, "I want to say again again my opposition to the plan." The absurdity robs the statement of force.

Many phrases do nothing but delay a sentence. "In reference to the matter under consideration, we have arrived at the decision that any student guilty of plagiarism should be immediately and automatically expelled." What does this lengthy sentence have that is not found in "We decided to expel all plagiarists"?

Directness in writing means don't waste words.

22m / Colloquialisms

Colloquialisms are terms that an educated person everywhere can and does use when he talks. Used in writing, they can make an essay as relaxed and warm as speech. Used without caution, without restraint, without judgment, they can make an essay as meaningless as babble.

Colloquialisms, in a strict sense, are informal terms which are so useful they have survived a particular time and a particular group: they are informal words that have become general and lasting.

Don't confuse colloquialisms, in our sense, with informal words that are still being tested by time or still limited to a group.

Slang words are inventive, figurative terms still being tested by time. Would you like to be a "man to ride the river with"? Can you "cut the mustard"? Can you even "cut a rug"? These terms, once meaningful to every American, are no longer in our daily talk. They were born slang and are dying slang. They didn't survive to become colloquialisms, in our sense. If you want your written discussion to remain meaningful even six months later, don't use slang—it has a high fatality rate.

If you read:

> When I asked her if I could carry her to the movies, she told me no, that I was too chinchy. I got mad and asked her what made her so salty.

Would it make sense to you? If not, it is because many of the words are *localisms*, terms used and understood only by persons in a limited geographical area. Someone in New Orleans would recognize "carry" as *escort*; "chinchy" as *stingy*; "salty" as *hostile*. Localisms are sometimes called *dialectal* words, and sometimes *provincialisms*: all mean words peculiar to a place.

The informal words that have become general and lasting—the colloquialisms useful to responsible writers—consist of idioms, contractions, and expressions that were once merely slang and localisms. Deciding when slang and localisms have been graduated into colloquialisms is, of course, difficult. But the decision must be made each time we write. What would you retain as colloquialisms and reject as slang in this passage:

> It's dangerous to assume that writing is a con-game, in which one man fools another by a fast flow of words. It won't work. At least, not for long. Con men have to get out of town fast; suckers have a habit of getting wise.

Should you accept *any* of these terms as proper and effective? Would you accept *all* of them? The decision in each case must be based on the intention of the writer and the effect on the reader. The question *always* remains the same: Are the words appropriate to the writer, the reader, and the subject?

22n / Jargon

Jargon means words peculiar to a profession or occupation. Occasionally, these words are not clear even to persons within the profession or occupation. Some writers, in an attempt to sound highly authoritative, use the most abstract, highly technical language they can find. The result is often both pompous and confused. The best writers within professions and occupations are as direct, clear, and economical as possible. They use the simplest, most concrete word possible. The sentence, "Emotional factors operating in various functional interrelationships with the somatic entity are capable of causing a physical debilitation, or conversely, a rehabilitation of the corporeal, organic structure," may mean "A man's mind can affect his body." But not even a person who knows the technical significance of *functional, somatic, organic,* can be sure.

22o / Obsolete and archaic words

An old word no longer in use is called *obsolete;* an old word rarely in use, except as preserved in religious and legal phrases, is called *archaic.* These words draw attention to themselves. They halt the flow of ideas. Use such strange and conspicuous words only if the reason is extraordinary: the gain must be great to outweigh the loss.

> She seemed the kind of person I fain would know. I introduced myself, saying I was yclept Arthur. We pleased each other well enow to sup together.

What does this passage mean? What does it intend? Is the writer poetic? Is he funny? Is he confused? Why does he jumble the speech of different times? Does *he* know what he is saying? Once he invokes old words and old meanings, he may be in danger of saying things he never intended. *Know*, in an archaic use, has a sexual meaning.

Archaic and obsolete words are obtrusive and disconcerting; they should be used only when strong purpose requires them.

22p/ Fine writing

Good writing *uses* words. Fine writing *displays* words. A writer must not parade words to make people admire him. Fine writing is worse than bad: it defeats itself. Words have a more important purpose. Use words to find out what you think—as clearly, as simply, as strongly as you can. Beauty in writing does *not* come from trying to be beautiful; it comes from trying to be clear.

The simplest way of saying something is best. To say a simple thing complexly is bad. To say a complex thing simply is good. If you always try to speak and write simply and clearly, you will always have what the subject demands—neither more nor less. You will have a complex statement only when the relationships of the subject are complex.

Use the simplest word the subject needs. If the meaning you intend requires an abstract word, then that word will be the simplest needed. Don't be so in love with impressive words that you lose all sense of rhythm, variety, and force. "Disputation among nations has necessitated the formulation of an international organization wherein solutions may be sought by rational means in order to avoid the holocaust of armed conflict." After the echoes have stopped bouncing in your head, what does the sentence mean? What simpler words would give this sentence rhythm, variety, force?

Don't confuse pretentious phrases with elegance. "The leonine orator, standing majestically before a seething mass of humanity, gazed into that sea of upturned faces and launched into an address that was destined to live through the ages as one of mankind's noblest utterances." Fine phrases heaped together do not make an elegant sentence—or even clear sense. In language, as in furniture, architecture, or clothing, the most elegant line is often the simplest line.

Don't write to be admired. Write to be clear. Then you will be admired.

22q/ Journalese

Journalese—a word as awkward as the fault it names—means the shoddy writing produced sometimes by a reporter in a hurry. Newspaper editors warn against it. Journalese is a jumble of clichés, mixed metaphors, pretentious phrases—and chop-chop headline syntax.

> PRODUCTION UPPED
> U.S. Figures Show
> —. Statistics released today by the United States Department of Commerce indicated that industrial output is booming despite pessimistic predictions that consumer demand would fall short of the needed goal. Economists warn that increased inventories will tax storage facilities to the utmost and that, unless steps are taken in the right direction, the economic structure will totter.

To warn against journalese is to emphasize again that good writing is appropriate, direct, and fresh.

22r/ Euphemisms

Euphemisms are terms used to veil meanings considered coarse or blunt. These terms often defeat themselves; intended to be genteel, their self-consciousness makes them unpleasantly suggestive or absurd. Words are perhaps least offensive when most brisk. Attention lingers in a peculiar way when *social disease* veils *syphilis*. A human being somehow is patronized when *senior citizen* veils *old man*. Perhaps, too, a janitor's dignity is reduced rather than enhanced when he is called the *building superintendent*. Is a mortician laying the departed to rest in a memorial park really less painful and more dignified than an undertaker burying the dead in a graveyard? Ultimately this phrasing reaches horror when we recognize that an official statement like "refractory elements were liquidated" can mean that hundreds of men and women were shot. Avoid euphemisms; language can be both delicate and direct.

22x / Exercises

1. Rewrite the Gettysburg Address on the familiar level. Avoid slang, but try for a relaxed, conversational style.

2. Rewrite the following passage in the familiar style.

Every man hath two birthdays: two days, at least, in every year, which set him upon revolving the lapse of time, as it affects his mortal duration. The one is that which in an especial manner be termeth *his*. In the gradual desuetude of old observances, this custom of solemnizing our proper birthday hath nearly passed away, or is left to children, who reflect nothing at all about the matter, nor understand anything in it beyond cake and orange. But the birth of a New Year is of an interest too wide to be pretermitted by king or cobbler. No one ever regarded the first of January with indifference. It is that from which all date their time, and count upon what is left. It is the nativity of our common Adam.

CHARLES LAMB

3. What label—slang, colloquialism, provincialism, formal English— would you use to classify the following:

get across a point	check up on
take in a show	chip in
kind of	you play ball with me,
sort of	I'll play ball with you
gents	cinch
mike	cop
prexy	goof
whirlybird	gripe
eyewash	highbrow
broke (without money)	rubberneck
lay an egg	flip your lid
kick the bucket	knucklehead
hit the ceiling	bonehead
fly off the handle	fatso
chew the fat	skinny
blow your top	

4. What other words are used in various parts of the United States for the following:

spring onion   peanuts
soda pop   porch
hot dog   fishing worm
Hoagie   Baltimore Oriole
bucket   doughnut
milk shake   dragonfly
bag

5. Find at least two synonyms for the following:

body (dead person)   drink
woman   horse
thin   stomach
janitor   man
stream

Now study the connotations of the synonyms. Discuss.

6. Make a list of words that mean "Under the influence of alcohol."

7. In how many different expressions can you use the word *dog*.

Example: It's a dog's life.

8. Consider the meaning of the word *free* in the following contexts:

free beer
free love
free enterprise

Can you think of any other uses of free? How many similar contexts can you find for the word *small?*

9. List several connotations of the following words:

cross (n.)   rocks
mother   lifeguard
snake   hay
Private Eye   apple pie
novelist   turkey
convertible (car)   fog
Pullman

10. What literal meanings are compressed in the following figures of speech taken from the Bible:
   a. The Lord is my rock and my fortress.

b. Our days on the earth are as a shadow.

c. And the Lord set a mark upon Cain.

d. Unstable as water, thou shalt not excel.

e. He kept him as the apple of his eye.

f. The people arose as one man.

g. Thou shalt come to thy grave in a full age, like as a shock of corn cometh in this season.

h. My days are swifter than a weaver's shuttle.

i. My cup runneth over.

Can you add ten more to this list?

11. Consider the appropriateness of the figure *iron curtain* to symbolize the lack of communication between Russia and the West. What does the term imply? How appropriate is *bamboo curtain?* What differences are there in relative effectiveness of the two terms?

12. Are terms like *table leg, eye of a needle, head of lettuce* metaphors? Defend your answer.

13. Submit definitions and examples of the following terms: *simile, metaphor, analogy, parable, trope, myth, symbol, personification, synecdoche, metonymy.*

14. Slang is colorful; clichés are stale, yet a dependence on slang can make a report stale. Slang can be more amusing than informative; used relentlessly, it is not even amusing. The effect becomes affectation. The habitual terms become dull and vague. They can frustrate both speaker and listener:

A: That cat blows a mean box, man; it's like endsville.

B: You mean you like the way he plays piano? Why?

A: Aw, you know, man. It's gone. It's like far-out.

B: What do you mean? Does he play better than other pianists? Or does he play differently from other pianists?

A: You trying to bug me, Dad? I mean he's tough. He's loose wig. He's close. You know, man.

B: No, I don't. I think you don't, either.

To what extent has dependence on slang obscured A's understanding of what he hears? To what extent does it prevent him from making the situation clear? Has slang become cliché?

Write a dialogue in which a person says precisely what he likes about a musician's performance; what distinguishes a musician's technique, invention, and interpretation.

15. How do the following sentences violate appropriateness? rewrite to correct.
   a. I had hoped that my employer would reward my industry and fidelity by increasing the amount of mazuma he slipped me every week.
   b. When he took and bopped me on the head, I thought he demonstrated paranoid tendencies.
   c. His attempt to change horses in mid-stream was nipped in the bud.
   d. After the doctor had established that the patient had passed away to eternal rest, he called the undertaker.

16. What words are wasted in the following passages?
   a. It was in the city of Philadelphia in the year 1776 that the document entitled "The Declaration of Independence" was written and signed.
   b. The club met together, as a usual rule, on Wednesday at 10:00 p.m. in the evening.
   c. The speaker did not make clear until the last sentence of his speech what the point of his speech was intended to be.
   d. The automobile mechanic at the garage overhauled the engine of my automobile. After the overhaul, the engine operated much more smoothly than before. The improved performance resulted in a more economical consumption of gasoline.
   e. The reason why he could not attend the Nature Lovers' Outing is because of the fact that he is subject to attacks of hay fever.

17. What faults made this passage weak and absurd?

His relationship with the fair sex left him sadder but wiser. The unhappy man would heave heart-felt sighs, reflecting that it was better to have loved and lost than never to have loved at all. But he could never forget that, at one fell swoop, the apple of his eye had thrown him over for a new swain. And, although he lived to a ripe old age, it goes without saying, that his heart was heavy as lead whenever he beheld a representative of the weaker sex. Finally, unnoticed and unwept, he shuffled off his mortal coil, delivered at last from this vale of tears.

18. The three passages that follow all deal with the same content. Yet each delivers the content in a different voice (see pages 101–102). Each has its own personality. The reader, in each case, reacts to the content-personality fusion. How, in each case, do the vocabulary, the phrasing, the sentence structure reveal a per-

sonality to which you react? All passages have the same theme. What is the virtue of each personality or voice? What is the defect of each personality or voice? Does each have to sacrifice something to gain something? What, in each case, is sacrificed? What gained?

a. In a sentence, which combines words to get meaning, each part exists because it does something only it can do—that is to say, each part of speech, punctuation mark, link of grammar. Each part exists by logic of function rather than because it is a law or a rule. So it is better to learn the function of sentence components rather than grammatical laws and rules. It wouldn't knock you out to learn the function of a saw or a hammer, would it? Well, then, if you want to be able to accomplish what you want to say, ascertain the function of each sentence part. Syntax is the logic of function.

The logic of sentence structure, which is simple, is merely that it uses words to render form and weight to an idea, thus making visible the relative importance of one idea to another. Ideas that are equally important are composed in structures of equal importance, and less important ideas are phrased in structures that are less important. A sentence structure, which makes an idea into a thing and gives weight to a meaning, has the effect of being the physical equivalent of a non-physical entity.

All right so far? Let's proceed. When you write, you may run smack up against two problems, and they are, what it is you are to communicate, and how you should say it. One person may not be able to recognize ideas and find it impossible to say anything clearly, while another may recognize ideas but say them clumsily and without taste. Could it be that the two problems are not two problems but merely two manifestations or degrees of the same problem? So what does this mean? It may mean that the degree of clarity with which the idea is expressed is affected by whether you recognize the idea clearly or not.

A person may say, "I know what I mean, but I can't say it," when the truth is that he is confusing two things: the *apprehension* of an idea with *comprehending* it. He does not yet know the identity of the idea, though he may be conscious of the fact that an idea is present. That is, though he hasn't yet surrounded the idea, he knows that it is around somewhere. And he will know *how* the idea should be expressed the moment he knows the identity of the idea itself. Which is to say that he does not have the idea if he has an idea that can be stated though he cannot state it. The statement of the idea is the comprehension of the idea.

Perhaps it might be a good thing for the student to try to write nakedly, to state ideas simply and make the relationship between them strong. You will present them with more grace and more forcefully than if you had tried to go all out for the ornamental and for complexity. One has to have attained simplicity before he can be complex; moreover, where he can be simple, he should never make his expression complex. Not only must nakedness have the virtue of honesty, but also it can be beautiful.

b.   A sentence combines words to get meaning. Each part of speech, each mark of punctuation, each link of grammar serves a function. Each exists because it does something only it can do. It exists not by law, not by rule—but by logic of function. Don't learn a law. Don't learn a rule. Learn the function. Learn the function of each as you would learn the function of a hammer or a saw. Then you will be able to say what you want to say. Syntax is the logic of function.

The logic of sentence structure is simple. It uses words to give an idea form and weight. The relative importance of ideas is made visible by sentence structure. Ideas equal in importance are put into structures equal in importance. Less important ideas are put into less important structures. A sentence structure is the physical equivalent of a non-physical entity. It makes a thing of an idea. It gives meaning weight.

When you write, you may face two problems: what to say, and how to say it. One person may be unable to recognize ideas and to say anything clearly. Another person may recognize ideas, but say them clumsily and tastelessly. The two problems may be simply two degrees of the same problem. It may be that the more clearly you recognize an idea, the more clearly you say the idea.

When a person says, "I know what I mean, but I can't say it," he may be confusing two things. He may be confusing the *apprehension* of an idea with the *comprehension* of an idea. He may be aware that an idea is present, but he does not yet know the identity of the idea. He knows that an idea is in the vicinity, but he hasn't yet surrounded the idea. The moment he knows *what* the idea is, he knows *how* to say it. If he has an idea which can be stated and he cannot state it, he does not have the idea. The statement of the idea is the comprehension of the idea.

Try naked writing. State ideas simply; relate them to each other strongly. Clarify your idea as directly as possible. Your presentation will be more graceful and forceful than it would have been had you tried for ornamentation and complexity. You cannot be complex until you have been simple. You should never be complex where you can be simple. Nakedness must be honest—and can be beautiful.

c.   It goes without saying that a sentence combines words to arrive at meaning. Each part of speech, each mark of punctuation, each link of grammar serves a function peculiar to itself, which function is its *raison d'etre.* This is the key to its existence—logic of function—not the compulsion of law or the reign of rule. Thus it is better to learn the function rather than the law or the rule, to learn the function of each sentence element as one would learn the function of a simple tool. If the writer will do this, he will be able to convey his intention in writing. Syntax, then, is the logic of function.

The logic of syntax, of sentence structure, is superlatively simple. It employs words to effect the materialization of an idea, to give it form and weight. Moreover, sentence structure makes visible the relative importance of ideas, equating structurally those of equal moment, relegating to subordinate structure those of lesser importance. Making a visible *thing* of an idea, and giving it an appropriate weight, a sentence structure is, it might be said, the physical equivalent of a nonphysical entity. It gives an idea corporality.

When one is to perform the act of writing, he may face two problems: the substance of his communication and the expression of his communication. One person may be unable to recognize ideas and to express anything clearly; another, though he recognizes ideas, may express them clumsily and tastelessly. It may be that the two problems are not mutually exclusive; rather, that they are simply variant degrees of the same problem. It may be that clear recognition of concept effects clear expression of the concept.

When a person says, "I know what I mean but I can't say it," he may be confusing the *apprehension* of an idea with the *comprehension* of an idea. Which is to say that, though he may be aware that an idea is present, he does not yet understand its identity; that, though he knows that an idea is in the vicinity, he has not yet encompassed it. Precisely with the *understanding* of the idea comes the ability to express it. So that, if he has an idea capable of being stated that he cannot state, then he does not have the idea. The statement of the idea constitutes the comprehension of the idea.

To try unadorned writing is to make a startling discovery. If the writer will school himself to state ideas simply, to relate them strongly, to clarify his idea as directly as possible, he will discover that his presentation will be more graceful, more forceful than if he had striven for ornamentation and complexity. The experiment will disclose two truths: that one cannot be complex until he has been simple; that he should never be complex if it is possible to be simple. Honest such writing *must* be; beautiful it *can* be.

19. Take notes as your instructor reads an unfamiliar essay to the class. Write an essay derived from your notes. Compare your essay to the original. What differences do you find in voice, development, syntax, diction, style, ordering, substance, tone? In each case which is better? Why?

PUNCTUATION:
OUTLINE OF USES

There are *seven* chief marks of punctuation. Each has a function. Each obeys logic. Each mark will either connect—or characterize—or terminate—or emphasize—parts of your thought. Once you recognize the function and the logic of a punctuation mark, you can use that mark to carry out your intention. Each mark says something. Punctuation is a part of a writer's vocabulary.

As a word has value because men recognize the idea or thing the word represents, so does a mark of punctuation. Recognize the idea basic to each mark; the many uses of each mark derived from that basic idea. Learn the meaning of a punctuation mark as you learn the meaning of a word.

□ PERIOD. The period terminates a sentence. It is flat, without emphasis. Its basic idea is that a sentence structure is complete. It indicates that whatever it terminates is to be considered complete, even though the structure may not be conventionally complete; for instance, in the passage "He would not talk to me. No wonder. He thought I had slandered him." the period confers upon the phrase *No wonder* the status of a complete structure. Secondary uses of the period are in the reference section which follows.

117

▢ COMMA.   The comma separates a sentence into parts. It, too, is flat, without emphasis. A sentence relates parts to each other. Two things must be clear: the identity of each part, and the relationship of all parts. The comma prevents one part from being confused with another.

Examples:

1.   He struck the table, and his wife left the room.

Without the comma, we would, for a moment, understand wrongly that he struck the table and his wife.

2.   When he began to choke, his friend pounded him on the back.

Without the comma, we would first think that an unfriendly act was taking place. Punctuation is essential to meaning; a change in punctuation is a change in meaning:

He loved only his friends, his dog, and his cat.
He loved only his friends: his dog and his cat.

Other derived uses of the comma are in the later reference section.

▢ SEMICOLON.   The semicolon shares the terminal function of the period and the separative function of the comma. Weaker than the period, stronger than the comma, the semicolon indicates a pronounced pause but not a stop, as between two statements, each complete in itself, but so closely related that they are contained within the same sentence:

I will not accept if nominated; I will not serve if elected.

Here the effect of the semicolon is that of a partial period. The semicolon also distinguishes a stronger use of the comma from a weaker one in the same sentence. The comma separates a sentence into parts, but how are parts separated into parts without confusion?

The stand had bins for apples, Mackintosh and Grimes Golden, oranges, grapefruit, bananas, potatoes, Idaho and Maine, lettuce, head and leaf, celery.

Where do commas separate items in this list—and where do commas separate one item into parts in this list? The semicolon provides an intensified comma:

> The stand had bins for apples, Mackintosh and Grimes Golden; oranges; grapefruit; bananas; potatoes, Idaho and Maine; lettuce, head and leaf; and celery.

The nature of the semicolon provides other uses discussed in the later reference section.

□ COLON. The colon anticipates. It establishes strong expectation: it promises that what follows will clarify, amplify, or itemize material discussed immediately before. It is emphatic.

Examples:

> He has one overriding desire: to win.
> He excels at many sports: baseball, football, tennis, soccer, and basketball.
> He doesn't want to be good: he wants to be best.

Other applications of the colon are discussed in the reference section.

□ DASH. The dash sets material off with special emphasis—or breaks into material with special emphasis—or simply breaks off a statement. It has a dramatic quality—and should be used sparingly, for situations that warrant the drama.

Examples:

> I want to show you slides of my trip through Europe, Asia, and South—Why are you putting on your coat?
> He has one overriding desire—to win. (*Here the dash can be used instead of a colon in order to add even more emphasis.*)
> He always claims—I wish I could believe him—that he wishes me well.

Other applications are described in the reference section.

□ QUOTATION MARKS. Quotation marks identify material the writer attributes to others. They may be used to indicate that the writer is repeating the words of someone else, or that the writer is reporting an opinion which is not necessarily his own.

Examples:

"The love of money is the root of all evil" indicates not that money is bad, but that our attitudes toward it may be bad.

The attitude of the censor who called the book "true, but harmful to public morality," is disturbing because it implies that truth and morality are opposed.

He may be "Responsible," but for what is he responsible?

Demonstrations are in the reference section.

□ PARENTHESES. Parentheses enclose information relevant to the statement, but not integrated into the statement. They identify, usually, a comment *about* the statement, an aside to the audience.

Examples:

We have decided (at least, for the present) not to ask his help.

The speaker thanked the audience for its courtesy and attention. (Half the audience was asleep.) Then he spoke for another hour.

See reference section for applications of parentheses.

The section which follows catalogues specific applications of punctuation marks. It lists uses and circumstances found in published writings. It provides guides for the use of each mark. Recognize that choices must be made, that no two marks are wholly interchangeable, that each will give the sentence a specific character. Each mark of punctuation establishes its own emphasis.

Choose the mark—the precise function—faithful to your intention.

23/ End Punctuation

23a/ The period

Use a period at the end of

1. A declarative sentence.

The notion of the artist as savior has been one of the most provocative literary ideas of our time.

2. An imperative sentence.

> Do not open the booklet until after you have read the instructions.

3. An interrogative sentence which makes a polite request.

> Will you please send me your free booklet entitled "Dividends over the years."

(Two typing spaces separate end punctuation marks and the start of a new sentence. A period is always placed inside the quotation marks.)

4. Use a period after an initial and after an abbreviation.

> J. H. Davis is the new representative to the Interstellar Relief Committee.

(One typing space follows periods after initials.)

Mc.	Mr.	c. o. d.
a.m.	Ph.D.	Mfg.
f.o.b.	Ky.	Ariz.

(One typing space follows periods after abbreviations and either one space or no space after the periods within the abbreviations themselves.)

5. Use a period for the decimal point in figures.

> 8.432
> 5.2 per cent

(No typing space follows a decimal.)

6. Use a period after the figures, letters, and Roman numerals of an outline.

> I.
>   A.
>   1.
>   a. (one typing space follows.)

7. Use three periods—four at the end of a sentence—to indicate the omission of words in a quotation.

> "In this design the bewildering and flamboyant Sir Walter Raleigh plays a prominent . . . part."

"In this respect Plato's thinking was perfectly consistent, though it made little sense. . . ."

The three-period sign of omission is called an ellipsis.

Omit periods in the following circumstances:

1. After items enumerated in lists

    5 lb. dark brown sugar
    1 doz. eggs
    2 cans blackeye peas

2. After chemical symbols

    H_2O H_2SO_4 CO_2

3. After a letter used as a label

    When grocer A fights with grocer B the whole trade suffers.
    Put this letter in file A before you go home.

4. After Roman numerals used in a sentence.

    His best work in Chapter VI was done while he was ill.

23b/   The question mark

1. A question mark follows a *direct question*. A period follows an *indirect question*.

    What was the temperature last night? [*direct question*]
    He wondered what the temperature was last night. [*indirect question*]

2. If a question is quoted, the question mark is placed inside the quotation marks.

    "What was the temperature last night?" Bill asked.
    A very good movie entitled "Can It Happen Here?" is playing at the Strand.

3. If a question is not part of quoted matter, place the question mark outside the quotation marks.

    Did any of you see the movie entitled "It Happened One Morning"?
    Have you ever heard Michael Ursprung read his parody of "The Raven"?

4. If an interrogatory sentence ends with a quoted question, the question mark within the quotation serves both interrogatory functions.

Did you see the movie "Can It Happen Here?"

Note: Do not leave a space between a question mark and quotation marks.

23c/ The exclamation point

1. An exclamation point will intensify the emotion in a phrase or sentence. But it should be used with care. If the language is emotional, the exclamation mark is superfluous.
Notice these two sentences:

    a. Come here right now.
    b. Come here right now!

The first is a calm request. The second, an angry demand. The exclamation point is necessary because the language alone cannot convey the meaning. But when Shakespeare says, "I had rather be a dog and bay at the moon than such a Roman," no emotion intensification is needed. The language is charged with it. (The spacing conventions for the exclamation mark are the same as for the question mark.)

24/ The Comma

24a/ Use commas to separate the members of a series—words, phrases, clauses, figures, numbers, signs, or letters.

Words: Please move the pipes, cigars, and cigarettes to another shelf.
Phrases: Reading a book, walking in the rain, hearing a cardinal whistle, smelling apples that bake on the hearth—these are all simple pleasures.
Clauses: When you can't think, when you walk two feet off the ground, when your heart pounds, when your head reels, you

may not be in love. You may simply have a low blood sugar level.

Numbers: Read sections 42, 65, 96, and 98 of the Motor Vehicle Code.

Figures: Dobrura has a population of 6,346,622.

[*Exceptions:* Figures containing not more than four digits (3600) in straight copy, serial numbers (13090413), and decimal fractions (1.62316).]

Signs: $, %, #, &, @, ¢

Letters: A, B, C, D, E, F

24b / Use commas between two or more adjectives of equal rank if the conjunction is omitted.

He was a direct, forceful, interesting speaker.

To test, supply the conjunction *and*. If it fits, you need a comma.

He was a direct *and* forceful *and* interesting speaker.

Do not use the commas if the adjectives are of unequal rank, i.e., if, when read aloud, there is no natural pause between the adjectives and if placing *and* between the adjectives would spoil the sense.

He bought a light brown suit.

24c / Use a comma before a conjunction (and, but, or, nor, for) in a compound sentence.

The sheep are in the meadow, and the cows are in the corn.

In very short compound sentences, the comma is usually omitted.

Peter sang and Marie danced.

Caution: Avoid the comma splice and the fused sentence.

Splice: The sheep, grazing hungrily, are in the meadow, the cows are eating stalks in the cornfield.

Supply the conjunction or use a semicolon.

Fused: The sheep are in the meadow the cows are in the corn.

Supply a conjunction and a comma, or use a semicolon.

24d / **Use a comma to indicate that a verb used in the first clause is omitted in the second clause of a compound sentence.**

Paul has joined the Air Force; his brother, the Marines.

24e / **Use a comma after certain introductory phrases and clauses.**

Introductory adverbial clause:

When I go to the theatre, I feel as though I were spending a few hours with my ancestors. . . .—MAURICE MAETERLINCK

Introductory infinitive phrase:

To be truly rich, one must first be poor.

Introductory participial phrase:

Believing in the continuity of nature, I cannot stop where our microscopes cease to be of use.—JOHN TYNDALL

Lost in the deep woods, I built a fire and waited.

Introductory gerund phrase:

By stealing a sailboat in Havana, he was able to make his way to Key Largo.

Long introductory prepositional phrase:

To a person uninstructed in natural history, his country or sea-side stroll is a walk through a gallery filled with wonderful works of art, nine-tenths of which have their faces turned to the wall.

THOMAS HENRY HUXLEY

No comma is used after a short introductory prepositional phrase:

In her eyes there was a strange light.

24f/   Use a comma to set off nonrestrictive (nonessential) elements.

Clauses and phrases that provide information necessary to the meaning of the sentence are called *restrictive*. They are essential to the sentence. Clauses and phrases that provide information which is additional rather than essential are called *nonrestrictive*. They are not necessary to the sentence.

Nonrestrictive:

> My brother Charles, who has just returned from Japan, spent the week-end with me.

Who has just returned from Japan is a nonrestrictive relative clause. It provides additional, but not essential information. The meaning of the sentence *My brother Charles spent the week-end with me,* is not changed by the elimination of the relative clause. The nonessential clause is, therefore, set off by commas.

Restrictive:

> All students who want to try out for the glee club should report to the Chapel at 1:00 p.m.

Here the clause, *who want to try out for the glee club,* is essential to the meaning of the sentence. *All students should report to the Chapel at 1:00 p.m.* is not the instruction intended. The clause restricts the number of students to those who want to try out for the glee club. It is necessary to the meaning of the sentence and is, therefore, not set off by commas.

Nonrestrictive adjective clause:

> The man, who had never dreamed of being so richly rewarded, was given an automobile.

The dependent clause *who had never dreamed of being so richly rewarded* here does not limit or identify the noun it modifies. It simply adds information about that noun. The clause is therefore nonrestrictive. It should be set off by commas.

Restrictive adjective clause:

The man who betrays his friends can expect no loyalty.

The dependent clause *who betrays his friends* is essential to the meaning of the noun *man;* it limits the man to a particular kind of man. The clause is therefore restrictive. It should *not* be set off by commas.

Nonrestrictive:

The DC-7, which was built to American Airlines specifications, made commercial aviation history.

Restrictive:

The DC-7 that left LaGuardia was over the Atlantic Ocean three minutes before the one at Kennedy took off.

Nonrestrictive phrase:

Mr. Carlton took the hats, *collected from the members the day before,* to the Salvation Army.

Restrictive phrase:

All the hats *collected from the members* were turned over to the Salvation Army.

24g /   Use commas to set off nonrestrictive appositives.

Gabriel Fielding, author of *Brotherly Love,* will speak to the creative writing groups tonight.

Restrictive appositives—those distinguishing their principals from other persons or things of the same name—are not set off by commas.

My uncle Charles is a deep sea diver.

I went to see my brother Charles.

[*The absence of a comma suggests that there are several brothers, but that only Charles was visited.*]

I went to see my brother, Charles.

[*The comma suggests that there is only one brother. In case anybody is interested, his name is Charles.*]

24h/ In general, set off parenthetical expressions or transitional words or phrases.

A partial list of such expressions follows:

however	as you know	on the other hand
moreover	in fact	in my opinion
in general	consequently	secondly
	accordingly	for the most part
		from time to time

Foreign cars, in my opinion, are enjoying a popularity they don't deserve.

Words like *also, perhaps, indeed* are frequently not set off by commas.

You will perhaps remember the way the sergeant wore his fatigue cap.

It is indeed certain that we shall win.

24i/ Use a comma after "Yes" or "No" at the beginning of a sentence.

Yes, we can deliver the order by 2:00 p.m.

24j/ Use a comma before "such as" when it introduces a short series of illustrations. If "such" and "as" are separated by a noun, omit the comma.

Evidences of a fight, such as torn clothing, bloody noses, trampled shrubbery, were obvious.

His desk contained such articles as pens, pencils, pipes, glue, paper clips, and index cards.

Also correct: Articles such as pens, pencils, pipes, and glue were on his desk.

24k / Use a comma after "for example," "that is," "i.e.," "e.g.," "namely," and similar expressions.

When the frost is on the pumpkin, i.e., when November comes . . .

24l / Use a comma to set off a name in direct address.

Mr. Johnson, you are absolutely right. On the other hand, Harold, you might have to wait another year.

24m / Use a comma between the day of the week and the month and between the day of the month and the year. If the year occurs in a sentence, use a comma after the date.

Mr. Roosevelt said that Sunday, December 7, 1941, was a day that will live in infamy.
He was born in 1920, in a small Pennsylvania town.

If the day, month, or year appears alone, no comma is needed.

24n / Use a comma between the name of a city and the name of the state and to set off the state from the rest of the sentence.

Springfield, Illinois, is the population center of the country.

24o / Use commas to separate a direct quotation from the rest of the sentence unless a question mark or exclamation is needed.

A WAC sergeant nodded toward the closed door and said, "Go right in, Lieutenant Jennings. The Colonel is waiting."
"Where do you come from?" Vic said.

24p / Use a comma between a name and Jr. or Sr., or any title or degree that follows a name.

J. Worthington Medlington, Jr.
Courtland Hassenplug, Ph.D.

24q/   Use a comma to prevent misreading.

Confusing: Before they ate their eight-month-old son fell out of the high chair.
Clear: Before they ate, their eight-month-old son . . .

24r/   Use a comma to indicate contrasting ideas.

To the victor, not the defeated, go the spoils.
He is an etymologist, not an entomologist as reported in the paper.

24s/   Use a comma to set off interjections.

Oh, I'm not so sure about that.

24t/   Unnecessary commas

Omit commas in units of weight, measure, time, and money.

10 lb. 6 oz.	2 hr. 10 min.
6 feet 4 inches	£5 8s. 6d.

Omit the comma before the ampersand in the name of a company.

Hart, Shaffner & Marx

Omit any comma which would separate subject and predicate or predicate and object, unless there is a phrase between them that needs to be set off.

Wrong: Members of the Fire Department, the Police Department, and the Board of Control, were there.
[No comma after *Control*.]

Don't use a comma to separate an indirect quotation from the rest of the sentence.

He said that it was not necessary to attend the party.
[No comma after *said*.]

25 / The Semicolon

25a/ Use the semicolon between coordinating clauses not connected by a conjunction.

Wadsworth is a very disorganized person; his desk is cluttered with half a year's neglected work.

25b/ Use the semicolon with coordinate clauses connected by a conjunctive adverb, such as "also," "moreover," "so," "therefore," "thus," "however," "accordingly."

It is available in models which project color or black and white images; therefore it should be useful to many schools and industrial training departments.

25c/ Use a semicolon between items of series if the items contain internal commas.

Last night the Loyal Order of Horned Toads elected the following officers: Leslie Johnson, Memphis, Tennessee, President; Howard Beckworth, Racine, Wisconsin, Vice-President; Wellington Harbaugh, Kennebunkport, Maine, Secretary; and Russell Thorne, Scarsboro, Iowa, Treasurer.

25d/ Use a semicolon between independent clauses joined by a coordinating conjunction if there are commas within one or both of the clauses.

Kingsley, our triple-threat halfback, is the best player we have; but, in my opinion, he is not good enough to get a professional contract.

25e/ When you use a semicolon in connection with quotation marks, always place the semicolon outside the quotation marks.

You should read Louis Kronenberger's "The American Sense of Humor"; the essay states that we have lost our sense of humor because we have ceased to be a serious people.

25f / It is correct to use a semicolon before "for example," "e.g.,"
"that is," "namely," "viz.," and "for instance"
when they introduce enumerations.

The use of the comma before such expressions is also well established, particularly if the enumeration is short.

A camper needs certain basic equipment; namely, tent, sleeping
bag, cooking set, insect spray.

One typing space follows a semicolon.

26 / The Colon

26a / You may use a colon to separate the clauses of a
compound sentence if the second clause is a
repetition or elaboration of the first.

A pair of lovers are like sunset and sunrise: There are such
things every day but we very seldom see them.—SAMUEL BUTLER

26b / Use a colon after formal or extended introductory
clauses or phrases.

Tell me: how can one man be so stupid?
Date of conference: August 28, 1965
We too have our religion, and it is this: Help for the living,
hope for the dead.—ROBERT INGERSOLL

Note: There is no consistent practice concerning capitalization
of the first word following a colon. When a formal statement follows,
the word is generally capitalized.

Doctors recommend the following prescription: Keep breathing.

26c/ Introductory words like "that is," "namely," "thus," "for example" may be preceded by a comma, a dash, or a colon.

_____, that is
_____—that is,
_____—that is:
_____: that is,

26d/ Use a colon after the formal introduction to a long quotation.

After the crowd had cheered and applauded for five minutes, the Prime Minister continued: "There will be no truce or parley with you or that grisly gang who work your wicked will."

Note: Two typing spaces follow the colon. The colon is *always* placed outside the quotation marks.

26e/ Use a colon after a general statement which introduces a series of particulars.

A writer has three sources of information: experience, imagination, and research.

27/ The Dash

27a/ Use the dash to indicate an abrupt change in the thought or the construction of the sentence.

The only way to handle such a problem is—oh, get out of my sight.

27b/ Use the dash to set off extended appositives.

For camping equipment—tents, sleeping bags, air mattresses, cook sets—see Joe at the Call-of-the-Wild Sporting Goods Store.

27c**/**   Use the dash to indicate an interrupted thought.
No period follows it.

I never felt better in my—

27d**/**   Use a dash—instead of a comma or parentheses—to
set off a parenthetical expression, if you
want special emphasis.

In spite of a look of depravity in the eyes—which everybody
has if you look deep enough—the man seemed honest.

27e**/**   Use a dash to emphasize a phrase or a clause.

All I can tell you is—don't.

28/   Quotation Marks

28a**/**   Use quotation marks to indicate the exact words
of another person.

If the quotation is divided, enclose both parts in quotation
marks. If a comma precedes the second part of the quotation, do not
capitalize the first word of the second part. If a period, a question
mark, or an exclamation mark precedes the second part, capitalize
the first word of the second part.

"I don't understand," Sandra said.
"They bought it," Vic said, "from a Mexican named Amado."
"Where in Nogales?" the officer said. "What's his full name?"

Do not use quotation marks to enclose an indirect quotation.

They said that they had bought it from a Mexican named
Amado.

28b/ For quotations that run to several paragraphs, place quotation marks at the beginning of each paragraph but not at the end of any paragraph except the last one.

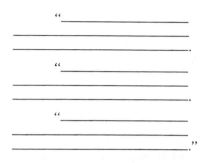

28c/ Use quotation marks to enclose the titles of short stories, booklets, poems, songs, magazine articles, chapters of books, sections of a report, and similar short items.

28d/ Use quotation marks to enclose words or phrases used in a special sense.

A problem like this is often solved by "grouting." Grouting simply means that materials are pumped in to fill the voids in the sand or rock.

Caution: Quotation marks around a doubtful word do not automatically make that word acceptable.

28e/ To indicate a quotation within a quotation, use single quotes.

"I shall conclude," said the preacher, "with the words of Celia Laighton Thaxter: 'Sad soul, take comfort, nor forget that sunrise never failed us yet.' "

28f/ Position of other punctuation marks when used with quotation marks.

Period: Always place the period inside the quotation marks.
Comma: Always place the comma inside the quotation marks.
Colon: Always place the colon outside the quotation marks.

Semicolon: Always place the semicolon outside the quotation marks.

Question mark: If the question is part of the quoted matter, place the question mark inside the quotation marks. If the question is not part of the quoted matter, place the question mark outside the quotation marks.

Exclamation mark: If the exclamation is quoted place its mark inside the quotation marks; otherwise, place it outside.

Dash: If the dash is part of the quoted matter, place it inside the quotation marks; otherwise, place it outside.

Parenthesis: Place the final parenthesis inside the quotation if it is part of the quoted matter; otherwise, place it outside.

Superior number or symbol: A superior number or symbol used to indicate a footnote is placed outside the quotation marks.

29 / Parentheses

29a / **Use parentheses to set off explanatory matter that could be omitted without destroying the sense of the sentence.**

There is no weapon that slays its victim so surely (if well aimed) as praise.—BULWER LYTTON

He directed his office with enough efficiency (and ruthlessness) to guarantee both his success and his destruction.

If the actor is standing, he pushes his weight forward, usually upon the upstage foot (one farthest from the footlights).

Note: Commas and dashes are also used in setting off parenthetical matter. In general, use commas if the matter is closely related to the primary material; dashes if you want to emphasize the parenthetical matter; and parentheses if the parenthetical matter is less important.

29b / **Place parentheses around the letters or numbers that designate the members of a series.**

The book can be used in (1) industrial training departments, (2) colleges of business, and (3) private offices.

29c/ Use parentheses to enclose figures confirming a statement.

Our check for four dollars and thirty cents ($4.30) is enclosed.

30/ Brackets

30a/ Use brackets to enclose an explanation inserted in a quotation.

The brackets indicate that the comment is not part of the original quotation.

> "It [London] has the sound of distant thunder."
> "They [bagpipes] are a trying instrument to perform upon."

31/ The Apostrophe

31a/ Use the apostrophe to form the possessive case of nouns.

For singular nouns add 's: One hour's work, John's book.
For plural nouns that end in s, *add only the apostrophe*: Two hours' work, The boys' books, The Reeds' car.
For plural nouns that do not end in s, *add the apostrophe and* s: The children's books, The men's comments.

Note: For the possessive singular of proper nouns, practice varies.

> *Correct*: Dickens's or Dickens'
> Charles's or Charles'

Avoid adding *'s* if the result would be three sibilant sounds. Use the apostrophe alone.

> Moses' law, not Moses's law

31b / Use the apostrophe to indicate the possessive singular
of indefinite pronouns.

one's house   the other's book   either's hat

Note: Personal and relative pronouns do not add the apostrophe.

Correct: hers, yours, its, theirs
Wrong: her's, your's, it's, their's

31c / Use the apostrophe in place of the omitted letters
in contractions.

don't, o'clock, you're

31d / Use the apostrophe to form the plurals of letters and symbols

a's, b's, c's
He wore size 12's

23–31x / Exercises in Punctuation

1. Clip an editorial from a newspaper or several paragraphs from a
popular magazine. Examine the punctuation. How would you
punctuate the same material differently? Why?

2. Compare the punctuation conventions followed by the *Reader's
Digest* and by *Time* magazine. Report the differences.

3. Copy from dictation a paragraph or two from a book or magazine.
Punctuate the passage. Compare and discuss.

4. Punctuate the following passages. Be prepared to defend your
choice.

a. Now Pip said he be careful
I will sir I returned
Dont commit yourself said Mrs. Jaggers and dont commit anyone you
understand anyone
Of course I saw that he knew the man had come
I merely want Mr Jaggers said I to assure myself what I have been told

is true I have been informed by a person named Abel Magwitch that he
is the benefactor so long unknown to me
That is the man said Mr Jaggers in New South Wales and only he said I
and only he said Mr Jaggers

from *Great Expectations* (adapted)

b. Love is no hot house flower but a wild plant born of a wet night
born of an hour of sunshine sprung from wild seed blown along the
road by a wild wind a wild plant that when it blooms by chance within
the hedge of our gardens we call a flower and when it blooms outside we
call a weed but flower or weed whose scent and color are always wild

The Man of Property
JOHN GALSWORTHY

c. When my eyes shall be turned to behold for the last time the sun in
heaven may they not see him shining on the broken and dishonored
fragments of a once glorious Union of States dissevered discordant belligerent on a land rent with civil feuds or drenched it may be in fraternal
blood

DANIEL WEBSTER

d. Think of all the changes ahead of you a bigger family new home
promotion at work and far in the future retirement

e. If youve ever been disappointed because the trim on your car rusts
pits or peels the next time you buy youll want stainless steel the extra
value metal created by research
Its stainless all the way through hard and tough stands up under abuse
that scratches and dents ordinary metals

GRAMMAR

32/ Grammar Connects Parts of Speech

Proper language is whatever makes meaning clear. The science of language reveals that when a man speaks he makes meaning clear in many ways: by intonations, by pauses, by gestures, by inflections, by body movements, by local references—by an intricate complex of sounds and movements. But *writing* is denied many of the instruments available to speaking. Therefore, in writing we must find a *pattern of words* to do what we, in speaking, accomplish with a *pattern of sounds and movements.*

What is done in speech by a rich variety of instruments has to be done in writing by a rigorously limited few: *words, grammar,* and *punctuation.*

Grammar, as an instrument of writing, has an intense and vast responsibility. It must make the relationship of words instantly and unmistakably clear. It must make the relationship clear without the help of sounds, intonations, gestures. It must make the relationship clear to more than an immediate audience at a particular time. It must make the relationship clear to whoever reads the message wherever he reads the message. It must enable the meaning to survive space and time.

The spoken word is evanescent; it disappears the moment it comes into existence. It can be extravagant, repetitious, digressive —because its effect depends upon the residue it leaves behind in the listener. The mass of the spoken word evaporates. An essence remains.

The written word is fixed. It does not disappear. It remains before the reader. It *is* the essence.

The written word does not reproduce the spoken word; it reproduces the *effect* of the spoken word.

In order, then, for grammar to make the written word clear, without aids, to many persons in many places, basic agreements on written-word relationships have been established and used.

Grammar shows what belongs to what. It responds to such questions as:

What thing belongs to what act?

Subject-verb agreement indicates the answer.

For what noun does a pronoun substitute?

Noun-pronoun agreement indicates the answer.

Is a thing acting—or being acted upon?

The case—especially of pronouns—helps reveal the relationship.

Does a word describe a thing—or an act?

Differences in form often distinguish an adjective from an adverb.

Which action in the past is deeper in the past?

Distinction in tenses reveals the relationship.

Grammar is clarity. It is not imposed on language. It is a quality of thought visible in language. When you are clear, you use elements of grammar—whether you can name them or not. Using them effectively is more important than naming them correctly. But recognize their logic: They relate words clearly to each other.

Here is a useful grammar for the written word:

The *parts of speech* name a way a word is used in a sentence. If we understand the name, we understand the use. We recognize the use wherever it occurs, however often it occurs. Parts of speech have *eight* names.

1. *Noun:* a word that names a person, place, or thing.

   Michael bought a *pen.*

2. *Pronoun:* a word that substitutes for a noun.

   Michael bought *it* for me.

3. *Adjective:* a word that describes a noun.

   The *green* pen had a *translucent* barrel and a *chrome-plated* clip.

4. *Verb:* a word that establishes action or being.

   Michael *went* to a jewelry store that *guarantees* its merchandise.

5. *Adverb:* a word that describes a verb, an adjective, or another adverb.

   Michael *carefully* counted the money.
   Michael is *unfailingly* careful.
   Michael *very* carefully counted the money.

6. *Preposition:* a word that connects a noun or pronoun to some other word in the sentence.

   Michael put the pen, *with* a birthday card, *into* a box; wrapped the box *with* decorated paper; and gave the package *to* me.

7. *Conjunction:* a word that connects word to word, phrase to phrase, or clause to clause.

   Because I was surprised, I held the pen *and* the card in my hands, able *neither* to laugh *nor* to cry.

8. *Interjection:* a word that exclaims, that expresses emotion, but that does not relate grammatically to anything else in the sentence.

   My goodness, I was surprised.

What does the word do in the sentence? How is the word used in the sentence? Your answer tells what part of speech that word is in that place and at that time.

33/ Subject and Verb Agree in Person and Number

Subject and verb belong to each other. In the active voice, the combination joins actor to act. To be sure that we know *who* is doing *what*, the act must have the same person and the same number that the actor does. The actor can have one of three identities —or persons: it can be the speaker (*I, we*), or *first person;* it can be the one spoken to (*you*), or *second person;* it can be the one spoken about (*he, she, it, they*) or *third person.* The act, or verb, must show the same person that the actor, or subject, established:

> He goes to town.
> I go to town.

The actor can be either one or more than one. If one, the number is *singular;* if more than one, the number is *plural.* So, for a singular subject, the verb must be singular. For a plural subject, the verb must be plural.

> He admires courage.
> They admire courage.

In the passive voice, the subject receives, rather than performs, the act. The subject, although not the actor, still determines the number and person of the verb:

> He *was elected* President.
> They *were named* to the Cabinet.

33a/ Words between subject and verb do not affect agreement.

> *Margaret,* like the other women, *wants* [not *want*] to know the cost.
> Each of the club members *pays* [not *pay*] a yearly assessment.
> His desire for wealth, prestige, and power *makes* [not *make*] him restless.

33b/   A collective noun, if the whole is discussed, needs a singular verb; if the parts are discussed, a plural verb.

The jury submits the verdict.
[The jury acts as a single unit.]
The jury disagree on the extent of guilt.
[Members of the jury act individually; if the sentence were "The jury disagrees on the extent of guilt" it could mean that the jury, as a unit, does not agree with a statement made by the prosecutor.]

Do not shift a collective noun from one number to another; do not say, "The jury *is bringing* in *their* verdict."

33c/   Two or more nouns joined by "and" need a plural verb.

Jack and Jill *are* workers in a water-transportation project.

But when the joined words have a single meaning, the verb is singular:

"Jack and Jill" is a nursery rhyme.
Ham and eggs is a favorite breakfast.
My friend and companion is a cocker spaniel.

33d/   When nouns of the subject are divided by "or," "either . . . or," or "neither . . . nor," the verb agrees with the nearer noun.

Neither his friends nor he is rich.
Neither he nor his friends are rich.
Either his brothers or he is responsible.

33e/   Some nouns plural in form but singular in use need singular verbs.

Mathematics is an interesting study.
The news is exciting.
His whereabouts is unknown.
Ninety dollars is a high price.
Two years is a long time.

Some words remain plural in use, although meaning tends toward the singular.

> Where are my trousers?
> The scissors are on the desk.

33f / **When "it" begins a sentence, a singular verb follows; when "there" begins a sentence, the verb agrees with the subject that follows the verb.**

> It is actions that count.
> It is they who are at fault.
> It is a pleasure to read.
> There is a horse in the field.
> There are a horse and two cows in the field.

It and *there*, when used to begin a sentence, are called *expletives*.

33g / **When a relative pronoun is the subject, the verb agrees with the noun for which the relative pronoun substitutes.**

> She is one of those persons who *hate* idle talk.
> [*Who* substitutes for *persons; hate* agrees with *persons*.]
> We who *are* about to die salute you.
> [*Who* substitutes for *we; are* agrees with *we*.]
> I who *am* about to go salute you.
> [*Who* substitutes for *I; am* agrees with *I*.]

34 / A Pronoun Agrees in Person, Number, and Gender with the Noun Which It Replaces

A pronoun can be either masculine, feminine, or neuter in gender. An inanimate object always requires a neuter pronoun; an animal, except when emphasis is on its sex, also requires a neuter pronoun.

> Jack disliked *his* employers, and *he* told *them* that *he* would resign.
> The boy gave the stewardess *his* white rat and asked *her* to give *it* some bread.

The pronoun, in each use, repeats the person, number, and gender of the noun to which it belongs. This noun, the word for which the pronoun later substitutes, is called the *antecedent*.

34a/ The pronoun refers to a single, expressed noun; not to a verb or adjective or adverb; not to a general idea implied in a phrase or clause.

Wrong: He sat for hours, practicing the piano étude; but *it* did not help him in the audition.

Wrong: He smokes aromatic tobacco in a white meerschaum pipe with a curved stem because he likes *it*.

Wrong: He drives his automobile as if it were a racing car, *which* frightens his friends.

Wrong: He is honest and industrious; *these* are his only virtues.

In special cases, a pronoun can refer to an idea contained in a group of words, if the idea is clearly stated and no ambiguity is possible.

Whether to speak or to be silent, *that* was my dilemma.

He bounced a ball against the blackboard while he lectured, which was distracting.

Your sentences can retain economy and gain clarity if you refer to the general idea by a single and summary noun.

When you lie to a man, be sure that you clasp his hand strongly; that you look him in the eye firmly; that you hold your shoulders back proudly. These *actions* will convince him you are honest.

34b/ A collective noun considered a unit needs a singular pronoun; a collective noun considered in its parts needs a plural pronoun.

The rifle team won *its* first match.

The rifle team ran to take *their* positions on the firing line.

A shift in the number of a collective noun confuses the sense: "The rifle team, eager to win *its* first match, ran to take *their* positions."

34c/   An indefinite pronoun singular in meaning ("one," "anybody," "each," "everybody," "everyone," "nobody," "someone," "either," "neither") needs a singular following pronoun.

Give to each *his* own.
Someone left *his* card.
Anybody who marries has *his* share of trouble.
Neither of the men had *his* wallet with *him*.
Nobody can take *his* wealth into the Promised Land.

The indefinite pronoun *none* can be either singular or plural.

We asked the desk clerk for rooms, but none *was* [or *were*] available.

An indefinite pronoun sometimes has a strong plural sense, and speakers use it to indicate *all* persons rather than *each* person. In the sentence, "Everybody in the room protested, and *they* had good cause," precision of words and intention of speaker are in conflict. To say ". . . and *he* had good cause," would clarify precision and confuse the intention. Since precision of words is important because it serves the intention of the speaker, either the intention must force the imprecision to stand, or the sentence must be re-phrased. Re-phrasing is safer: "All in the room protested, and they had good cause."

34d/   A noun that does not specify the sex of the person to whom it refers takes, for brevity, a masculine pronoun.

A person who wants to act must train *himself* to watch.
When one reads a classic, *he* discovers that no word is wasted.
Each of us must take *his* chances.
Let everyone examine *his* conscience.

When the sex is established by the sense of the sentence, the pronoun obeys that sense.

Everybody in the sisterhood did *her* part.

34e/ A pronoun which immediately follows the noun to provide further identification needs the same case used by the noun.

The trio—Sam, John, and I—sang in the auditorium.
The audience booed the trio—Sam, John, and me—after the first three bars.

A pronoun in apposition repeats the function of its antecedent and therefore shares its case.

34f/ Two nouns joined by "and" need a plural pronoun; two nouns divided by "or" or "nor" require that the pronoun agree with the nearer noun.

The Indians and the cowboy loaded *their* rifles.
Neither the Indians nor the cowboy wanted to risk *his* life.
Neither the cowboy nor the Indians wanted to fire *their* rifles.

35/ A Noun or Pronoun Takes a Form Which Shows Whether It Is Used as a Subject, an Object, or a Possessor

In English, a noun or pronoun can have one of three relationships to the rest of the sentence. Each relationship is called a case. As the subject of a finite verb, the noun or pronoun is in the *nominative* (subjective) case. As the object of a verb or preposition, it is in the *accusative* (objective) case. As a possessor, it is in the *genitive* (possessive) case.

A noun changes form only to show possession. A pronoun, however, has a distinctive form for each case.

He	hit	*her*.
(nominative)		(accusative, object of verb)
She	hit	*him*.
(nominative)		(accusative, object of verb)

She	hit	*his* face.
(nominative)		(genitive)
She	was	tired of *him*.
(nominative)		(accusative, after preposition)
He	was	afraid of *her*.
(nominative)		(accusative, after preposition)

35a / **A relative pronoun takes its case from its use in the relative clause, regardless of the use of the relative clause in the sentence.**

My house is open to *whoever* comes.
[The clause "whoever comes" is the object of the preposition *to*: the relative pronoun "whoever" is the subject of the verb *comes*.]
He did not hire the man *whom* I recommended.
["Whom" is the object of the verb *recommended*; "I" is the subject.]
He hired the man *who* had no recommendations.
["Who" is the subject of the verb *had*.]
Whomever I recommend has two strikes on him from the start.
[The relative clause "Whomever I recommend" is the subject of the sentence; "Whomever" is the object of the verb recommended within the relative clause.]

When expressions such as *I think, I hope, he says, one expects,* are only interjections; they do *not* affect the case of the relative pronoun.

I gave my money to a broker *who* I trust will double it.
[*Who* is the subject of *will double; I trust* is parenthetical.]

If the sentence read, "I gave my money to a broker *whom* I trust," *I trust* is integrated, not interjected, into the sentence. *Whom* is then the object of the verb *trust.*

35b / **A pronoun acting as the subject of an infinitive takes the accusative (objective) case.**

We asked *him* to come.
We waited for *him* to arrive.

35c/ A pronoun or noun before a gerund (a verb form acting as a noun) takes the possessive case.

I was asked to do *my* singing elsewhere.
We approved *their* going on vacation.
John's taking command prevented a panic.

For emphasis on the pronoun rather than on the gerund, the pronoun takes the accusative case:

I cannot imagine *him* giving orders to anybody.

35d/ A personal pronoun never uses an apostrophe to form the possessive.

The horse lost its *shoe*.
The dress is *hers*.
The trophy is *ours* to cherish; *theirs* to envy.
Yours is the large cup.
He is the man *whose* nose was broken.
[The relative pronoun *who* changes case forms as personal pronouns do.]

35e/ Form of pronoun shows relationship of pronoun to implied verb.

He likes her more than *I* like her.
[*I* is the subject of implied verb *like*.]
He likes her more than he likes *me*.
[*Me* is object of implied verb *likes*.]
John deserves the medal as much as *they* deserve it.
Are you as indignant as *I* am indignant?

36/ An Adjective or Adverb Indicates by Its Placement and Form the Word It Modifies

An adjective or adverb specifies, intensifies, or limits the meaning contained in another word. An adjective serves a noun or pronoun.

An adverb serves a verb, an adjective, or another adverb. In general, an adjective links a quality to a thing; an adverb links a quality to an action, or a quality to a quality.

> He is ill. [A quality specifies the condition of *he*; *ill* is used as an adjective.]
> He is *seriously* ill. [A quality intensifies the quality *ill*; *seriously* is used as an adverb.]
> His illness is *serious*. [*Illness* has become a thing under examination; *serious*, used as an adjective, specifies its quality.]
> A *serious* illness must be treated *carefully*.
> [The adjective *serious* serves the noun *illness*; the adverb *carefully* serves the verb *must be treated*.]
> It must be treated *very carefully*.
> [*Carefully*, an adverb serving the verb *must be treated*, is itself served by *very*, another adverb.]

Phrases and clauses often perform the function of an adjective or an adverb:

> An illness *of such severity* must be treated *with great care*.
> [The prepositional phrase *of such severity* specifies the quality of *illness*: The function is that of an adjective. The prepositional phrase *with great care* links a quality to the verb *must be treated*: The function is that of an adverb.]
> The doctor *whom we called* is a specialist.
> [The dependent clause *whom we called* is used to limit the meaning of *doctor*: The function is that of an adjective.]
> The doctor acted *as if he were pleased*.
> [The dependent clause *as if he were pleased* specifies the nature of the verb *acted*: The function is that of an adverb.]

Although many words can be used either as adjectives or adverbs, the ending *-ly* often identifies an adverb. This observation would be helpful if some adjectives did not also end in -ly: *dastardly, goodly, saintly, sprightly*. Rendering the *-ly* ending still less reliable as the test of an adverb is the fact that an adverb may drop the *-ly* in cases of brief, abrupt commands: *Go slow. Hold tight.*

A word, phrase, or clause doing the work of an adjective will answer the question *How many?* or *What kind?* or *Which one?* A word, phrase, or clause doing the work of an adverb will answer the question *How?* or *When?* or *Where?* or *How much?*

36a/ An adjective is placed, most often, either before the noun
it serves or after a linking verb.

The *happy* bride seemed *beautiful*.
[*Happy* modifies bride; *beautiful* modifies bride. Since the verb
intervenes between the noun and the adjective, *beautiful* is here a
predicate adjective.]

Verbs that establish being (*am, is, are, become*), appearance
(*seem, appear*), and sensation (*feel, look, smell, taste, sound*) usually link the subject with a descriptive or qualifying word—a predicate adjective. Verbs of being, appearance, and sensation are called
linking or *copulative* verbs. When these verbs emphasize an act
rather than link subject and quality, an adverb can follow to describe
the act. The difference between "He smells bad" and "He smells
badly" is the difference between an offensive condition and an impaired faculty.

The coffee smells *strong*.
The man seems *eager*.
The band sounded *weak*.
[Emphasis could be shifted to the verb; the adjective *weak*
would become the adverb *weakly*; the sentence would be "The band
sounded (its opening chord?) weakly."]
He looks angry. [Or, if emphasis is on verb rather than subject:
"He looks angrily (at us?)."]

Adjectives, for grace or special emphasis, are sometimes placed
after the noun.

The officer, *cool* and *precise*, seemed efficient.
The old man, *exasperated*, slammed the door.

36b/ A noun may be used as an adjective

A noun can do the work of an adjective well: a *paper* cup, a
cloth coat, an *oil* furnace, a *gold* mine. But when a series of nouns
attempts to modify a noun, confusion and clumsiness often result.

He is a University of Mandota graduate faculty behavior psychology professor.

[Does he study the behavior psychology of a graduate faculty? Or of the graduate faculty of the University of Mandota? Is he a professor on general staff of the University of Mandota? Or is he a professor on the graduate faculty of the University of Mandota?]

Prepositional phrases improve the sentence:

He is a behavior psychology professor on the graduate faculty of the University of Mandota.

36c / **An adjective or adverb indicates by its form its degree of comparison.**

An adjective or adverb can establish a *positive degree* of comparison:

The girl is *pretty*.
She smiles *warmly*.

The positive degree has no explicit object of comparison. Implicit in the word *pretty* is the assumption that if the girl's appearance were *less* pleasing, she would be plain; and if her appearance were *more* pleasing, she would be beautiful. The adverb *warmly* implies, too, that smiling would have a different effect if it had *less* heat, or *more* heat.

A modifier in the *comparative degree* establishes a relative value between two things:

She is *prettier* than her friend.
She smiles *more warmly* than her friend.

A modifier in the *superlative degree* establishes a relative value among three or more things:

She is the *prettiest* of the quartet.
She smiles *most warmly*.

Many modifiers add *-er* to the positive degree to establish the *comparative* degree, and *-est* to establish the *superlative* degree.

Other modifiers, especially those with three syllables, establish the comparative degree by adding *more* or *less* to the positive, and the superlative degree by adding *most* or *least* to the positive.

Words used as adjectives

sweet — sweeter — sweetest
beautiful — more [less] — most [least]
beautiful beautiful

Words used as adverbs

near — nearer — nearest
sincerely — more [less] — most [least]
sincerely sincerely

Some words exist only in the positive degree, because they establish an absolute state which cannot be diminished or enlarged. A thing cannot be *more unique* or *less unique*. *Unique* means that only one of a kind exists. Attempt to make the word comparative or superlative, and meaning disappears. Words like *possible, perfect, dead, absolute,* forced into comparative and superlative degrees, are robbed of meaning and effect.

When two degrees are included in the same sentence, one degree must be completed before the other is begun:

She is as pretty *as*—if not prettier *than*—her friend.
She is as pretty as her friend, if not prettier.

36d / One negative modifier cancels another.

Although in some languages one negative intensifies another, in English one negative nullifies the other. When writers want to make a positive point in a restrained, reserved way, they use the principle of the double negative: "He is *not un*intelligent." But a writer who wants to make a negative point and uses two negatives defeats himself: "I don't want *no* trouble." For the precise—or, perhaps, over-precise—he has said, although he does not mean, "I do want trouble."

Most deceptive, however, are the approximate negatives such as *scarcely, hardly, can . . . but.* "I can *hardly* believe it," means that something is difficult to believe. "I *can't hardly* believe it," means, technically at least, that something is easy to believe "I can but marvel at his energy," means that I can only marvel at his energy. "I can't but marvel at his energy," means that I can't only marvel at his energy. The intention of the double negative, especially in idioms, is often clear; but a double negative intended as an emphatic single negative runs the risk of confusion. The effect is rarely worth the risk.

37 / The Form of a Verb Reveals Tense, the Time Lapse Between Actions or Between Action and Statement; Mood, the Speaker's Attitude Toward His Statement; and Voice, the Relationship of Subject to Action

"He came home." The statement is made now about an action before now. *The tense is past.* The speaker considers his statement a report of fact. *The mood is indicative.* The subject "he" performed the action "came." *The voice is active.*

37a / Tenses place actions in time.

Verbs have six tenses. Each of the three major areas of time—*present, past,* and *future*—uses, for special purposes, a *perfect* tense.

Tense	Conventional Form	Progressive Form	Emphatic
1. Present:	I go	I am going	I do go
2. Present perfect:	I have gone	I have been going	—
3. Past:	I went	I was going	I did go
4. Past perfect:	I had gone	I had been going	—
5. Future:	I shall [or will] go	I shall [or will] be going	—
6. Future perfect:	I shall [or will] have gone	I shall [or will] have been going	—

The *present perfect* establishes an action in the past near or continuing to the present. The *past perfect* establishes an action in the past concluded *before* another action in the past. The *future perfect* establishes an action that will have been completed before some specific time in the future.

A dictionary gives for each verb its *infinitive, past tense,* and *past participle:* [to] go, went, gone. From these forms the other forms can be derived.

A verb that requires an object to complete its meaning is called a *transitive* verb. *Transitive* means that the movement must pass to an object. "He raised the anvil." An *intransitive* verb needs go no further; it, in a sense, completes itself: "The anvil rose."

37b / Verbs obey the logic of time.

The logic of time requires that an action take place in some *consistent* area of time. The reader's mind reels when exposed to flickering time:

> He *drew* his revolver and *captured* the criminal.
> He *snaps* the handcuffs on the cowering man.
> They *went* to the police station, where the prisoner is *finger-printed*.

The present tense can be used in passages of past action if a dramatic effect of immediacy is needed. This use is called the *historical present*. It must be used sparely, carefully, skillfully.

> We crept toward the building. We dared not even whisper in the blackness. Groping along the wall, we found the door. Ed turned the knob, pushed the door open, and POW! a blinding flash and we *fly* through the air.

The present tense can be used at any time to establish a continuing and general truth. This use is called the *universal present*.

> We depended on the fact that day *follows* night to show us where we were.

Establishing which actions are earlier and which are later in areas of time require the use of tenses in *sequence*. An action in the

past is put into the past tense. A second action further in the past
is put into the past perfect tense.

> He *had gone* when I *called.*
> (past perfect)   (past)

The meaning is changed when the past tense is used for both
actions:

> He *went* when I *called.*
> (past)   (past)

An action in the future is put into the future tense. An action
between now and another time in the future is put into the future
perfect tense.

> By this time next Tuesday, I *shall have passed* my fortieth
>   (future perfect)
> birthday.

An action in the present is put into the present tense. An action
in the near past continuing to the present is put into the present perfect tense.

> He *has gone* to the office and *is talking* to the client.
> (present perfect)   (present)

37c/ Verbals obey the logic of time.

Verbs in derived forms can serve as nouns, adjectives, and adverbs. These derived forms are called verbals. They can, as verbs
do, take subjects and objects; but they cannot make independent
statements. The *infinitive*—a verb form preceded by the characteristic *to*—can act as noun, adjective, or adverb:

> She wanted *to cry.*
>   (noun: object of verb)
>
> *To protest* is useless.
> (noun: subject)

It is a wonder *to behold.*
>(adjective: modifier of the noun *wonder*)

He rose *to be* king.
>(adverb: modifier of the intransitive verb *rose*)

The infinitive has two forms: the *present* (*to speak*); and the *perfect,* with an auxiliary verb (*to have spoken*). A peculiarity of the infinitive is that its subject is always in the accusative (objective) case:

I wanted *him* to *speak.*

Sometimes the characteristic *to* of the infinitive is absent:

He dared not [*to*] speak.
He helped me [*to*] compose a speech.

The second verbal, the *participle,* acts as an adjective. It has three forms: the *present,* which ends in *-ing;* the past, which usually ends in *-ed;* the *perfect,* which uses an auxiliary verbal.

Present participle
The *crying* woman ran from the room.
>(adjective, modifier of *woman*)
She cried for her *departed* lover.
>(adjective, modifier of *lover*)

Perfect participle
Having cried, she wiped her eyes.
(adjective, modifier of *she*)

The third verbal, the *gerund,* ends in *-ing,* but acts as a noun:

Crying relieves the tension.
(noun: subject)
She stopped *crying.*
>(noun: object of verb)
She never tires of *crying.*
>(noun: object of preposition)

Both the participle and the infinitive forms are determined by the tense of the verb in the sentence. If the action in the verbal and the action in the verb take place at the same time, the participle or the infinitive takes the *present* form:

Laughing, I struggled for breath.
(present participle and verb establish simultaneous actions)
I struggled *to get* my breath.
(present infinitive and verb are involved in the same action at the same time)
I was glad *to escape*.
(verb and infinitive establish simultaneous actions)

If the action in the verbal takes place before the action in the verb, the participle or the infinitive takes the *perfect* form:

Having laughed, I apologized.
(perfect participle establishes action prior to action of the main verb)
I am sorry *to have laughed*.
(perfect infinitive establishes action prior to action of the main verb)
I would give a fortune *to have been* there.
(perfect infinitive establishes action prior to action of the main verb)

37d/ Verbs change tense when direct discourse becomes indirect discourse.

Verbs in a quotation move back one degree in time when the statement is given indirectly as summary or paraphrase.

Direct Discourse: She said, "I *hate* him.
Indirect Discourse: She said that she *hated* him.
Direct Discourse: She said, "I *hated* him.
Indirect Discourse: She said that she *had hated* him.
Direct Discourse: She said, "I *will hate* him if he *does not come*."
Indirect Discourse: She said that she *would hate* him if he *did not come*.

Present tense in direct discourse changes to past tense in indirect discourse; past to past perfect; future to conditional.

37e/ The verb takes special form for subjunctive mood.

The verb in English can distinguish among three general attitudes a speaker has toward what he says. The mood may be *indicative:* the speaker states a fact, offers an opinion, or asks a question:

"I *read* the book. The book *is* interesting. *Have* you read it?" The mood may be *imperative:* the speaker commands or requests. The subject is often understood; the tense is present; the person is second: "*Get* out; *go* far away; *don't come* back." The mood may be *subjunctive:* the speaker doubts, supposes, wishes.

The subjunctive has many uses. It expresses uncertainties, conditions contrary to fact, improbabilities, possibilities, concessions, emphatic commands.

> If they *had selected* me, wouldn't they notify me?
> (uncertainty)
> If my aunt *were* a man, she would be a pirate.
> (condition contrary to fact)
> He acts as if he *were* sick.
> (possibility)
> If I *were* immortal, I wouldn't worry.
> (improbability)
> I insist that you *be* here.
> (emphatic command)
> *Be* it as the council requests.
> (concession)

The subjunctive is used in three structures. In main clauses, it expresses a wish:

> The Lord be praised.
> Long wave the flag.
> The public be damned.

In independent clauses with *if* meanings, it establishes a supposition or a condition contrary to fact:

> If I *were* in charge, I would listen to suggestions.
> I will speak though he *punish* me.
> *Were* I king, I would abdicate.

In independent clauses introduced by *that,* it establishes wish, request or command:

> We voted that he *be* commended.
> The judge requested that the defense attorney *approach* the bar.
> The sentry commanded that we *advance* and *be recognized.*

The subjunctive mood has characteristic forms. For all persons in the present tense, the form of *to be* is *be*; for all persons in the past tense, *were*; for all persons in the present perfect tense, *have been*. Other verbs have a characteristic form for the subjunctive mood only in the third person singular, present tense. The *s* or *es* ending of the indicative is omitted: the indicative "he merits" becomes the subjunctive "if he merit."

The words *would, could, should* often indicate that a subjunctive idea is expressed.

Although the indicative mood is used often as though it were interchangeable with the subjunctive mood, only the subjunctive mood can provide certain shades of meaning. Each mood has a specific function. The shift of mood within a sentence is ungraceful and confusing. The *indicative*, the *imperative*, the *subjunctive* each establishes an attitude of the speaker toward his statement. When the moods are jumbled, the attitude loses definition.

> Go to your employer and you should tell him your complaints, however apprehensive you be, and he will listen.

Is the speaker indicating a fact, or expressing a wish, or uttering a command? The mixture of moods obscures the speaker's attitude.

37f / Verbs should be in the active voice generally; in the passive voice for special purposes.

When the subject does something, the voice of the verb is *active*. When something is done to the subject, the voice is *passive*.

> The subject *does* something.
> (active voice)
> Something *is done* to the subject.
> (passive voice)

In English, the two voices are *not* equal and parallel in form. Verbs are usually conjugated in the active voice. The passive sense is made by adding a past participle to the conjugated forms of *to be*.

Passive Construction: Verbs *are* usually *conjugated* in the active
                                (present   (past participle)
                                form of
                                to be)
voice.

Passive Construction: The passive sense *is made* by adding a
                                (present of *to be* plus
                                past participle)
past participle.

Life is action. When we see someone do something, we understand a direct, natural sequence: actor, action, accomplishment.
When the order is reversed, our understanding is less instinctive,
less immediate. The passive voice inverts natural sequence, imposes
complexity, slows comprehension. When used, it had better be
worth its cost.

The passive voice can provide variety and special emphasis.
It is an effective construction, used sparely and purposefully.

Why use the passive voice?

Use the passive voice when the act is known, but the performer
is not:

> I *was hit* from behind.
> The paintings *were cut* from their frames.

Use the passive voice when emphasis is on the act, not on the
performer:

> The paintings *were mutilated.*
> I *was distracted.*

Often the passive is used to *weaken* the effect of an embarrassing situation: "I need money" becomes "Financial assistance is
needed." The stark verb *need* is softened to *is needed.* The badly
exposed *I* has gone into hiding somewhere.

Do not shift active and passive voices arbitrarily. Mixing the
voices attempts to view the same thing from two directions. The
senses are confused. Don't write:

> Sharpen your pencils; then the paper is laid out; then the sub-
> ject is chosen; now you begin to write.

Except for special intentions, the passive voice is unwieldy and diffusive (See 20b). Use the active voice. It will force you to be clear and direct—or expose you when you are not.

37g / For special purposes, "shall" is distinct from "will"; "should" from "would."

For simple anticipation, *shall* is used with the first person; *will* with the second and third persons. *I shall, you will, he will; we shall, you will, they will.*

To show resolve or determination about the future, *shall* and *will* exchange places. *I will, you shall, he shall; we will, you shall, they shall.*

> "Will you go?"   "You shall go!"
> "No, I shall not go."   "I will not go!"

In general use, however, *will* indicates the future for all persons. And writers often depend—not upon the *shall-will* reversal— but upon the context to emphasize resolution or determination.

The relationship between *should* and *would*, when the future is involved, exactly parallels that between *shall* and *will*. *Would* tends, like *will*, to eclipse its partner.

Should and *would*, as past tenses, replace *shall* and *will* when direct discourse becomes indirect discourse:

> He said, "I *shall* go."
> He said that he *would* go.
> He said, "You *will* go."
> He said that I *should* go.

In practice, *would* and *should* are interchangeable for direct discourse.

Should has other uses. It can mean "ought to," to express obligation or expectation:

> We should help each other.
> We should be there by dawn.

Should can express condition:

If I should come, would I be welcome?

Would, too, has other uses. It can express a wish: .

Would that there were peace on earth.

It can express habitual or repeated action:

After the meetings, we would have informal discussions.

Would, like *could*, can express condition:

I would come, if you would invite me.

32–37x/ Exercises: Grammar

1. In the sentences that follow, find the subject of each clause. If necessary, change verb to agree with subject.
   a. Mr. Hoffman, with his three sons and four other men, are building a house.
   b. The club is willing to contribute, but are not agreed on the amount.
   c. She is one of those cooks who hates food.
   d. There is a chair in the kitchen and two more in the hall.
   e. Ethics determine the rightness of our actions.
   f. Neither the men nor the officer were happy.
   g. This tribute to the men in the laboratory for their discoveries and their contributions in the fields of the sciences and the humanities are well deserved.
   h. The food I like best are steaks.
   i. Rifles, tents, cots, and the rest of the trail supply was carried by porters.

2. In the sentences that follow, find the word which the pronoun replaces. If necessary, change pronouns to agree with its antecedent. Change sentence if pronoun has no specific expressed antecedent.
   a. When the alarm sounded, everyone ran to their stations.
   b. No matter how cleverly a person makes out his income tax

report, they can always tell whether he is telling the truth or not.

c. We—Edward, Mary, and me—signed our names to the letter.
d. Neither the girls nor their mother wanted to sign their names.
e. The committee, in its first meeting, offered their resignations.
f. Each member rose and listed his or her complaints.
g. The chairman will not listen to any complaints, which makes it unpleasant for the other members.
h. I like nursing because they help sick persons.

3. Correct, where necessary, the case of the pronoun in the following sentences.
   a. We will give the mission to whomever volunteers to go.
   b. It is impossible for he to go.
   c. The second house on the block is their's.
   d. My mother took my sister, my brother, and I to the airport.
   e. I resented him muttering during my speech.
   f. We will give the mission to whoever the president recommends.
   g. He is no better than me.
   h. I have done as much for the welfare of our town as him.

4. Correct sentences in which elements acting as adjectives or adverbs are misused.
   a. He is a real good musician.
   b. His phrasing is very unique.
   c. He seems tense, but he plays relaxed.
   d. The bride looked sweet in her gown and veil.
   e. The bride looked sweet at her husband.
   f. Of the two sisters, Amy is the prettiest.
   g. He plays the piano as good, if not better than many professional musicians.
   h. I can't hardly stand hearing a piano played bad.
   i. I cannot talk or write without he corrects me.
   j. He felt badly about having offended his hostess.
   k. He was most positive in identifying the suspect.
   l. Teetering on high heels, he saw her walking down the street.
   m. The lemon tasted sourly.
   n. He is a Civil Service Commission, Planning and Procedures Section, regulations writer.
   o. I feel some better than I felt yesterday.
   p. I sure hope that you state your case clear.
   q. I know that the other attorney will make his point clearly to the jury.

r. Most everyone in town attended the trial.

s. He will be considerable relieved when I tell him how good the critics thought he acted the role.

5. Correct sentences in which the logic of verb *tense, mood*, and *voice* is violated.

   a. After Mary went home, Janice told us the reason.

   b. I would have been glad to have come.

   c. He said that he will send the book.

   d. He struts as though he was the cock of the walk.

   e. I wish I was a rich man.

   f. The officer ordered that we are there at 10:00 A.M. tomorrow.

   g. We require that each applicant has two years experience.

   h. Rise and face the future like a man, and then you should act boldly and vigorously, and success will be yours.

   i. The dress was bought by a young woman, and she added to it a belt and four ornamental buttons.

   j. I was expecting you ever since I received your letter.

   k. The lecturer said that the world was round.

   l. Beginning two weeks ago, he finished building the wagon yesterday.

   m. If we are to work effectively, we would plan our time allocations.

   n. I wanted to have gone with you.

MANUSCRIPT
MECHANICS

38/ *Titles*

A good title attracts favorable attention to your essay without promising more than the essay delivers. Word your title economically but not so cryptically that it fails to state or at least suggest the contents.
    A good title may be:

1. A challenging question
>   Is Speed Reading Really Reading?
>   Can We Get Rid of Featherbedding?
>   Can Science Prolong Our Useful Years?
2. A polite imperative
>   Let's Give Santa Claus Back to the Children!
>   Don't Just Sit There—Reach for the Switch!
3. An arresting statement
>   You Can Have Your Cake and Diet Too
>   Good-by, Measles
>   Americans Talk Too Much

4. A label
> Birdman to the World
> The Indian Napoleon

5. A play on words
> Ghost Raider in the Sky
> Big Changes in the Big Woods
> Home, Home Off the Range
> Daring Dive for Derelict Gold

6. A plain assertion
> He Manufactures Useless Ideas
> We Should Scrap Civil Defense

39/ Manuscript Form

To invite reading, themes must be neat and legible. The following directions, based on well-established custom, should help you prepare satisfactory manuscripts.

□ PAPER AND INK. Type (double space) on unruled 8½ × 11 inch paper or write neatly in blue or black ink on ruled or unruled paper of the same size. Use only one side of the sheet. Be sure your typing ribbon (black only) is fresh and type is clean.

□ MARGINS. Leave about an inch and a quarter at the top and the left-hand side of the sheet and about three-fourths of an inch at the bottom and at the right-hand side of the page. Paragraphs should be indented about an inch.

□ PAGE NUMBERING. Number pages after page one (top center) and arrange pages in proper order.

□ FOLDING AND ENDORSING. Bring the left edge of your paper even with the right edge and fold. Write the following information on the outside sheet:

> Name of Student
> Course and Section Number

Title or Number of Theme
Date Due
Instructor's Name

40 / Capitals

40a / Capitalize the first word of every sentence.

The footmen were serving hot coffee.
We were the first to arrive.

40b / Capitalize the first word of a direct quotation.

"Sit down, sit down," said the Colonel.
"Don't wait for the others."

40c / Capitalize all proper nouns and proper adjectives.

Willard Anthony   The African jungle
The Netherlands   Chinese poetry
Bethlehem, Pennsylvania

40d / Capitalize the names of religious, educational, fraternal, political, and business organizations.

Delta Sigma Phi
Marine Truck and Equipment Service
Lancaster Shelter Home
The Boy Scouts
Democrats
Hamilton College

40e / Capitalize titles used with a name or in place of a name.

The Honorable Homer Wright
Ambassador Glick
Sir John Carruthers
The Senator

40f/   Capitalize an official title used in an address.

> Mr. Adolph Becker, Principal
> East Overshoot High School
> Kersey, Pennsylvania

40g/   Capitalize common nouns that are used in place of names.

> May I ask you a question, Mother?

Here the word *Mother* is used in direct address in place of name—
May I ask you a question, Bertha? In the sentence, "I asked my
mother for help," *mother* would not be capitalized since one would
not say "I asked my Bertha for help."

40h/   Capitalize the names of the days of the week,
the months of the year, and of holidays,
but not of seasons of the year.

> This spring Easter falls on the second Sunday in March.

40i/   Capitalize the first word and all important words
in titles of books, articles, etc.

> George Gamow wrote *The Birth and Death of the Sun.*
> *The Mystery of the Fiery Murders*

40j/   Capitalize the first word of every line of poetry.

> Such epithets, like pepper,
>   Give zest to what you write;
> And, if you stew them sparely,
>   They whet the appetite;
> But if you lay them on too thick,
>   You spoil the matter quite!
>   LEWIS CARROLL

40k / Capitalize the first word and each noun in the salutation of a letter and the first word of the complimentary close.

My dear Miss Carew: Yours truly,

40l / Capitalize the names of compass points when referring to sections of a country but not when indicating directions.

Bill was educated in the South.
Walk east on Beacon Street.

40m / Capitalize initials, abbreviations of titles, abbreviations of proper nouns, degrees, etc., and such words as "Street," "Avenue," "Road," "River," "Lake" when they are part of a name.

On his trip along the Missouri River, Professor E. D. Fisher, Ph.D., visited his old friend, Marvin Lowe, of Central Boulevard, Indian Lake.

40n / Capitalize the word "Bible" and the names of its books, reference to the Deity, and names of churches and religious denominations.

The Saviour reigns.
He read the Bible from Genesis to Revelation.
The Unitarians are building a chapel.
You can feel secure in the power of His love.

40o / Capitalize words like "Department," "Company," "University," when they refer to a specific proper noun.

He studied in England for nine months and visited the *Continent* during the summer.
The *University* reserves the right to change fees without giving notice.
The *Department* will not tolerate excessive tardiness.

40p / Capitalize movements, periods, events in history.

The Civil War   The Middle Ages   The Renaissance

41 /   Abbreviations

In general, avoid abbreviations in formal writing. A few, of course, are established conventions that must be used.

> Abbreviations for courtesy titles used with proper names—Mr., Mrs., Messrs., Hon.
> Abbreviations for academic degrees—Ph.D., A.B., LL.D., M.D.
> Abbreviations with time and dates—B.C., A.D., A.M., P.M.

Do not use the ampersand (&) for *and* in conventional writing.

42 /   Italics

Words to be set in italic type in printed matter are underscored in handwriting and in typewriting.

42a /   Underscore titles of books, magazines, newspapers, plays, motion pictures, long poems, and other long works.

> Carlyle's *The French Revolution* was published in 1837.

42b /   Underscore the names of ships and the titles of famous works of art.

> John will sail Monday on the *Queen Mary*.
> The subject of Manet's *Luncheon on the Grass* is a somewhat unconventional picnic.

42c /   Use (sparingly and with caution) the underscore to indicate emphasis.

> "Save *me*," he cried.

Avoid underscoring for emphasis in places where the context itself conveys the meaning.

"Save me first," he cried.

No underscore is needed.

42d/ Underscore a letter, word, or phrase used as such,
not as part of the context of the sentence.

The word *Susquehanna* ripples on the tongue, and *pillow* invites
sleep.
His habit of saying *you know* spoils his lectures.
Be sure to cross your *t's* and dot your *i's*.
Very is generally used as an adverb.

42e/ Underscore foreign words that have not become
a part of the English language.

In 1920 he published a kind of *cronique scandaleuse* of his
own family.
The West Germans do not want reunification because they
fear to jeopardize the *Wirtscheftswunder*.
The title was taken by the interpreter of modern *révoltées*,
Janet Achurch.

43/ *Syllabication*

43a/ Divide words according to pronunciation, not derivation.

pri ma-ry   prepar a-tory
prim i-tive   pro bate
prep-a-ra tion

43b/ Do not separate two consonants which
are pronounced together.

bank-ing (not ban-king)   find-ing (not fin-ding)

43c/ In general, separate double consonants when
they fall between two vowels.

syl-la-ble   pro-ces-sion   omit-ted   run-ning

Exceptions:

    suc-cess-ive   dwell-ing   tell-ing   bill-ing

43d /   **Do not divide words of one syllable.**

    through   passed   their   leaves   horse

43e /   **Divide according to pronunciation two vowels sounded separately even though they occur together.**

   cre-a tion   zo-ol o-gy

43f /   **Do not divide two syllable words of only three or four letters.**

   ever   any   also   into

43g /   **Do not leave one letter on a line or carry forward only two letters.**

   Wrong: e-   a-   want-
                    nough   gainst   ed

43h /   **Do not separate dollars from cents, whole numbers from related fractions (or decimals), or titles and initials from the names to which they belong.**

   Wrong: Major   Mr. H. Y.   Mr. Homer Martin,
                  Harry Bowman   Cox   III

                  33-   7,825.-
                  ⅓ per cent   25

43i /   **In certain troublesome words where a vowel stands as a separate syllable, keep the vowel with the preceding syllable.**

   singu-lar   para-mount

43j /   **Avoid dividing the endings "able" and "ible."**

   suit-able   cred-ible

43k / Divide a compound-word at the hyphen already part of the word; try to avoid adding additional hyphens.

mass-production   self-control

Note: Consult a dictionary whenever you are in doubt about dividing a word.

44/ *Hyphens*

44a / Use the hyphen to indicate compound words.

mass-production
letter-perfect

Note that as compound words become established the hyphen is dropped.

air-lines   airlines

44b / Use the hyphen for syllabic breaking of a word at the end of a line.

44c / Use the hyphen in writing out compound numbers: twenty-one, forty-two, eighty-eight.

38–44x / Exercises: Manuscript mechanics

1. Supply capital letters where needed in the following passage.

the cape cod art association has now spent eight years in the captain's house, on main street, where it has been the guest of the town of barnstable. the fine old house, with the blue and pink slate roof and the gingerbread trimmings, was built by captain owen bearse about 1840, after he had retired from the sea and become a dealer in rare woods, some of which are found in the interior of the house.

later when the maritime academy was located in hyannis, the building was promoted; it became the admiral's house. it is not slated for demolition; the land belongs to the federal government, and is required for an extension to the post office.

the close neighborhood of the new cape cod community college makes this a particularly suitable location. fortunately, the president and board of directors were able to buy the hyannis woman's club building nearby. it is located on ocean street, a few doors from main street, and is directly across from the town parking lot. the building lends itself to development as a gallery and stands on a valuable site.

the association, in acquiring property of its own, has taken a step forward and passed into a very different period, one in which it can use the support and creative ideas of all members. everybody will be able to co-operate in the interesting time ahead.

money is being raised to finance the purchase of the new gallery and for the remodeling, which will make it functional.

2. Show the correct syllabication of the following words and terms. If the word should not be divided, place a check mark after it.

seance	carriage	fitted
graduate	repetition	spilling
biological	triumphant	gunning
weakling	referring	chiming
mediation	couldn't	losses
separate	business	structure
woebegone	knowledge	responsible
ogre	learned	regular
balminess	control	fixes
conspicuous	62⅝ per cent	partial
strapping	$165.21	treated
submitting	extension	controlling
occasioned	depth	expressed
edible	suitable	seized
self-use	around	upon
departure	calamity	cheaply
	sensible	cross-eyed

SPELLING

45 / Spelling

If you are not a perfect speller, there is at least one good reason: English spelling is a mess. A foreigner learning English can be driven crazy by combinations like *cough, bough, through; smile, aisle; rude, move, true, new; sugar, nation, fuchsia, shoe*. Part of the trouble comes from the fact that we have five vowel symbols (*a, e, i, o, u*) that we must use in various combinations to represent possibly thirty-six vowel contrasts. We could make use of a few extra consonant symbols, too—something to take care of the *sh* sound in words like *shall*; the *z* sound in words like *rouge, treasure*; the *ng* sound in *sing*, and the difference between the *th* sound of *this* and *thin*. Although it is fun to speculate on the chances for some kind of spelling reform in the future, it is foolish to go on misspelling while you wait. It's better to make use of the few rules and hints available:

1. Correct pronunciation is often a help in correct spelling. Note the difference in pronunciation of the following words:

    advice, advise   immigrant, emigrant
    lose, loose   persecute, prosecute
    accept, except   precede, proceed
    quiet, quite

2. For homonyms—and all troublesome words—the best re-
   course is memorization:

dual, duel	wave, waive	principle, principal
coarse, course	root, route	aught, ought

3. Don't confuse words that have similar sounds but different
   meanings. Here is a partial list of such words:

accede, exceed	formally, formerly
accept, except	loose, lose
access, excess	miner, minor
addition, edition	its, it's
affect, effect	ordinance, ordnance
allusion, illusion	passed, past
already, all ready	personal, personnel
bare, bear	principle, principal
brake, break	respectively, respectfully
coarse, course	stationary, stationery
compliment, complement	their, there, they're
decent, descent, dissent	whose, who's
eligible, illegible	your, you're

   Sometimes memory tricks help.
   Example:

   The princi*pal* is my *pal*.
   There is *a rat* in sep*arate*.
   You don't "wanta" *tary* in a ceme*tery*.
   Think of pap*er* in station*ery*.

   It doesn't matter how ridiculous the association is, so long
   as it works for you.

4. The little jingle

   i before *e* except after *c*
   or when sounded as *a*
   as in *neighbor* or *weigh*

   is helpful if you can remember the exceptions: *seize, counter-
   feit, foreign, forfeit, weird, leisure, either, neither, sheik,
   height, sleight, seismograph, kaleidoscope, financier.*

5. When to double the final consonant
   If the suffix begins with a consonant (*fy, hood, less, ly, ness,
   ward*), do not double the final consonant of the root word:

quick, quickly	man, manhood

If the suffix begins with a vowel (*able, ed, en, ant, ent, ing, ish, ist, ous*) —

Double—	Do not double—
If the final consonant of the root word is preceded by a single vowel:	If the final consonant of the root word is preceded by two vowels:
plan, planned sit, sitting	retail, retailing claim, claimant
If a word of more than one syllable accents the final syllable:	If the word ends with two consonants:
admit, admitting defer, deferring	rest, resting
	If a word of more than one syllable does not accent the last syllable (after addition of suffix):
	prefer, preference

Note: There are exceptions; *traveled, travelled* are both correct.

6. Change of *y* to *i*
Change *y* to *i* when the *y* is preceded by a consonant:

cry, cried   modify, modifier

Do not change *y* to *i* when *y* is preceded by a vowel:

attorney, attorneys

7. Visualize the words you have trouble spelling. Good spellers have good visual memory. When they need to write a word, they merely copy the word off the screen of their minds. Poor spellers tend to have aural memories. When they need to write a word, they can hear it but they can't see it. Such people can improve visual memory by writing words in big purple letters or imagining them on billboards—perhaps with the troublesome letters underscored or printed larger than the others.

8. Don't trust your spelling ability. If you have the slightest hesitation about a word, look it up.

45x/ Exercises

Check your spelling ability on this list of words frequently misspelled:

accept	apparatus	brief	compel
accommodate	appearance	broadcase	compensation
accountant	applicant	brokerage	competent
accumulate	appraisal	budget	complaint
acknowledg-	appropriation	bulletin	complimentary
ment	approval	bureau	concession
acquainted	argument	business	condemn
acquire	arrears		conference
acquisition	arrival	calculator	confirmation
acquitted	articles	calendar	congestion
actually	assessable	campaign	conscientious
additionally	assignment	canceled	consequence
address	assistance	candidate	considerable
adjustable	associate	capacity	consignee
administration	assured	capitalization	consolidated
advances	attached	carbon	construction
advertisement	attorney	carrier	consumer
advisability	attempt	cartage	container
advise	attendance	carton	contemplating
affects	attractive	certificate	contemporary
affidavit	auditor	chattel	contingent
affirmative	available	circular	convenience
agency	aviation	clearance	conveyance
aggravate		coincidence	cooperate
allotment	baggage	collapsible	corporation
allowance	balance	collateral	corroborate
all right	bankruptcy	collision	corrugated
alphabetic	banquet	column	counterfeit
aluminum	barrel	combination	coupon
analysis	barter	combustible	courteous
analyze	becoming	commerce	credentials
anniversary	beneficiary	commission	creditor
announcement	benefited	committee	cylinder
anthracite	biased	commodity	curiosity
anticipating	bituminous	community	currency
anxiety	bookkeeping	companies	customer
apology	borrower	comparative	

decision
defendant
deferred
deficit
definite
defray
demonstration
depreciation
description
desperate
destination
deteriorate
determination
develop
dictionary
director
disappear
disappoint
disastrous
disbursements
discernible
discontinued
discrepancy
discuss
dispatch
dissatisfaction
dissolution
distinction
distinguish
distributor
dividend
document
doubt
duplicate
durable

earliest
earnest
easier
economic
eighth

elevator
eligible
embarrass
emergency
enormous
enterprise
envelope
equally
equipped
especially
estimate
essentially
eventually
evidence
exaggerate
examination
exasperate
excellent
except
exchange
executive
exhibition
existence
expedite
explanation
extension

facilitate
February
financier
foreclosure
forehead
forfeit
formally
formerly
forty
franchise
fundamental
furniture
futile

generally
genuine
government
grammar

handkerchief
hastily
hazard
height
hoping
hosiery
humorous

illegible
immediately
impracticable
inasmuch
inconsistent
inconvenience
incorporated
incredible
increment
indelible
indemnity
indispensable
inducement
industrial
inevitable
inferred
inflation
infringement
initiate
inquiry
insolvency
inspection
instance
institution
instructor
insurance
integrity
intelligence

interpretation
inventory
investigate
invoice
involved
itemized
itinerary
its

jobber
journal

keenness
knowledge

laboratory
ladies
latter
leased
ledger
legitimate
leisure
liabilities
library
license
likable
liquidation
literature
lucrative
luscious
luxury

machinery
maintenance
management
manila
manufacturer
margin
material
maturity
mechanical

medicine	overhead	principal	ridiculous
memorandum	oxygen	principle	rural
merchandise		privilege	
mercantile	pamphlet	procedure	sacrifice
merge	parallel	process	salutation
middleman	parenthesis	professional	sanitary
mimeograph	parliament	prominence	satisfactory
miniature	particularly	promissory	schedule
miscellaneous	pavilion	pronunciation	scissors
misrepresent	peaceable	prospectus	secretarial
misspelled	peculiarities	psychology ·	security
moistener	pecuniary		seize
monopoly	per cent	qualification	separate
mortgage	perforation	quantity	several
movie	performance	questionnaire	significance
mucilage	permanent	quotation	similar
municipal	permissible		simultaneous
	perpendicular	readjustment	sincerely
necessary	perseverance	really	sociable
ninth	personal	reasonable	society
notary	personnel	rebate	solemn
noticeable	persuade	receipt	solvent
notwithstand-	perusal	recognize	sometimes
ing	petition	recommend	source
nowadays	petroleum	reconstruction	southern
	photostat	reference	souvenir
obliging	physical	regardless	specialize
observation	physician	register	specify
obsolete	plaintiff	reimburse	spectacular
obstacle	plausible	reinforcement	speculate
occasionally	policy	relations	statement
occurred	practically	relevant	stationary
omission	precedence	remedied	stationery
oneself	precise	remittance	statistics
opportunity	preface	representative	straightened
optimism	preference	requisition	strenuous
option	prescription	resign	strictly
ordinance	presence	respectfully	sublet
organization	presidency	respectively	subsidize
outrageous	prestige	responsible	substantial
overdraw	primitive	restaurant	substitute

subtle	tangible	typewriter	vicinity
successful	tariff	typographical	volume
suggestion	tendency	typical	voucher
summary	testimonials		
superfluous	tickler	unanimous	waive
superintendent	together	university	warrant
surplus	transferred	unmistakable	Wednesday
surprise	transparent	utilities	whatever
susceptible	treasurer	utilize	wholesale
syllable	triplicate		wholly
syndicate	Tuesday	verification	women
systematize	turnover	visible	

GLOSSARY OF ERRORS

46/   Glossary of Errors in Thinking

You may carefully organize your writing plans, execute them with precision and economy and still fail, if your facts are wrong or if your thinking is illogical. *Responsibility* is the key word. People tend to believe what they read. It's your responsibility to be valid. It is not enough to be believable. The purpose of your writing is to uncover the truth. The language mechanism in human beings—whatever it is that turns wants into words—is a very skillful deceiver. It has learned many tricks to "make the worse appear the better cause." The best defense is reason.

46a/   Fact and opinion

In writing, you must (1) make judgments. And you must (2) enable your reader to judge your judgments. In the first, you provide opinions. In the second, you provide facts.

Before you can provide either, you must be able to distinguish between *opinion* and *fact*.

Q. What is the distinction between *fact* and *opinion?*
A. A fact can be verified; it is objective. An opinion is an attitude toward fact; it is subjective.
Q. What is the relationship between fact and opinion?
A. Opinions are drawn from facts. The more facts that support a judgment, the more valid the judgment tends to be.
Q. We are concerned with the *truth* of facts and the *validity* of opinions. What is the difference?
A. *Truth* means "in accordance with reality," *validity* means "well grounded on evidence." Evidence, or facts, consists of testimony of the senses, testimony of witnesses, testimony of authorities.
Q. The validity, then, of a judgment depends on the facts that support it. What should the ratio be, roughly, between facts and judgment?
A. The fewer the judgments, the more the facts, the greater validity the judgments have.

The facts justify the opinion, then, as the particulars justify the general, and the concretes justify the abstract.

Again we examine a previous passage: What here is fact—matter which can be verified? What here is opinion—a judgment based on the verifiable matter?

Scum floated on the water. The glass sat on a sodden paper napkin. Heavy and sweet in the air was the smell of hot, stale fat. Flies pulled wildly at a brown strip spiralling from the overhead light. The waitress threw silverware on the table, pushing aside the crusted bottle of catsup. A tine on the fork was scabbed with yellow. Changing brilliant lights squirmed in the plastic casing of the juke box. Music blared and rebounded. The waitress pulled a pencil from her hair and stood, waiting. The restaurant was unpleasant.

Which convinces *you* more: someone's opinion—or facts that enable you to form an opinion? Which would convince your reader more?

Terms multiply for this fact-opinion principle. Recognizing the principle whatever its disguise; realize that you are not learning many different things, but simply reinforcing one essential understanding.

Here are some opposed terms which involve fact and opinion:

Fact	*Opinion (Attitude toward Facts)*
1. Denotation	1. Connotation
2. Objective	2. Subjective
3. Exposition	3. Persuasion
4. Summary	4. Criticism
5. Evidence	5. Verdict
6. Paraphrase	6. Interpretation
7. Particular	7. General
8. Concrete	8. Abstract

46b / Hasty generalization

Things and events come to us as particulars. But the mind likes to assume that there are universal connections or relations in nature. It is easy, therefore, to generalize. Don't jump to conclusions. One hundred Republican enthusiasts in Centreville do not necessarily mean a Republican landslide in the November national election.

If you have had low grades in three courses taught by blue-eyed instructors, don't make the hasty generalization that blue-eyed teachers mark harder than brown-eyed ones. (See 7f, p. 55.)

46c / Post hoc reasoning

You know that events have causes. You know that causes precede effects. When an event occurs—an accident, an illness—you look among preceding events for the cause. This is proper reasoning. The danger comes from assuming that just because a certain event preceded another it must necessarily have caused the other. A black cat crosses a hunter's path. He gets no game that day. His bad luck is caused by the cat's crossing his path. A baseball player has an unusually good day at the plate. He wonders about the cause of his new success. In the locker room after the game, he discovers that he had put his undershirt on backwards before the game. Obviously this simple move has placated the baseball gremlins and caused his good luck. From now on he will wear his undershirt backwards. Political debate, superstitions, home remedies, magic, old wives' tales are full of this kind of error.

Ask this question before assuming the cause of anything. Do I have lots of representative cases and no instances of counter results?

46d / False analogy

Analogies, although helpful in revealing relationships between things or events, are misleading if carried too far. A whale lives in the water and is shaped like a fish. Yet he has more in common with a cow. A university administration is a governing body. A federal government is a governing body, too. Must they, therefore, have the same type of organization? James I of England held that Republicanism was a false philosophy of government. The monarch is the head of the state, he said. When the head of a body is cut off, the other parts cannot live. The analogy is false. A government and a human body are not comparable in any literal sense. "Life is like a mountain railroad," the old song says. "Keep your hand upon the throttle and you eye upon the rail." Anyone who tries to push that analogy much further will certainly be derailed. Analogies are safest when used to clarify a point already proved by some other means. (See 7i, p. 58.)

46e / Equivocation

A word sometimes changes from one meaning to another during a discussion. The shift is equivocation. The shift converts a genuine discussion into a sham discussion. The result is deception and confusion. If a writer equivocates intentionally, he is dishonest; if unintentionally, he is incompetent.

If you accept, because you do not recognize equivocation, a shift in meaning, it is futile and frustrating, however much you sense a wrongness, to attack a subsequent argument: the argument can be perfectly valid, once the premise upon which it is based is accepted. Much poor writing results from a writer attempting to compensate for his own unrecognized equivocation.

A word like *right* is most seductive. "Capital punishment is right because it deters crime." So far, what do you think *right* means? If you disagree with the statement, are you going to argue that capital punishment does *not* deter crime? If you do, then you think *right* means *necessary*. Another person might argue that capital punishment is not right even if it does deter crime. He thinks *right* means *moral*. He may agree that it is necessary, but not that it is right. Yet another person might think that *right* is *good*, and refuse to agree that capital punishment is good, although he might agree that capital punishment is an evil less evil than some other evils. If all these persons were in the same discussion, they would end up in a fury. They thought they were all discussing the same question. They were not. They were discussing three questions:

Is capital punishment *necessary?*

Is capital punishment *moral?*

Is capital punishment *good?*

Without immediate, common definition, a word like *right* splits into many identities, each considering itself the true *right* and furious at the imposters.

46f / Fallacies of composition and division

If you argue that the boys in your college are wealthy, and use as evidence the fact that your fraternity brothers drive sports cars and wear expensive clothes, you are committing—among other things—the fallacy of composition; that is, you are attributing to the whole something that is true only of a part.

The fallacy of division is the converse: What holds true for all members of a class taken together is necessarily true for each alone. "Since I am not obligated to help all the poor people in the world there is no reason why I should help this one poor man." If you say, "Mr. Katz must be an irresponsible drunk. He is a member of the American Veterans' Society and every time they have a convention the newspapers are full of stories about their carousing," you are assuming that a reputation earned by the group as a whole must be attached also to each individual of that group (see 7f, p. 55).

46g / The fallacy of simple extremes (false dilemma)

This is the "either—or—" mistake. If you're not for me you must be against me. It is the assumption that there is no middle ground, no shades between black and white.

Bill: "I think there's a great deal more to get out of college than a Phi Beta Kappa key."
Harry: "You mean grades don't count?"

A parent says to his teen-age son, "Don't you think you've been to too many parties this week? Why don't you stay home and study for a change?"

Son: "Oh, you want me to be a bookworm and wear thick glasses like Hogarth McGillicuddey."

The son has presented the parent with a false dilemma. He is saying, "I'm either going to be a party boy or a bookworm. Take your pick." The desirable middle-ground of "work-a-little, play-a-little" is ruled out as a possibility.

Worrier: If I devote myself to my worldly interests, I shall lose my soul, and if I devote myself to religious duties, my business will fail and my family be ruined. Since I must devote myself either to religion or to worldly interests, it is obvious that I must either lose my soul or ruin my family.

This is a false dilemma. It avoids a third possibility—attending to the interests of both.

46h / Faulty classification

The world is filled with things, and time crammed with events. If we had to deal with each item or event on an individual basis, we would be immobilized within hours; so we group things according to certain common attributes. The creatures that fly may form one group; those that slither on their bellies, another, and so on. We put items in a *class* and give it a name. This is classification. It helps us reduce the multitudinous world to manageable proportions. Sloppy classification can lead to irresponsible writing. Therefore, a few rules:

1. The classification must be exhaustive. An automobile manufacturer has classified auto noises into seven categories: *squeak, scrape, grind, rattle, thump, knock,* and *hiss*. If no one turns up a *crunch* or a *blip*, this classification may serve. Whenever one item cannot find a home in the existing cate-

gories, you can be sure that the classification is not exhaustive.

2. The categories must be mutually exclusive. A classification of baseball players into infielder, outfielder, and left-handers is faulty since both infielders and outfielders may be left-handed.

3. A definite single basis of classification will insure mutually exclusive categories. Baseball players classified according to defensive positions: Infielders, Outfielders. Baseball players classified according to handedness: left-handed, right-handed, ambidextrous. Baseball players classified according to state or country of birth: Pennsylvania, Nevada, Puerto Rico, etc.

46i / Vagueness

Responsible thinking should lead to clear writing. Vagueness is the result of muddled thinking.

The strength of middle-class society today comes from its incorporation of the objectist tradition; its weakness arises from its subjection of that tradition to the non-ironic Enlightenment Orientation which drains two opposites of their opposition and reconciles the irreconcilable.

The writer means *something*. The reader will have to guess. The old warning still applies: If it *can* be misunderstood, it *will* be.

46j / Over-precision

In a struggle to make ordinary vocabulary as precise as scientific vocabulary, some people reject whole areas of useful human inquiry and discovery. This pedantic rejection is called logic-chopping, hair-splitting, over-precision. It rejects thought constructions that are sometimes the best available and quite adequate for the matter under discussion. In many cases it is all right to say that a man is tall or fat without giving dimensions for tallness and fatness.

46k / Misusing authority

Your reader will believe you if your assertion is supported by evidence. The testimony of a qualified expert is useful evidence. The expert's authority must be recognized by his peers. His identity must be clearly established. You can't just say, "impartial experts agree . . ." The testimony he gives on your subject must be in the field of his special knowledge. A famous military general's opinion on a certain battle is valuable; but his opinion on medicine should not be enhanced by his special knowledge of military science.

46l/ The "bandwagon" fallacy

This is the argument that seeks to convince because "everybody's doing it." This argument is most successfully used in advertising. "In Philadelphia, nearly everybody reads *The Bulletin*"; "The nicest people vacation at San Marcos." Try to find better evidence than mere *numbers*. Perhaps the idea you promote is healthful, fun, educational, or beneficial in some other way. Numbers can be a valid *additional* support if basic proof has been established by other means.

46m/ Ad populum appeals

This fallacy is popular with demagogues and political campaigners. It is any appeal to popular prejudices and passions on a matter that should be argued on its own merits.

> If this bill becomes law, radicals and long-haired professors will be telling us how to run our business.

46n/ Ad hominem attacks

If you are more interested in crushing an opponent as a person than in uncovering the truth, then the *ad hominem* attack is your weapon. It consists of abuse, sarcasm, recriminations. There is a legitimate use of argument against the person in discrediting the testimony of a proved liar, but otherwise there is little likelihood that you can make legitimate use of this device.

> *Ad hominem:* Only a subversive would ask such a question.

46o/ Non sequitur

Drawing a conclusion from premises with which it has no logical connections is to commit a *non sequitur*.

> No cat has eight lives.
> One cat has one life more than no cat.
> Therefore, one cat has nine lives.

46p/ Begging the question

An argument which gives the conclusion as a reason for the conclusion commits the fallacy of begging the question.

Three boys are walking along a creek. They find five arrow-heads. "Good," one of the boys says. "Now we can start an Indian tribe." He gives one arrowhead to each of his friends and keeps the other three. "You two will be the braves," he says, "and I will be the chief." "But why should you be chief?" a boy asks. "Because I have the most arrowheads," the question beggar replies.

46x/ Exercises

Comment on the responsibility, devices, appeals, logical constructions of the following items:

1. A reader reports that a recent poll of women drivers reveals that 89 per cent believed radiator hose had to be a brand of nylons, 72 per cent were positive a brake drum was a percussion instrument, 61 per cent advocated a change in the ignition system, 48 per cent thought fan belts could be used to hold up fender skirts, and 65 per cent were of the opinion that universal joints are an international disgrace.

2. Forever, End/Run, Sheerloc and Ultra No. IV are names of new ladies' nylons that are being touted by some manufacturers as "indestructible" due to their weaving technique. Other makers claim just as loudly that this is false.

We have no fear that the American woman will be fooled by claims of indestructibility. The women we know have been complaining about run-resistant stockings that weren't for so long that if some came along that were runless they might buy only one pair—just to make up for all the money lost on runners. At least one producer has admitted what women have long known: hose-makers are not planning to put themselves out of business.

From the *Pittsburgh Post Gazette*

3. U.S. agricultural department has come up with an astounding discovery: If a tomato is dropped on a hard surface it will be damaged more than if it is dropped on foam rubber.

Furthermore, says a press release announcing the results of a study on bruising injuries to tomatoes, "injury was found to be cumulative . . . that is, when tomatoes were dropped two or more times, the damage was found to extend to more and more internal parts." A tomato dropped often enough becomes inedible.

This all sounds reasonable. And the claim is that the information is of scientific value. The experiment was conducted to find out how tomatoes can best be packed to arrive on the consumer's table in the best possible shape.

The press release didn't provide one piece of information that taxpayers might be interested in: What grade does a scientist have to reach in civil service before he's qualified to bounce tomatoes?

From *Milwaukee Journal*

4. Perhaps the United States had better forget any future space projects which raise the ire of world scientists.

There have been two recently, and both have fared rather poorly.

The first was the plan to circle the earth with a belt of tiny copper needles, released by a satellite. Some scientific voices were raised against this experiment on the grounds that it would needlessly interfere with astronomic observations and, possibly, with communications for an indefinite period of time.

We went ahead anyway and shot the satellite into a perfect orbit— but the needles never made it, presumably because of a malfunctioning in the system designed to release them.

Now it's the high-level "rainbow" nuclear explosion, with a device to be carried to the edge of the atmosphere in the nose of a missile. This experiment is designed to show us what effect this sort of explosion might have in knocking out detection devices prior to a nuclear attack.

The scientific complaints have centered on the unknown effects such a blast may have on the Van Allen radiation belts. Again we have proceeded, but twice now the missiles have had to be destroyed in mid-flight.

These failures have had one good feature. They have proved that a nuclear warhead won't go off accidentally if something goes wrong and the missiles have to be destroyed. Our safeguards against such an accident apparently work quite well.

U.S. scientists say they want to check the entire system before trying again, which sounds like a wise thing to do. Or should they give up
on these controversial experiments? It looks as if international scientists
have an unscientific "whammy" on us.

From the *Harrisburg Evening News*

5. A monopoly of the sugar-refining business is beneficial to the
sugar-refiners; and of the lumber business to the lumber dealers; of tex-
tiles to the clothing industry; and of labor to the laborers. All these
classes of men make up the whole community. Therefore, a system that
eliminates competition is beneficial to the community.

6. The recent growth of Los Angeles is a very ominous sign because
Los Angeles is the heart of California and an enlarged heart is a sign
of disease.

7. The president should eliminate all executive bureaus that came
about since the war. We got along without them before the war. We
can get along without them now.

8. I can't see why some claim that hunting is a cruel sport. The
firearms industry employs a lot of people and hunting is a lot of fun.

9. No body can be healthful without exercise, neither natural body
nor politic, and certainly to a kingdom or estate, a just and honorable
war is the true exercise. A civil war indeed is like the heat of a fever;
but a foreign war is like the heat of exercise, and serveth to keep the
body in health; for in a slothful peace, both courages will effeminate
and manners corrupt. But howsoever it be for happiness, without all
question, for greatness it maketh, to be still for the most part in arms;
and the strength of a veteran army (though it be a chargeable business)
always on foot, is that which commonly giveth the law, or at least the
reputation, amongst all neighbour states; as may well be seen in Spain,
which hath had, in one part or other, a veteran army almost continually,
now by the space of six score years.

BACON, of *The True Greatness of Kingdom and Estates*

10. In the following account, what is fact, and what is opinion?

The mother of the fighter sat silently with her head bowed, her
eyes half-closed, her fingers ripping at the rolled-up piece of Kleenex
in her lap.

When her son, George Chuvalo, climbed into the Madison Square
Garden ring to meet Pat McMurtry on Friday night, she made the sign
of the cross, but did not watch the fighters. She wore black.

She had never been to the Garden before, and did not like prize
fighting, but she came down from Toronto at the insistence of her husband and daughter, who sat next to her.

Zora, the daughter, in a fur-trimmed suit, smoked a cigarette, and
called, as the bell rang, "Okay, George; come on, George!" The father,

a floridly robust little man with his arms crossed, his eyes large and deep-set, said nothing.

George Chuvalo, the Canadian heavyweight champion was an awkward, inept figure and, after the second round, blood from his nose showed on his white trunks. McMurtry chopped at the nose repeatedly. George looked pathetic. Zora seemed angry and she jumped up and yelled:

"George, George, what's the matter with you?"

The father said nothing. Some of the 2,500 customers began to boo. The mother, her head still down, pressed her thin lips, seemed to be praying.

Zora lit cigarettes, but the parents did not smoke.

"Stop the fight!" someone yelled from the rear.

"Hit the bum again!" yelled another.

Soon it was over. George was soundly beaten, and misshapen about the nose and eyes. Nobody booed the unanimous decision for McMurtry.

The father put on his jacket, which had been in his lap, and he moved with the mother and daughter into the crowded aisle. They would wait outside for George. The three of them did not talk. Under the mother's chair were twisted shreds of Kleenex.

By GAY TALESE

47 /   Glossary of Errors in Diction

The following glossary lists many of the common problems of usage. Some of the expressions are definite violations of good usage and should never be used. About others, there is some disagreement. The comments on each item are intended to guide you to sound choices for formal writing, not to set arbitrary standards of right and wrong. For more information consult an unabridged dictionary.

ACCEPT, EXCEPT.   As a verb, *accept* means to receive; *except* means to exclude. *Except* in the sense of *but* is a preposition.

> All the winners accepted the money *except* [but] Bill. He decided that his essay should be excepted [excluded] from the list.

AD.   Clipped form for *advertisement*.

A.D.   *Anno Domini,* "In the year of our Lord." Place it before the date: A.D. 1954. Do not say 18th century A.D. B.C., "Before Christ," follows year or century.

AFFECT, EFFECT.   *Effect* as a noun means *result. Affect* has no common noun use. As verbs, *affect* means to influence or change; *effect* means *to accomplish.*

"I was not affected [influenced] by the new law."

"The airplane effected [accomplished] a landing in the narrow pasture."

AGGRAVATE.   Means *to increase* or *intensify.*

> Sub-zero weather aggravated supply problems.

Don't use *aggravate* in formal writing for *annoy, exasperate, irritate,* or *provoke.*

ALIBI.   Colloquial for *excuse.* Acceptable in Standard English when used in its legal sense.

ALLOW.   Means to *permit.* Don't use for *think* or *admit.*

ALL THE FARTHER, ALL THE FASTER.   Use *as far as, as fast as.*

ALLUDE, REFER.   To allude is to make an indirect reference.

> "When he mentioned 'Hangman's Hands,' we all knew he alluded to *Macbeth.*"

To refer to is to mention the specific name: "For further details, I refer you to the Census Bureau."

ALLUSION, ILLUSION, DELUSION.   Allusion means "an indirect reference." Illusion means "a false impression," or "deceptive appearance." Delusion means "false belief."

> He made an *allusion* to *Hamlet.*
> He gives the *illusion* of being clear.
> He has the *delusion* that he is indispensable.

ALOT.   Two words: a lot. Colloquial for *many* or *much.*

ALREADY, ALL READY.   Already is an adverb meaning *before* or "by this time." *All ready*—two separate words—means "everything is ready" or "everyone is ready."

ALRIGHT.   Use *all right.*

ALTOGETHER, ALL TOGETHER.   *Altogether* means *entirely.*

> "You have been altogether too friendly with that man."

All together means individual people joined in some group.

> "The Smiths were all together at the picnic."

A.M., P.M., a.m., p.m.   Either upper or lower case is acceptable. Do not add "in the morning," "in the afternoon" or "o'clock." "Classes begin at 8:00 A.M. [not 8:00 A.M. in the morning]." For 12 o'clock say *noon* or *midnight.*

AND ETC.   Redundant. Use *etc.* alone, *et* [and] *cetera* [so forth].

ANYWAY, ANY WAY.   *Anyway* is an adverb meaning *in any case.*

"Anyway, he's not available for conversation."

Any way is a noun phrase.

"I don't think there is any way you can find the answer."

ANYWHERE NEAR.   Colloquial for nearby, close.

"He doesn't live close [not *anywhere near*] to Bowmansville."

ANYWHERES, NOWHERES, SOMEWHERES.   Substandard for *anywhere, nowhere, somewhere.*

APT.   See *liable.*

AS.   Avoid using *as* in place of *that, whether,* or *like.*

Wrong: "I don't know as I like your remark."

Don't use *as* in the sense of *because.*

Wrong: "I can't come to the party as I'll be out of town."

AT ABOUT.   The *at* is unnecessary.

AWFUL, AWFULLY.   Avoid *awful* and *awfully* as intensives.

Bad: "We had an awful good time."
Better: "We had a very good time."

BADLY.   Don't use *badly* with verbs like *feel, look, taste.*

Correct: "I feel bad." "It looks bad." "It tastes bad."

BALANCE.   There is still objection to the use of *balance* for *remainder* or *rest.*

BANK ON.   Colloquial for *rely on.*

B.C.   See A.D.

BECAUSE.   Avoid using *because* to introduce a noun clause.

Wrong: "Because you have money is no excuse for feeling superior."

Acceptable as predicate nominative: It's because you mistake money for worth.

BEING AS, BEING THAT.   Do not use *being as* or *being that* for *since* or *because.*

BESIDE, BESIDES.   *Beside* means *at the side of:* "I stood beside him." *Besides* means *in addition, moreover.*

"I don't like movies; besides I haven't the money to go."
"Does the detective know anything besides what was in the papers?"

BETWEEN, AMONG. Avoid the common error, *"between you and I."* *Between* is a preposition. Both pronouns must be in the objective case. A few authorities may insist that *between* should apply to only two items and *among* to more than two, but careful writers know that *between* is sometimes the only reasonable choice when more than two items are involved: "There was a lot of space between the infielders on that play."

BLAME ON, BLAME IT ON. *Blame it on* is a colloquialism. Say, "They blamed Bill for it," rather than, "They blamed it on Bill."

BOY FRIEND. Although *boy friend* and *girl friend* are widely used on the colloquial level and although there are no satisfactory substitutes (suitor, fiancé, escort, lover), they are still unacceptable in formal writing. Find another way to express the idea.

BRAINY. Colloquial for *intelligent.*

BROKE. Slang for *out of money.*

BUST, BUSTED, BURSTED. Colloquial for *break, broke, burst.* Do not use these to suggest financial ruin. Burst is a good word, meaning *to break* in the sense of *explode.* Its past participle is *burst,* not *bursted.*

BUT THAT, BUT WHAT. Colloquial. Say, "I have no doubt *that* he will pay the bill" not *"but that* or *but what* he will pay the bill."

CALCULATE, RECKON. Provincialisms for *intend, plan, expect.*

CAN, MAY. In American usage there is still objection to using *can* in the sense of *to have permission. Can* means *to be able. May* means *to have permission.*

CANNOT HELP BUT. A hybrid (considered by many an impropriety) fusing two idioms (1) *cannot help* and (2) *cannot but.*

> *Standard:* "One cannot help being sad."
> *Standard:* "One cannot but be sad."
> *Questionable:* "One cannot help but be sad."

CAN'T HARDLY. A double negative. Use *can hardly.*

CAN'T SEEM. There is some objection to using *can't seem* in sentences like "I can't seem to get to sleep." (Purists would substitute "I can't sleep.") The construction is regarded as acceptable by some dictionaries.

CLAIM. Acceptable in the sense of *demand.* "The janitor claimed the reward." Do not use for *assert* or *state* unless there is doubt about the truth of the assertion.

> "The man claimed that he had been an army general." [doubt]
> "Omar Bradley stated that he had been an army general." [no doubt]

COMPLECTED.   Dialectal or colloquial. Use *complexioned* instead.

CONSIDERABLE.   Colloquial for *a large quantity of*: "They say he has a great deal of [*not considerable*] money."

CONTACT.   Overused for *get in touch with*, etc.

CONTEMPLATE.   Should not be followed by *on*: "We contemplate going to Europe."

CONTEMPTIBLE, CONTEMPTUOUS.   *Contemptible* means deserving contempt: "That's the most contemptible act I've ever witnessed." *Contemptuous* means *showing* or *expressing* contempt. "Why should you be contemptuous of Harry?"

CONTINUAL, CONTINUOUS.   Continual means *frequently recurring*: "He is continually asking me for money." *Continuous* means *without interruption*: "His nose bled continuously."

COULDN'T HARDLY.   See *can't hardly*.

COUNCIL, COUNSEL.   *Council* is an advisory body. *Counsel* means advice.

"At a special meeting of the council, counsel was given to two delinquent boys."

CREDIBLE, CREDITABLE, CREDULOUS.   *Credible* means *believable*: "It was a credible account of the trip." *Creditable* means *worthy of praise*: Although his hand was injured, he played a creditable game." *Credulous* means *very ready to believe*: "A man as credulous as he is will believe anything."

CUTE.   Overworked colloquialism for *pretty, clever, attractive*, etc.

DATA.   Technically plural of *datum* but used widely as singular: "*This data is more accurate than that*" is acceptable since one may regard data as a unified mass of information. Of course, "*these data* are more accurate than those" is also correct.

DISINTERESTED, UNINTERESTED.   *Disinterested* means impartial.

"An umpire must be disinterested in the outcome of the game."

Uninterested means *not interested*.

"I am uninterested in baseball."

DUE TO, CAUSED BY.   There has been objection to use of these constructions as prepositions to introduce an adverbial phrase. Although the objection is weakening, you may want to substitute *because of, owing to*, or *on account of*.

EACH AND EVERY.   Redundant. Use *each* or *every* but not both together.

EFFECT. See *affect*.

ELSE BUT. Do not fuse the similar terms *else than* and *but* into the meaningless term *else but*.

> *Right:* "That remark is nothing but blackmail."
> *Right:* "That remark is nothing else than blackmail."
> *Wrong:* "That remark is nothing else but blackmail."

ELUDE, ALLUDE. *Elude* means *to evade*. *Allude, to refer to indirectly*.

> *Right:* "The deer eluded the dogs."
> *Right:* "He alluded to *Macbeth* in his sermon."

EMIGRATE, IMMIGRATE. *Emigrate* means to leave one's country for permanent residence in another country. *Immigrate* means to come into a country.

ENTHUSE. Colloquial for *to be enthusiastic* or *to make enthusiastic*.

EQUALLY AS GOOD. Wrong for *just as good* or *equally good*.

ETC. Avoid in formal writing. It should never be preceded by *and*. Don't use it after a series introduced by *such as*.

EXCEPT. Archaic in the sense of *unless*.

> *Biblical:* "Except the Lord build the house, they labor in vain who build it."

EXPECT. Colloquial for *think* or *suspect*.

EXTRA. Avoid as a substitute for *very* or *unusually*.

FARTHER, FURTHER. Interchangeable except in the sense of *more* or *in addition* where only *further* is acceptable ("I will take no further action"). Some authorities may insist that *farther* be used for distance and *further* to indicate degree, time, or quantity.

FAZE. Colloquial for *bother, annoy, disturb, worry*.

FEEL LIKE. Colloquial when used to express *desire* or *inclination*.

> "I feel like going to the movies."

FELLOW. Colloquial for *man, boy, person*.

FEWER, LESS. *Fewer* refers to items that can be counted. *Less* refers to *masses, weights, quantities* that are not usually counted.

> "There are fewer people in this room than in that room, but there is less coal in my cellar than in your cellar."

FIX. As a noun, fix is colloquial for *predicament*. As a verb, it is colloquial for *repair, arrange,* or *prepare*.

FOLKS.   Colloquial for *relatives*.

FOLLOWING.   Do not use for the preposition *after*.

> *Wrong:* "Following the game there will be a party in the Student Union."

FORMER, LATTER, FIRST, LAST.   Use *former* in referring to the first item in a list of two. If there are more than two items, use *first* and *last*.

FUNNY.   Avoid using funny to mean *odd* or *peculiar*.

GENT.   Use *gentleman* or *man*.

GET, GOT.   Be careful in using the many possible expressions involving *get* and *got*. Most of them are colloquial or slang: *get around, get ahead of, get away with, get next to, get with it*, etc. Many of the approximately seventy uses of *get* and *got* are indispensable in conversation, but should be avoided in formal writing.

GIRL FRIEND.   See *boy friend*.

GOOD.   *Good* is an adjective. It is the correct choice following a linking verb.

> "Bill says he feels good."
> "Apples taste good."

Do not use as an adverb.

> *Wrong:* "Harry swims good."
> *Right:* "Harry swims well."

GOOD AND.   On the colloquial level *good and* is useful:

> "The water is good and hot" meaning
> "The water is very hot."

GOTTEN.   Frequently used as a past participle of *get*, especially in American English. *Got* is the more generally accepted choice.

GUESS.   Colloquial for *believe, suppose, think*.

GUY.   Colloquial for *man* or *person*.

HAD HAVE, HAD OF, HADN'T OF.   Avoid these substandard forms. Use *had* alone.

HAD OUGHT, HADN'T OUGHT.   Avoid these substandard forms. *Should* and *shouldn't* are acceptable substitutes.

HUMANS.   Not to be used instead of *human beings, persons*, or *people*.

IMPLY, INFER.   The speaker or writer *implies*. The listener or reader *infers*. In his speech before the U. N. the delegate implied that his government would intervene.

I infer from his remark that he intends to change jobs.

IN BACK OF. Still objected to in formal writing. Substitute *behind, at the back of, back of.*

IN REGARDS TO. Substitute *in regard to* or *as regards.*

INSIDE OF. Colloquial for *within:* "He should be here inside of three days." *Inside of* is entirely acceptable in sentences like "The inside of the house is more attractive than the outside."

IRREGARDLESS. A vulgarism for *regardless.*

IT. See *they.*

KIND OF. Colloquial when used adverbially as in "He looks kind of hungry."

KIND OF A. Avoid the *a.* "This is the kind of house I like best."

LADY, GENTLEMAN. Use *woman, man* to indicate sex differences. *Lady, gentleman* can be used when the person referred to is cultivated, refined, or of high social standing.

> *Wrong:* "Three ladies and one gentleman came out of the Post Office."
> *Right:* "Three women and one man came out of the Post Office."

LAY, LIE. *Lay* is a transitive verb meaning to put or place something. Its principal parts are *lay, laid, laid. Lie* is an intransitive verb meaning to rest or recline. Its principal parts are *lie, lay, lain.*

> *Correct:* "The rug lies on the floor."
> *Correct:* "Please lay the linoleum in the kitchen."
> *Correct:* "The papers have lain there for two days."
> *Correct:* "I laid the gloves on the shelf."

LESS, FEWER. *Less* refers to quantity; *fewer* refers to number.

> "There is less coal in this pile than in that pile."
> "There are fewer people in this room than in that room."

LIKE, AS, AS IF. *Like* is a preposition; *as* and *as if* are conjunctions. In formal English, write "He looks as if he hasn't slept for two days" rather than "He looks like he hasn't slept for two days."

LIABLE, APT, LIKELY. Although these words are interchangeable on an informal level, careful writing requires a distinction. *Liable* means *subject to:* "He is liable to arrest if he speeds through town." *Apt* means *to have aptitude for:* "He is a very apt pupil." *Likely* implies *probability:* "She is likely to report this to the principal."

LINE. Avoid the slang or vague uses of this word.

Slang: "Don't hand me that line."
Vague: "He sells fishing rods, shot-guns, and things in that line."
Better: "He sells sporting equipment."

LOCATE.   Avoid using *locate* for *settle.*

Correct: "John Good's ancestors settled [*not located*] in the Conestoga Valley."

LOTS, LOTS OF.   Colloquial for *much, many, a great deal.*
LOVELY.   Overused in the sense of *very pleasing.* Hunt the exact word demanded by the context.
MAD.   Colloquial for *angry.*
MATH.   Write *Mathematics.*
MIGHTY.   A colloquial intensive.

Formal: "This is a very [*not mighty*] important project."

MOST.   Colloquial when used for almost. "Almost [*not most*] all the fish have been caught."
MUST.   Avoid using *must* as a noun or an adjective, as in the following:

"On your trip West the Grand Canyon is a *must.*"
". . . a must book."

MYSELF, YOURSELF, HIMSELF.   Correct when used as reflexives or intensives.

Intensive: "If you can't do it, I'll do it myself."
Reflexive: "I cut myself."
"For further information, ask my father, my sister, or me [*not myself*]."

NOWHERE NEAR.   Not to be used for *not nearly.*

"It's not nearly so cold today."

OFF OF.   *Off* is sufficient. *Of* is redundant. "He got off the train."
OUTSIDE OF.   Colloquial as a synonym for *execpt.*

"Every team had a player in the All-Star game except [*not outside of*] the Lions."

POSSESSIVES WITH VERBAL NOUNS.   An *ing* form of a verb used as a noun should be preceded by a possessive: "He was awakened by the hunter's snoring."

QUOTE. When used as a noun, colloquial for *quotation*.

REAL. Don't use in place of *really* or *very*.

"He plays baseball really—or very—well [*not real well*]."

REASON IS BECAUSE. Not an acceptable substitute for *reason is that*.

REFER BACK, REPEAT AGAIN. Both these combinations are redundant. Use *refer* alone and *repeat* alone.

SHALL, WILL; SHOULD, WOULD. *I* takes *shall* and *should*. The others take *will* and *would*. To express determination, switch them: "I *will* speak." "They *shall* not perish." These distinctions are usually disregarded in informal English.

SO. Avoid as an intensive—"so beautiful," "so wonderful." Be careful in using it as a connective. Usually *so, that, therefore, consequently,* or *thus* will express the relationship more exactly.

THEY, YOU, AND IT. Generally avoid using the indefinite *you* in formal writing.

Informal: "You should never underestimate your reader's intelligence nor overestimate his knowledge."
Formal: "one should never . . ."

Avoid the indefinite use of *they* in sentences like "They grow a lot of corn in Iowa." Use "A great deal of corn is grown in Iowa" or "Iowa is a great corn-producing state." The indefinite *it* is correctly used in expressions like, "It is raining." "It is cold." But don't use it in expressions like "It says in the paper that rain is coming."

TOO. Avoid as an intensive.

Weak: "The Yankees didn't hit too well."
Better: "The Yankees didn't hit very well" or (better yet) "The Yankees didn't hit well."

Do not use *too* as a conjunctive adverb: "Too, the American had the better aircraft."

TRY AND. Don't substitute for try to: "Try to finish [*not try and finish*] the job by noon."

OUTSIDE OF. Colloquial as a synonym for *except*.

"What type of [not simply *type*] berry is this?"

UNIQUE. Do not use in the comparative and superlative degrees or with *most,* unless you also use a qualifying word like *nearly.*

Illogical: "This is the most unique discovery that we have made."

Logical: "This is a unique discovery."

Logical: "This may not be unique but it is more nearly unique than the others."

UNINTERESTED.   See *disinterested.*

WAIT ON.   Colloquial for *wait for.*

WAYS.   Substandard for *way.*

"He has come a long way [not *ways*], but he still has a long way [not *ways*] to go."

YOU.   See *they.*

APPENDIX

48/ *The Research Paper*

48a/ Definition

A research paper is the record of an inquiry and (hopefully) of a discovery. It illuminates a situation or clarifies a relationship.

Every research paper, therefore, must be a new creation. Like all new creations it will be fashioned from existing materials; but the raw materials will be assimilated, refined, recast; and the product will be like nothing else. It will be unique—hence its value.

48b/ Primary and secondary sources

A research paper gathers together evidence from original sources and testimony from investigators and brings them to bear on a specific subject. Collecting evidence and testimony is not enough; their application to the subject must be made clear. Your research paper must:

1. Reproduce pertinent parts of original sources.
2. Report correctly what investigators have to say.
3. Identify precisely each investigator, and indicate his authority.
4. Establish the significance of the collected information.

Information is everywhere. Where you go to find it depends on many things. You can test at first-hand whatever elements you are equipped to test. Your own tests, observations, and experiments are *primary* sources of information. If your absence from the event, or your lack of a specific training disqualifies your testimony, then you have to depend on the testimony of others, or *secondary* sources of information.

If you write about a novel, that novel is a primary source. A critical essay about it is a secondary source. If your study is the stature of a novelist in the eyes of critics, then a critical essay may be a primary source. There is no profit in attempting a theoretical identification of sources without reference to a problem. After you define your problem, get all the information you can and get as close as you can to the item of interest. A soldier's letter can sometimes tell more than a historian's guess.

48c / A working bibliography

Much of the usual research paper consists of your examination of other people's examination of the thing or event. Therefore, much of your work takes place in the library. After you learn your way among the card files and the indexes, you will need to make a working bibliography.

Use 3 × 5 inch or 4 × 6 inch cards. Make a record of every promising source. You can later discard the ones that are without value. The ones you use will form the basis of your final bibliography. See examples on pp. 242–243.

Note (demonstrated on card) that citing the publisher is optional. If the publisher is omitted between the place and date, the colon is changed to a comma.

Berky, Andrew S. *Practitioner in Physick*. Pennsburg: The Schwenkfelder Library, 1954.

or

Berky, Andrew S. *Practitioner in Physick*. Pennsburg: 1954.

Bibliography card for a book. One author.

Library
Call Number

Borland, Hal. *How to Write and Sell Non-fiction*. New York: The Ronald Press Company, 1956.

Or: Borland, Hal. *How to Write and Sell Non-fiction*. New York, 1956.

Bibliography card for a book, one author.

McPherson, Hugo. "Carson McCullers' Lovely
Huntress." *Tamarack Review*, XI (Spring 1959),
28–42.

Bibliography card for a periodical item.

Call
Number

Craig, Hardin and Thomas, J. M. *English
Prose of the Nineteenth Century.*
New York: Appleton-Century-Crofts, Inc.,
1929.

Bibliography card for two authors.

Call
Number

Richardson, Harlow C. and others.
Practical Forms of Exposition. New York:
The Macmillan Company, 1934.

Bibliography card for book with more than three authors.

Books printed by Albright Wright and Sons.
Earltown, Pennsylvania: Albright Wright,
1838.

Bibliography card for book with no author named.

Kazin, Alfred, editor. *The Open Form.*
New York: Harcourt, Brace and World, Inc., 1961.

Bibliography card for an anthology.

Flaubert, Gustave. *Madame Bovary.*
Translated by Marx Averling.
New York: Harper & Row, 1950.

Bibliography card for a translation.

College Entrance Examination Board.
Advanced Placement Program:
Course Descriptions, 1960.

Bibliography card for book prepared by a Board or Committee

Encyclopedia Britannica, 1956, Vol. 8,
p. 307. Article, "Electrochemistry."

Bibliography card for Encyclopedia article. If an encyclopedia article is signed by initials, look up the name of the author (in a list at the front of each volume) and record the name as in the case of a magazine article.

Alpert, Hollis. "Are Movie Critics
Necessary?" *Saturday Review*, XLV (October 13, 1962).

Bibliography card for a magazine article.

"U.S. Denies Compromise on Berlin,
Cuban Issues." *The Daily Collegian*,
October 16, 1962, p. 1, cols. 1–3.

Bibliography card for a newspaper article.

Duryea, E. D. "Management of Learning."
New Dimensions in Higher Education, No. 5.
Edited by Winslow R. Hatch. United States
Department of Health, Education, and Welfare,
Office of Education, 1960.

Bibliography card for signed Government Bulletin.

48d / Note taking

As your bibliography cards accumulate, you can begin taking notes from the books and periodicals they identify.

Take notes on cards or slips of paper of uniform size, not in a notebook where they soon become unmanageable, and not on bibliography cards.

Your tentative outline will direct your reading, and the information you gather will naturally fall into categories. You must recognize these categories as you read, label the categories in your note system, and record the information. Don't try to treat more than one subtopic or more than one source on a single card.

Take time to prepare your notes accurately and legibly. An orderly worker can write on both sides of a card without confusion. Others should establish a rule: *Write on one side only.* The success of your system will depend on the accuracy and appropriateness of your subject headings. If your project is carefully outlined and its parts properly labeled, finding the information to fill the cards will be a pleasant experience.

The following skeleton card shows the components of a good note card:

Subject Heading

Body of note which may be:
1. An outline
2. A summary
3. A direct quotation
4. A commentary
5. A paraphrase

Source including page number. This can be an abbreviation since you already have a full bibliography card for the source. Some people identify the source with a number given to the bibliography card.

48e / Assimilating material

While you take notes, protect yourself against plagiarism. Be sure to translate all notes except quotation notes into your own words. In summarizing, be sure that you have assimilated whole ideas, that you command the ideas, and that you can state the ideas in several different ways. In paraphrasing, don't just change a word here and there. Instead, paraphrase larger elements and avoid the apt expressions of the original author. Record your source so you can show your debt to it when you write your paper. When you quote, quote exactly. You should be able to tell an hour or five years after taking a note just what its status is. If it's a quotation note, you must have confidence that it is exact. If it is not in quotation marks, you must be confident that the wording is yours. If you want to leave out material from a quotation, indicate the omission by three spaced periods: ". . ." (an ellipsis). Be sure the omission will not change the sense of the original.

If you add words, place the addition in brackets: "They [i.e., the Gothic novelists] liked heroes sullied by unmentionable crimes, persecuted heroines, castles with secret passages and haunted rooms, and a plentiful sprinkling of supernatural terrors." Use the Latin

word *sic* in brackets to indicate an error in the original: "William
Wadsworth [*sic*] was born in Cumberland in 1775 [*sic*]."

Don't overquote. Most of your notes should be paraphrase notes.
If the original is so striking or so complex that paraphrasing might
weaken it, don't hesitate to quote. But you don't want your paper to
be a mosaic of quotations held together by a few sentences of transition.

48f / Organizing and interpreting data

As your file of cards grows, your view of your project will
change, and you will revise your tentative conclusions. Try to formulate a thesis: "Senator Skipjack was a crooked politician who enriched himself by aiding the underworld." Will your material prove
such a thesis, or does it prove something different? "In spite of his
allegiance to the Gunther Gang, Senator Skipjack was a courageous
public servant." Or do your findings justify clearing the Senator's
name: "The much-maligned Senator Skipjack brought about the
dissolution of the Gunther Gang while seeming to work with it?"

48g / Speculating

Let speculation lead you to facts. Let facts lead you to a conclusion. Distinguish between a *speculation,* an idea which will lead
you to investigate, and a *conclusion,* an idea at which you arrive after
investigation. Distrust a conclusion which arrives at the speculation
from which it began: Has your investigation revealed *no* new aspect?

You are looking for truth. You are *not* looking for proof of
what you already think is truth. If you are concerned only with supporting a prejudice, you will ignore evidence that contradicts the
prejudice. Ignoring contradictory evidence is neither honest nor
profitable. Besides, you leave your presentation unarmored: Anybody with knowledge can destroy it.

Let your idea direct you to an area, but examine that area thoroughly. Don't let your idea blind and halter you; it is your guide, not
your master. Don't hesitate to discharge your guide if you find a
better one.

48h / Writing the paper

After you have completed your research, you can arrange your cards for your final outline. The value of the card system will now be obvious. You can try certain cards in one section, then in another. After you have fixed the best arrangement, you are ready to begin the rough draft.

1. Use the third person. Don't refer to yourself. Keep the style formal (a matter of diction), but not stiff.
2. Get the story down. Write freely. The time for polishing is later.
3. Don't bother to recopy exact quotation notes that you plan to use. Simply staple them to your working paper. They can be typed on the second draft. Source references for footnoting will be there, too. Paraphrase notes that were carefully made can also be stapled to the rough draft. Write transitions and go on to succeeding notes.
4. Write footnotes into the text. Draw a horizontal line above and below the note so that it can be easily spotted in the revision.

Your first draft will be something of a mess—crossed-out words, paper clips, scotch tape, marginalia—but the controlling idea and attitude should be clear and the organization sound. Go through it again to correct spelling and punctuation errors, to improve transitions, to tighten prose, to check documentation. You should be able to salvage many pages for the final draft, but some pages you will have to re-write. Making the final draft is just a matter of copying perfected text.

48i / Footnoting

You place a footnote in your paper whenever you want to indicate the source of an idea or a quotation. The footnote says to the reader, "Here's exactly where I got this idea or this phrasing. You can check it for additional information."[1] You will soon develop a "documentation sense" that will guard you from the common fault of students—over-annotating. You need not show sources for facts in common knowledge or general information that can be taken for granted. Nobody will expect you to indicate a source for your statement that the earth is round or that eight minutes in boiling water will hard-cook an egg. You do not need to show a source for your statement that Fyodor Dostoevski was born in 1821 or that his final great masterpiece was *The Brothers Karamazov*, but if you say that he was sentenced to death for socialistic activity, reprieved, and banished to Siberia, you should assume that your reader might like details; and you will show him, by a footnote, where to get them.

The best way to develop quickly a documentation sense is to read scholarly papers in the field of your interest. Note the natural, unobtrusive way the notes add authority to the analysis.

After you learn *when to footnote*, your remaining problem is *how to* write a footnote. The following list shows models. (See also the specimen research paper, pp. 224–243.)

First References

BOOKS

[1] Hal Borland, *How to Write and Sell Non-fiction* (New York, 1956), p. 26. [One author]

[2] Hardin Craig and J. M. Thomas, *English Prose of the Nineteenth Century* (New York, 1929), p. 89. [Two authors]

[3] Harlow C. Richardson and others, *Practical Forms of Exposition* (New York, 1934), p. 65. [More than three authors]

[4] Alfred Kazin, ed. *The Open Form* (New York, 1961), p. 10. [Edited work]

[5] Gustave Flaubert, *Madame Bovary*, translated by Marx Averling (New York, 1950), p. 212. [A translation]

MAGAZINES AND NEWSPAPERS

[1] *Pittsburgh Press*, April 2, 1964, p. 8. [Unsigned news article. For a signed news article include author's name and the title of the article as in the case of a magazine article.]

[2] Hollis Alpert, "Are Movie Critics Necessary?" *Saturday Review* CXL (October 13, 1962), p. 59. [Magazine article]

---

[1] You may also use a footnote for additional explanation of a point. Overuse of the explanatory footnote confuses a reader, so use it sparingly.

ENCYCLOPEDIAS
 [3] "Electrochemistry," *Encyclopedia Britannica,* 1956, VIII, 307. [Unsigned Encyclopedia article. For a signed article, place the author's name before the title as in the case of a magazine article.]

PAMPHLETS OR BULLETINS
 [4] *Massachusetts Salt Water Fishing Guide,* Massachusetts Department of Commerce (Boston, 1962), p. 64.
 [5] *Cape Cod Art Association* (Hyannis, 1962), p. 5.

Second References

BOOKS
 [6] Borland, p. 31.
 [7] Craig and Thomas, p. 102.
 [8] Richardson and Others, p. 201.
 [9] *Ibid.* [Same work (Richardson and Others), same page as footnote #8.]
 [10] *Ibid.,* p. 202. [Same work as in preceding footnote, but different page.]

MAGAZINES AND NEWSPAPERS
 [11] Alpert, p. 58. [Only one item by Alpert in bibliography.] Second references to newspaper articles follow the form of the first reference unless the second reference is to the same article, in which case the date may be omitted—*Pittsburgh Press,* p. 8.

ENCYCLOPEDIAS
 [12] "Electrochemistry," *Encyclopedia Britannica,* p. 307. [If no other encyclopedia was consulted in the study, the words *Encyclopedia Britannica* could be omitted. If the first reference was to a signed encyclopedia article, the second reference would give just the author's name and the page number, as in the case of a book or a magazine article.]

PAMPHLETS OR BULLETINS
 [13] *Massachusetts Salt Water Fishing Guide,* p. 17.

48j / Abbreviations in footnotes

More than likely, *Ibid.* is the only abbreviation that you will need to use in your paper. A few other common ones are listed here to help you in your reading of scholarly papers. Practice varies on the use of the underscore (to indicate italics) for footnote abbreviations derived from Latin. There is a growing tendency to omit the underscore of such abbreviations. Whatever your choice, be consistent in carrying it out.

cf. "Compare." The word *see* is commonly used instead of *cf.*
ch., chs.   Chapter, chapters
ed.   Editor or edition
f., ff.   And the following page, pages
fig.,   Figure
i.e.,   That is
l., ll.   Line, lines
loc. cit.   In the place cited
n.   Note
n.d.   No date given
op. cit.   In the work cited
p.   Page
pp.   Pages
passim.   Here and there [used after a title to indicate reference
    to various places in the work.]
rev.   Revised
viz.   Namely

48k / Specimen paper

APOSTATE APOSTLE: H. L. MENCKEN AS
SHAVOPHILE AND SHAVOPHOBE*

by Stanley Weintraub

It is ironic that we owe to the self-publicizing paradox

purveyor Henry Louis Mencken, more than to any other American

critic, the popular misconception of Bernard Shaw as self-

advertising clown and coiner of cheap paradoxes. Though once

a Shavophile, in middle age Mencken was wont to look back upon

his disciplehood as a youthful indiscretion, fostering the

impression that George Bernard Shaw: His Plays, his first major

publication, was more biological necessity than pioneering work.

One of his earliest biographers even wrote: "Mr. Mencken had

his attack of Shavianitis at the appropriate age, when there

was some merit in 'discovering' Shaw, and before it was too

late to recover from the generous illusions of one's critical

nonage."[1] This became the orthodox interpretation, although a

close look at Mencken's "escape" from Shavian disciplehood may

indicate other motivation. "Schoolboy admiration"[2] was a term

another Mencken biographer applied; and certainly the twenty-

five year-old Mencken (with a modesty he was soon to shed) in-

dicated as much in inscribing a presentation copy of his book

_____

[1] Ernest Boyd, H. L. Mencken (New York, 1925), p. 23.

[2] Edgar Kemler, The Irreverent Mr. Mencken (Boston, 1950), p. 115.

* Reprinted by permission of the author.

-2-

to Shaw with an apology for his youthful zest and inexperience,
and the hope that he would have the pleasure of meeting
the playwright some day.[3]

What time Mencken could spare from his duties on the
Baltimore Sun in 1904 had been devoted to reading of Ibsen,
Conrad and Thomas Huxley. During that year, Will A. Page
of the Washington Post added Bernard Shaw to the young
journalist's reading list. Before long Mencken decided to
do for Shaw what Shaw had done for Ibsen. During that summer he spent his spare time outlining a critical study of
Shaw's plays--a "Quintessence of Shavianism." The job done,
Shaw's American publisher of The Quintessence of Ibsenism--
Brentano--rejected the proposal, and the disappointed critic
turned to John W. Luce, a small Boston firm which had published a slender volume of Shaw's, the essay "On Going to
Church." Through the early part of 1905 the manuscript was
prepared, and, after exchanges of long letters, rewritten to
mutual satisfaction of author and publisher, and to the intended greater glorification of GBS.

Contemporary American reviews of Shaw's own work were often
emotional but seldom flattering; it was not to be expected that
reviews of Shavian exegesis would receive any better treatment,

---

[3]From the copy of the book in the Hanley Collection,
University of Texas Library.

-3-

especially when the preface ended, as Mencken's did, with the

line, "Even the worst of Shaw is well worth study." Still it had

a gratifyingly respectable sale, and Mencken's first success-

ful book thus resulted from his Shavian disciplehood.

To the young critic, Ibsen now paled beside Shaw, whom

Mencken saw as more than a "mere imitator." "In some things," he

wrote, "indeed—such, for instance, as in fertility of wit and

invention—he very often exceeds the Norwegian."[4] Furthermore,

he thought that no other contemporary dramatist, with the pos-

sible exception of Ibsen, had so stimulated the public's thinking:

> Pick up any of the literary monthlies and you will
> find a disquisition upon his technique, glance
> through the dramatic column of your favorite news-
> paper and you will find some reference to his plays.
> Go to your woman's club, O gentle reader! and you
> will hear your neighbor, Mrs. McGinnis, deliver her
> views upon "Candida." Pass among any collection of
> human beings accustomed to even rudimentary mental
> activity--and you will hear some mention, direct or
> indirect, and some opinion, original or cribbed, of
> or about the wild Irishman.... And so we may take it
> for granted that Shaw tries to make us think and that
> he succeeds.[5]

At this stage in Mencken's Shavolatry it was possible that

a play by Shaw could have some serious faults, but each flaw

was vastly overshadowed by its preponderant merit. Captain

---

[4]H. L. Mencken, George Bernard Shaw: His Plays (Boston,
1905), p. xix.

[5]Ibid., pp. xx-xxi.

-4-

Brassbound's Conversion, for example, was "decidedly inferior"
to most of Shaw, chiefly because the exposition in the first act
required "an immense amount of talk without action." Yet the
piece was "a melodrama of the true Shaw brand, in which the play
of mind upon mind overshadows the play of club upon skull."
Even Caesar and Cleopatra, which Mencken described as "sweeping"
and "spectacular" as well as "more human and more logical"
than Shakespeare's Caesar play, admittedly had a serious flaw—
Caesar himself, who was "scarcely a Roman." But Mencken's
innate iconoclasm was whetted most by the gargantuan Man and
Superman, which he described with pre-Hollywoodian fireworks:
it was "the most entertaining play of its generation" as well
as "a tract cast in an encyclopedic and epic mold—a stupendous,
magnificent colossal effort to make a dent in the cosmos with
a slapstick."[6]

When Mencken became literary critic for Smart Set several
years later (and particularly when he rose to co-editor in
1914), a different approach to Shaw became inevitable. The
early apostolic enthusiasm had not quite worn off, but Shavian drama no longer needed a Paul; it had already been
noisily received on American shores and was now more than a
curiosity peddled by crackpots. Amateur and professional groups

[6]Ibid., p. 37.

were successfully presenting You Never Can Tell, Candida, Arms

and the Man, The Devil's Disciple, Man and Superman—and New York

police had successfully blocked presentation of Mrs. Warren's

Profession, causing Mencken to boast in 1914, "To see Shaw's

'Mrs. Warren,' I had to go to Germany."[7] However, his pos-

ition as literary critic and editor demanded more objectivity

than hero-worship, and the tone of Smart Set demanded as much

irreverence as reverence. Furthermore, his emotions seem to

have become affected by messianic impulses. The older genera-

tion—Ibsen, Shaw, Nietzsche—had served its function by clear-

ing away much of the Victorian rubbish; it was now time for

Mencken's generation—with Mencken as its spokesman—to impose

its more freshly jaundiced view of the times.

Mencken's approach to this design was the announcement—

actually an elaboration of the obvious—that Shaw (now nearly

sixty) was slowing down and becoming more repetitious. Reviewing

Misalliance, Fanny's First Play and The Dark Lady of the Sonnets

for Smart Set, he raised himself to peerage with GBS through the

leverage of his pen and condescendingly referred to "our loud

and bold friend, George Bernard Shaw," adding further:

----

[7]Mencken, "Thirty-Five Printed Plays," Smart Set,
XLIV (Sept., 1914), 154.

-6-

> Is it time to add "tiresome"? For one, I protest
> against it....The long preface to "MISALLIANCE"
> (Brentano)--it runs to 121 closely printed pages,
> perhaps 45,000 words, a good sized book in itself--
> is one of the best things, indeed, he has ever
> done.... You will be constantly chuckling and glow-
> ing and murmuring, "How true! How true!" This is the
> special function of Shaw, the steady business of his
> life: to say the things that everybody knows and
> nobody says, to expose the everyday hypocrisies, to
> rout platitudes with super-platitudes....[8]

Though Mencken scoffed, his heart was obviously not in

it, for nowhere yet had Shaw torn into so many human foibles

so dear to Mencken's own iconoclastic heart as in Misalliance

and its preface. The Brobdingnagian preface, with seventy-

five such topics as "Wanted, a Child's Magna Charta," "How

Little We Know about Our Parents," "Children's Rights and

Duties" and "Natural Selection as a Religion," Mencken had

to admit was one of the best things Shaw had done. Still he

felt obliged to add, "No, these new plays will not lift Shaw

nearer Shakespeare--he has yet to do anything better than the

earliest fruits of his fancy--'Mrs. Warren,' 'Candida,' and

'Arms and the Man.' But though he thus stands still as a

dramatist, he yet remains a surpassing entertainer."[9]

---

[8]"Thirty-Five Printed Plays," p. 160

[9]Ibid.

-7-

By August, 1916, Mencken was, as Irvin S. Cobb once re-
marked, "drunk with the power which he has found in his pen."
Certainly it was a different Mencken than had written Bernard
Shaw: His Plays a scant decade before. His new theme had
appeared in milder terms in the review of Misalliance two
years earlier--the accusation that GBS was guilty of announcing the obvious in terms of the scandalous. Now Shaw was
the "Ulster Polonius," who in Androcles and the Lion had
fooled the world with a "veritable debauch of platitudes"
and "embalmed ideas." Moreover, Mencken announced, Shaw was
"not at all the heretic his fascinated victims see him, but
an orthodox Scotch Presbyterian of the most cock-sure and
bilious sort." He took little stock in the "theory" that
Shaw was Irish, demonstrating to his own satisfaction that
Shaw's name and background were Scotch. The playwright's
"ethical obsession," he railed, had founded in England "the
superstition that Ibsen was no more than a tinpot evangelist."[10]

With more leisure, Mencken expanded the review of
Androcles into an article-length diatribe, also entitled
"The Ulster Polonius." Here Mencken's claim to authority was
that he had written the first book about Shaw's works and

----

[10]"The Ulster Polonius," Smart Set, XLVI (August, 1916),
140.

-8-

still read and enjoyed them. But the earlier praise was

hedged, ex post facto: "Yet so far as I know, I have never

found an original idea in them. . . . What is seriously

stated in them is quite beyond logical dispute. . . . As

well try to controvert Copernican astronomy." Why then, asked

Mencken, is the Ulster Polonius regarded as an arch-heretic?

"Because he practices with great zest and skill the fine

art of exhibiting the obvious in obvious and terrifying

lights."[11] The "most searching and illuminating observa-

tions" which Mencken had praised in Man and Superman in

1905 were, in a reappraisal of the play, exposed as platitudes:

evidence, perhaps, of Shaw's success in gaining wide intel-

lectual acceptance. Also, by proclaiming Shaw now to be

merely an entertaining windbag, Mencken was (it seems implied)

setting himself up to be Shaw's successor as arch-heretic

of the English-speaking world. Mencken had the need "like

so many of his fellow-critics since," as Louis Kronenberger

put it, "in raising one thing up, to pull another down."[12]

Thus to Mencken, Shaw became now "almost the archetype of

the blue-nose," a "Scotch Puritan" to whom "Beauty is a

lewdness, redeemable only in the service of morality." In

_____

[11]Prejudices, First Series (New York, 1929), p. 182.
[12]"An Ill-Will Tour of the American Mind," Saturday
Review of Literature, August 6, 1949, p. 42.

conclusion he sniped, "And this is Shaw the revolutionist,
the heretic! Next, perhaps, we shall be hearing of Bene-
dict XV, the atheist. . . ."[13] To Mencken's satisfaction, at least, GBS was unmasked.

When necessary, Mancken even (to use his own terms)
"dredged" reasons to deflate Shaw's reputation from the works
of naive and specious Shavolators whose panegyrics could
only have served to embarrass their subject. In 1918 the
unlucky offender was Robert Blatchford, an English socialist,
who wrote, "Shaw is something much better than a wit, much
better than a politician or a dramatist; he is a moralist,
a teacher of ethics, austere, relentless, fiercely earnest."[14]
"What could be more idiotic," Mencken commented. "Then Cotton
Mather was a greater man than Johann Sebastian Bach. . . ."[15]
Blatchford was merely a convenient soapbox from which to blast
Shaw's didacticism. Mencken had no quibble with Shaw's
playwriting, steadfastly praising his dexterity in the
theatre while insisting that Shaw "smothers his dramaturgy in
a piffish iconoclasm that is no more than a disguise for

---

[13]*Prejudices, First Series*, p. 190.
[14]Quoted in Mencken, <u>Damn! A Book of Calumny</u> (New York,
1918), p. 39.
[15]Ibid.

-10-

Puritanism."[16]   The Sage of Baltimore obviously had designs

elsewhere than on Shaw's playwriting reputation.

Mencken's admiration for Shaw remained, for the most

part, elaborately concealed beneath a bushel of repetitive

tirades. Still, between assaults, in 1922, he journeyed to

England:

> [He] walked the streets of London within easy reach
> of Shaw's flat, but he hesitated to pay his respects.
> Frank Harris, or some other intermediary, had told
> him that GBS was very angry. Nor did Mencken have
> it in him to make the first gesture. In his youth
> he had shyly stood apart during a Sunpapers recep-
> tion for Mark Twain, and in his maturity he was
> still unwilling to intrude upon his heroes.[17]

At about the same time, Shaw's biographer Henderson was in

London, recording the Master's "Table Talk" for posterity.

Regarding American letters, GBS confessed to him, "I am ob-

viously and ridiculously out of date." He had never heard of

Willa Cather, Edith Wharton and Sherwood Anderson, and thought

James Branch Cabell was a senator. But he had (apparently

without rancor) read Mencken, and had found him "an amusing

dog, and a valuable critic, because he thinks it more important

---

[16] A Book of Prefaces, Second (revised) Edition (New York,
1918), p. 26.
[17] Kemler, p. 116.

-11-

to write as he feels than to be liked as a good-hearted,
gentlemanly creature."[18]

Before Shaw's warmly admiring gesture was published in
The Fortnightly Review in 1924, Mencken appeared in print with
more abuse, this time somewhat contradictory to his own
earlier apostasy. Shaw was still a "Scotch blue-nose dis-
guised as an Irish patriot and English soothsayer" who
attempted "heroic but vain struggles to throw off Presby-
terianism." But now Mencken found that the "discussion
plays" such as Misalliance and Getting Married, which he had
condemned earlier as theatrical platitudes, were the only
Shavian plays "which contain actual ideas," although they
"failed dismally on the stage."[19] Many of his aphorisms
were now inversions of his earlier convictions: Ibsen and
Shaw had served their purpose; there were no ideas in the
so-called "drama of ideas." A decade earlier, the Baltimore
soothsayer, already by then an apostate, was still praising
such plays as Candida, Arms and the Man, and Man and Superman.
Now he lumped them with Androcles as idea-less:

_____

[18]Archibald Henderson, "Literature and Science. A
Dialogue between Bernard Shaw and Archibald Henderson,"
Fortnightly Review, October 1, 1924, p. 512.
[19]Prejudices, Third Series (New York, 1922),
pp. 304-05.

-12-

> The successful plays contain no ideas; they contain
> only platitudes, balderdash, buncombe. . . . Shaw
> has given all these pieces a specious air of pro-
> foundity by publishing them hooked to long and
> garrulous prefaces and by filling them with stage
> directions which describe and discuss the char-
> acters at great length. But as stage plays they are
> almost as empty as 'Hedda Gabler'. One searches them
> vainly for even the slightest novel contribution
> to the current theories of life. . . . Shaw's pref-
> aces, of course, have vastly more ideational force and
> respectability than his plays. If he fails to get
> any ideas of genuine savor into them it is not
> because the preface form bars them out but because
> he hasn't any to get in.[20]

The middle twenties found Mencken firmly atop his _Ameri-_

can Mercury platform at the zenith of his fame and influence.

Perhaps it seemed to him no longer necessary to work at deflat-

ing Shaw in order to inflate Mencken. After Shaw's philosophic

excursions in _Heartbreak House_, _Saint Joan_ and _Methuselah_,

Mencken sounded almost orthodox when he mourned that GBS,

"once so agile and diverting, becomes a seer and a pro-

phet."[21] Writing on Mark Twain in _The Chicago Tribune_, he

compared the American to such literary giants as Wagner,

Tolstoy—and Shaw. Like them, Mencken thought, "he was a

great artist, but also a great mountebank."[22] By 1930 he

---

[20] Ibid.

[21] "The American Novel," reprinted in _Prejudices, Fourth
Series_ (New York, 1924), p. 281.

[22] _The Bathtub Hoax and other Blasts and Bravos_, ed.
Robert McHugh (New York, 1958), p. 86.

-13-

could be even more objective about his master, acknowledging

(according to a Mencken biographer) that Shaw was both the

most accomplished stylist and the most successful of contem-

porary intellectual demagogues. Shaw and he, Mencken admitted,

were "working the same side of the street"--that is, "stating

the obvious in terms of the scandalous."[23] Yet this is what

Mencken had been denouncing Shaw for doing during the twenty

previous years of apostatehood.

To the depression generation of the thirties, Mencken,

no longer editor of the now-declining Mercury, was also no

longer hero and cause.[24] Still as reactionary as ever in his

politics, he may have seen common ground between him and the

Shaw of the political plays, such as On the Rocks and The

Apple Cart, who, without rejecting his Fabianism, had become

disillusioned with the waste and stupidity he thought inherent

in Democratic processes. While sneering about GBS's socialism

to associate editor Charles Angoff,[25] Mencken was writing in

one of his last reviews for the Mercury that Shaw's socialism

was only "a blackjack for clubbing the heads of the orthodox."

[23]Kemler, p. 115

[24]As Mencken's Shavophobia lessened it was still to breed
such embarrassing phenomena as Benjamin de Casseres' near-lib-
elous volume of fulminations in praise of Mencken and in scorn
of Shaw, Mencken and Shaw (New York, 1930).

[25]Letter to the author from Mr. Angoff, July 3, 1958.

-14-

Though--admittedly here--both <u>were</u> working the same side of the

street, almost by reflex action, it seems, Mencken repeated his

well-worn Scotch Puritan epithets. Even some lukewarm and

condescending praise was in order now, however, as, in one

of his interviews, he defended Shaw's comic style:

> Is there anything discreditable about being a
> really first-rate clown? Is it a sin against the
> Holy Ghost to go through life pricking bubbles? I
> incline to think not. What Shaw has to say is almost
> always what has been said before, and often it has
> been better said. Sometimes it is sense and some-
> times it is nonsense. . . . He has not made life
> better for anyone, but he has made it more amusing,
> more exciting, and hence more endurable. It is thus
> idle to sneer at him, and silly to denounce him. He
> is a lightweight, true enough, but he has a long
> reach and knows how to use his feet, and he has
> brought many a heavyweight clattering to the floor.[26]

Here again was evidence that Mencken hadn't changed much.

Through a quarter of a century--whether apostle or apostate--

he had continued to demonstrate his inability to understand

Shaw's religion and philosophy. Though he had done much to

cause the thinking minority of the public to take Shaw

seriously, his admiration was generally limited to a super-

ficial aspect of Shaw. It is for this reason, perhaps, that

it is to Mencken more than any other American critic that we

owe the popular notion of Shaw as a self-advertising clown and

------

[26]"Harris on Shaw", <u>American Mercury</u>, XXV (February, 1932), 255.

coiner of cheap paradoxes. Mencken consistently treated GBS
as primarily a satirist with a slapstick, a modernized and
better humored Swift or Voltaire. This was a confusion of
ends and means, for although Shaw used satire and irony
freely, it was not merely to expose hollow idols, sham
ideals and feet of clay, but to expound his partially de-
rivative "original morality"--which Mencken looked on as
nonsense. Furthermore, Mencken the individualist, could
not understand Shaw, the socialist, who considered his
socialism not as an end but as a first faltering step in the
grand design of Creative Evolution. Mencken's journalistic
and superficial individualism was undirected but ego-satis-
fying as long as it refused to recognize his own creed as
essentially negative.

Following his retirement from the American Mercury at
the end of 1933, Mencken undertook a complete rewriting of
his major exhibit in evidence that scholarship can be enter-
taining--The American Language. First published in 1919, it
had three revisions thereafter. For his fourth and final
version, he had some business correspondence with another sage
fascinated by language study--Bernard Shaw. In one exchange
of notes, regarding permission to insert a Shavian quotation

-16-

in The American Language, Shaw unbent sufficiently to reply,
"Yes, and you may go the limit."[27] But that was also the
limit that familiarity ever went between the old warriors.

In the 1936 edition were several graceful nods to GBS
in his role as innovator and conservator of the English
language. Mencken praised Shaw's activities as the dissenting
member of the BBC's Advisory Committee on Spoken English and
his reasonable approach toward accepting change in the language.
As Mencken mellowed, he burrowed even deeper into philological
researches, coming out regularly to issue blasts against the
New Deal and Franklin Roosevelt, FDR having replaced GBS
as radical villain. When Supplement One—a work almost as
large as the final version of the original work—was published
in 1945, again Shaw was present--as contributor of Comstockery
to the American language.[28] Here Shaw's cause was one particularly dear to Mencken's heart, and the Sage of Baltimore
spent a long footnote detailing the Shavian term's exposure
of America's moral provinciality. Another contribution from

----

[27]Kemler, p. 116.
[28]The American Language. Supplement One (New York, 1945),
p. 350 fn.

-17-

GBS was the lessening of the horror of <u>bloody</u> (already quite

innocuous to Americans) to Englishmen after its use by Mrs.

Pat Campbell in <u>Pygmalion</u>. Again Mencken's pleased reference

was to Shaw's part in accelerating the decline of prudery.[29]

Yet only a dozen years earlier Mencken had still been repeating

in print his assertion that GBS was a "Scotch blue-nose."

Though Time's wheel had worked its metamorphosis upon

Mencken, it could not turn full-circle. Nostalgic as the

old faith might have seemed to the mellowing Mencken, recan-

tation was impossible. We may infer from Mencken's last

publications that he preferred to let his writings on Shaw

be forgotten out of neglect. In <u>A Mencken Chrestomathy</u>

(1953), "a collection of choice passages" edited and annotated

by the author, he explained his selections by prefacing,

"I have occasionally allowed partiality to corrupt judgment."[30]

None of his many past references to Shaw, <u>pro</u> or <u>con</u>, appear

in the hundreds of closely printed pages, not even in the sec-

tion on "Literati," although names several degrees lesser in

literary magnitude wither again or are re-enobled under the

---

[29] <u>Supplement One</u>, pp. 678-79.
[30] <u>A Mencken Chrestomathy</u> (New York, 1953), p. vi.

-18-

Mencken pen. In <u>Minority Report</u> (1956), the jottings from his

notebooks published in the year of his death, the ailing

curmudgeon would only admit about his Shavolatrous landmark of

a half-century before: "I succumbed to more sophisticated and

tortured devices, and there was a good deal of empty ornament

in my first prose book, 'George Bernard Shaw: His Plays.'"[31]

So Shaw--once prophet and cause to Mencken--appeared and dis-

appeared in the wan light of Mencken's last years.

---

[31]<u>Minority Report</u> (New York, 1956), p. 292.

Bibliography

Angoff, Charles. Letter to the author, July 3, 1958.

Boyd, Ernest. H. L. Mencken. New York, 1925.

de Casseres, Benjamin. Mencken and Shaw. New York, 1930.

Henderson, Archibald. "Literature and Science. A Dialogue
    between Bernard Shaw and Archibald Henderson." Fort-
    nightly Review (October 1, 1924), 512.

Kemler, Edgar. The Irreverent Mr. Mencken. Boston, 1950.

Kronenberger, Louis. "An Ill-will tour of the American Mind".
    Saturday Review of Literature (August 6, 1949), 42.

McHugh, Robert, ed. The Bathtub Hoax and other Blasts and
    Bravos. New York, 1958.

Mencken, H. L. The American Language. Supplement One. New
    York, 1945.

————. A Book of Prefaces. Second (revised) Edition. New
    York, 1918.

————. Damn! A Book of Calumny. New York, 1918.

————. George Bernard Shaw: His Plays. Boston, 1905.

————. "Harris on Shaw." American Mercury, XXV (February, 1932),
    255.

————. A Mencken Chrestomathy. New York, 1953.

————. Minority Report. New York, 1956.

————. Prejudices, First Series. New York, 1929.

-20-

———. Prejudices, Third Series. New York, 1922.

———. Prejudices, Fourth Series, New York, 1924.

———. "Thirty-five Printed Plays." Smart Set, XLIV
(September, 1914), 154.

———. "The Ulster Polonius." Smart Set, XLVI (August,
1916), 140.

Note: In the final bibliography, listings are alphabetical and page numbers are given for articles in collections and for periodicals.

INDEX

Homeopathy
In Practice

DOUGLAS BORLAND, M.D.

MB, ChB, FFHom

Edited for publication by

KATHLEEN PRIESTMAN, M.D.

LRCP, MRCS, FFHom

Keats Publishing, Inc. New Canaan, Connecticut

Note: The spelling of homeopathy herein follows the British style as it appears in the original text. Where new material has been added (cover text, bibliography, introductory copy, list of companies making and selling homeopathic products, etc.), Americanized spelling has been used.

Preface

I have found it very interesting to be able to help in preparing Dr Borland's manuscript for publication in book form. I attended a number of his original lectures myself, and possess the notes of other lectures attended by my former senior partner, Dr Agnes Moncrieff. I found these notes of great value during my years in general practice, and referred to them frequently, as well as to his books on *Children's Types* and *Pneumonias*.

The material in this book does not represent the entire balance of Dr Borland's hitherto unpublished lectures. It does, however, represent all of them that were taken down in shorthand. They are published here because Dr Borland's homoeopathic insight remains as important and as fresh today as it ever was. Wherever current practice has moved on from his time, notably in the availability of antibiotics and in the development of modern surgical techniques, I have edited the text to point this out.

One of the difficulties in homoeopathic prescribing is to distinguish between remedies with similar symptomatology, and Section II of this book examines a number of major groups of related remedies. The individual remedies are not presented in alphabetical order – Dr Borland frequently linked remedies by their common characteristics or differences, and excelled in leading on from one to another, as the reader will appreciate.

There are a number of occasions throughout the book where Dr Borland was explaining the use of homoeopathic remedies in a busy general practice surgery, and the word 'routine' is sometimes used. This is against the basic principle of homoeopathy, which is that an individual remedy is chosen for each patient according to the symptoms presented at the time. In practice there are certain common ailments which present with the same symptom picture in many individuals, so that the same remedy is indicated, and it is in this sense that the word 'routine' is used. Dr Borland warns the prescriber to be on the watch at all times for patients who do not fit the common symptomatology, and who therefore require another remedy.

Books on homoeopathic practice have sometimes been criticised for being too anecdotal, and for this reason most references to patients have been omitted. However, the picture of Lachesis, as demonstrated by Dr Borland's patient, is so typical that it has been included (Chapter 12).

This publication, small though it is, should be a most valuable tool in the hands of anyone using the homoeopathic method of treatment.

K. G. Priestman, LRCP, MRCS, FFHom

Explanation of
Homoeopathic Terms

Potency

This is used to indicate the strength of the remedy. Samuel Hahnemann found in his original experiments on himself and on those testing the remedies – usually known as 'provers' – as well as when treating patients, that material doses of the substance he was using caused such unpleasant symptoms in the 'provers', and side effects in the patients, that he gradually reduced the dose. As he increased the dilution, he introduced a method of shaking the substance in dilution, finding by experience that the medicines used in this way had a more beneficial effect than when used in material doses.

The method of shaking he called succussion, and the result of dilution plus succussion he called 'potency'. In the past, the use of these very small doses has brought disbelief and ridicule to homoeopathy, but in these days of electron microscopy and the microchip, disbelief in the smallness of anything may well reflect more on the mind of the disbeliever than on the subject of his disbelief.

Hahnemann used two scales for his dilutions, the decimal and the centesimal. His method was as follows. Taking the original substance, he made a strong solution in either water or alcohol. The solution was then filtered and the filtrate was known as the 'mother tincture'. Using a new clean glass bottle and pipette for each step, one drop of the mother tincture was placed in the first bottle, and either 9 or 99 drops of alcohol (as pure as possible) were added. The bottle was corked and then shaken vigorously by striking it hard on a book or the palm of the hand ten times.

Then, taking one drop from this bottle, either 9 or 99 drops of the alcohol were added and the shaking or succussion repeated. This process was continued until the desired potency was reached.

The scale in which 9 drops of alcohol are used is denoted by the Roman numeral X and is known as the decimal scale. Where 99 drops of alcohol are used, the scale is designated by the Roman numeral C and known as the centesimal scale. That is, for example, Belladonna 1x, 2x, 3x, etc., or 1c, 2c, 3c, etc. The x potencies are known as 'low' potencies and also the lower scale of the c potencies. Potencies of the C scale have been taken to very high figures, even as far as the CM, and are known as high potencies from the 30c upwards. In modern times mechanical means are used for succussion. Hahnemann used his manual method as far as the 30c potency.

In this book, wherever no specific potency is mentioned, it is safe to use either 6c, 12c or 30c.

Modalities

These are the differences and modifications of symptoms. They are very important in relating the symptoms of the patient to the homoeopathic remedy, and concern the circumstances or conditions which make them better or worse. For example, a pain or sensation may be affected by:

1) Temperature, open air, weather, time of year, etc.;
2) Motion, touch, noise, position, eating, sleeping, etc.;
3) Time in 24 hours, etc.

Constitution, Constitutional Remedy or Type

Hahnemann was insistent that sickness in a person relates to the whole man and not to one particular part or organ of the body.

The people who tested or 'proved' remedies for him were asked to note every change or symptom that occurred in their thoughts, feelings and emotions, as well as physical sensations in every part of the body. These were carefully recorded under systematised headings, and gradually a pattern emerged for each remedy. This pattern became known as the 'drug picture' for that particular remedy.

It has been found that certain remedies are indicated very frequently, and that many people exhibit symptoms which correspond to the symptom picture or 'drug' picture of each of these remedies. Therefore they have become known as 'constitutional' remedies. The patients are said to have, for example, a Pulsatilla constitution or be a Pulsatilla type, or a Sulphur or Lycopodium type, according to which of these particular remedies their temperament most closely responds.

Unfortunately, over the years, it has become a common habit for homoeopathic doctors to speak of the remedies as if they were the patients and vice versa. It is to be understood, for instance, that the 'Kali Carb. backache with pain shooting down the thighs' may be used of a patient suffering from this condition, or also in a description of the Kali Carb. symptomatology.

To state that Pulsatilla is a certain person's constitutional remedy indicates that the individual's habitual personality resembles the 'picture' of Pulsatilla as it was brought out in the 'provers'. In any sickness where those Pulsatilla symptoms are intensified, Pulsatilla is the remedy that will bring the patient back into a state of health.

In acute conditions, patients may exhibit symptoms that indicate some remedy other than their constitutional one. In these cases, the prescription must always follow the homoeopathic law of similars. When the acute condition is resolved, it may well be that a dose of the patient's constitutional remedy will be needed to restore them to full health.

K. G. P.

Contents

Chapter 1

Injuries and Emergencies

SPRAINS AND DISLOCATIONS

Among the commonest minor surgical complaints seen in general practice are sprains, fractures and dislocations of all kinds. Much can be done to diminish the pain and shorten the period of disability. After an accident with general aching pain, whether it is a sprain, a dislocation or a fracture, where the part feels bruised with a dislike of movement which is painful, the first remedy to give is Arnica.

After a dislocation has been reduced but where there is still pain around the dislocated joint, or after a sprain where the patient is complaining of considerable pain, the affected joint being more comfortable when the patient moves it about but stiffening up when he keeps it still – i.e. so long as it is kept moving it is easier – give Rhus Tox.

In all acute cases, any potency may be used, 30c or higher. Give several doses, usually three doses two hours apart. That is the ordinary routine treatment.

One other allied condition is rupture of a muscle. This may occur with a severe sprain or dislocation. There are some indications for Arnica – very painful on movement, must keep as still as possible – and yet Arnica does not give relief. The patient finds it very difficult to move, and gets sharp pains in the torn muscle, rather than the bruised feeling of Arnica. A few doses of Bryonia help this condition just as much as Arnica helps the others. It is more commonly met with in back strain than anywhere else – a man has lifted something too heavy, something gives in his back and he is in great pain. A great many of these cases in general practice are a problem. Quite a few will respond to Arnica, but the majority respond very much better to Bryonia.

One warning: in a sprain with Rhus Tox. symptoms (where the affected area stiffens up with rest and is better for movement). In the typical warm-blooded, gentle Pulsatilla patient, Pulsatilla will be far more effective than Rhus Tox. Pulsatilla has exactly the same modalites as Rhus Tox., stiffens up in the same way, and Rhus Tox. does not seem to do much good. It is better to prescribe Pulsatilla in the first instance. Pulsatilla patients are rather the loose-jointed type and tend to get sprains. In spite of the Rhus Tox. symptoms, Rhus Tox. does not act in the typical warm-blooded gentle Pulsatilla type.

With persistent stiffness and weakness after sprains in the neighbourhood of a joint, Ruta can be given as a routine. Ruta has very much the Rhus Tox. modalities; the muscles tend to get stiff when not in use and to become easier with use. If Rhus Tox. has been given without effect, follow it up with Ruta, which will usually clear up the condition.

There are two remedies to consider for weakness of a joint following a sprain, or where there is a tendency to recurring dislocation. With a loose joint which tends to turn over and is weak, e.g. ankle, a few doses of Calcarea Carb. will strengthen the ligaments. Where the looseness and weakness of the joint is accompanied by a certain amount of stiffness as well as being easily dislocated, it will improve after a few doses of Strontium Carb. A patient who had received treatment for repeated subluxation of the right sacro-iliac joint without benefit was manipulated, and given Strontium Carb. Because the subluxation occurred when she used the brake on the car, she was also forbidden to drive for two months. She had no further trouble.

Muscular fatigue or general exhaustion from walking too far or driving too long can be helped by having a hot bath to which two tablespoonsful of Arnica tincture have been added, after which the individual feels completely refreshed.

For synovial effusion into a tendon sheath, or a pre-patella bursa or ganglion of the wrist, Ruta is almost specific. If a pre-patella bursa does not clear with Ruta it will usually do so on Apis.

FRACTURES

As an ordinary routine, start the patient on Arnica. There is considerable pain, effusion of blood and bruising, and the typical aggravation from movement. When dealing with a comminuted fracture, with a number of spicules of bone, particularly in the neighbourhood of a joint, or where a nerve has been injured by splinters of bone with pain shooting along the course of the nerve, Hypericum gives greater relief than Arnica. Where bony union is slow, callus formation can be stimulated by a few doses of Calc. Phos., the commonest remedy for slow union. The other possibility is Symphytum. These are often very helpful, as in many of these cases it is difficult to get any indication on which to prescribe, apart from the local injury.

HEAD OR SPINAL INJURY

For a head injury with concussion, or for a spinal injury, again with a degree of concussion, certain routine prescriptions can be given. In the case of head injury with mild concussion, the best prescription is Arnica. Where the concussion has been much more a spinal concussion rather than a head concussion, the best prescription is Hypericum. That is an immediate prescription. For concussion with persisting drowsiness with obviously increasing intra-cranial pressure, do not persist with Arnica but go on to Opium at once. When dealing with the later effects of concussion, the post-concussion headache, there are again certain routine prescriptions available. The most useful remedy is Natrum Sulph. Arnica is disappointing for a post-concussion headache. Natrum Sulph. is the commonest remedy for these cases, and the next most useful is Opium.

When dealing with the neuraesthenic symptoms which may be associated with a spinal concussion, the most commonly indicated remedy is Actea Racemosa, followed by Hypericum. (An alternative name for Actea Racemosa is Cimicifuga.) These remedies may all be given in the 30c potency.

SMALL WOUNDS AND LACERATIONS

For small wounds, lacerations and similar conditions there are three commonly indicated remedies. The commonest is Calendula. The ordinary homoeopathic routine of putting a Calendula dressing on wounds gives extremely good results, but they will be even better if Calendula in potency is given orally at the same time. Give three doses two hours apart of 30c or 200c potency. A wet Calendula dressing helps the bruising as well as the laceration.

With a wound involving any very sensitive area, such as the tips of fingers, beds of nails, or toes – where there is a great deal of pain, particularly shooting pains – before any red streaks indicate an infection, it can be prevented altogether by putting on a Hypericum dressing and giving Hypericum orally.

After a confinement, where there has been instrumental interference and damage to the coccyx, with coccygeal pain, or in a patient with a history of injury to the coccyx from a fall, Hypericum will relieve the pain. Hypericum is always indicated for the very sensitive areas plentifully supplied with nerves.

Lacerated fingers should be soaked in Hypericum lotion, followed by a Hypericum dressing, and Hypericum given in potency orally.

For a badly lacerated hand the same treatment should be given using Calendula. Not only does healing take place very rapidly but sepsis does not occur.

Arnica is most useful internally, but should not be used externally on any injury where the skin is broken as it may cause inflammation. Hamamelis will reduce bruising and is a safe external application in these conditions.

SEPSIS

For an inflamed area, very hot, puffy, tender, aggravated by hot applications which increase the swelling and congestion and increase the pain, with red streaks running up the lymphatics – as a routine, give Ledum. That is in the earlier stages. With a similar condition, but comfort from hot applications, the prescription is Hepar Sulph.

For a more virulent condition, with a rapid spread of sepsis and obvious early necrosis of tissue, there are three remedies to consider. Where there is very severe, stabbing pain accompanied by nervous excitement of the patient, the best prescription is Tarentula Cubensis. Where the infected area is dark purple, very hot, not so sensitive, throbbing rather than the stabbing pains of Tarentula Cub., the best prescription is Lachesis. In a typical Lachesis picture the whole part looks puffy and purple, purplish blue, swollen, with a tendency for the infection to spread very rapidly. Where there is a more advanced condition, with sloughing and great offensiveness, and oozing a quantity of black blood mixed up with pus, the best prescription is Crotalus Horridus.

For pustular eruptions after a septic infection the best prescription is Calc. Sulph.

The prescription for paronychia depends on the character of the pain, and on the response to heat and cold. The acute paronychia is acutely painful at the start and, during that extremely painful stage, if it is relieved by hot fomentations the best prescription is Hepar Sulph. If it is very much aggravated by hot applications, with swelling and tenderness, and stabbing, shooting pain, the best prescription is Apis. These two remedies in the majority of cases will abort an acute paronychia.

For a peri-anal inflammation, or inflammation round a faecal fistula, where there is any possibility of B. Coli contamination of an infection, give Rhus Tox. This seems to have an almost specific effect in these conditions.

(*Note*. Since the use of antibiotics, the very severe infections described by Dr Borland as needing Lachesis or Crotalus Horridus are rarely seen; also, if the *correct* homoeopathic remedy is given in the early stages of an infection the majority will clear up without the need for any more drastic measures. Ed.)

FAINTING

Where this is caused by the sight of blood, or by being in a crowded room, Ignatia is the remedy of choice. If the faintness is due to the heat and stuffiness of the room, and if standing is also intolerable – use Pulsatilla. Fainting due to shock will respond to Aconite.

INJURIES TO THE EYE – THE 'BLACK EYE'

If Arnica is given within a short time of the injury, there will be no 'black eye' – Arnica stops the effusion of blood. There may be some discolouration, but not the deep purplish swelling. If the patient is seen some time after the injury, with discolouration and swelling already present, there is a much better response from Ledum. With an injury to the eyeball itself Symphytum will relieve the pain more quickly and more definitely than Arnica.

EAR – ACUTE OTITIS MEDIA

In a case of acute otitis, with violent pain spreading to the mastoid region, there are three remedies to be considered. Aconite, Chamomilla and Capsicum.

Aconite
In a case where the symptoms have come on very suddenly, with a history of the patient having been out in a very cold north east wind, the patient is intensely restless, and the pains are very violent, usually burning in character. The patient is irritable, frightened, with a rising temperature and extreme sensitivity to touch. With that history, a few doses of Aconite will abort the acute inflammatory process.

Chamomilla
Another type of case is usually seen in children. There is not the same definite history of chill, although that may be present. The pain is even more intense and the patient is practically beside himself with pain, will not stay still, is as cross and as irritable as can be, with extreme tenderness, and gives the impression that nothing his parents do can satisfy him. After a few doses of Chamomilla the inflammatory process will rapidly subside.

Capsicum
In yet another type of case there is much more tenderness over the mastoid region, possibly a little swelling, with the ear beginning to look a little prominent on the affected side. The external ear is very red and there are very acute stabbing pains in the ear. Capsicum almost always clears up the condition which is a little relieved by hot applications, and where the patient is very sorry for himself, miserable, wanting to be comforted, probably a little tearful, but without the irritability of Chamomilla.

Pulsatilla, Mercurius, Hepar Sulph.
In addition to the above three remedies, bear in mind the possibility of a Pulsatilla child requiring a dose of Pulsatilla for the condition. And not infrequently one sees a case giving indications for Mercurius or Hepar Sulph.

ACUTE NEURALGIAS

For typical acute neuralgias, facial neuralgias or acute sciaticas, where relief is required as soon as possible, there are a number of remedies which may be used almost as a routine.

Consider acute facial neuralgia, acute trigeminal neuralgia; there are two outstanding drugs, Mag. Phos. and Colocynth. Spigelia is a third one which is sometimes indicated.

Magnesia Phosphorica

Take a case with very violent sharp stabbing pain, or twinges of pain running along the course of the nerve, coming on from any movement of the muscles of the face, very much aggravated by any draught of air, with extreme superficial tenderness over the affected nerve. If it is also much more comfortable from warmth – applied warmth – and much more comfortable from firm supporting pressure, such a case almost always responds to Mag. Phos. It does not really matter which branch of the nerve is involved, or which side, though it is more usually the right side than the left.

Incidentally, this does not apply to dental neuralgia. Dental cases are much more difficult and there are quite a number of remedies to choose from.

Colocynth

The same condition, with practically the same symptoms and the same modalities, affecting the *left* side, almost always responds to Colocynth.

The side usually determines the choice between Mag. Phos. and Colocynth, but occasionally either remedy may relieve neuralgias involving the opposite side.

Spigelia

In orbital neuralgia, with sharp stinging pains, or pain 'as if a red hot needle were stuck into it' – a very common description given by patients in these cases – the pains radiating out along the course of the nerve. In the majority of cases Spigelia will give relief.

One very useful point about Spigelia is that the patient sometimes says that, in spite of the burning character of the pain, there is a strange cold sensation in the affected area after it has been touched. This indicates Spigelia and no other remedy.

These three remedies are the most useful in a routine way for treating facial neuralgias.

As a rule, high potencies may be used. Sometimes, in these very painful conditions, a very high potency will aggravate the pain for 10 minutes or so, giving unnecessary suffering, so with acute pain a 30c potency is preferable.

POST-HERPETIC NEURALGIAS

Another group of conditions of the same type, the post-herpetic neural-gias, are sometimes very troublesome. In ordinary shingles neuralgia, the patient comes in with acute burning pain along the course of an intercostal nerve and gives a history that he has had a small crop of herpetic blisters, very often so slight that he paid little or no attention to it. Mag. Phos. will relieve if the same modalities are present as in the facial neuralgias under Mag. Phos. But much more commonly these post-herpetic cases respond to Ranunculus.

Ranunculus Bulbosus
The particular indications for this remedy are that the very sharp shooting pains extend along the course of the intercostal nerve, that the painful area is very sensitive to touch, and that the pain is induced or aggravated by any movement, particularly by turning. If the condition has been in existence for a little time, and the pains come on in wet weather and are certainly aggravated by it, the patient becomes extremely conscious of any weather change because it will start the neuralgia again. That type of case responds in almost every instance to Ranunculus.

Mezereum
There may be a few of these cases which have not responded to Ranun-culus. There is much the same distribution of pain, much the same modalities, but without the marked aggravation in wet weather. The affected area is sensitive to any cold draught, particularly sensitive to any bathing with cold water, and the pains are extremely troublesome at night, with a marked hyperaesthesia over the affected area. These cases will respond very well to Mezereum.

SCIATICA

Magnesia Phosphorica
There are helpful indications for certain remedies for another type of neuralgia – the sciaticas. In a case of sciatica, pure sciatica, with no indications except the ordinary classical symptoms of acute pain down the sciatic nerve, which is aggravated by any movement, is very sen-sitive to cold and more comfortable if kept quiet and warm, then the remedy indicated depends on which leg is involved. If it is a right-sided

sciatica, Mag. Phos. will relieve; if it is a left-sided sciatica use Colocynth. A large number of cases obtain almost immediate relief from either Mag. Phos. or Colocynth.

Kali Iodatum

In a few patients with sciatica, the pain increases the longer they keep still and they are compelled to move. There are two remedies which seem to relieve the majority of these cases. If the patient is a warm-blooded person, and if the sciatic pains tend to be more troublesome when warm – particularly warm in bed – and if better when moving about, Kali Iod. will give relief in the majority of instances.

Rhus Toxicodendron

If there are the same modalities with a patient who is sensitive to the cold, particularly if he is sensitive to damp as well as cold, and is more comfortable while moving about, Rhus Tox. will relieve a great many of the cases.

Gnaphalium

There are one or two curious indications which sometimes help in a sciatica with few other symptoms. For instance, in a sciatica which has marked numbness associated with the acute sciatic pain, there are two remedies which cover most cases. One is Gnaphalium, which has this sensation of numbness associated with the pain and tenderness over the sciatic nerve, more markedly than any other remedy in the Materia Medica.

Plumbum

The second remedy which has this numbness associated with pain and tenderness of the sciatic nerve is Plumbum. The main indication for Plumbum is extreme constipation in addition to the pain and numbness.

ACUTE COLIC

Fortunately, the indications in acute colics are usually definite.

Aconite

A first attack of colic, whether it be biliary or renal, is a very devastating experience for the patient and he is usually terrified. The pains are extreme. If, in addition, the patient feels very cold and very anxious, feels faint whenever he sits up or stands up and yet cannot bear the room being hot, Aconite will very often give relief within a very short time.

Aconite is seldom indicated in repeated attacks. The patients begin to realise that although the condition is exceedingly painful it is not fatal, so the mental anxiety necessary for the administration of Aconite is not present, and without that mental anxiety Aconite does not seem to act.

Belladonna

Belladonna will bring almost immediate relief in a patient having repeated attacks of either biliary or renal colic, each one quite short in duration, developing suddenly, stopping suddenly, associated with a feeling of fullness in the epigastrium. The attacks are induced, or very much aggravated, by any fluids. The patient has a hot, red face, dilated pupils and a full bounding pulse.

Chelidonium

A patient who has had some liver symptoms for some time, just vague discomfort, slight fullness in the right hypochondrium, a good deal of flatulence, intolerance of fats, and who is losing weight, becoming sallow and perhaps slightly jaundiced, may be helped by Chelidonium. He develops an acute colic, an acute hepatic colic, with violent pain going right through to the back, particularly just at the angle of the right scapula. This pain subsides and leaves a constant ache in the hepatic region. Then the attack recurs, and again subsides. If the pains are relieved by very hot applications or drinking very hot water, Chelidonium will relieve these attacks very rapidly.

An X-ray of a patient with these symptoms will often show a number of gallstones. An X-ray taken again after an attack for which Chelidonium has been prescribed may show that the gallstones have passed, if they are small.

One or two other remedies are also very helpful for colic.

Berberis

Berberis often gives relief in colic, whether it is a renal colic or a gallstone colic. The outstanding point about the Berberis colics, of whatever type, is the fact that from one centre the pain radiates in all directions. In a renal colic – and when Berberis is indicated, it is more commonly a left-sided one than a right – the colicky pain may start in the renal region, or along the course of the ureter. There is one centre of acute pain and from that centre the pain radiates in all directions. In a hepatic colic the centre of acute intensity is the gallbladder, and from there the pain radiates in all directions, going through to the back, into the chest and into the abdomen.

In addition, with a renal colic there is an acute urging to urinate, and a good deal of pain on urination. A biliary colic is usually accompanied by a very marked aggravation from any movement. This is present to a slight extent in the renal colics, but less markedly. In both, the patient is very distressed and has a pale, earthy-looking complexion. The pallor is more marked in the renal cases, and there may be jaundice where there has been a previous gallstone colic.

No other remedy has the extent of radiation of the pain that is in Berberis.

With renal colic the urine usually contains a quantity of greyish white deposit which may be pus, and a quantity of amorphous material, usually phosphates, sometimes urates. It is not blood-stained. It is a very dirty-looking urine, but surprisingly inoffensive.

Magnesia Phosphorica

Two remedies frequently indicated for colics of any kind are Colocynth and Mag. Phos., whether the colic is uterine or intestinal, biliary or renal. The difficulty about these remedies is that they are almost identical. Always in their colics the pain is very extreme, and the patients are doubled up with it. In both cases the pains are relieved by external pressure, and in both cases the pains are relieved by heat. In Mag. Phos. there is rather more relief from rubbing than in Colocynth; Colocynth prefers steady, hard pressure. Their colics are intermittent. The patients get spasms of pain, which come to a climax and then subside.

There are one or two distinguishing points which help in making the choice. In Colocynth the patient is intensely irritable and impatient, wants immediate relief, and is liable to be violently angry if the relief is not forthcoming. In Mag. Phos. there is not the same degree of irritability, and the patient is distraught because of the intensity of the pain rather than being violently angry.

Another point that sometimes helps is that Colocynth tends to have a slightly coated tongue, particularly if it is the digestive tract that is upset, whereas Mag. Phos. usually has a clean tongue.

Both of these remedies have a marked aggravation from cold, a little more marked in Mag. Phos. than in Colocynth. For instance, Mag.

Phos. is exceedingly sensitive to a draught; Colocynth, though it likes hot applications, is not so extremely sensitive to cold air in its neighbourhood.

Another distinguishing point between the two is that in Colocynth there is a tendency to giddiness, particuarly on turning – especially on turning to the left – but this is not present in Mag. Phos.

Where there is a report that the colic – more commonly uterine than intestinal colic – has followed on an attack of anger, it is almost certainly Colocynth that will be required, and not Mag. Phos.

If the colic is the result of over-indulgence in cheese, Colocynth is indicated. If, on the other hand, the colic is the result of exposure to cold, either a dysmenorrhoea or an abdominal colic, it is much more likely to be Mag. Phos.

These are two of the most useful remedies in the Materia Medica for colics, and it is surprising how much relief can be obtained from their administration.

Dioscorea
This is another remedy which is very useful as a contrast to Mag. Phos. and Colocynth, and which has very much the same sort of pain – a very violent, spasmodic colic coming on suddenly, rising up to a head, then subsiding. It has the same relief from applied heat, and is sometimes more comfortable for firm pressure. But in contra-distinction to the other two remedies, instead of the patient's being doubled up with pain, they are hyper-extended; they will bend back as far as possible. Dioscorea is the only remedy which has that violent abdominal colic and gets relief from extreme extension.

Ipecacuanha
Ipecac. is one other remedy to consider for colic, and the indications for it are very clear and definite.

The character of the pain described in Ipecac. is much more cutting than the acute spasmodic pain occurring in most of the other colic drugs. But the outstanding feature is the feeling of intense nausea which develops with each spasm of pain, yet, in spite of the nausea, the patient has a clean tongue. Quite a number of adolescent girls have violent dysmenorrhoea. Characteristically they are rather warm-blooded people, and with the spasms of pain – they very often describe it as cutting pain in the lower abdomen – they become hot and perspiring, with acute nausea. They cannot stand up and any movement makes them worse. They have a perfectly clean tongue and a normal temperature. Very often Ipecac. will stop the attack as well as the tendency to dysmenorrhoea. It is one of the very useful remedies for colic, and tends to be overlooked.

Occasionally a case of renal colic, associated with the same intense nausea, will respond to Ipecac. but that is unusual. The indications for it are more commonly found in uterine cases.

Lycopodium, Opium and Raphanus

These are three remedies where the colic is accompanied by violent abdominal flatulence. It is always an intestinal colic in which they are indicated. It may be associated with a gallbladder disturbance – if so, it is much more likely to be Lycopodium than either of the other two. In all three there is a tendency for the flatulence to be held in various pockets in the intestines, giving irregular areas of distension. All three are likely to be indicated in post-operative abdominal distensions, or semi-paralytic conditions of the bowel. In a paralytic ileus following abdominal resection there are more likely to be indications for Raphanus and Opium than for Lycopodium; but if the paralytic condition is in the region of the caecum the indications are probably for Lycopodium rather than for the other two.

Lycopodium

That is the general distinguishing point. Then there are one or two extra points which help. For instance, in Lycopodium the colicky pain is likely to start on the right side of the abdomen, towards the right iliac fossa, and spread over to the left side, whereas in the other two it remains more or less localised in one definite area.

In Lycopodium there is liable to be a late afternoon period of extreme distress, the 4–8 p.m. period of aggravation of Lycopodium.

There is likely to be more rumbling and gurgling in the abdomen in Lycopodium, and more tendency to eructation, whereas in the other two the patient does not seem able to get the same relief. Where there is eructation the patients usually complain of a very sour taste in Lycopodium.

In Lycopodium, the patient is rather emaciated, with a sallow, pale complexion.

Opium

There are one or two points that lead to Opium instead of the other two. In Opium, there is apt to be a definite area of distension, and the patient will say that he gets a feeling as if everything simply churned up to one point and could not get past it. It is as if the intestinal contents were trying to squeeze past some obstructing band, or as if something were being forced through a very narrow opening.

Another point of selection is that with these attacks of colic the Opium patient tends to become very flushed, very hot, feels the bed distressingly hot and wants to push the blankets off. After the spasm has subsided he tends to become very pale and limp, and often stuporous.

The area of distension in Opium is likely to be in the centre of the abdomen rather than in the right iliac fossa, and it is one of the most commonly indicated drugs in a paralytic ileus.

Another point that sometimes indicates Opium is that when the pains are developing and coming up to a head the Opium patients become hypersensitive to noise.

Raphanus

The Raphanus type of post-operative colic is slightly different. Instead of getting the right side of the abdomen distended as in Lycopodium, or the swelling up in the middle as in Opium, in Raphanus there are pockets of wind. A small area comes up in one place, gets quite hard and then subsides, and a fresh small area does exactly the same. These pockets of wind may be in any part of the abdomen. In the acute attacks of pain the patients tend to get a little flushed, but not so hot as the Opium patients, and they do not have the tendency to eructation that is associated with Lycopodium. They do not seem to be able to get rid of their wind at all, either upwards or downwards. It is the small isolated pockets of wind coming up in irregular areas throughout the abdomen that give the indications for Raphanus.

Podophyllum

There are, of course, endless other remedies which have colic, but these are the ones that are most useful in emergencies. Podophyllum is one other which is useful to know, and it is mainly useful in biliary colics. It is also useful in intestinal colics associated with acute diarrhoea.

Where Podophyllum is indicated in biliary colic, there is always infection of the gallbladder. One of the first things indicating Podophyllum is that the temperature reaches a peak in the morning and not in the evening.

In addition, Podophyllum patients are always very miserable and depressed. They are disgusted with life. Podophyllum patients with biliary colic are always jaundiced.

In the majority of cases, the pain is not localised in the gallbladder area, but is more in the epigastrium, and tends to spread across from the middle of the epigastrium towards the liver region. The pains are described as twisting in character, and are very much aggravated by taking any food.

In Podophyllum, the subsidence of acute pain leaves a feeling of soreness in the liver region. Podophyllum patients lie stroking the liver area, which gives them a great sense of comfort.

Chapter 2

Headaches

Apis

Apis is indicated for headaches which occur as a result of emotional stress, excitement, or the checking of some discharge; for instance, catarrh checked suddenly by a potent spray, or a menstrual period checked by sudden shock or cold. The patients say that the headache starts in the morning as a violent, stabbing pain running through the head, associated with a general congestion throughout the whole head. They are flushed, with facial congestion and usually slight swelling. There is often some conjunctival congestion, the eyes are unduly bright and the pupils are dilated. They are excited and have an intense aggravation from heat. They get violent shooting pains through the head, from side to side, and aggravated by movement. These headaches are usually relieved by pressure and cold applications, yet the whole scalp becomes tender to touch due to the severe pain. The skin, particularly of the forehead, is moist. In addition, these patients have the usual Apis general nervous excitement, irritability and dislike of being disturbed or interfered with.

Belladonna

At first sight the headaches are very similar to the Apis headaches. They come on under the same circumstances, but there are other conditions which also cause them. For instance, any heat, particularly of the sun; and under the opposite conditions, exposure to cold. Sensitive people may get a headache from washing the hair and not drying it properly before going out, or after a haircut. The headaches are also caused by emotional shock or fright.

The appearance is not unlike that of Apis. The patients have a hot head and are very flushed, but it is a much brighter flush than in Apis, and there is not the same degree of puffiness of the face as in Apis, or the same degree of conjunctival congestion. There is intense photophobia and, with the headaches, they are incredibly sensitive to any motion, jar or mis-step. With the pain there is a general pulsation; it may be temporal or it may be all over the head. On stooping, it is as if the whole head were throbbing. Another thing that distinguishes Belladonna from Apis, although there is such intense heat of the head, is that the patients themselves are chilly and like to be covered up warmly. They do not have the Apis desire for cold applications on the head, and the head is not damp but very definitely dry. In spite of the aggravation from motion, they do not want to lie down. They like to be propped up, often with their heads well back, because there is a degree of tension in the posterior cervical mucles, and bending the head back gives relief.

The headache comes on at 4 or 5 o'clock in the afternoon and persists right through the night. The patients are much worse from using the eyes, particularly from turning the eyes or attempting to follow any movement. Very often they not only complain of pulsation in the head but the pulse is visible beating in the temple. The headache is relieved by firm pressure. There may be a marked degree of mental excitement – it is always present in children, and children suffering from exposure to the sun are almost certain to become delirious during the night.

Bryonia

Bryonia gives a different picture altogether. The headaches usually come on during the night, patients waken with a headache, but are not acutely conscious of it until they get up and begin moving about. They complain of a dull aching pain in the frontal region, as if deep in the front part of the brain, and this aching, heavy pain tends to spread right through the head into the occiput. The pain comes on when getting up in the morning, and persists throughout the whole day. A Bryonia headache may develop during the day, but as the result of some definite exciting cause. The commonest time is during the night. Generally, the patient has been rather over-doing it the day before, and has been up late, possibly drinking too much or eating too much – more likely over-eating than drinking – and in the morning has a typical Bryonia headache. Sometimes a typical Sepia comes up to town for a day's shopping, enjoys a visit to a theatre, and then will often develop a Bryonia headache before the day is out. Another thing which will cause a Sepia patient to develop a Bryonia headache is ironing; she gets hot, tired and headachey, and if given Bryonia the headache will be relieved very rapidly.

With the aching pain in the head there is a feeling of heaviness and heat, accompanied by a general feeling of chilliness and particularly cold hands and feet. This is unlike ordinary Bryonia patients, who are generally worse from heat.

During the headaches the eyes are heavy, and any use of them is very painful. If the headache is really severe, the head is very tender. Even the hair is sensitive to touch, but in spite of this the headache is relieved by firm pressure.

Like all the other Bryonia symptoms the headaches are very much worse from motion, or jarring. The patients are irritable and, with a headache, cannot bear talking to people; the effort of speaking makes the headache so much worse. If the headache is associated with any dietetic indiscretion, the bowels frequently fail to act on the morning of the headache. In other words, the old custom of taking an aperient after an unwise and excessive dinner was not at all a bad idea. On stooping, the patients experience a sensation as if the whole head would burst. Lying still and putting cold applications on the forehead will give relief.

China Sulphuricum

A China Sulph. headache is always associated with a digestive upset. The typical patients are the rather delicate, chronic dyspeptics. Sometimes people of this type who have had a rather strenuous week or two, and become exhausted, will develop a violent headache. It starts in the back of the neck, spreads over the head and settles in the forehead, and they complain of a violent aching pain. One definite diagnostic point is the appearance of the patients, who give the impression that they are just about to vomit. They are pale, clammy, sweaty, look unwell, and have the peculiar greyish-green colour that people get prior to vomiting. Associated with the headaches, such patients get intense, troublesome flatulence, and are constantly bringing up small amounts of slightly sour-tasting gas. They develop an artificial hunger, feeling hungry all the time, but food does not relieve them. Lycopodium patients have the same sensation, but their headache is relieved by food and the flatulence is relieved by eructation, while in China Sulph. patients it is not so. China Sulph. patients get marked relief from pressing the head against something cold, although in general they are definitely chilly. They want to keep the head as still as possible, because the pain is very much aggravated by turning the head or using the eyes; it is also very much aggravated by moving about in the open air.

Cocculus

There are two circumstances in which indications for Cocculus are present. First, the patients develop a very typical headache after a long journey. Second, the headache is one which starts after a period of strain. For instance, a mother who has been looking after a sick child and has had no sleep for a couple of nights, or a businessman who has been through a crisis, or round about examination time in people who are studying hard and getting too little sleep.

Cocculus people will often say that they feel dead tired, exhausted, and rather giddy. They have a peculiar sensation of the head being empty and numb, followed immediately by a sensation as if it would burst with pain, as if the skull were opening and shutting. The pain is very severe, particularly at the back of the head, and the intense pain is almost always accompanied by nausea and may go on to actual vomiting. It is aggravated by sleep; after having a little sleep they always waken with the headache much worse. It is greatly aggravated by any stimulant such as coffee, alcohol and especially tobacco. During the headaches they develop intolerance for hot rooms, and want cold air. When the pain is severe in the occiput, the back of the head becomes extremely tender and they cannot bear to lie down. If the headache has continued for some time, particularly the occipital type, it extends down the back of the neck and the patient feels as if a tight cord were pulling the head back and down the spine. The pain is aggravated by motion, particularly any sudden motion, also by mental effort, and by any use of the eyes.

Gelsemium

It is a little difficult to know whether to place Gelsemium among the acute or the chronic remedies, as it has acute headaches but also recurring periodical headaches.

In the acute type, the headache comes on in association with some other disturbance, such as an acute cold, or after exposure to cold, with signs of acute coryza. There is always some degree of disturbance of sight; it may be simply a slight haziness of vision, it may be diplopia, it may be partial blindness, or it may be a flickering before the eyes.

With the headaches the patients have a very heavy, sleepy, drowsy appearance, and they always have some degree of heaviness of the eyelids, with difficulty in keeping the eyes open. They say they feel heavy and sleepy with the pain. Usually the headaches start during the forenoon and subside towards evening. If the patients lie down, as a rule the headache becomes worse at first, but if they continue lying it gradually subsides. The pain is usually a boring pain, often situated in the frontal region, most often over the right eye, and associated with a sensation of coldness at the back of the head. When the headache is very severe it produces a sensation of faintness. If the patients can get a good sleep this normally clears the headache; or, at least, it eases the pain. It is made much worse by motion and there is always some degree of photophobia. As the pain begins to ease there is an increase in the amount of urine excreted – this is a strong indication for prescribing Gelsemium. Vomiting will also practically always relieve the headache.

Glonoinum
Glonoinum, the next of these remedies, has a very definite symptom picture, the typical picture of sunstroke or heat stroke.

The first impression is that it is very like Belladonna but much more severe. There is a very marked degree of congestion, but the patient has a rather duskier colour. Belladonna patients are bright red, whereas Glonoinum patients are purple. There is rather more puffiness of the face in Glonoinum than in Belladonna. The skin is moist in Glonoinum and there is not the dry heat of Belladonna.

The complaint of the patient is always that the head feels as if it is going to burst, the whole head feels full, and the skull feels as if it were actually swelling. Accompanying the headaches there is usually some degree of eye disturbance. There are flashes of light before the eyes, or everything seen is red, or there may be temporary loss of sight. The pains in the head are very much aggravated by any motion or jarring or by any physical exertion. These all make the head throb and feel as if it would burst. There is amelioration from ice-cold applications and from keeping quite still. In typical cases of sunstroke, the patients sit with their elbows on their knees and the head gripped in their hands. They will answer if spoken to but will not look up, as they keep their head as still as possible.

Occasionally, after exposure to the sun, a headache of that type occurs as a hemicrania instead of the usual generalised headache. There may then be a peculiar symptom – a flushing of one side of the face with dilatation of the vessels on that side, and comparatively little on the other side. Sometimes these patients give a history of having had sunstroke in the tropics, and they are now liable to get the same type of headache in summer in more temperate climates, though not so severely. The headaches start at sunrise, are worst at mid-day, and tend to go with sunset. As a rule, Glonoinum will altogether cure the headache in a patient with this history of sunstroke and this time modality.

Melilotus
Occasionally a patient gives all the symptoms of Glonoinum, but does not respond to it at all. Melilotus has almost the same symptoms as Glonoinum, except that there is a little more excitement in Glonoinum, and a little more dullness, sleepiness and duskiness in Melilotus. They are rather more sensitive to thundery weather than Glonoinum, which has no definite thunder aggravation at all. Another point is that Melilotus and Glonoinum patients describe their discomfort slightly differently. In Glonoinum the whole head feels as if it is going to burst, it is so full. In Melilotus it feels as if a vessel would burst inside the head. So, if headache of this type does not respond to Glonoinum, give Melilotus. The most useful potency for the patient to carry with him is 30c – otherwise the 200c may be given.

Iris
It is not easy to decide whether to include Iris with the acute remedies or not. The headaches are as acute as any, but they also tend to be recurrent. The patients give a history of getting over-tired, and they tend to get a day or two when they are particularly tired, heavy and sleepy before the headache. Then they wake up at 2 or 3 a.m. and know that the headache is coming on. It is always preceded by disturbance of vision, hemianopia, fortification spectra or something similar. The attack usually develops – and this is a differentiating point from a number of other remedies – with the eye disturbances, vomiting and nausea, before the headache actually begins. The type of vomit is very suggestive. It is similar to Kali Bich. – white, tenacious, stringy fluid, often quite tasteless. After some hours the patient develops a violent headache, with a feeling of heat and fullness in the head, and an absolutely stupefying, stunning sort of pain. This pain is usually worse on the right side, but so severe that it involves practically the whole head. It is worse on keeping still, and better by moving about gently. It is slightly relieved by a draught of cool air, though it is aggravated by cold air; cool air is definitely comforting. The patient is liable to get a peculiar boring pain just in the middle of the epigastrium if the vomiting has gone on for more than two or three hours. It is in the pancreatic region, and it is interesting that Iris patients are sensitive to sugar. If they are over-tired they tend to get a sugar hunger. Then they are apt to indulge in too many sweets, and the result is that they develop a typical Iris headache. This is quite a usual history, and is easy to link up with the pancreatic pain.

Another point about the Iris headache is that each attack develops at exactly the same hour of the twenty-four hours.

The indications for Iris are always found in a very definite type of patient. They are artistic, thin, delicate and nervous,and they are usually very charming people to meet.

Lachesis

Lachesis headaches occur most frequently during the menopause. In addition they occur from exposure to heat, sun, fright, shock or grief.

Patients usually complain of a sensation of a rush of blood to the head. This is followed by a pressing, burning pain, most commonly in the vertex, with a sensation of a weight on the head, or a feeling that the head is expanding because it is too full. Another sensation is an acute pulsation, particularly in the temples. Associated with their headaches they get a flushed face, even a dusky appearance, accompanied by emotional excitement.

With these headaches patients are very sensitive to motion, any movement increases the feeling of fullness, and the pain is aggravated by pressure. The patient likes to sit propped up, as any stooping or lying down increases the congestion and increases the pain. Also, emotional excitement of any kind increases the congestion and the headache, and brings on the pain. Any stimulant may precipitate a bad headache, and Lachesis patients are peculiarly sensitive to them when a headache threatens.

The headache is aggravated by sleep. This is increased during the menopause, when a slight headache will become a blinding one after sleep. This is greater the longer the sleep – after a doze it is not quite so severe.

These patients often develop flooding during the menopause, and the flow always ameliorates the headache very quickly. Occasionally with the violent headaches and congestion they get shortness of breath, and the usual Lachesis sense of constriction, but this is by no means constant.

Magnesia Phosphorica and Silica

Mag. Phos. has two definite types of headache. One is a superficial, neuralgic headache, with neuralgic pains shooting over the head along the course of the superficial nerves of the head. The other is a very severe deep-seated headache starting at the back of the head, spreading through it and settling over the right eye. This Mag. Phos. headache can be confused with Silica, in which the pain also tends to develop in the back of the neck, spreads right over the head, and settles over the right eye, and in which there is also marked aggravation from cold. In Silica, however, there is no relief from pressure – in fact, wearing a tight hat is often enough to bring on a Silica headache. The types of patient will also probably be different. Silica patients tend to be fine skinned, fine haired and small boned. Mag. Phos. patients tend to have a fairly well developed bony framework, they are rather emaciated and somewhat sallow and greyish complexioned, and have dark rings under the eyes.

The two types of Mag. Phos. headaches come on under different circumstances. The acute neuralgic ones come on from cold and exposure to cold winds, though sometimes also after extreme nervous strain with the history of exposure to cold. The deep-seated headache always occurs in exhausted patients in poor health, and these tend to be recurring. These recurring headaches tend to be worse from 9 to 11 o'clock in the morning and from 4 to 8 o'clock in the evening. With the neuralgic type the patients are usually pale, but with the chronic type of headache the patients tend to be rather flushed. They develop marked sensitiveness to touch, whether it is a neuralgic or a deep-seated headache, and, although they develop this superficial hyper-aesthesia, the headache is definitely relieved by firm pressure. They are extremely sensitive to cold, no matter which type of headache they have. They are also better from warm applications, so much so that they have a dread of uncovering the head for fear of any cold air blowing on it.

Students are particularly liable to develop Mag. Phos. headaches. There are two types of students' headaches, the commonest being the one that tends to develop over the forehead just above the eyes, associated with intense eye weariness. The other develops in the back of the head and spreads right through it to settle over the right eye. This is the one that is so difficult to distinguish from Silica.

Nux Vomica

The Nux Vomica headache is the typical 'morning after' headache due to alcoholic excess, although it occurs from over-eating as well as over-drinking. The patients complain of a general fullness in the head with a feeling of congestion and pressure. The pressure is usually on the upper part of the head, often in the higher frontal region. The headache is always associated with constipation, but is not necessarily accompanied by vomiting. One useful point, which distinguishes it from the Bryonia headache, is that the Nux Vomica headache is present on waking in the morning, whereas the Bryonia headache does not come on until the patients begin moving about.

Nux Vomica patients are usually very chilly during their headaches and always bad tempered. They do not like to be spoken to or disturbed, and they hate to move. If they have to go and work, the headache is very much aggravated by any mental concentration. They usually have a feeling of nausea and if they force themselves to take food it aggravates their headache. This is a useful distinguishing point from Lycopodium, when the headache is eased by taking a little food. If Nux Vomica patients have to go out in the morning into the cold air they immediately get an increase of the frontal headache. Any noise greatly aggravates the headache and they are very irritable. The headaches are better from lying down, and aggravated by taking any stimulant, such as wine or coffee.

One clinical point – most of these patients tend to be thin and dark. With the same history in a fair patient and little response to Nux Vomica, consider Lobelia. Nux Vomica is much more likely to be useful in thin, irritable, dyspeptic, dark patients.

Sanguinaria and Gelsemium
The remedy most likely to be confused with Sanguinaria is Gelsemium. The actual pain in Sanguinaria is rather more intense than in Gelsemium. Instead of the general dusky, heavy, sleepy appearance of Gelsemium, there is more likely to be a generalised flush of the cheeks in Sanguinaria. Again, in Gelsemium the patients usually feel chilly down their backs, whereas in Sanguinaria they are likely to get a distressing, uncomfortable, burning heat of the palms of the hands and soles of the feet.

The patients complain that the whole head feels as if it were full of blood and as if it would burst, or they have a feeling of fullness at the back of the eyes, as if they were being pushed forward. This is similar to the symptoms in Bryonia, but in Bryonia the sensation is rather different. It is a sensation of fullness in the forehead with a feeling of weight settling right down on top of the eyes, making the lids feel heavy. As a rule, the pain of a Sanguinaria headache starts in the occipital region and spreads over the whole head. It tends to be rather more intense on the right side. With violent headaches there is not infrequently tenderness of the face and neuralgic pain involving the whole of the upper jaw. The headaches come on in the morning and last until evening, and a good night's sleep generally clears them. The patients are more comfortable keeping as quiet as possible in a dark room. Another distinguishing point between Sanguinaria and Gelsemium is that there is no definite urinary increase at the end of the headache in Sanguinaria, whereas in Gelsemium the patient knows that the pain is about to subside because the urinary output is increased.

There often tends to be a certain amount of periodicity in these headaches, usually about a seven-day recurrence.

Spigelia

Spigelia is only called for in cases of typical nervous headaches. They usually start at the back of the head, spread up over it, and settle over the left eye or in the left temple. The pain is pulsating, throbbing, and stabbing. Associated with the headaches, the patients get some degree of pain in the eyes, often more marked in the left. It is described as a sensation as if the eye was too big for its socket. This is a distinguishing point from Sanguinaria, in which there is a feeling of the eye being pushed out. The patients complain of stabs of pain radiating back through the head, coming on in the morning, usually about mid-day, and tending to decrease towards evening. The pain is aggravated by using the eyes for any purpose at all, as well as by motion in general, particularly jarring, sudden motion. The head is sensitive to touch and the pain is increased by noise. The most comfortable position is lying on the right side – not the painful side – and keeping the head and shoulders supported with pillows. These headaches usually come on after some emotional upset.

Theridion

Theridion headaches usually start about puberty, though they also occur round about the menopause. There are one or two outstanding features about them. The pain is a pressing one just at the back of the eyes, and from there it spreads backwards through the head. Associated with it the patients have a definite and intense giddiness which is particularly marked when they close the eyes, whatever their position. The giddiness is accompanied by nausea. With frontal headaches, patients usually want to keep their eyes closed – with Theridion patients it is exactly the opposite.

These patients are abnormally sensitive to noise, which causes throbbing pain in the head, shooting to the face and down the spine. With most of their headaches they develop hyper-sensitivity all down the spine to touch and jarring. The headaches are relieved by lying down and keeping quiet. This is the patients' most comfortable position.

When considering Theridion, the main points are giddiness, nausea, pain on closing the eyes, hyper-sensitivity to noise, and the headache occurring either at the start or cessation of menstruation.

Two other remedies should be considered. They are very difficult to distinguish and they come on in the same type of people and under the same circumstances – Aconite and Ignatia.

Aconite

With either of these remedies the patients are liable to headaches as a result of definite emotional crisis, or fear, or excitement. These are the commonest causes, but in Aconite, in addition, headaches may occur from exposure to either heat or cold. There the similarity ends.

During their headaches, Aconite patients always suffer from extremely violent pain, so severe that it makes them almost delirious. A typical instance of this is an Aconite sunstroke, with sudden onset of very violent, agonising pain, intense fear, and marked excitement. The patients complain of burning, throbbing, tearing pains in the head and a feeling of congestion as if the brain was too big for the skull and would burst out through the front of the head. They get marked congestion of the whole head and face. The headache is aggravated by light, noise, heat or any motion. During their headaches they get the usual Aconite restlessness, fear and anxiety, and yet any movement will increase the pain in their head. The indications for Aconite are the history of exposure, acute emotional crisis and fright, also the intense emotional excitement of the patient and the intense fear; it is a most violent condition.

Ignatia

In Ignatia, on the other hand, the indications are the general Ignatia make-up of the patient, with the history of emotional crisis as the result of disappointment or grief, though occasionally the cause of the headache will be a fright. They do not suffer from headaches which are due to exposure, and they are not liable to sun headaches, though a headache may develop during the course of a cold.

The pain is nothing like so violent as in Aconite. Ignatia patients are always the sensitive, slightly hysterical type. Anyone of that type who has suffered a severe disappointment and spent the day weeping is almost certain to need Ignatia to relieve a headache before night. With their headaches they often have an artificial hunger, a feeling of emptiness in the stomach. For a time their headaches are rather better from taking food; but it is only for a very short time and quite soon after eating the headache returns with increased severity.

Usually the headaches are most troublesome in the forehead, and patients complain of a general fullness and congestion in the forehead.

If they are disturbed at all, or have to move or talk, they get spasmodic pains over a small area of the head. In that condition they get relief from lying on the painful side. They develop a certain amount of nausea, and during the headache they become sensitive to coffee, tobacco or alcohol. They are better from keeping absolutely quiet. The headache is ameliorated by pressure, and the patients are very sensitive to noise or light, and particularly to looking up. Any increase of emotional disturbance will greatly aggravate the headache, also any excitement or talking, and particularly contradiction.

The different types of headaches tend to recur more at one season of the year than another. For instance, Bryonia headaches are much more frequently met with in winter. Of course, during a period of financial crisis or at examination times, the nerve strain headaches are common. After dietary indiscretions Nux Vomica will probably be indicated.

Chapter 3

Sore Throats

Rhus Toxicodendron and Arnica

In a patient with an uncomfortable sore throat after tonsillectomy, with stiffness of the muscles of the throat in the morning, Rhus Tox. is the remedy to prescribe. If after the operation there is complete inability to swallow, also pain of head and neck, Arnica is indicated; it eases the pain and the inflammation decreases. If the patient has stiffness and swelling in the throat on waking, and a quantity of sticky mucus in the throat, with pain on first swallowing, becoming easier if persisted in, again Rhus Tox. is indicated. With these two remedies, Arnica and Rhus Tox., the patient will improve very quickly. Rhus Tox. is not indicated the first day – it is usually Arnica. On the second day Rhus Tox. may be needed. There is a tendency to prescribe routinely – then the odd case occurs and the usual remedies are no use at all. One case in ten requires a different remedy, and the majority of the tenth cases need one of the Mercurius salts. These patients have a very inflamed throat with exudate on the surface and a pale tongue. They feel alternately hot and cold and are sweating slightly, with a raised temperature. They are much worse from any hot fluid, and cold drinks ease them. The breath is offensive. The condition should improve rapidly if Merc. Sol. is prescribed.

If there is slight bleeding from the throat, it is better to give Merc. Cyanide rather than Merc. Sol. These remedies will deal with almost all post-tonsillectomy cases.

(*Note.* Mercurius Solubilis and Mercurius Vivus are interchangeable, and are abbreviated as Merc. Ed.)

Aurum Muriaticum

This may be required in patients with a history of a cold and persistent sore throat. There is congestion, enlargement of the tonsils, redness of the fauces, and possibly ulcers in the mouth or throat, or a history of ulceration during the acute stage of the cold. There is a quantity of sticky mucus in the throat, which is very difficult for the patients to clear away. They cannot get the throat quite free, and the effort to clear it is painful. There is a sensation of heat round the tonsils and in the upper part of the pharynx, and the throat is much more comfortable after taking food. There may be enlargement of the glands in the neck. The patients are rather flabby and pale, and the tongue is swollen. They are chilly and have rheumatic pains, mainly a feeling of stiffness, particularly at the back of the knees, as if the hamstrings were a bit short, or they have stiffness in the muscles of the shoulders, elbows and particularly the hands. There is a tendency to sweat on their extremities, particularly their feet. Three or four doses of Aurum Mur. should clear the symptoms.

Baryta Muriaticum

The patients give a history of frequent colds which always affect the throat. On examination the patient is flushed, the lips are rather dry and there is a slightly coated tongue, white and rather greasy, and a heavy breath rather than an offensive one. The throat is congested, and the tonsils are enlarged and somewhat dusky in colour. As a rule there is a tendency for the right side to be more involved than the left. Associated with this enlargement of the tonsils and the fact that there is a recurring sore throat, there is a tendency to obvious enlargement of the veins of the posterior pharyngeal wall. It is covered with a good deal of mucus and secretion. The patients complain of difficulty in swallowing, as if there was a plum in the throat. Usually it is not very painful, but sometimes there is pain shooting up into the ear. That pain is relieved by a sip of cold water. There is enlargement of glands under the angle of the jaw. The patients usually say that the symptoms start in the evenings and that they have had a very uncomfortable night — they were hot and damp during the night and had very little sleep. They are often more comfortable in the morning and often have quite a good appetite in spite of the sore throat. These patients will respond to Baryta Mur. They may run a temperature up to 38·5°C.

Calcarea Sulphurica

In the very rare event of a quinsy, the drug most commonly indicated after it has been incised is Calc. Sulph. Instead of the white-coated tongue, the tongue tends to become yellow at its base. The patient's temperature is higher than when Baryta Mur. is indicated. He perspires more freely and is more flushed in appearance, possibly a little more dusky. The throat is obviously more swollen, more oedematous and darker red than the typical Baryta Mur., and the choking sensation is definitely worse – it is a real choking instead of just the plum sensation of Baryta Mur. The glands of the neck become more enlarged and the patients tend to be acutely thirsty. Calc. Sulph. patients want air, and are uncomfortably hot, whereas Baryta Mur. are hot in the night, but not uncomfortably hot. The extremities are hot, more especially the feet, and patients often complain of itching of the hands and feet.

Dulcamara

This is another remedy which may be difficult to identify, but which is quite frequently indicated. The typical history is of the patient having been chilled and within a short time developing an uncomfortable, painful throat, associated with a good deal of hoarseness. On examination, the throat is red, dark red in colour, rather shiny and dry, with profuse post-natal catarrh. The patients complain of a yellow, slimy discharge, particularly in the mornings. The tongue is dry and rough and the patients develop herpetic spots about the lips. There is a tendency for patches of urticaria to occur, with itching aggravated from heat and better from cold, and worse from scratching. Unlike the ordinary tingling of urticaria, it begins to burn if it has been scratched. There are general aching pains and general heat of the head and body, with coldness of the extremities. With these symptoms the patients should respond to Dulcamara.

Guiacum

This is very useful in acute attacks of tonsillitis which have developed suddenly, with painful glands of the neck. The pain in the neck and in the tonsils is very much more comfortable from external pressure, and the patients will sit up in bed holding the neck. The temperature is always high. The tongue is always furred. As a rule the patients are obviously toxic – the face is puffy and the colour ashen. They tend to have dilated pupils, which is suggestive of this remedy. They all have joint pains and they may get a little swelling, particularly about the fingers, and are more uncomfortable when hot, so they keep their hands outside the bedclothes. Rather than acute pain in the throat they complain of intense heat. They complain of headache, with a very severe, intense pain at the nape of the neck. There is a night aggravation from about 6 o'clock in the evening till about 4 o'clock in the morning. These symptoms will clear with Guiacum.

Aethusa

This remedy is required for the more chronic sore throat, the chronic pharyngitis. The patients complain of a hot uncomfortable throat, of which they are very conscious all the time. The condition never quite clears, and every now and then the symptoms become worse, and when troublesome there is always increased catarrh, particularly post-nasal. It occurs most commonly in patients who have had their tonsils removed in childhood, so they have no definite tonsillitis. On examination of the throat there is an atrophic condition of the mucous membrane, which is covered with streaks of white or yellowish mucus, and possibly the pharyngeal wall is mapped by dilated, often tortuous veins. The patients will remark that on attempting to clear this rather adherent mucus they very often get a little bleeding from the back of the throat. They are sensitive to cold, damp air, which makes the throat much worse, and may also have a nondescript flatulent dyspepsia. They may have quite a high colour, with a tendency to rather dilated veins on the cheeks and a tendency to swelling of the extremities. In this condition the remedy most likely to help is Aethusa.

Mercurius

In Mercurius cases there is a more septic type of throat than in simple tonsillitis. The patient's mouth tends to be dirty, the tongue heavily coated with the impression of being swollen, and it may show the imprints of the teeth on the sides. The outstanding indication is its offensiveness.

Mercurius throats are extremely painful. The patients often complain of the throat feeling very dry in spite of the fact that there is always very marked salivation. Patients will often say that the saliva trickles out of the mouth at night when they are asleep, although the throat feels hot and dry.

They complain of the throat feeling very full. It is accompanied by stiffness in the neck, and the tonsillar and cervical glands are enlarged. Any effort to swallow is extremely painful. On examination, the throat is swollen and dusky red, with a quantity of dirty mucus stretching over the tonsils.

At a slightly later stage, small patches of darker red appear over the generally congested tonsils. These Mercurius throats may go on to an acute quinsy, with isolated dusky spots tending to coalesce, forming a bulging area – a typical quinsy throat.

Mercurius patients always perspire. They feel hot, and yet when uncovered they promptly become chilly and cover up again. There may be small superficial ulcerated patches on the tonsil or there may be deeper pus formation.

That is the typical Mercurius picture.

Mercurius Cyanatus

In Merc. Cy. the throat is a little more dirty, with a greater tendency to ulceration. There is less tendency to abscess formation, and if swabbed, a Merc. Cy. throat will almost certainly bleed.

Another distinguishing point in the Cyanide is that an area of ulceration will frequently have a very bright red area of demarcation, as if it has been edged round with a red ink pen.

But so far as the choice between Merc. and Merc. Cy. is concerned, it is purely a question of intensity – the Cyanide is more virulent, more rapid in its onset, more ulcerative in type, and there is much more tendency to bleed.

Mercurius Iodatus Rubrum or Mercurius Iodatus Flavus

Occasionally a patient with indications for Merc. does not respond sufficiently well. The condition responds up to a point, but not really satisfactorily, so one of the other Mercurius salts, either Merc. I. R. or Merc. I. F. should be considered.

If a case is not responding very well, with definite Mercurius indications and affecting the right side, better results may be obtained from Merc. I. F. than from Mercurius. If, on the other hand, it mainly involves the left side of the throat, it may be found that Merc. I. R. sometimes takes up the work in place of Mercurius, just as Merc. I. F. does for the right side. It is a help to remember that the Rubrum, the R, applies to the left not to the right.

Phytolacca

The next most useful remedy for these throats is Phytolacca.

Phytolacca patients have a very similar type of throat to that of Mercurius, but there are one or two points which distinguish it. In Phytolacca there is a tendency for the glandular enlargement to be a little more obvious than it is in Mercurius, and not infrequently it will extend to the cheek, rather than to the neck. In fact, parotitis may be suspected because swelling of the glands spreads beyond the angle of the jaw.

The tongue in Phytolacca and Mercurius patients is almost identical; although possibly in some cases with a generally coated tongue, in

Phytolacca the tip of the tongue may be red, in Mercurius there is a general coating all over.

In Phytolacca there is a common tendency for the pain to shoot into the ears on swallowing, whereas in Mercurius the pain is generally in the throat, only occasionally shooting into the ear.

The temperature reaction is slightly different. Instead of the very hot, sweaty state of the Mercurius patient, with shivering if they are uncovered, Phytolacca patients feel hot but also feel shivery without being uncovered.

Patients with a marked aggravation from hot drinks are much more likely to require Phytolacca than Mercurius. Mercurius has the aggravation slightly, Phytolacca acutely.

In Phytolacca the face is very flushed, with a feeling of great heat in the throat and mouth, and patients often say that their tongue feels as if it had been scalded. They always complain of a feeling of fullness in the throat, and an incessant desire to swallow, and yet the act of swallowing is extremely painful. The pain is situated right in the base of the tongue more than in the throat itself, and from there it tends to shoot up into the ears. The discomfort from the throat is very much aggravated by any hot application, hot drinks particularly. There is usually a yellow coating, particularly down the centre of the tongue – very often the edges of the tongue or the tip are quite clear. The tonsillitis may be accompanied by aching pains, usually in the legs or lumbar region, or moving from joint to joint, possibly amounting to a general bruised sensation all over. With these general aching pains the patients are restless. They want to move but they get no relief; rather, there is an aggravation of the pains from movement. The throat appears considerably swollen; it is almost oedematous, particularly the uvula. There may be ulceration of the tonsils, typically a yellow sloughing ulcer on the tonsil, which is extremely sensitive. As a rule, there is more involvement of the right side of the throat than the left. In spite of the general restlessness, these patients almost always complain of giddiness on sitting up or getting out of bed for any reason. They are liable to faint and are always distressed. At first, if undisturbed, they are sluggish. The temperature is high and they are always apprehensive and depressed. In spite of the local aggravation from warmth and hot drinks, they themselves are usually chilly. They feel the cold and they like to be covered up.

They have much the same difficulty in swallowing as in Mercurius, a feeling as if the throat was obstructed. There is not the same degree of salivation in Phytolacca as in Mercurius.

Phytolacca has one very distinctive feature – an acute pain in the base of the tongue when it is protruded. It is an almost diagnostic symptom of Phytolacca if there is any doubt between Phytolacca and Mercurius.

The throats considered so far are all fairly common types. There are one or two others which are not so common, but which give very useful indications for homoeopathic remedies.

Apis

A sore throat which has developed very acutely, which is much aggravated by heat or hot drinks and relieved by cold, and in which any attempt to swallow fluids produces a sensation of acute constriction in the throat with complete inability to swallow, may indicate Apis. The patient feels extremely hot, is very much aggravated by any heat, a hot room, and particularly by radiant heat.

On examination, the throat is very red. In addition to the acute inflammatory appearance there is a very marked oedematous tendency. The whole soft palate, uvula and pillars of the fauces look oedematous, as if they were full of water, and there may be a certain amount of swelling of the tongue also.

As a rule the inflammation starts or is more marked on the right side of the throat, and spreads from there.

These cases respond very well to Apis, prescribed on the oedematous appearance of the throat, accompanied by the marked aggravation from heat, either general or local.

These patients have a high temperature. Incidentally, quite apart from throats, marked oedema is associated with Apis in other conditions as well. Acute angioneurotic oedema will respond well to Apis. Many years ago a woman was seen with angioneurotic oedema which came on suddenly during the night, affecting the whole side from below the neck right down to underneath her costal margin. The condition cleared up almost at once on Apis.

Fish poisoning cases with oedema also respond to Apis, usually in the 200c potency.

Oedema, bright red colour, a burning sensation and an aggravation from warmth are indications for Apis.

Belladonna

Belladonna is needed for acute sore throats which are extremely painful, with a sensation of dryness of the throat and burning pain. It develops very suddenly, with a feeling as if the throat is swelling up, and there is inability to swallow. Any attempt to swallow is attended by violent pain and seems to set up an acute spasm of all the throat muscles. It is accompanied by a very high temperature, a good deal of nervous excitement, and a full bounding pulse, red face and dry skin. On examination, the throat is bright red, very often with small aphthous patches on the tonsils, usually with a dry tongue, slightly coated. There is extreme sensitivity of the throat to touch. These cases clear up very quickly with a few doses of Belladonna, 30c or 200c.

Baptisia

For septic throats the most commonly indicated remedy of all is Baptisia.

The patients are obviously toxic, they look heavy and bloated, they are uncomfortable, the skin is hot and moist, the sweat is offensive, and the mouth is particularly offensive. There is always a very dirty tongue. It may be brownish-yellow and greasy to touch, or it may be brown and dry, or else yellowish with a thick brown streak down the middle. There is an early tendency to ulceration of the tonsils, and the ulcers are dirty-looking. Baptisia is one of the remedies to consider for Vincent's Angina – that is the type of throat. There is always a quantity of very sticky, ropy saliva about the mouth, and particularly the throat. There is always swelling in the neck and round the pillars of the fauces.

The throat itself is dusky in colour, and the patients give the impression of being dusky. They are a bad colour.

Any attempt at swallowing solids is impossible; the patients simply choke, but swallowing fluids sometimes gives a certain degree of comfort.

As a rule these throats are extremely painful. Occasionally one may present with all the general symptoms of the toxic state, offensiveness, the appearance of the tongue, but be almost painless – and yet Baptisia is indicated. It is one of the really severely infected throats, and the cases in which it has been most clearly indicated have often been cases of Vincent's Angina. It is worth remembering that diphtheria and Vincent's Angina may be combined, a very nasty proposition. These cases do best by tackling the Vincent first and the diphtheria afterwards. Given Baptisia to start with, the Vincent's Angina clears in about 24 hours; then treat the diphtheria, which responds very well to Mercurius or Merc. Cy. in most cases and complements the effect of antitoxin.

Two other remedies for septic throats are Lachesis and Hepar. Sulph. They are a very useful contrast, because the Lachesis patient is hot and the Hepar Sulph. patient is cold.

Lachesis

Lachesis patients typically complain that the throat feels swollen and that the fullness extends into the neck, yet on examination there is very little swelling to be seen. Very often they complain that as they fall asleep they have to sit up in bed – they feel as if the throat had completely closed and they are choking.

Lachesis patients with sore throats are always dusky in colour, and look congested. They are very liable to get a pain right through to the base of the skull, extending down the back of the neck, and they complain of the neck being extremely stiff.

In the throat there is always a quantity of very tough mucus which they have great difficulty in clearing. There is a constant desire to swallow, and yet any attempt at swallowing is extremely painful. It is less painful for them to swallow fluids or solids than just to attempt to swallow the saliva. Any attempt at swallowing hot fluids produces an acute spasm in the throat, making swallowing impossible. Hot fluids increase the discomfort in the throat, whereas cold fluids give a degree of relief.

Looking at the throat, some ulceration may be present, but much more commonly there is a very dusky, purplish swelling of the tonsils. And in Lachesis there is a tendency for the trouble to start on the left side, spreading from there to the right.

Lycopodium takes the place of Lachesis for septic throats, just about as painful as the Lachesis ones, but without the aggravation from warm drinks and with an amelioration from warmth. This is particularly true where the trouble starts on the right side instead of the left, and where the patient is not so hot and not so generally congested. But do not prescribe Lycopodium because a condition appears to be right-sided if it has definite Lachesis indications. Lachesis will work in a right-sided inflammation provided the general Lachesis indications are there.

Hepar Sulphuricum

The other remedy frequently indicated for acute septic throats is Hepar Sulph. In Hepar Sulph. the pains in the throat are much more acute and stabbing, in contrast to the feeling of general swelling and choking of Lachesis. Instead of the general toxic state accompanying Lachesis sore throats, Hepar Sulph. patients tend to be much more irritable.

There is the same tendency to early suppuration in the two remedies, but in Hepar Sulph. the patients are always intensely chilly. They want to be covered up, and any draught of air is complained of. They are impatient and very difficult to please.

The Hepar Sulph. throat is always acutely sensitive, and the patients resent examination. There is not the same tendency to glandular enlargement in Hepar Sulph. as there is in Lachesis.

In addition to their chilliness, in Hepar Sulph. there is always a tendency to sweat, particularly about the head. It is often a cold sweat, whereas in Lachesis the skin is hot and sticky.

As a rule, in Hepar Sulph. associated with the acute sore throat, patients develop a very irritable cough – a sort of barking cough, which is very distressing to the throat.

Chapter 4

Respiratory Conditions

COLDS

Gelsemium and Eupatorium

There are two outstanding remedies in the Materia Medica for the usual types of cold, and these are Gelsemium and Eupatorium. The cold which requires either Gels. or Eupatorium is the typical feverish one. The patients say they have a feverish cold, a slight headache, they feel cold and ache, they shiver in the cold air, the shivers going up and down the spine, their nose becomes obstructed in a hot room, and they feel unwell generally. That is the typical Gels. cold. If it progresses further, and instead of just feeling unwell they are aching from head to toe, if it is painful to move and there are signs of a catarrhal cold with an increased feeling of weariness, and a definitely increased sensitiveness to change of temperature – that is the typical Eupatorium. These two remedies will cover the majority of the ordinary feverish colds.

Allium Cepa

There are two outstanding remedies for the ordinary streaming cold in the head. The commonest is Allium Cepa. The patients have a profuse watery nasal discharge with a feeling of heat and burning in the nose, a tendency to excoriation of the upper lip, maybe a slight rise of temperature, but with very little in the way of general symptoms. If it has been untreated for 48 hours or so it usually sets up a laryngeal irritation with a very sensitive larynx. There is excoriation of the upper lip and apparently excoriation of the larynx as well. That is the later stage of the ordinary Allium Cepa acute coryza, and is much the most common.

Euphrasia

The other type is one in which there is a similarly profuse nasal discharge, but where the discharge is not excoriating and is accompanied by a good deal of conjunctivitis, congestion of the eyes, a certain amount of photophobia and redness of the eyelids. In other words, the lachrymal discharge is irritating but the nasal discharge is not. That case responds to Euphrasia.

Arsenicum Album

Occasionally a patient appears as a fairly typical Allium Cepa patient; there is the excoriating, burning, nasal discharge, but there is rather more temperature, rather more chilliness and the burning tends to extend back into the fauces. There is a certain amount of post-nasal discharge which is again hot and burning, accompanied by thirst and general chilliness. That case usually responds to a few doses of Arsenicum Album in a low potency.

Mercurius

In a patient where the cold starts with irritation in the throat, either pain or burning in the tonsillar region with difficulty in swallowing, a feeling of fullness and a few hours later they have a pouring coryza, a few doses of Mercurius are usually indicated.

It is impossible to cover the whole Materia Medica that applies to colds. These above are the most common useful remedies in general practice.

BRONCHITIS

Moving a little further down the respiratory tract and considering acute bronchitis, there are three remedies which will help greatly in treating the average case.

A child starting an attack of acute bronchitis, with rapidly increasing mucus secretion, very distressing cough, an obvious temperature and râles all over the chest, will almost always respond to Ipecacuanha. If it is a little more severe, the child obviously more ill, the râles more extensive in the chest, the child becoming rather cyanotic, and the tongue definitely coated, instead of Ipecacuanha give Antimonium Tart. These two remedies will deal with most cases of acute bronchitis in the child.

Acute bronchitis in the adult; the patient who comes every winter with an acute bronchitis, which is really only an aggravation of his chronic bronchitis, will be relieved by Ammonium Carb. almost every time. There is often a certain amount of arterial sclerosis, a certain amount of emphysema and a sticky sputum, the patients getting a profuse, watery sputum, as well as a tough sputum which they cannot expel due to the chronic condition. These patients will respond well to Ammonium Carb. It diminishes their sputum, relieves their heart and loosens their cough. Several doses of the 30c potency should be given.

There are three remedies to consider when dealing with the child who has a dry wheezing distressing cough, depending very largely on the time of day at which they are most distressed. If the paroxysm of coughing begins early in the evening with a dry chest, a few doses of Aconite will relieve it. If the main distress is round about the early hours of the morning, midnight to 2, 3 or 4 a.m., a few doses of Spongia will alleviate. If there is relief from either Aconite or Spongia but it does not hold them, or if the cough begins later in the night – after 4 a.m. – or is mainly troublesome in the day, then Hepar Sulph. is the main standby.

The tiresome, irritating, tickling cough of tracheitis is usually controlled by Drosera. An acute feverish tracheitis that has spread downwards from the throat will usually respond to Allium Cepa.

PNEUMONIA

Bryonia and Phosphorus

For the treatment of pneumonias there are two remedies much more commonly indicated than any others, Bryonia and Phosphorus. The main distinguishing features between Bryonia and Phosphorus pneumonias are that Bryonia patients are more toxic, heavy and slightly cyanotic. They dislike being disturbed, usually have a very painful cough, with a good deal of pain in the chest which is relieved by pressure – either lying on the affected side, or by holding the side when coughing. The patients have a white-coated tongue and are thirsty for fairly large quantities of cold water. Not infrequently the paroxysms of coughing are relieved by hot drinks, which is not what the patients feel they want. It does not matter which lung is involved; it is probably more commonly indicated in the right side, but Bryonia will act equally well in a left-sided pneumonia.

In the Phosphorus pneumonias the patients are more anxious, much more awake, flushed, not cyanotic, and are as thirsty as the Bryonia patients, often for ice-cold drinks. But they do not have nearly such a coated tongue, dislike any pressure on the affected area, and tend to lie on the unaffected side. Again it does not matter what area of the lung is involved, although it is probably more commonly the lower lobe that is involved in a Phosphorus pneumonia.

The probability is that the Bryonia pneumonia has developed rather more slowly, and the Phosphorus pneumonia has come on fairly acutely.

POST-INFLUENZAL COMPLICATIONS AND SEQUELAE

Probably the most common sequela of influenza is a persisting infection of one or other of the accessory nasal sinuses, antrum, ethmoidal cells or frontal sinus. Next in frequency is persistent catarrh of the eustachian tube and middle ear. These two complications not infrequently occur at the same time.

Another very common and trying result of an influenzal attack is persistent trouble in the respiratory tract, showing itself as an obstinate, distressing and often intractable cough.

Less commonly, but still quite frequently, are cases in which the digestive system seems to have been upset, with symptoms suggestive of a subacute gastritis, gastro-duodenitis, or even cholecystitis or hepatitis.

The most common general sequelae are persistent weakness and nervous depression.

As a rule, where prescribing for the acute attack has been accurate such trials are not met with, but even with the best endeavours, they do still occur.

Taking the sequelae in a little more detail; first the accessory sinuses and naso-pharynx, the remedies most frequently indicated are Kali Bich. and Silica.

Kali Bichromicum

In patients needing Kali Bich. there has been a persistence of sticky discharge, associated with pain or a sense of fullness,or pressure over the frontal sinuses or the antra, and usually a sense of obstruction at the bridge of the nose. These post-influenzal Kali Bich. patients are always classical examples of post-influenzal debility, and their symptoms are acutely aggravated in cold damp weather and better in a warm bed. If they complain of sharp, pressing pain over the affected sinus, that is a confirmatory symptom of great value.

Silica

Contrast that picture with the one presented by Silica. At first sight the two appear to be almost identical. Both show signs of general debility, both show aggravation in cold damp weather, and in both there is a complaint of fullness or pressure in the affected sinus. In Kali Bich. this involvement is accompanied by profuse discharge, while in Silica there is no discharge and a steadily increasing tension in the affected sinus.

Pulsatilla

There is a different type of case in which the symptoms of the patient are aggravated by heat, close rooms or a stuffy atmosphere, suggestive of Pulsatilla. There is not so much active involvement of the sinuses in Pulsatilla, but the patient complains that the nose is blocked, often very marked on waking in the morning and getting worse again towards evening, and especially in a warm room. It is better in the open air. This is not infrequently associated with a very unpleasant odour of which the patient is acutely conscious.

Pulsatilla, though seldom indicated for involvement of the sinuses, is quite often indicated in catarrhal involvement of the ear in cases which may go on to acute otitis media with sharp stabbing pains in the ear.

Mercurius and Kali Iodatum

Where there is involvement of the sinuses in patients who are sensitive to heat, enquire for indications suggesting either Mercurius or Kali Iod. Both have acute involvement of the sinuses with acute pain. In Mercurius the patient has marked aggravation from radiant heat, associated with a sense of fullness in the affected sinus, a tendency to perspire and violent pains. The Mercurius patient is very sensitive to draughts and will exhibit the typical pale flabby indented tongue of Mercurius.

When dealing with a case showing such acute sensitiveness to draughts it is always worth while to remember that a case of that kind, improving but not cured by Mercurius, may later be helped by Hepar Sulph.

In Kali Iod. patients there may be trouble in any of the sinuses, with an acute sense of tightness, often accompanied by stabbing pains. There is marked aggravation in a warm room, with a sense of general weariness, and the patient is much better walking about in the open air. It is more frequently indicated in infections of the frontal, sphenoid or ethmoid sinuses rather than the antra.

Pyrogen
When the deeper sinuses are involved, Pyrogen may be indicated. There is usually a marked toxaemia with general aching, slight attacks of shivering alternating with a feeling of heat, and a pulse temperature discrepancy.

Hydrastis
Post-influenzal coughs can be particularly troublesome. There are the cases in which the patient complains of rawness and irritation of the naso-pharynx, with a bad cough aggravated by talking or smoking and which is often worrying at night. For this condition Hydrastis is the greatest help, especially for cases with a reddened congested pharynx and streaks of yellow muco-pus trickling down from the posterior nares.

Alumina
Alumina is another remedy increasingly indicated in such cases of persistent pharyngitis. There is not nearly so much secretion, in fact the pharynx often has a somewhat dry appearance. The patients complain of its being very sensitive and sore, with sticking pains. Periodically there seems to be an accumulation of ropy mucus which must be expectorated, and this is accompanied by a feeling of soreness in the larynx and trachea, with a hacking cough.

Two other medicines frequently indicated are Nux Vomica and Conium.

Nux Vomica
Indications helpful in the Nux Vomica patient are acute irritation in one or other tonsillar region, setting up a violent cough which continues until there is the expectoration of some mucus or muco-purulent sputum, after which they have peace for a time. This, when associated with a tendency to nasal congestion in a hot room, and accompanied by some gastric acidity, is a strong indication for Nux Vomica.

Conium
There appears to be a close similarity in Conium, in that the patient has a violent paroxysmal cough due to irritation in the throat. The irritation, however, is in the pharynx or larynx rather than in the tonsillar region. It is liable to come on when the patient is lying in bed or on taking a deep breath. It is unaccompanied by the heartburn met with in Nux Vomica. Though the patient may say he has to sit up and

cough to clear the irritation, this does not mean, as in Nux Vomica, that there is relief immediately on the expectoration of some sputum.

LARYNGITIS AND TRACHEITIS

Further down the respiratory tract, the cases with persistent irritation in the larynx and trachea must be considered. With their clear-cut indications of irritation at the level of the supra-sternal notch and their aggravation from change of temperature, Phosphorus or Rumex immediately come to mind, and they do cover a large number of cases. The next most frequently indicated remedy is Carbo Veg. for people who are below par generally. Their colds do not clear and the inflammation extends to the larynx and trachea. They become husky, particularly in the evening. They get attacks of most exhausting cough, almost like whooping cough, in which they become red in the face and damp with sweat, gasping for air, and after which they are exhausted. The larynx feels raw and is often tender to touch. These are indications for Carbo Veg.

Never think of whooping cough without considering Drosera. Drosera is occasionally called for in post-influenzal coughs which come on after eating or drinking, or are liable to be very troublesome on lying down at night or round 3 a.m., and are of this violent spasmodic nature with a most distressing irritation in the larynx.

Then never think of spasmodic coughs without recalling Hepar Sulph. and Spongia. Hepar Sulph. with its hypersensitiveness to any cold air or becoming cold, with rattling in the chest. And Spongia with its cough coming on just after midnight, a dry cough, accompanied by anxiety, cardiac oppression, and aggravation in a warm room but amelioration from warm drinks.

One of the commoner laryngeal troubles which persist is hoarseness. Here, consideration of a fresh group of remedies is required in addition to those already mentioned. Carbo Veg. and Phosphorus are often needed, but even more frequently there are indications for Causticum. The patient complains of hoarseness in the morning which usually improves during the day. There is violent coughing in an endeavour to clear the mucus from the respiratory tract and patients often say that they cannot cough deeply enough to clear it, but if they can expectorate the voice improves. The attacks of coughing may be relieved by a drink of cold water, and the patient may have loss of urinary control during the violent attacks of coughing. This hoarseness, if accompanied by the general aching tiredness of the post-influenza period, especially if symptoms are worse in cold dry weather, is almost certain to respond to Causticum.

Causticum is similar to Arum Triphyllum, which has all the symptoms of an ordinary influenza, especially the aching in the bones. As a rule, the patient will say that the condition started with a very excoriating nasal discharge accompanied by intense irritation in the nose, most marked on the left side. This was followed by a raw feeling behind the sternum with loss of voice, the peculiarity being the ability to speak on either a higher or lower note than usual, progressing to complete loss of voice.

In other cases where the voice is lost with use there may be indications for Rhus Tox. The patients have the dry tormenting cough, coming in paroxysms, with aching pains all round the ribs, and the general mental and physical restlessness of Rhus Tox.

It is not practicable to discuss all the possible remedies which may be required in cases showing persistent chest trouble. However, apart from the use of a nosode, the remedies likely to be indicated are Silica, Phosphorus, Carbo Veg., Calcarea Carb., Lycopodium, Sulphur and Pulsatilla in the chronic and Kreosote, Sanguinaria, Senega, Kali Carb. and Antimonium Tart. in the more acute stages.

DIGESTIVE SEQUELAE

Kali Bichromicum

The common digestive sequelae of influenzal attacks are usually catarrhal in nature, and the remedy most commonly indicated in these cases is Kali Bich. The symptoms are usually somewhat vague, such as weakness of digestion and being upset by the simplest of foods. The disturbances are of two kinds, either distension and obstructed flatus in stomach and bowel with repletion after the smallest meal, or sharp pains. The pains are cutting or burning in character with soreness and tenderness in the epigastrium, usually towards the left in a small spot – rather suggestive of a gastric ulcer – coming on usually after 1 a.m., between 1 a.m. and 3 a.m. There is often a sense of emptiness with aversion to food, and a marked aggravation from starchy food, especially potatoes. X-ray may reveal a marked excess of mucus, increased gastric mobility and exaggeration of the normal pattern of the mucous membrane. With such symptoms, consider the possibility of Kali Bich., but the symptomatology suggests the possibility of several other remedies being required: Lycopodium, for instance with its flatulence, empty feeling and repletion after a small meal. The patient would have the typical Lycopodium make-up of the tired, thin, wrinkled, chronic dyspeptic, aggravated by cold drinks and relieved by warm, and sensitive to beer, coffee and fruit. China presents a very similar picture with its feeling of hunger yet aversion to food, its acute flatulent distension and its general debility. China is also indicated for the extremely sensitive nervous patient liable to attacks of diarrhoea after a meal, upset by fruit, fish and particularly wine, and likely to have violent attacks of colic coming on at midnight. In cases with extreme flatulent distension after any food, Carbo Veg. is needed. In Carbo Veg. there is outstanding relief from eructation: without this, Carbo Veg. is not indicated, no matter how suggestive the other symptoms may be.

Bryonia
In the digestive complications of influenza, as opposed to the sequelae, the drug most frequently indicated is Bryonia. This has a classical picture of acute gastritis, with extreme abdominal sensitivity, intense nausea, aggravated by any movement, better after eructations and with relief from hot drinks. This complication yields very readily to Bryonia.

Antimonium Crudum
Antimonium Crudum is indicated in those cases in which the catarrhal symptoms have persisted with a tendency for the nose to be blocked up in the evening in a warm room, and with digestive symptoms. There is a thickly-coated white tongue, and the patient complains of a constant sensation of fullness and heaviness in the stomach, as if they had overeaten. There is a feeling of acute distenstion though there is no swelling of the abdomen, and aversion to the thought or smell of all food. All digestive symptoms are greatly aggravated by becoming cold or by drinking anything sour.

DEPRESSION

Aurum Metallicum
Depression is a common sequela of influenza. The first remedy which immediately comes to mind is Aurum, with its acute depression and feeling that everything is wrong, looking on the black side of everything, expecting trouble and looking for it. The patients are obstinate,

irritable and very easily annoyed. They have flushes of heat and are better in the open air, frequently they suffer from palpitation and often have slight exophthalmos. They may have oedema of the ankles. Not infrequently Aurum is indicated in cases of post-influenzal arthritis, with pains which are worse at night compelling the patient to get out of bed and move about.

Pulsatilla

Another type of depression usually responds to Pulsatilla. Here there is the same sensitivity to heat and a somewhat similar depressed state, where the patient tends to be miserable and sits about saying nothing, but the picture is in essence very different. In Pulsatilla the patients are sensitive. There are liable to be tears and irritation. They feel that they are being misunderstood or slighted in some way, and hate to be interrupted in what they are doing. Often they think that no one realises how ill they feel and they are miserable about it. They are restless and better when moving about and occupied. They are hot-blooded and hate a lot of clothing, are difficult to feed and complain of feeling full up hours after a meal.

Silica

Silica is another remedy which may be required for post-influenzal depression. The patients are depressed because they feel incompetent, that they cannot cope with life and especially with the problems of the moment, although in reality they manage perfectly well. They are shy and retiring, and liable to be irritable when aroused. After an attack of influenza there may be persistent enlargement of the cervical glands. They feel tired and suffer from headaches spreading over from the back of the head, accompanied by dampness of the forehead and extreme sensitiveness of the head to cold air. These patients are aggravated by cold and becoming cold, but they cannot stand extremes of either heat or cold.

EXHAUSTION

For post-influenzal nervous exhaustion there are three remedies of the greatest value, namely, Picric Acid, Phosphoric Acid and Cocculus Indicus. In all of them there is the same feeling of weariness and inability to sustain any mental effort.

Picric Acid

The main complaint in Picric Acid is that any attempt at mental application produces a violent headache, accompanied by trembling, faintness, numbness and extreme lassitude. The patients feel they simply must lie down. They become indifferent and do not want to do anything. Typically they are useless during the day and are much better during the evening. They are sensitive to heat and are often relieved by bathing the head with cold water. Any physical exertion is followed by a feeling of complete exhaustion.

Phosphoric Acid

The Phosphoric Acid picture is somewhat different. Here there is a state of torpor associated with the mental weariness. The patients do not want to talk, they feel so tired. They suffer from headaches with a sense of pressure on the top of the head, which is brought on by any exertion. They complain of cold extremities and are liable to have cold damp hands. They are sensitive to cold, though they cannot stand a stuffy room. Frequently they complain of acute skin irritation on any part of the body. Often they say that since influenza their hair has been falling out. They may complain of giddiness and a sensation of floating. Usually Phosphoric Acid patients suffer from indigestion with a sense of the food taking hours to digest, and are liable to attacks of diarrhoea, which surprisingly seem to brighten them up. They quite often complain of bone pains, described as if the bones were being scraped.

Cocculus Indicus

Lastly there is Cocculus Indicus. The typical picture is that of mental and physical prostration. All the reactions are slowed down and convalescence is correspondingly slow. The patients cannot be hurried, they want a long time to do everything, all the movements are slow. There is a tendency to incoordination and they are liable to drop things, and complain of sudden jerking of the limbs. They are liable to suffer from violent headaches with nausea and vomiting. These may be brought on by any form of travelling, by car, boat, train or aeroplane. They suffer from great weakness in the knees and back, often with a sense of stiffness in the joints and a feeling of being almost paralysed, frequently coupled with a feeling of numbness. They are very sensitive to noise, jarring, or any sudden movement. The appetite is practically lost and there may be an acute aversion even to the thought of food. They suffer from sleeplessness and are prostrated by any loss of sleep.

Chapter 5

Heart Conditions

The simplest way to group cardiac emergencies from a remedy point of view is to look at them under three headings: 1) Acute cardiac failure, 2) Gradual cardiac failure with a tendency to dilatation, and 3) Acute cardiac angina.

ACUTE CARDIAC FAILURE

For acute cardiac failure, most cases require one of four remedies. These are Arsenicum Alb., Antimony Tart., Carbo Veg. and Oxalic Acid. There are various points which help in the selection of these individual remedies and it is not difficult to distinguish between them.

Arsenicum Album
Arsenicum Alb. patients demonstrate the typical Arsenicum Alb. mental distress, with extreme fear, extreme anxiety, and mental and physical restlessness. They have constant thirst, with a desire for small sips of cold water.

The main complaint is a feeling of extreme cardiac pressure, a feeling of great weight or constriction of the chest. At the same time the patients feel as if they cannot get enough air into the lungs and that they are going to die.

As a rule Arsenicum Alb. patients are cold, they feel cold, though they may complain of some burning pain in the chest.

In appearance they always look extremely anxious. They are grey, their lips are rather pale, maybe a little cyanotic, and they are very dangerously ill. They often have a peculiar pinched, wrinkled, grey appearance.

As a rule there is a history that the attack has developed quite suddenly, and the response to Arsenicum Alb. should be equally quick. The first response is a diminution of the patient's mental anxiety and extreme fear, the restlessness begins to subside, and they begin to feel a little warmer.

Arsenicum Alb. seems to act very much like a temporary cardiac stimulant, and in the majority of these cases it is necessary to repeat the dose frequently and to give it in a high potency.

There is a very important practical point in connection with these cases. A patient has responded well to Arsenicum Alb., his condition has improved and then in 3, 4 or 6 hours he has a relapse. If Arsenicum Alb. is repeated the patient does not improve a second time. To avoid this it is necessary to prescribe a second remedy within 4–6 hours of the primary collapse, while the patient is still responding to the Arsenicum Alb. This should prevent the secondary collapse. This seems to be one of the very few instances which appears to ride right across the dictum that so long as the patient is improving, continue with the same remedy. In these acute Arsenicum Alb. cases, if the patient improves, a second remedy needs to be prescribed within 2–3 hours.

The remedies which frequently follow Arsenicum Alb. in the reactive stage are Phosphorus or Sulphur, but that is by no means constant. One can easily picture that grey, pinched, anxious Arsenicum Alb. patient responding, getting a little warmer, a little less grey, a little less pinched and drawn, a little less anxious and restless and becoming a typical Phosphorus patient. Equally one can see them going to the other extreme, where they are too hot, with irregular waves of heat and cold, tending to push the blankets off, with air hunger and requiring Sulphur.

These are the two commonest remedies, but one other that can be helpful following Arsenicum Alb. is Carbo Veg. Here the air hunger persists and the patient has to sit up to get comfortable, he has troublesome flatulence, the extremities are very cold, but the thirst is subsiding. The patient is slightly cyanosed, perspiring and has a craving for fresh air, moving fresh air, and asks to be fanned. With these symptoms Carbo Veg. is indicated.

Antimonium Tartrate

Antimonium Tart. patients present a somewhat similar picture to Arsenicum Alb., but there are clear points of difference. Antimonium Tart. have a greater tendency towards cyanosis than Arsenicum Alb. This may involve the whole of the extremities or it may be confined to the nails.

There is never the same kind of mental anxiety in Antimonium Tart. They are more exhausted, much more hopeless, more depressed. They are never quite as restless and never quite so pale as Arsenicum Alb. They are not thirsty, and drinking seems to increase the patient's distress.

Another contrast is that Antimonium Tart. are very much aggravated by heat, and especially by a stuffy atmosphere. As a contrast between Antimonium Tart. and Carbo Veg., Antimonium Tart. patients do not like a stream of air circulating round them; they want the room fresh, but they like the air to be still.

In most of these Antimonium Tart. cases there is an early tendency to oedema of the lower extremities.

Another indication for Antimonium Tart. is that practically all these patients have a very white thickly-coated tongue, with a rather sticky, uncomfortable mouth.

They have a feeling of fullness in the chest, rather than the feeling of acute pressure found in Arsenicum Alb. Frequently, generalised, diffuse râles are present in the lower part of the lungs on both sides.

In contrast to the Arsenicum Alb. patient with collapse after a cardiac crisis, patients responding to Antimonium Tart. will continue to improve without the need of a follow-up remedy as is necessary in Arsenicum Alb.

Carbo Vegetabilis

Carbo Veg. patients present the classical picture of collapse. They have the cold clammy skin, are mentally dull and confused, and have no very clear idea of their surroundings or what is happening to them. They have the most intense air hunger, and in spite of their cold clammy extremities want the air blowing on them. They cannot bear to have the bedclothes round their necks and they benefit from oxygen.

They are much paler than the Antimonium Tart. patients; the lips tend to be pale rather than cyanotic.

Like the Antimonium Tart. patients, any attempt to eat or drink tends to increase their distress, and they have none of the Arsenicum Alb. thirst.

An apparent contradiction in Carbo Veg. patients is that, in spite of their desire to be uncovered and their intolerance of the blankets round the upper part of the neck or chest, they complain of ice-cold extremities. They feel as if the legs are just lumps of ice and they cannot get them warm at all.

Once the patient is responding to Carbo Veg. – perspiring less, the surface becoming warmer and the distress less acute – it is wise then to look for a second remedy in case of need, because some Carbo Veg.

patients relapse although many of them make a complete recovery on Carbo Veg. Often when the patient has made some improvement after the administration of Carbo Veg., the follow-up remedy will be found to be Sulphur, although Kali Carb. should always be considered.

Oxalic Acid

The last of these remedies for acute cardiac failure is Oxalic Acid. Oxalic Acid has one or two very outstanding symptoms which are often met with in cases of collapse, and which are a great help in the selection of the remedy.

First, the patients always complain of a feeling of the most intense exhaustion. Associated with that exhaustion there is usually a sensation of numbness. They very often say that their legs and feet feel numb and paralysed, or they feel as if they had no legs at all.

The skin surface is about as cold and clammy as it is in Carbo Veg. but Oxalic Acid patients have a peculiar mottled cyanosis not present in the other remedies. The fingertips and finger and toe nails will be cyanotic but in addition, the patients have a peculiar mottled appearance of the hands and feet which is quite distinctive to Oxalic Acid. This mottled cyanotic condition also occurs on the face, usually over the malar bones.

These patients, in contrast to Arsenicum Alb., want to keep absolutely still; movement of any kind increases their distress.

In addition to their general distress, most Oxalic Acid patients complain of sharp pains in the chest. The pain is not typical anginal pain; it is a sharp pricking pain which usually comes through from the back and extends up the left side of the sternum towards the clavicle, or down the left side of the sternum into the epigastrium.

GRADUAL CARDIAC FAILURE WITH A TENDENCY TO DILATATION

Now to consider cases where the heart is gradually failing, beginning to dilate, becoming slightly irregular, and the patients are obviously going downhill. In many of these patients with early cardiac failure, the heart improves and the dilatation disappears in response to ordinary routine prescribing, and it is not necessary to consider the cardiac symptoms particularly. The patients respond to the remedy for their general symptoms. For instance, quite frequently in pneumonia – a severe pneumonia, with a failing heart, with dilatation – after the administration of Lycopodium, the pulse steadies and the dilatation of the heart disappears. This occurs in all acute illnesses where the patient is responding to the particular remedy indicated. However, there are cases in which the patient improves but the cardiac failure does not respond to the individual remedy, and here it is necessary to prescribe for the cardiac failure.

These patients most readily respond to the Snake remedies, especially Lachesis and Naja, less commonly to the plants Lycopus and Laurocerasus.

It is very difficult to distinguish one Snake remedy from another for such conditions. In appearance the patients are all very similar, but much the most commonly indicated are Lachesis and Naja.

Lachesis and Naja

The Lachesis picture is typical of all the Snake remedies, but there are a few indications which make Naja the choice in preference to Lachesis.

All patients for whom the Snake remedies are indicated have a cyanosed, bloated appearance. They all complain of a feeling of tightness or constriction in the chest, more commonly in the upper part of the chest, and they are all intolerant of any weight or pressure of the bedclothes or any tight clothing around the upper part of the chest or the neck. All are sensitive to heat, they feel hot and they dislike a hot stuffy room. They all have a marked aggravation after sleep. They get acute suffocative attacks when they fall asleep, and they wake up in increased distress.

All of these patients in their cardiac distress have a marked aggravation from being turned over on the left side. All of them have a very marked tremor. And most of them, as they get worse, become mentally dull and confused, and often tend to become difficult and suspicious.

If these were all the symptoms, Lachesis would be the indicated remedy. A certain number of patients have acute stitching pains which go right through the chest from the precordium to the region of the scapula, associated with numbness, particularly in the left arm and hand. These are the indications for Naja in preference to Lachesis.

If the pain – stitching pain – is more marked, Naja is indicated. If the feeling of constriction is more marked, give Lachesis. Their general symptoms are identical. Possibly Naja patients are a little less congested, less bloated looking and a little paler than Lachesis patients, but that is not very striking.

Apart from the Snake remedies there are two others which are very useful in these conditions, Lycopus and Laurocerasus.

Lycopus

Indications for Lycopus may occur in patients with early signs of heart failure. Their pulse is slightly irregular and the heart beginning to dilate. The patients tend to be pale rather than cyanotic, and they are always restless.

The outstanding symptoms of Lycopus cases is that the patients complain of a tumultuous sensation in the cardiac region. Their heartbeat is completely irregular, and they experience a feeling of intense throbbing extending up into the neck and head. The tumultuous sensation in the chest is usually accompanied by a desire to cough.

Another symptom which distinguishes Lycopus patients is that their discomfort is greatly increased by turning over on to the right side – a contrast with the patients needing Snake remedies, whose cardiac discomfort is worse turning on to the left side.

Lastly, Lycopus patients have an intense dislike of any food, and particularly the smell of food.

Laurocerasus

The Laurocerasus patient presents a definite picture, and the easiest way to remember it is to recall the appearance presented by a congenital heart patient of about 16 to 18 years of age. Think of the peculiar bluish-red complexion, clubbed fingers, which are rather congested, and the peculiar bluish appearance – almost like ripe grapes – of the lips. That underlying colour is associated with Laurocerasus.

These patients always suffer from extreme dyspnoea, which is nearly Cheyne Stokes in character. They take a sudden gasping breath, then two or three long breaths, then the breathing gets gradually shallower, then a pause, followed by two or three gasps, and this pattern of breathing continues. This dyspnoea gets very much worse if the patients sit upright. They are easier in a semi-recumbent position.

There is a marked tendency to the early development of hypostatic pneumonia in such cases, and once this has appeared, the cough is more troublesome unless they are reasonably supported. When lying down the cough is worse, yet sitting upright produces a feeling of extreme constriction of the chest, so that semi-recumbent is the position of choice.

These patients are always cold; they feel cold to touch and want to be kept warm, and any movement or exertion causes an acute aggravation.

Two other remedies are of great value in treating heart conditions, namely Crataegus Oxyacantha and Latrodectus Mactans.

Crataegus Oxyacantha

Crataegus is of the greatest value in myocardial degeneration with a steadily failing heart. In such a condition there will be the usual accompanying symptoms, increasing pulse rate, signs of pulmonary congestion, a certain amount of oedema, slight cyanosis and aggravation from any exertion.

In such a condition, Crataegus in low potency may produce a dramatic effect and a considerable amount of recovery in the apparently irreparably damaged heart. Give Crataegus 3x every 3 to 4 hours for several weeks.

Latrodectus Mactans

The indications for Latrodectus are also in cases of cardiac failure such as those with a definite valvular lesion.

As in Crataegus, there are the usual physical signs of a failing heart, but Latrodectus patients are in addition always very irritable. They complain of numbness of the left hand and arm, and they usually have precordial pain which may be of any degree of severity.

These patients will get great relief from the administration of Latrodectus 12c or 30c, given at short intervals, say every 2 to 4 hours, for 24 hours, and then repeated only when necessary.

ACUTE CARDIAC ANGINA

Patients with true or pseudo-angina often give cause for anxiety, but there are a few homoeopathic remedies which give great relief to many of them.

Aconite

The outstanding characteristic of the majority of patients in their first attack of angina pectoris is an overwhelming fear. The patient is certain he is going to die and that he is going to die very speedily, and he is terrified. He is quite unable to keep still, and yet any movement seems to aggravate his distress. In a patient with these symptoms, a dose of Aconite in a high potency will give relief almost instantly.

The patient may have a similar attack at a later date, and the anxiety, the distress and the fear are not so marked because he has recovered from a previous attack, and Aconite may give no relief at all. In the first attack, when the patient is quite certain he is going to die, Aconite relieves the symptoms straight away, but it has no effect in a second or later attack. In the later attacks of angina pectoris, Cactus is the remedy most likely to give relief.

Cactus

Cactus patients have a good deal of anxiety and fear, but it is quite different from that of Aconite patients. It is not a fear that the immediate attack will kill him, it is more a conviction that he has an absolutely incurable condition which will eventually be fatal.

Another point is the type of the actual distress of which the Cactus patient complains. He feels as if he has a tight band round the chest which is gradually becoming tighter and tighter, and that if this tightness does not let up soon the heart will be unable to function. That feeling of increasing tension gives the Cactus indication.

In addition to the constriction, there may be stabbing, radiating pains from the precordium, but they are not so characteristic of Cactus as the intense feeling of constriction. This is, of course, exactly how the majority of patients with angina pectoris describe their pain.

In these acute conditions, give the remedy in a high potency, because it acts much more quickly and the patient needs relief as quickly as possible.

Arsenicum Album

Occasionally a patient experiences an attack of angina with very similar constricting pain, not quite as intense as in a Cactus patient where the constricting pain seems to dominate the whole picture, but still a feeling of constriction. The patient has been unwell for some time. He is pale, rather anxious and worried, and feels cold, and the feeling of constriction in the chest is accompanied by a rather acute, distressing, burning sensation. These patients respond very well to a dose of Arsenicum Alb.

Iodum

Other patients may complain of very much the same sensation, but the feeling of constriction, the feeling of tension, is described as being actually in the heart itself rather than involving the whole of the side of the chest.

The patients are just about as anxious as Arsenicum Alb. – but instead of the intense coldness of Arsenicum Alb. they are uncomfortable in heat and in a stuffy atmosphere. They are about as restless, but instead of the pale, drawn appearance of Arsenicum Alb., they tend to be rather flushed and, as a rule, are dark-haired, dark-complexioned people. They are usually underweight, in spite of the fact that they often have an appetite above the average. These cases respond exceedingly well to Iodum.

Spongia

Yet another type of case is one in which the complaint, instead of being constriction, is of a sensation of progressive swelling in the heart region. The patients feel as if the heart is swelling more and more and will finally burst, and the sensation of fullness spreads up into the neck.

This sensation of fullness and swelling is very much aggravated by lying down, when the patients feel as if they will choke, and it is accompanied by acute pain.

The patients are chilly, and any draught of air increases their distress. In addition to their discomfort in the chest, they usually complain of numbness, particularly of the left arm and hand, or numbness of the hand without any involvement of the arm. Not infrequently they also complain of numbness of the lower extremities.

As a rule, the face and neck look congested, they do not have the pale, drawn wrinkled appearance of Arsenicum Alb. patients. These cases respond well to Spongia.

Spigelia

Another useful remedy for patients who do not have the typical anginal constriction, but the pseudo-anginal stabbing, radiating pains – sharp, stabbing pains starting in the precordium, spreading up into the neck, maybe across into the right side or down the left arm. These shooting pains may be followed by numbness involving the whole affected area, and as a rule, the pain is a little eased by turning over on to the right side.

Accompanying the stabbing pains there is a degree of hyperaesthesia over the precordium. Any movement aggravates the pain, or brings on a violent attack. These patients respond to Spigelia.

Lilium Tigrinum
There is a condition which is not a true angina but which is met with in hysterical women. No cardiac lesion is demonstrable, but the patients will produce a symptom picture which is difficult to distinguish from a true anginal attack. They have marked stabbing, radiating pains, often an intense hyperaesthesia of the chest wall. They are very depressed and frightened, and they are intensely irritable. They are sensitive to heat, and their distress is aggravated by any movement. In addition to their stabbing pains, they have the anginal sense of constriction, tightness of the chest wall.

If these patients also have a pelvic lesion or a history of having had some gynaecological complaint, they will respond to Lilium Tig.

Chapter 6

The Gastrointestinal Tract

DYSPEPSIA

The ordinary dyspeptic patient seen in the surgery has either an acute attack of indigestion following some indiscretion in diet, or chronic dyspepsia and chronic constipation.

Consider the acute attack. The patients fall quite easily into one of two classes. First, the adult who has been out, eaten and drunk too much, and comes to the surgery next morning feeling indisposed, probably with a slight headache, and very little inclination for breakfast. This type will respond in the majority of instances to a few doses of Nux Vomica in a low potency.

The other type of acute digestive upset is met with more commonly in the child. The child who has been out to a party, eaten too many cakes and ices, been vomiting all night, and is brought in next morning pale, irritable and tired. In the majority of cases all the child needs is a dose of Pulsatilla in either the 6c or 30c potency.

The next type of dyspeptic disturbance is the tired out, weary patient with chronic flatulence. There are mainly two types. There is the thin, nervous patient whose digestive upset has followed some minor acute illness, who has chronic indigestion, a good deal of flatulence, and is rather chilly and irritable. A few doses of China in a low potency will usually clear the symptoms.

In contrast there is the heavy, sluggish, fat, lethargic type with a tendency to eat too much starchy food, a tendency to flatulence and a feeling of fullness and discomfort round the waist. A few doses of Carbo Veg. puts that temporary indiscretion right.

Patients must be considered as individuals. These are broad outlines. Each of these remedies may be used as a heading for a number of others which are complementary. Include with the Nux Vomica patients all the nervy, excitable people who are upset by over-rich food. They may require Nux Vomica, Lycopodium, Ignatia, Arsenicum Alb.

or Phosphorus. All patients of that type are upset by similar things, and Nux Vomica can be put at the head of the group, but the others must be considered.

In children – Pulsatilla, Argentum Nit. and Calcarea Carb. are all liable to be upset in similar circumstances, but Pulsatilla is much the most commonly indicated member of the group.

Another group is the emaciated China type. A similar type of patient may need Sepia, Natrum Mur., Natrum Carb. and occasionally Lycopodium.

In the Carbo Veg. group they may require Graphites, Anacardium, Calcarea Carb. or occasionally Petroleum. That is the way to group them. Always try to get a clear picture of the outstanding member of the group and then fill in the exceptions. As a start, the four remedies – Nux Vomica, Pulsatilla, China, Carbo Veg. – cover most cases of dyspepsia, but those that do not respond must be reconsidered.

GASTROENTERITIS

There are very few remedies to consider for acute diarrhoea and vomiting. For instance, for acute gastroenteritis poisoning, which is very violent and develops within a few hours, Arsenicum Alb., Carbo Veg. and Veratrum Alb. are the three to be considered. For more slowly developing diarrhoea and vomiting there are other useful remedies, a number of which are also described here. With a good knowledge of these remedies, most acute cases can be treated.

Arsenicum Album
In Arsenicum Alb. cases there will be very violent vomiting and diarrhoea, purging and vomiting at the same time. The patients say they get constant little gushes of diarrhoea which seldom stop, and which are associated with violent burning pains in the rectum. There is constant retching with a burning pain in the stomach, and extreme exhaustion.

These Arsenicum Alb. patients are at first extremely restless, and have violent distressing tenesmus after the bowels act. As the condition progresses they get more and more prostrated, they become very cold, look very anxious, and have marked tenderness all over the abdomen.

Between the vomiting, Arsenicum Alb. patients very often get relief from little sips of hot water, and the abdominal distress is relieved by hot external applications. In acute diarrhoea and vomiting they have a very dry mouth and may take sips of cold water, but this will be vomited at once, whereas a sip of warm water often seems to quieten the stomach temporarily.

During the acute diarrhoea, Arsenicum Alb. cannot lie still in bed, they get up and move about, and are liable to have an involuntary stool.

There is nothing very characteristic about the appearance of the stool, except that it is small, frequent, rather watery and very offensive.

Arsenicum Alb. is the typical food poisoning remedy. The attacks may be induced by any impure food, such as rancid meat, bad sausages, over-hung game or blown tinned meat. Occasionally an Arsenicum Alb. diarrhoea will be brought on by over-indulgence in ice cream in warm weather – from chilling the stomach when the patient is hot.

Carbo Vegetabilis

Patients needing Carbo Veg. do not have such severe vomiting as the Arsenicum Alb. patients, but there is a very violent, exhausting diarrhoea, with marked tenesmus and the passage of small stools, usually liquid, brown and offensive.

The patients have none of the restlessness of Arsenicum Alb. They look ill, the face is pinched, drawn and pale, and they are covered with cold, clammy sweat. They feel intensely cold, complain of the legs and feet being icy cold, and yet have a marked air hunger and cannot bear a close, stuffy room. They like to feel a movement of air.

There is burning in the abdomen, though not so marked as in Arsenicum Alb. and there is none of the Arsenicum Alb. dryness and thirst.

Another pointer to Carbo Veg. is that, in acute attacks, Carbo Veg. patients have a great deal of flatulent distension. They feel the abdomen is very distended, and pass large quantities of flatus. They have frequent eructations which give very marked relief. That is an important point as a distinction from Lycopodium, where in spite of eructating the patients still feel distended and there is no relief. It is important to remember that Carbo Veg. as well as Lycopodium may be needed in shellfish poisoning, although Lycopodium is the main antidote to oyster poisoning.

Carbo Veg. may be needed for patients suffering from food poisoning, or from eating too much ice cream when they are hot.

Veratrum Album

The third of these remedies is Veratrum Alb. Many cases requiring Veratrum Alb. have already had Arsenicum Alb. without benefit.

Arsenicum Alb. is considered the typical remedy for food poisoning with diarrhoea and vomiting, and is given automatically, whereas many of these cases need Veratrum Alb. and not Arsenicum Alb.

The indication for Veratrum Alb. is that there are gushes of large quantities of fluid material. There is as much vomiting and purging, or even more, in Veratrum Alb. as in Arsenicum Alb. The quantity of fluid lost is considerable. the stool is often odourless in Veratrum Alb.

The patients are always icy cold and bluish in colour. They are just about as pinched-looking as Carbo Veg. patients, and are drenched in sweat, in spite of losing so much fluid from the bowel. It is not quite so clammy as in Carbo Veg. but it is a cold sweat, and the patients themselves feel cold. The sweat is all over the body in Veratrum Alb., whereas in Carbo Veg. it is mostly on the face, hands and feet – not the general sweating as in Veratrum Alb.

Another indication for Veratrum Alb. is that after the bowels have acted, there is the most deathly faintness. In severe cases, with almost continuous vomiting and diarrhoea, the patients may become unconscious. In a patient with acute diarrhoea and vomiting, who is sweating profusely, with profuse discharge and a tendency to faint, Veratrum Alb. in a high potency should give rapid relief.

Camphor

There are one or two cases which present a less usual picture, and which will need other remedies. Occasionally a patient is seen in a late stage where the history seems to suggest Arsenicum Alb., but has progressed beyond the anxious restless stage to one of acute collapse. On enquiry it will be found that there have been alternating waves of heat and cold during the acute stage. In the state of collapse, the patient is icy cold to touch, although he complains of burning internally. He wants to be uncovered in spite of the external coldness, because of the burning heat internally. The skin is dry.

There is constant tenesmus, small dark stools, and the patient is on the point of collapse, pulse rate increasing, colour becoming greyish-blue.

These patients should respond very well to Camphor, given a high potency. They warm up very quickly, and when warm they can be covered up; while the surface of the body is cold they are much more comfortable uncovered.

Cuprum

Cuprum is another remedy that is sometimes useful in a case of diarrhoea and vomiting, with very profuse discharges from both the stomach and the bowel. The patients feel very chilly and have a mottled, dusky appearance, with blueness round the finger nails, and the extremities look rather dusky, but – unlike Camphor – with the chilliness, the patients want to be covered up. The skin is moist and there is a tendency to slight jerking of the muscles, jerking of an arm or jerking of a leg, and violent cramping abdominal pains. With the action of the bowels they are liable to get acute cramp in the gluteal muscles. They may get cramps in the calves of the legs and have a tendency to spasm of the hands, where the thumb flexes inside the fingers. These cases respond exceedingly well to Cuprum.

Lycopodium

Lycopodium is almost a specific for people who are oyster sensitive. In a case of violent diarrhoea and vomiting following a meal of oysters, Lycopodium is almost always indicated.

As a rule, Lycopodium patients have a great deal of eructation, which may be accompanied by vomiting. But they still feel uncomfortably distended in spite of the release of wind.

There is a great deal of rumbling and gurgling in the abdomen before the diarrhoea comes on, and then the most violent, liquid stool. These attacks seem to be more common in people who are habitually constipated, with a history that the attack has started with flatulence, distension, rumbling and a certain amount of colic. The first stools that were passed were rather lumpy and hard, and the later ones were liquid and accompanied by the passage of a large quantity of flatus.

Another symptom that helps in the selection of Lycopodium, in preference to any other remedy, is the fact that the abdominal distress is relieved by hot drinks. They must be really hot, not the warm fluid of the Arsenicum Alb. patients. A hot drink seems to get rid of a good deal of the flatulence and makes them more comfortable. As with Arsenicum Alb. patients, the abdominal discomfort is also relieved by hot applications

There is not the same degree of anxiety and restlessness as in Arsenicum Alb. Lycopodium patients tend to be anxious, but are much more miserable and depressed than the acutely apprehensive Arsenicum Alb. patients. It is much more on the history of the cause of the attack of diarrhoea than on the actual symptomatology that Lycopodium is prescribed.

Phosphoric Acid

The characteristic of Phosphoric Acid is that the patients have the most copious, watery diarrhoea, which is almost painless. It just gushes out and they may have complete incontinence. It is always very urgent, and the stool is almost entirely odourless.

The next indication for Phosphoric Acid is that patients seem unaffected by their diarrhoea. There is always a history of completely painless, watery diarrhoea, with extreme urgency and difficulty in controlling it. It may be accompanied by a certain amount of flatus, which is quite odourless. It may be induced after eating ice cream, or being chilled, or after a period of stress, and occasionally as an anticipatory diarrhoea from fear. Phosphoric Acid may also be indicated for patients suffering from diarrhoea after eating sour fruit. Patients requiring Phosphoric Acid rarely vomit.

Aconite

In conditions where Aconite is indicated, there is a history of a very sudden onset: the patients were in good health, then exposed to some food poisoning, or to being chilled or a similar situation which has precipitated the enteric attack. Occasionally an acute enteritis, which is the result of shock or fright in a highly nervous, excitable patient, will respond to Aconite; but the commonest cases are the result of chill or exposure. With their enteric attacks the patients suffer from acute burning and agonising, griping pain.

Aconite enteritis patients have an almost incessant urging to stool, with constant pain, heat and burning. They frequently have recurrent attacks of colic, with a burning pain in the rectum and acute tenesmus while the bowels are acting. As a rule there is a sense of relief in the bowels when they have acted, but the patients feel very exhausted and nauseated.

The stools in typical cases are always small and frequent, and consist mainly of blood and mucus. The blood is usually bright red, and the stools may consist of almost pure blood. It is a very acute inflammatory condition.

Always where Aconite is indicated, there is the extreme nervous anxiety and distress, a feeling of apprehension and restlessness that Aconite has in all its acute conditions. In acute bowel disturbances there is one symptom that is not so frequent in other Aconite conditions – the patients feel faint and may actually faint on sitting up. With the attacks of diarrhoea, Aconite patients are always intensely thirsty; their lips and mouth are dry and often have a slightly bitter taste. They may complain of a tingling sensation in the mouth. There is an apparent contradiction – with the diarrhoea they have intense thirst for cold water in fairly large quantities, but the colic is relieved by hot drinks, and the abdominal pain is relieved by hot applications. The abdomen is tender to touch because there is an intensely inflamed bowel, so any heavy hot water bottle will be resented, although warmth is comforting. Another thing about Aconite patients in their acute enteric attacks is that they are often pale and have a cold sweat about the head, but have a hot sweat when they are covered up.

A further distinctive symptom of Aconite is that, accompanying the enteritis attacks, patients have a certain amount of bladder irritation, but pass quite a large quantity of urine. The bladder is irritated but the urine is not suppressed. This is the opposite in Cantharis patients, for instance, who have scanty urine – a useful distinguishing point. One other symptom occurring with all Aconite acute inflammations, no matter where they are, is marked sleeplessness. The symptoms in most patients becoming suddenly very violently ill will be eliminated by Aconite, if given early enough. The symptoms are so intense that the highest potency can be used, and repeated frequently about every 15 minutes. If the symptoms are not subsiding within a couple of hours, do not continue with Aconite; some other remedy will be indicated. If the patient is responding, the mental anxiety subsides first, then the stools become less frequent and less painful. Continue the Aconite and the symptoms will probably clear in 18 hours.

Colocynth

Colocynth is indicated for a very similar sort of attack. There is a similar history of onset. It develops either from a digestive indiscretion or from exposure, and the symptom that always indicates the possibility of Colocynth is the intensity of the abdominal colic. This colic begins before the diarrhoea develops and is extremely severe. As a rule it starts as a somewhat indefinite griping pain, usually on the left side of the abdomen. Frequently before the diarrhoea develops, the colic tends to spread up into the epigastrium, producing intense nausea and often vomiting. This subsides a little and the colic spreads further down. There is then a violent, sudden urge to stool which is so urgent that the patient has the greatest difficulty in retaining the stool. When the bowels are acting, there is violent rectal tenesmus associated with generalised abdominal colic. One of the characteristic symptoms is that the patients often complain of a violent pain in the forehead during a stool, during this tenesmus and colic. As a rule they get relief from colic after a stool, but it leaves a burning pain in the rectum and round the anus. That is the typical picture. Patients will occasionally get the violent urging to stool and feeling of inability to control the bowels unaccompanied by any colic at all, the colic developing only after the bowels have acted; but that is less common.

At first the stool is profuse and liquid, containing mucus which quickly becomes bloodstained, the mucus and blood increasing with the frequency of the stools. The next constant thing in Colocynth enteritis is that any food or drink tends to produce an attack of colic, followed by an action of the bowels.

There is a good deal of bladder irritation, with urging to urinate, and often a statement that while passing urine, abdominal colic tends to develop and then the urge to stool. Colocynth patients have acutely inflamed bowels, the abdomen is tender and they dislike any weight on the abdomen because of the inflammation; for that reason they lie with their legs drawn up, to take the tension off the abdomen. But they are more comfortable and the colic is relieved by hot applications and gentle, steady, firm pressure.

One outstanding difference between the Colocynth and Aconite is that there is not the same fear of death in the Colocynth patients. Colocynth dislike being disturbed, dislike being interfered with and would much rather be left alone. All Colocynth patients are thirsty, but that is so common in an acute enteritis that it is not of great importance.

One point, which is sometimes a help, is that with a Colocynth colic the patients frequently say that the colic is eased and made more comfortable by taking coffee or by smoking. Smoking tends to relieve the abdominal irritation in Cololcynth patients. This is exceptional and therefore of value. They are restless, which is a useful point, because patients requiring some of the other remedies are only comfortable when they are keeping still.

Given early, Colocynth should clear the symptoms altogether. If symptoms have been present for some days and the inflammatory condition in the bowel has been extensive, and the colic is tending to become less intense and the tenesmus greater, the remedy needed to follow will probably be one of the Mercury salts.

Mercurius

The best way to consider the Mercury salts is to take Merc. Sol. or Merc. Viv. as typical of them all, because in enteritis, considering Mercury or one of its salts is purely a question of intensity. Merc. Sol.

and Merc. Viv. are interchangeable, and one of these two is intended whenever the abbreviation Merc. is used. If the stool appears to consist of almost nothing but blood, the condition will respond better if the patient is given Merc. Cor. or Merc. Cy. If the stool consists mainly of mucus, there will probably be a better response from Merc. Sol. or Merc. Viv.

The main distinguishing point between Colocynth and Merc. Sol. is the fact that the colic has subsided or has not been present, and there is very much more inflammatory disturbance in the pelvis, colon and rectum, with the most violent, frequently recurring urging to stool. This is a Merc. Sol. characteristic. With this urging to stool there may be a feeling of nausea without actual vomiting, and the patients complaining that they feel intensely chilly. Merc. patients feel alternately hot and cold. There is severe rectal tenesmus before the bowels have acted. During the action of the bowels the tenesmus becomes even more marked and the action produces very small, very slimy, bloody stools, which feel as if they were scalding the anus. During the time the bowels are acting the patients feel even more chilly than before, yet often break out into a hot sweat on the head. After the bowels have acted, the tenesmus continues and there is no relief from the evacuation.

With their bowel disturbances Merc. Sol. patients have very little colour in their face. During the action of the bowel, they may become a little flushed with a hot head and tend to perspire, particularly on the head and face. They always give the impression of being toxic and their eyes are heavy. Their mouths tend to become unpleasantly offensive very rapidly in their attacks of acute enteritis, and the tongue gives the impression of being large, flabby, pale and shiny. During their attacks they complain of nausea with salivation, and that their saliva is unpleasantly sticky.

In most of these diarrhoeas the patients are thirsty for cold drinks, just as Merc. Sol. patients are in all their other conditions. The attacks of diarrrhoea are exhausting and the patients very quickly become weak and tremulous. With their recurring attacks of tenesmus they usually get urinary frequency, but not the same degree of bladder spasm and bladder irritability that occurs in some of the other remedies. If these patients have severe bladder tenesmus and rather scanty urine, Merc. Cor. or Cy. is usually indicated rather than Merc. Sol. If the urine is markedly bloodstained, Merc. Cy. is the remedy. With rather scanty urine, it is Merc. Cor. There is severe tenesmus in both.

Kali Bichromicum

A remedy which is not so often indicated in the acute stage, but which may be needed as a follow-up in some of these very intense cases, when the condition has improved a little but has not cleared, is Kali Bich. The main indications for Kali Bich. are cases having intense inflammatory disturbance in the bowel and very small, frequent stools with a great deal of blood, mixed up with a lot of mucus, where the intensity is subsiding, the tenesmus easing, the stool less bloodstained, and the mucus less watery and becoming thicker. Kali Bich. patients with enteritis have abdominal flatulence, not very marked colic, with considerable urging to stool. This is accompanied by straining and the passage of strings of mucus, very little blood; but after the passage of the mucus, intense burning in the anus and rectum.

Kali Bich. will often clear up that type of case. During this stage patients often feel very tired out and develop the Kali Bich. desire for stimulants. If the inflammatory condition has spread into the stomach and there is an acute gastritis with mucus, that is an additional indication for the administration of Kali Bich.

Aloes

In acute conditions the Aloes stools are typical dysenteric stools. There is a marked tendency for Aloes patients to develop incontinence. When Aloes is indicated, the diarrhoea is always associated with flatulence, and the patients have incontinence of the bowel when passing flatus or passing urine. There is a peculiar sensation experienced just before the bowels act. It is as if the whole pelvis had filled up, accompanied by griping pain in the abdomen. That may subside with the passage of just flatus without any stool, or else the patients think that they are going to pass flatus, and a little of the bloodstained mucus comes away almost unconsciously. Another symptom is a griping pain high up in the abdomen, spreading downwards with this feeling of filling up of the pelvis and intense tenesmus, as if the whole rectum was in a state of spasm. As a rule there is a sudden, violent evacuation of the bowels, with complete relief of the urging and colic by the evacuation. There is also a tendency to develop a prolapse of the rectum or very painful piles. Associated with the diarrhoea, whether piles have developed or not, the patients have a sense of heat and burning in the rectum. Their piles are relieved by cold applications and aggravated by greasy ointments such as petroleum jelly. Quite frequently Aloes patients will say that before the griping pain develops there is a feeling of disturbance in the abdomen, with gurgling in the bowel, tending to come on immediately after any food or drink, but particularly after food. In the acute stage, they say that any movement or effort to pass urine tends to bring on the diarrhoea, and they may have incontinence of stool with the passage of urine.

As far as general symptoms are concerned, Aloes patients are irritable with their abdominal conditions. They are sensitive to heat and complain of a burning sensation in the extremities, particularly their feet. They are usually thirsty in spite of the fact that fluids aggravate their diarrhoea. The tongue is usually clean and they may complain of a bitter taste. During the griping attacks the abdomen is tender to touch, and there is a good deal of general abdominal distension. In spite of the abdominal disturbance and aggravation after food, Aloes patients with diarrhoea usually have a good appetite, which is an unusual symptom. The diarrhoea tends to be worse in the morning, often quite early – 6 a.m. onward – similar to Sulphur. But in the Aloes patients the diarrhoea is attended by a feeling of fullness in the rectum and pelvis generally. They have more colicky pain than Sulphur patients and the urge to stool is more violent, accompanied by more flatus. As a rule, Aloes patients are more irritable than Sulphur patients. They have a peculiar state of dissatisfaction with what is being done for them, and a state of almost childish anger when the colic is developing. Sometimes this is a help in distinguishing between Aloes and Sulphur, as their heat and cold aggravations are almost identical. Sulphur patients as a rule like meat, and Aloes have an aversion to meat. Alcoholic patients occasionally suffer from a morning diarrhoea, which can usually be checked by having some beer before getting out of bed. This condition can nearly always be cleared up with Aloes.

Podophyllum

It is very difficult to distinguish Podophyllum from Aloes in the textbooks. At the start of the diarrhoea the symptoms of both are very much the same. Podophyllum patients have the same aggravation after eating or drinking, and the first sensation they have is the same kind of gurgling in the abdomen and throughout the bowel generally. They develop a similar griping pain after the gurgling has stopped, but it is much more colicky in character. They get a sudden urging to stool, which is much more acute than in Aloes patients. There is not the same tendency to develop piles, but there is a more marked tendency to rectal prolapse with the stool. Podophyllum patients experience a very violent, aching pain when the bowels are acting, which Aloes do not. This is a real distinction between the two.

In Podophyllum patients the stools tend to be much larger, much more fluid, and the flatus is mixed up with the fluid stool so that it is expelled noisily. The appearance of the stool may be anything from a watery mucus stool to a very offensive bloodstained stool. Practically all the diarrhoeas which respond to Podophyllum are offensive.

Aloes patients, as a rule, are more peaceful for a while after the bowels have acted. In Podophyllum, the colic continues for some time after the bowels have acted, with a feeling of exhaustion. The stool is very forcibly expelled. Often the patients feel cold, alternating rapidly with flushes of heat that spread over their backs. Another distinguishing point about Podophyllum patients with diarrhoea is that quite frequently, just before the bowels act, they are not quite sure whether they are going to have an action of the bowels or whether they are going to vomit. They may start retching and gagging, and then have a sudden violent, watery stool. Cramp in the thighs or legs may accompany the abdominal colic.

As far as the abdominal condition itself is concerned, there is very little to distinguish the two remedies. In both, the patients have abdominal tenderness and are not particularly aggravated by either heat or cold. As far as appearances are concerned, they are quite distinctive. Podophyllum patients with diarrhoea look ill, as if they were going to vomit, and they are cold, clammy and sweating. Immediately after an attack, they experience waves of heat, during which they may become flushed; but in the attacks they become cold, pinched and distressed.

They have a night aggravation, not early in the morning, as in Aloes. It may be any time during the night, but is usually about 3 to 5 in the morning. They get a definite aggravation from being bathed. Podophyllum patients are usually lacking in thirst and usually have a coated tongue, either white or yellow.

Cantharis

Cantharis is the next remedy that should be considered for very violent bowel inflammations. It is never needed except in the very acute stage. The stools are always small, frequent and burning, and consist of a mixture of mucus and blood with shreds of tissue. The symptoms felt by the patients before and during the action of the bowel are a very intense, abdominal colic and urging to stool, with general abdominal pinching pains. The colic continues right through the action of the bowels and is accompanied by intense burning pain in the anus and rectum. There is always intense straining, often with a degree of prolapse of the bowel. After the bowel action the colic subsides, but the rectal tenesmus and pains are often worse. During this period the patients often shudder with the pain, describing the sensation as if cold water was being poured over them, and yet inside they were being burned up. They get a good deal of bladder irritation, either frequent urging to urinate, or suppression of urine. There is always burning pain during the passage of urine, and often burning in the bladder after the urine has passed.

Cantharis patients are always anxious and restless. They are very pale, particularly during the pains, although they may become flushed in between.

If the inflammatory condition spreads up to the stomach, they are thirsty whereas, with diarrhoea, they are thirstless and have an aversion to all food or drink. The abdomen is usually somewhat distended and is always very tender to touch.

All Cantharis patients tend to have a general night aggravation. This aggravation starts in the evening and usually lasts throughout the whole night. The acute symptoms in these cases can be controlled with Cantharis but, as a rule, some other remedy will be needed to cure, and by far the commonest one to follow is Kali Bich. This is indicated when the colic is beginning to subside and the stools are beginning to get a little less bloodstained with more stringy mucus, but with the tenesmus persisting.

Capsicum

In the typical Capsicum diarrhoea, there is a history that the patient has a good deal of general abdominal flatulence. Then, before the diarrhoea starts, there is generalised abdominal colic, tending to become more intense while the bowels are acting. There is spasmodic tenesmus in the rectum, during the action, and after the bowels have acted this tenesmus becomes much worse. The first distinguishing Capsicum symptom is that with the tenesmus after the bowels have acted, the patient becomes intensely cold and thirsty for cold water. .Yet if they drink cold water, it often produces a sensation as if they were almost frozen, with acute discomfort in the abdomen and general shivering. During this acute tenesmus they often complain of intense drawing pain in the back, coming on after stool. Nux Vomica patients experience a similar sensation before stool, continuing during the action of the bowels, but not after. The typical stool of Capsicum patients is a rather thin, very slimy, adherent stool containing mucus and streaked with very dark blood. The upper part of the large intestine is mostly affected, so the blood is dark in colour. The patients stress that the stool tends to be very difficult to clear away, as it is small, adherent and slimy. Associated with their attacks of diarrhoea, they complain of feeling very tired and sleepy, and they may be yawning and stretching during the interview. The lips are rather swollen, and dry and cracked, and the patients often complain of a sour, offensive taste. They are acutely sensitive to cold and sensitive to draughts of any kind, even of hot air. They are not usually thirsty, except after the bowels have acted, but drinking water produces the peculiar cold shuddering sensation. They are usually rather fat people and sluggish in their movements. They tend to be pale, but often become very flushed during the action of the bowels. One useful symptom is that in their attacks of diarrhoea they often develop a craving for coffee, yet, if they drink coffee during an attack, they become nauseated. If the diarrhoea persists, bladder irritation may develop. This is sometimes severe, though as a rule it is slight. Occasionally there is very marked irritation with constant straining, but retention of urine. This is not a suppresssion of urine, which distinguishes it from Apis and Cantharis, and which patients requiring either of these remedies may develop.

Nux Vomica
Nux Vomica patients may experience a feeling as if their back was breaking before and during the action of the bowels. The general abdominal symptoms in Nux Vomica patients are generalised abdominal soreness and colic. Before the bowels act, they develop a very intense rectal tenesmus, a constant feeling as if the bowels were going to act lasting for some considerable time before the action takes place. After they have cleared the rectum there is almost immediate relief. They complain of a good deal of burning in the anus after the bowels have acted. The typical stools are frequent, small and usually semi-solid, and are dark in colour, mixed with mucus and thin bloodstained liquid. The patients complain that the stools are hot, burning and offensive. During the attack there is some bladder irritability, but never difficulty in passing urine – just urinary frequency. The rectal tenesmus eases for a time after passing urine, but soon returns.

In their acute attacks, Nux Vomica patients always have very severe abdominal tenderness. It is always much more sensitive than would be expected from the degree of inflammation. They always have a thickly coated tongue, which may be white or brown, but is usually yellow. They complain of an unpleasant taste, usually bitter, but it may be very offensive, almost putrid. With their acute abdominal conditions there is always nausea to a greater or lesser degree, aggravated after food. A distinguishing symptom is that Nux Vomica are drowsy after meals, or sleepy during the greater part of the day, and then disturbed and restless at night. As a rule they are thirsty and very chilly. In their digestive upsets they are acutely sensitive to smell, also to jarring and motion, due to the abdominal tenderness. They are very irritable and become very sensitive to noise and often to light. In appearance, they are under-nourished. They are thin, worried-looking, very often sallow, and may be jaundiced.

CONSTIPATION

A common condition seen in general practice is chronic constipation. It may be due to irregular habits, often accompanied by over-use of aperients, leading to an inactive atonic condition of the rectum. The usual advice about habit and diet, including fruit, vegetables and bran should be given.

There are three homoeopathic remedies which may help. Where the patient rarely gets an urge to stool, and the condition appears to be one of insensitivity and inactivity of the rectum, Opium in the 6c potency will often correct the condition.

In patients who habitually take large doses of aperients, where there is an urge to stool but inability to expel it, there is often a good response to Nux Vomica 6c given three times a day.

Some patients have bouts of severe constipation which are associated with haemorrhoids, which are painful and bleed. Hydrastis in a 6c potency will usually help.

In each case the remedy should be taken three times a day until a good response is obtained, then reduced to twice, and finally to once a day as the condition improves.

HAEMORRHOIDS

The treatment of haemorrhoids depends on the local modalities. If they are inflamed and acutely painful, and the patients obtain relief from hot applications, then Kali Carb. is the remedy. If they are relieved by cold applications, Pulsatilla will usually ease the pain.

A certain number of patients complain of a continuous throbbing pain in the haemorrhoids, which are hypersensitive. If they obtain relief from cold applications, Lachesis is the remedy.

Chapter 7

Obstetrics and Some Gynaecological Conditions

From the obstetric point of view there are various remedies which are useful and which have clear indications. Where there is a delayed or prolonged labour there are certain remedies with definite indications, which give a very much easier confinement.

OBSTETRICS

Caulophyllum

Consider a confinement where progress is slow, the mother is having indefinite pains coming at long intervals, making very little progress, and is just becoming exhausted. If there are no individualising symptoms at all, a few doses of Caulophyllum 200c given at hourly intervals stimulates the uterine muscle and brings on a labour that has not been progressing. Caulophyllum will also bring on the labour peacefully and successfully for the patient who has some contractions during the day, which quieten down at night when she goes to sleep, with no further progress, and who is becoming more exhausted.

Gossypium

Gossypium is not a very well known remedy, but is very useful in a similar condition. There is a history of a mother who has had a certain amount of abdominal discomfort and a definite show. On examination, labour has started, but she is having singularly painless contractions. As well as being painless, the contractions are intermittent and accompanied by a feeling of intense weariness. Very little progress is being made and, again, there are few indications except that the pains are so tiresome and exhausting, and yet not acutely painful. The mother is getting tired out of all proportion to what she is suffering. That is the kind of case which responds to Gossypium.

These two remedies, Caulophyllum and Gossypium, are the routine remedies to give to stimulate the progress of a labour supposing there were no other indications to go on.

Pulsatilla

In slow labours the most commonly indicated remedy is Pulsatilla. The reason is that the Pulsatilla type of patient tends to get distressed during labour. They are very mild, tearful and apprehensive, their uterine contractions are poor and they become worried and anxious. They feel hot, become breathless and may feel faint, wanting the doors and windows open, or to be fanned, and they make very little progress in labour. One of the indications for Pulsatilla in these mothers is that with each uterine contraction they tend to have an increased feeling of distress and suffocation, and often palpitation. On palpating the uterus, quite a good contraction can be felt starting, the uterus hardening up, and then the patient experiences this faint fluttering feeling and the contraction fades. It is the emotional stress that interferes with the normal progress of the uterine contraction and prevents their making any progress.

Another confirmatory point is that, whereas in most confinements the mothers are intensely thirsty – they are working hard and their mouth tends to become dry and they are very thirsty – Pulsatilla mothers remain entirely or comparatively thirstless. That thirstlessness is a confirmatory Pulsatilla indication.

In that type of case Pulsatilla will soothe the patient. It removes the nervous apprehension and the tendency to faintness and palpitation, and it strengthens and regularises the uterine contractions. After making no progress for hours, given Pulsatilla, four doses a quarter of an hour apart, the mother makes steady progress and labour is completed easily.

Kali Carbonicum

The next most indicated remedy in that type of delayed labour is Kali Carb.

The Kali Carb. patient is a woman who is getting weary with the slow progress of her confinement. She is very tired and probably a bit chilly, and is liable to be irritable. The indication for Kali Carb. is the manner in which the pains develop. The contraction starts and then the patient develops a violent pain in the back, just in the lower lumbar region or at the junction of the lumbar region and the sacrum; it is a sensation as if the back would split open. As the uterine contraction increases, the pain, instead of spreading round the sides as described by a normal patient, tends to shoot down into the gluteal region and into the buttocks. With that extension down into the buttocks, the patient arches the back and is unable to make any voluntary pressure.

In their confinement all Kali Carb. patients tend to get general abdominal discomfort, particularly flatulence. If they can get rid of a quantity of wind – usually upwards – they feel very much easier and as if labour could progress, whereas until they do get rid of wind they feel as if they could not make any effort. After some Kali Carb., the patient loses the intense pain in the back altogether, the contractions become more regular and more forceful, and labour progresses satisfactorily.

Chamomilla

One of the chief indications for Chamomilla is the patients' inability to bear pain. Whether the cause be purely mental or an actual hyperaesthesia, they become distraught with the discomfort and pain that they are enduring. Their mental irritability seems to check the normal uterine rhythm completely. A pain starts normally, the uterus is beginning to contract and then, instead of it going on to a full contraction with the voluntary muscles coming into play, the patient shrieks out, 'I can't bear this any longer', and the contraction ceases. She cannot bear any touch or any kind of examination. Often a Chamomilla patient complains that the pains in the uterus radiate in all directions, very often down the thighs, which seems to annoy her even more, and she always feels that much more should be done for her than is being done. She is the kind of person who is always asking for hypnotics, or else forceps to end labour when the cervix is only about one finger dilated.

After a dose of Chamomilla the patient begins to have pains of which she is barely conscious. It seems to relieve the hyperaesthesia more than anything else. Instead of the pains driving her nearly distraught, she does not seem to feel them until the cervix is half dilated. It is not unusual to see Chamomilla patients in confinements who do not require any anaesthesia until the child's head is on the perineum, although in the early stages of labour the mother gives the impression that early sedation will be required.

Sulphur

Sulphur mothers are sometimes very difficult to distinguish from Pulsatilla mothers. It is an interesting point that a patient who has needed Pulsatilla during the earlier part of a confinement, if the placenta is very slow to separate, will almost certainly require Sulphur and not Pulsatilla to bring it away.

The typical picture of Sulphur is that of a mother who is becoming very exhausted. She is very weary, and complains constantly of having distressing flushes of heat. It is not the same stifling, hot, faint feeling of the Pulsatilla mother. It is much more a general wave of heat, often associated with a feeling of intense coldness in the legs and feet. And, as a contrast to the Pulsatilla mother, although she is feeling so hot and sticky, she is very sensitive to any cold draughts, whereas the Pulsatilla mother wants the doors and windows open.

The next point about the Sulphur mother is that when the uterus contracts, she often complains of feeling faint. It is much more a sinking faintness, rather than the stifling, palpitating faintness of the Pulsatilla mother. Very often, accompanying the feeling of faintness, a commencing uterine contraction can be felt just fading out and the uterus becoming soft and flabby.

Another point that distinguishes her from the Pulsatilla mother is that the Sulphur mother is usually thirsty. One thing she definitely does not want is cold drinks – she wants something hot and stimulating and feels better for it.

Sepia
When dealing with the typical elderly primipara, with a rigid, fibrous cervix in a poorly developed, thin, weary and sallow patient, always consider the possibility of Sepia.

One of the distinguishing points about Sepia is that as labour commences, and as dilatation starts in the lower uterine segment, the mothers frequently complain of localised stitching pains in the lower part of the uterus with the contractions, and these stitching pains often stop quite a strong contraction from progressing. Sepia mothers often have a very acute, distressing backache with each pain. It feels exactly as if the back were going to break. They do not get radiating pains down into the hips, and this distinguishes them from Kali Carb.

As the pains become more severe, and are obviously just about as severe as she can bear, as the contraction reaches its maximum, the patient develops a weird shuddering, the contraction subsides and she lies back exhausted, cold and very often somewhat faint. It is more a feeling of weariness and tiredness than actually a faint. Before the shuddering sensation comes on she may complain of feeling too hot, and yet she wants to be covered up. The Sepia patient is one who cannot be allowed to get out of bed and walk about, particularly if the room is at all cold, because unless she is kept warm she makes no progress at all in her labour.

In these mothers, Sepia will help to shorten the labour.

Nux Vomica

There are one or two remedies which are not frequently required, but which have definite indications and are very useful when needed. One of these is Nux Vomica.

The odd symptom that distinguishes Nux Vomica is that every time the patient has a contraction, she feels that she must get out of bed and either have her bowels opened or pass urine, and makes no progress in labour.

This is an unusual symptom and is useful to remember.

Cocculus Indicus

There is another type of case which is difficult to treat, illustrated by the following. A patient was progressing in labour very slowly. She would have one strong contraction and then three or four of which she was very conscious but which did not reach their full potential. Then she would have another good contraction, followed by three or four more coming to nothing. She just went on like that for twelve hours, making no progress at all. In addition, she complained of a general congestive headache and a feeling of numbness in her legs, as if they were losing all sensation. The feeling of numbness is fairly common, but it was particularly marked in this patient. She was very tired and sleepy, and slept practically all the time between her pains. After receiving Cocculus, the patient became alert, the contractions regular and strong, and labour progressed normally.

Lobelia

Two other remedies should be mentioned, because they help a difficult type of case, the one with the failing heart.

A patient with a mitral stenosis, the highly coloured, florid patient who tends to become very cyanotic, with acute dyspnoea as the pains become more intense, responds very well to Lobelia. The cyanosis clears, the respiratory distress eases, and the tendency to acute oedema of the vulva, which is so often troublesome in these patients, is very much lessened.

Carbo Vegetabilis

The other drug for patients with a failing heart is Carbo Veg., and it is given on the general indications for Carbo Veg. The patient is tired out, the pulse rate is increasing, and volume poor. The contractions are becoming weaker. The skin surface is cold and clammy. There may be a history that there has been a tendency to oedema of the ankles in the later months of pregnancy, probably with very troublesome varicose veins, and varices of the vulva. There is blueness of the lips and a feeling of air hunger. The legs and feet are icy cold, and the patient wants to get warm, wants to be covered up all the time, but also wants to feel movement of air. In that type of case, where there was a possibility of a difficult delivery, the patient should have quite a normal delivery after some doses of Carbo Veg., which can be given in high potencies.

Phosphorus
One type of mother that causes anxiety is the Phosphorus patient, because Phosphorus are liable to postpartum haemorrhage. With any known Phosphorus patient it is advisable to give her Phosphorus before the child is born, particularly if she is showing any signs of distress towards the end of labour, to avoid the haemorrhage.

There is one odd symptom to remember. After the infant is born, and before the haemorrhage, the patient may complain of a feeling of acute emptiness in the abdomen, accompanied by intense heat running up the back and a certain amount of eructation of wind. In such a case give Phosphorus immediately.

POSTPARTUM HAEMORRHAGE

Prescribing for postpartum haemorrhage is very difficult. These cases are very acute and treatment is urgent, so it is necessary to know the remedies, and a good knowledge of the homoeopathic Materia Medica may save a patient's life.

Ipecacuanha
The most commonly indicated drug in a postpartum haemorrhage is Ipecac. The patients usually get a feeling of sudden, intense nausea and collapse. They look deathly pale, they feel extremely ill, even from the first gush of blood.

Sabina
The other drug that may be needed is Sabina, which has almost the

same symptoms as Ipecac., a sudden collapse and faintness, but without the acute nausea. There is just the same gush of bright red blood, although the Sabina patient has large blood clots and then gushes of blood alternating. The Ipecac. patient tends to get gushes of unclotted blood.

Postpartum haemorrhage is an urgent and alarming condition, but it very rarely occurs in patients who have been treated with homoeopathic remedies throughout their pregnancy and confinement.

ACCIDENTAL MISCARRIAGES

The commonest causes of accidental miscarriages are falls, jars or over-exertion, stresses or shocks. Working on these lines there are clear indications for homoeopathic remedies.

Arnica
Arnica is the remedy if there is a history of a fall, which has been followed by the commencement of either haemorrhage or uterine pain, but without any definite signs of an inevitable abortion – merely a threatening without a great deal of pain, but just a little oozing of blood or bloodstained mucus or serum. Alternatively, if there is a great deal of aching or pain in the uterine region without definite uterine contractions, but possibly with a slight sticky discharge, a few doses of Arnica given at that stage will almost always prevent an abortion taking place.

The 200c potency may be given, about half a dozen doses, four hours apart for twenty-four hours, and by next day the danger of abortion should have disappeared.

Cinnamon
Probably the next commonest mechanical cause for a miscarriage is over-lifting. Strangely enough, cases of abortion coming for that reason do not respond nearly so well to Arnica as might be expected.

The patients usually complain of a good deal of dragging pain – a feeling as if everything had settled down into the pelvis, and a good deal of tenderness in the region of the round ligaments, and possibly some blood loss. That kind of case responds very well to Cinnamon.

One distinguishing point is that the Cinnamon type of patient is usually restless. She is extremely uncomfortable; she finds it difficult to get a comfortable position and tosses about. Arnica patients are made very much worse by any movement.

Rhus Toxicodendron

The third common cause for an abortion is over-exertion, the patients getting tired out, being much too strenuous and finally having a threatened miscarriage. That type of case usually responds very well to Rhus Tox.

These patients have the general weariness and tiredness of Rhus Tox. They have general aches, particularly backache, very often in the part they are lying on, aches which make them restless and want to move. There is always a certain amount of anxiety, they are tired and nervous, and their pains are severe. It is the type of case where abortion seems almost inevitable; but if treated early enough with a few doses of Rhus Tox., all the symptoms subside.

These three are by far the commonest types.

Ignatia

Another case which presents in the accidental class is the miscarriage from shock – nervous, emotional shock – and it is necessary to differentiate between the effect the shock has on different patients.

With the acute emotional disturbance and acute hysterical reaction, the patients find it very difficult to keep still. They are either moving about, wringing their hands or weeping, and they start having irregular uterine pains. In that type of patient, the miscarriage is usually prevented by a few doses of Ignatia.

Opium

For patients in whom the shock has caused prostration, with dullness and depression, where they are completely overcome by it, the remedy is Opium rather than Ignatia.

Aconite

A third type is one where the patient suffers a terrible fright, and after falling asleep at night wakes up in terror. One such case was a woman who came downstairs and found one of her children standing in front of the fire with her frock alight. The woman was three and a half months pregnant. She dealt with the emergency, but that night she woke up in terror, screaming out, and within half an hour she had started definite uterine contractions and a discharge of blood. That is the kind of case that responds to a few doses of Aconite.

So far as these emotional disturbances are concerned, it is necessary to differentiate the kind of shock and the effect it is having on the patient.

IDIOPATHIC MISCARRIAGES

Sabina

Apart from accidental miscarriages there are women who seem to miscarry for no particular reason. A perfectly healthy young woman starts a normal pregnancy, and then miscarries about the third month. If there is no uterine displacement, and no reason can be discovered for it, there is one remedy that will often help and that is Sabina. The main indication is that so long as the patient keeps perfectly still there is very little loss, but any movement at all starts up a haemorrhage. That is the usual story in this type of miscarriage. The patients say that in previous pregnancies they stayed in bed from about the middle of the second month to the middle of the third month, and as long as they were lying still they were all right; if they got up and moved about again there was a little show. There is apparently no cause for the threatened miscarriage. The blood coming away is quite bright and fresh looking, and as a rule it has a normal tendency to clot. Usually, if the condition is progressing, the patients tend to get a good deal of dragging, forcing pain from a point situated behind the uterus, between the uterus and the lumbar spine, and coming right forward towards the pubis – the premonitory symptoms of a miscarriage. That type of case responds very well to Sabina.

These are the remedies that might be considered for routine work. Beyond that, it is a question of prescribing for each miscarriage as it occurs. For instance, in a patient with a low lying uterus, think of one of the remedies which has the sensation of the dragging in the pelvis, such as Sepia. If the patient is a hot-blooded individual, consider Lilium Tig. If the patient has albuminuria, think of one of the remedies with a relationship to kidney disturbance, either one of the snake remedies, or Terebinth, or a similar remedy. Where it is associated with an ovarian tumour, consider the supportive use of Apis. Otherwise, prescribing is purely on the local symptoms and any remedy in the Materia Medica may be required.

The constitutional medicine can be expected to prevent a miscarriage, provided there are no clear indications for any other remedy. For instance a Kali Carb. patient tends to miscarry very easily, and Kali Carb. should stop this tendency. They suffer from persistent backache, the uterus is low, and they are very liable to miscarry if they get over-tired.

The remedy that helps most women who tend to abort in the later months is Sepia, because they cannot carry the weight of the full uterus. It is lack of tone that frequently causes the seven-months miscarriage in that situation. Sepia is the remedy for the cold-blooded patient, and Lilium Tig. for the warm-blooded patient.

SEPTIC MISCARRIAGES

(*Note.* Such cases will be treated with antibiotics now. It is to the patient's advantage to use the correct homoeopathic remedy as well, since this will speed full recovery. Ed.)

The three remedies most frequently needed for septic miscarriages are Secale, Sulphur and Pyrogen, and the indications for them are very distinct. They all have a very offensive discharge and of the three, the one with the greatest quantity of discharge is Secale. It has a purulent discharge mixed with dark, decomposing blood. In Pyrogen and in Sulphur the discharge is less in quantity, less bloodstained, more purulent and more offensive.

Secale
Secale patients are very restless, very anxious, uncomfortably hot, and yet have a strange feeling of coldness in the abdomen. This is apt to be forgotten about Secale because it is looked upon as one of the hot drugs, and the fact that the patients complain of a feeling of coldness is confusing. They are always thirsty and they are very frightened. As a rule they have a dry skin.

Sulphur
The typical Sulphur patient feels very hot, but it is not a constant feeling of heat. They experience waves of heat with perspiration and very often feel cold and shivery up the back. Their sweat and everything about them is offensive. They are much more heavy and dull and toxic, and far less anxious and worried than Secale. They are usually thirsty, though the thirst is nothing like so marked as it is in Secale, and

they tend to develop a purple congested look of the lips and mucous membranes in general. They are often very restless and complain of generalised aching pain.

Both Secale and Sulphur patients are liable to get a high temperature and, in Sulphur particularly, the infection spreads early from the uterus out into the pelvic fascia.

Pyrogen

In Pyrogen cases there are more general toxic symptoms – increased general aching, headache, aching in the back, aching in the legs. The patients may develop an early pelvic thrombosis. They are hot and sweat profusely, but they do not experience the same waves of heat that are present in Sulphur.

Both Sulphur and Pyrogen may have rigors, but they are more common in Pyrogen.

LEUCORRHOEA

There are four remedies which are more commonly indicated for pelvic lesions than any others – Sepia, Sulphur, Pulsatilla and Sabina.

Sepia

With Sepia patients there is always uterine displacement, usually accompanied by a mild degree of pelvic infection, with a rather bulky, unhealthy uterus, usually in a multiparous woman with a relaxed pelvic floor. They may have a cystocoele or a rectocoele, and very often a torn perineum. There are two types of discharge, either of which may indicate Sepia. One is a thick, greenish, acrid discharge, usually a B. Coli infection, definitely purulent in character. The other is a much more milky, profuse discharge, the type associated with a chronic endocervicitis.

The symptom that indicates Sepia is the feeling of dragging down, bearing down, of weakness in the lower abdomen, a feeling as if the perineum or the abdominal wall must be supported. These patients are almost incapable of standing for any length of time because of the dragging, which produces a severe backache, so they are more comfortable moving about. The other Sepia characteristic in these gynaecological cases is the feeling of emptiness, often described as a kind of false hunger, with not much desire for food.

Sepia patients have a general visceroptosis and suffer from chronic constipation. Occasionally a case presents in which, with a marked retroversion of the uterus, there is a feeling of something pressing against the rectum and a desire for stool, often associated with very severe, troublesome haemorrhoids.

Characteristically Sepia patients are tired out, miserable and irritable. They get cross with their surroundings, they feel they are badly used, that life is too much for them, and they just cannot bear things. Their inability to bear things may either show itself as breaking down and weeping or getting very angry. They are chilly and very sensitive to any disturbance about them, such as sudden noises or anything similar.

Sulphur

Two types of case present indications for Sulphur. One is the patient who has had a mild pelvic infection, either an incomplete abortion, or a subinvolution of the uterus. The other has irregular periods associated with the menopause, with a mild degree of pelvic infection. In both cases there is the same sort of local discomfort. There is a consciousness of weight, fullness in the pelvis, the uterus is bulky, very often tender to touch – more often in the infected case than in the menopausal one.

Definite Sulphur indications are that the discharge may be yellow, yellowish-white, or even faintly bloodstained. But no matter what its colour, it is always a very unpleasant, sticky sort of discharge, and always offensive, and very often the Sulphur patients themselves are acutely conscious of this offensiveness. The discharge is always very irritating. It either produces a sensation of heat and burning or intense irritation, becoming very much worse whenever the patient is warm. One of the characteristics is that any attempt to bathe, although it relieves the patient temporarily, tends to increase the irritation later.

Another Sulphur indication is that with these pelvic disturbances the patients tend to have disturbances of the circulation. They have flushes of heat from exertion or stress, and very often after eating, quite frequently followed by shivering.

Pulsatilla

Pulsatilla is indicated in patients with a profuse yellowish discharge, not noticeably offensive, probably with redness and swelling of the vulva and an uncomfortable feeling of heat. The uterus is enlarged and the patients complain of a feeling of weight in the pelvis. There may be actual prolapse but, as a rule, there is only a slight dragging down of the uterus, often associated with a good deal of thickening along the broad ligaments and probably an enlarged Fallopian tube, which is surprisingly non-tender. There is always a feeling of unpleasant, often distressing, fullness in the abdomen. Sometimes it is very marked, amounting almost to a sensation of being bloated with great discomfort from anything tight around the abdomen. It is accompanied by a feeling of heat with a tendency to faint, particularly in any stuffy atmosphere. The patients are usually somewhat overweight. Occasionally the vaginal discharge is completely non-irritating, although that is unusual in a Pulsatilla patient. Most Pulsatilla discharges are quite bland, but the vaginal discharges are usually irritating although they do not get the intense itching of Sulphur.

That picture in rather a mild, gentle patient with the usual Pulsatilla likes and dislikes, its desire for company, dislike of being left alone, desire for sweet things, dislike of fat, gives indications for Pulsatilla. It will clear most cases without any local treatment at all.

These are only the key-notes of these remedies; they are to help to identify them easily.

Sabina

(*Note.* Antibiotics are the recognised modern treatment for venereal disease. Before they were discovered, homoeopathic remedies had proved very effective in such cases and remain a valuable supportive therapy. Ed.)

If a patient presented with acute gonorrhoea and cauliflower growths, most prescribers would give Thuja, and be very disappointed with the result. Thuja will clear up a chronic gonorrhoea but it does not clear the acute condition. The remedy for acute gonorrhoea is Sabina, and in Sabina there are two conditions. One, the frank gonorrhoea with a pouring greenish-yellow discharge, with masses of soft cauliflower growth all round the vulva and extending back round the anus. These cauliflower growths are, like most of the gonorrhoeal growths, soft and insensitive, which is the distinguishing point between Sabina and Thuja. Chronic gonorrhoeal warts are much smaller and more sensitive, and indicate Thuja. The Thuja discharge is nothing like so profuse, or so thick, and not so deep in colour; it is not the greenish-yellow colour, but pale yellow and more liquid.

That is the classical Sabina acute case. The other case with indications for Sabina is the patient with a uterine fibroid who has the kind of discharge associated with a fibroid – the sticky semi-purulent discharge. They are usually overweight, with a florid complexion. They become pale owing to loss of blood from the fibroid. They have profuse periods, followed by intermittent loss, and become steadily more anaemic. The loss gets less and finally stops, and they are clear for a month or two, with just a slight leucorrhoea. During that time they improve in general condition, their colour begins to return and then the haemorrhage starts again. That is the typical Sabina history.

UTERINE INFECTION

After these four remedies, there is another pathological condition needing another group of remedies. It is a mild uterine infection with a quantity of not very purulent but very persistent discharge. For this condition, with typical viscid, whitish or yellowish-white, sticky discharge associated with a mild infection of the cervix or the uterus, there are frequently indications for Hydrastis, one of the Kali salts, or Natrum salts. They all have a similar type of viscid, sticky discharge, and in all of them there may be a torn, eroded cervix, or just a mild pelvic infection with a slightly enlarged uterus.

Hydrastis
There are certain distinguishing points between the three groups of remedies. Hydrastis has that type of discharge, but it tends to have colour in the sticky discharge – it is deeper yellow than in either the Potassium salts or the Sodium salts. Also in Hydrastis the discharge is more irritating; there is itching and general soreness. In the case of an eroded cervix, on examination the cervix is very friable and bleeds very easily. It is this tendency to easy bleeding which is the indication for Hydrastis.

Kali Salts
The Kali salts have a similar type of discharge, but there are certain minor points that decide their individual selection. If there is a history of a sub-involution of the uterus and the discharge persisting since a pregnancy, the probability is that Kali Bich. is needed in preference to the other Kali salts. It must be remembered that in leucorrhoeas, the Kali Bich. discharge is more yellow than the rest of the Kali Bich. discharges. The nasal discharge, for instance, is rather like white of egg; this leucorrhoeal discharge is of much the same consistence, the same stickiness, but it is yellow.

   Another point in favour of Kali Bich. is that with the bulky uterus there is a sensation of prolapse, a dragging down in the pelvis. The patients generally tend to be very much worse in hot weather, and in particular their dragging sensation.

The type of discharge in which Kali Carb. is indicated is associated with fibroids rather than with an infected uterus. It is much the same in character as the Kali Bich. discharge, but almost always the patient gives a history of excessive periods. Finally, all Kali Carb. patients have the typical Kali Carb. prostrating backache, a low-down sacral backache which feels exactly as if the back were going to break, tending to be particularly bad at a menstrual period. They cannot keep on their feet during the first two days of the period, partly because of the excessive loss but mainly because of the intense backache.

The indication for Kali Phos. in preference to the other Kali salts is the fact that, in addition to the typical discharge, Kali Phos. leucorrhoea is always very offensive. It is also excoriating, the vulva becomes quite raw. The discharge also tends to be more profuse in Kali Phos., and there is probably a secondary infection, possibly a B. Coli infection.

Natrum Salts

Of all the Natrum salts, the most frequently indicated is Natrum Mur., which has a very characteristic white-of-egg discharge. Apart from the ordinary Natrum general indications, the point that indicates Natrum Mur. in preference to the other remedies for sticky discharge is that it is intermittent. There are days when the discharge is profuse and very troublesome, and other days when there is very little discharge and the patient complains of acute dryness, burning, itching and smarting in the vagina.

Another characteristic of the Natrum salts is that with their leucorrhoea, as with their other discharges, they tend to get herpetic patches on the mucous membrane over which the discharge is flowing, either on the mucous membrane or on the skin surface. These herpetic patches burn and smart, and are seen on speculum examination of the vagina.

LEUCORRHOEA COMPLICATED BY MALIGNANCY

(*Note.* In any case where cancer is suspected it is necessary that the fullest investigation be carried out, and every form of treatment considered, in the best interests of the patient. But whether surgery, radiation or chemotherapy are used, homoeopathic treatment is always a valuable supportive therapy. Ed.)

Kreosote
The commonest remedy for the palliation of a malignant growth in the body of the uterus or in the cervix is Kreosote. The first characteristic is the typical malignant odour, easily recognisable; it is a most penetrating, indescribable sort of odour. It is present in all the remedies for malignancy, but is worst in Kreosote.

In Kreosote, the discharge is intensely irritating; the surfaces with which it comes in contact become almost raw, and they are extremely sensitive to touch. Always with Kreosote indications there is a purulent discharge mixed with streaks of blood, which is partly decomposed. There may be streaks of bright blood, but there will be black streaks in among it, and with this type of discharge, Kreosote will give great relief.

Carbo Animalis
There is another type with malignant ulceration of the cervix, where there is a much more watery type of discharge than occurs with malignancy of the body of the uterus. In Carbo Animalis the discharge is particularly irritating, much more extensively so than in Kreosote. The inflammation seems to spread down the thighs much more than it does in Kreosote. As with all malignant disease of the cervix, the discharge is bloodstained, but the cervix is not nearly so friable as in the typical Kreosote case. The discharge is very offensive, but not quite so penetratingly offensive as in Kreosote, and it seems to be more foetid than the horrible decomposition smell of the other. Then the patients requiring Kreosote have been fairly well-nourished originally, whereas Carbo Animalis patients have always been rather emaciated. On first looking at them they may suggest Sepia; they have the same sort of brownish discolouration of the face associated with Sepia, but Sepia does not help in malignant cases. In a patient with the Sepia exhaustion, weary, depressed and miserable, with the dragging down sensation, and the Sepia staining of the face, Carbo Animalis rather than Sepia will give greater relief.

Arsenicum Iodide
There is only one other remedy to mention and that is Arsenicum Iod. When dealing with a malignant uterus in a patient who gives the Arsenicum Alb. indications, extreme restlessness and anxiety, burning pains, incessant and excoriating scalding discharge, Arsenicum Iod. will give better results than Arsenicum Alb.

Chapter 8

Sleeplessness

There are no homoeopathic remedies which act specifically as hypnotics in the same way as those which are normally given for sleeplessness, yet they are very helpful when given on the right indications.

There are two remedies which may be indicated when the sleeplessness is caused by stress of apprehension, such as going into hospital before an operation, taking an examination, or before an important business meeting.

If the patient is restless, unable to stay in bed but must get up and walk about, or tries to sleep in a chair and then goes back to bed again, becoming exhausted and increasingly apprehensive, Arsenicum Alb. is the remedy.

If, with the restlessness, the patient is miserable and depressed, and afraid to be alone, possibly becoming weepy and slightly hysterical, Ignatia will help.

In other patients the sleeplessness is caused more by activity of their thoughts rather than fear. Patients in hospital will be worrying over their families as well as their own condition and its possible outcome. The examinees will be going over all possible questions they may have to face, and the businessmen cannot stop thinking of the next day's meeting. These patients will be helped by Coffea. They are acutely sensitive to noise. They become restless and may experience tingling sensations in various parts of the body.

Other patients, not unlike them, who also tend to become more mentally active and more sensitive to their surroundings in the late evening, and cannot sleep, require Nux Vomica. They become very irritated and angry by their inability to sleep.

Both Nux Vomica and Coffea are very helpful for the sleeplessness caused by excessive coffee drinking. (The coffee should also be stopped.)

Another type of patient similar to those requiring Nux Vomica is one who is oversensitive, particularly to pain. This person is helped by

Chamomilla. The main difference is the type of irritability. It is a much more petulant, peevish state rather than the angry irritation of Nux Vomica. Chamomilla is also helpful for patients who have been in the habit of taking sedatives, when it is desirable to bring them back to a normal pattern of sleep. They very often respond to Chamomilla during the difficult phase of withdrawal, when they are particularly irritable and peevish.

Opium is another remedy which may help those who are trying to leave off regular hypnotics and who are in a state of acute nervous excitability.

Sometimes, more particularly in children, homesickness may be a cause of sleeplessness. They feel the strangeness of their surroundings acutely and want to be with the family. They are really miserable, and in these circumstances Capsicum will help.

There are also patients who have had long periods of stress, or broken nights from looking after someone through a prolonged illness, and who reach the stage when they find it almost impossible to sleep. They will require Cocculus Indicus to help them back to a normal sleep pattern.

Sleeplessness is uncommon in children, but for the nervous, excited, frightened child who cannot sleep, Aconite is the remedy.

Belladonna is also useful for the excited child with a flushed face, hot head and widely dilated pupils, perhaps seeing faces or black shadows in the corners of the room after getting over-excited at a party.

Sleeplessness may also be caused by pain. In hospital practice, the homoeopathic remedies used for this type of sleeplessness are mostly determined by the nature and site of the operation, and are mainly prescribed for relief of pain rather than the sleeplessness itself.

After an abdominal operation involving the stomach, liver or gallbladder, the most useful remedy is Phosphorus.

The most commonly indicated remedy after appendicectomy is Rhus Tox., where the patient is restless. If the patient is flushed, hot, thirsty and wants to keep quite still, Bryonia is needed.

Sepia is the most useful remedy after operations on the uterus, and Apis after operations on the ovaries and Fallopian tubes.

Where there is post-operative distension of the bowel, Carbo Veg. is the most helpful remedy if the abdomen is generally distended, Raphanus if there are small, localised areas of distension.

In conditions where sphincter muscles have been stretched, such as cystoscopy or sigmoidoscopy, or after operation for haemorrhoidectomy, Staphisagria is the most frequently needed remedy, although occasionally it will not help and then Hypericum should be given.

Sometimes Nitric Acid is needed after haemorrhoid operations, when the patient is intensely irritable and complains of acute stabbing pain.

After breast amputation, if the patient complains of severe aching pain, Arnica will help, or if the patient is very restless, Rhus Tox.

For neuralgic pains, shooting, cramping pains, whatever the site of the operation, Mag. Phos. is the most helpful remedy.

For sleeplessness, the homoeopathic remedies act most satisfactorily if they are prescribed in low potencies 2 or 3 times a day, or 2 or 3 doses during the evening, with the last dose on getting into bed. They should be stopped as soon as there is a good response.

Arsenicum Alb. and Opium should never be given in potencies lower than a 6c. The other remedies mentioned may be given in 1x, 2x or 3x. The remedies that are prescribed for post-operative pain should be given in the 12c or 30c potency, commencing as soon as the patient has recovered from the anaesthetic, and the dose repeated every half hour to every 4 hours according to the severity of the pain, until relief is obtained.

When prescribing for sleeplessness from anticipation, it is not usually necessary to treat the patient for more than 24 hours before the event. This may be difficult to arrange for a patient who is in hospital awaiting an operation but, if it is possible, the homoeopathic remedy will give them great relief from their anxiety and distress.

Chapter 9

Pre- and Post-Operative Treatment

The use of homoeopathic remedies in post-operative treatment is determined to a very large extent by the type of operation.

EYES

Hypericum

The eye is an intensely sensitive organ, and patients are liable to get very acute pain. After an eye operation, Hypericum may be given for the relief of pain as a routine.

Aconite and Stramonium

If the patient has a marked nervous reaction, becoming very excitable, restless and distressed, as eye patients do, the routine treatment is to prescribe Aconite, when they will settle down quite quickly. The best plan is to give the Aconite frequently at 15-minute intervals in acute and very painful conditions.

If the condition is more acute still, after the first stage is over, the patient verging on delirium, the remedy that controls it is Stramonium.

These are the three drugs that help after most of the serious eye operations. Use the 200c potency in each case.

Coccus Cacti

After the removal of a foreign body from an eye, if the patient declares that something has been left behind, prescribe a few doses of Coccus Cacti. This removes the sensation of a foreign body, due to abrasion.

THROAT AND NOSE

Arnica and Symphytum

After any operation on the nasal septum, removal of turbines or submucous resection, the indications are almost always for Arnica or Symphytum.

Usually the patient will say it is exactly as if he has had a blow on the front of the face, which feels swollen, and that he feels he cannot breathe. These patients respond to Arnica. Occasionally a patient does not respond to Arnica, in which case use Symphytum.

After operations on the antrum, in the first instance it is wise to prescribe Arnica. Some of these patients suffer very severe pain after drainage of an antrum, and Arnica will give them almost immediate relief, although previously they were complaining that their face was feeling exactly as if it was going to burst and that they were getting pains right up the side of the face from the area that had been punctured.

Arnica and Rhus Tox.

For tonsil and adenoid operations the indications are either for Arnica or Rhus Tox. In Arnica, the patient wants to keep the throat as quiet as possible, and obtains relief from cold applications to the neck and cold drinks. As long as the patient makes no attempt to swallow, the throat is fairly comfortable. The Rhus Tox. patient has relief from hot applications to the neck and hot drinks to relieve the throat and, so long as he goes on taking little sips of hot water, the throat is fairly comfortable. He wants to keep the throat moving. If he keeps it still, it is very painful when he starts to move it again by swallowing. This is the ordinary Rhus Tox. aggravation from keeping still and pain on beginning to move again, and the ordinary Rhus temperature reactions – amelioration from heat as opposed to the Arnica amelioration from cold.

After 48 hours these tonsillectomies may have a very offensive exudate, dirty tongue and foul breath. Merc. Cor. will improve the condition rapidly in the majority of cases.

ABDOMEN – RIGHT UPPER QUADRANT

In the abdominal region, prescribing becomes a little more complicated, but there are certain broad indications to follow. In the majority of cases that have had an operation in the right upper quadrant of the abdomen there are indications for either Phosphorus or Arnica. Occasionally Carbo Veg. or Chelidonium are required for operations about the gallbladder or in the region of the duodenum.

Phosphorus

The indications for Phosphorus are a sensitive stomach, a tendency to bilious vomiting, pains in the right upper quadrant of the abdomen. The patients are thirsty with a desire for cold water. They have a certain amount of anxiety and fear, want company and dislike being alone. They complain of a burning pain in the affected region. That is the ordinary Phosphorus case.

Arnica

Arnica patients will probably complain that they feel as if they have been kicked under the ribs. They have a bruised pain in the affected area with very marked aggravation from any movement, and the breathing is shallow in order to keep as quiet as possible. They feel far too hot, and have very little thirst. If it is a gallbladder operation they have a tendency to become jaundiced. A few doses of Arnica will give them relief.

Carbo Vegetabilis

Carbo Veg. patients are obviously shocked and cold, with clammy skin. They very often complain of cold legs and feet, a feeling of extreme abdominal distension, the feeling being out of all proportion to the amount of flatulence. They have a choking sensation and like to feel a movement of air, and may ask to be fanned. There is not very much thirst, but they want their drinks hot. They have a feeling of extreme distension after any drink. A few doses of Carbo Veg. will relieve these symptoms.

Chelidonium

Chelidonium patients have much more acute pain in the right upper abdomen. It is stabbing in character, tending to go through to the back, aggravated by any movement. They are more comfortable with a fairly firm bandage round the affected area. They are thirsty, have a tendency to jaundice and a desire for hot drinks.

ABDOMEN – RIGHT LOWER QUADRANT

Rhus Toxicodendron, Arnica and Bryonia

Passing to the right lower quadrant – the appendix, ileo-caecal region, right iliac fossa – the two great standbys there are Rhus Tox. and Arnica for the immediate post-operative treatment. If Rhus Tox. is given immediately after the operation it will prevent much of the post-operative pain and restlessness. The differences between Rhus Tox. and Arnica are just the ordinary differences between these two remedies in general – Arnica with intense aggravation of pain, discomfort and distress from any movement, and relief from keeping still. The patients feel hot, too hot, and have a general bursting, aching feeling in the side. Rhus Tox. patients on the other hand are definitely restless and, although it hurts to move, they cannot keep still. They have a dry tongue, thirst, recurring spasms of pain, and a desire for hot applications, which give relief.

These are the routine remedies for the appendix region. One other very commonly indicated remedy is Bryonia, and it is sometimes difficult to distinguish between an Arnica and a Bryonia. In both cases there is marked aggravation from movement, the feeling of being too hot and the dislike of being turned over or touched. But in Bryonia the tongue is thickly coated, white and with a feeling of nausea, and there is always a constant thirst with a desire for cold drinks – that is the main differentiating point between Arnica and Bryonia.

Note. In the following discussion of serious septic conditions and intestinal stasis, it is certain that chemotherapy will be used. It is still in the best interests of the patient that homoeopathy is also used as supportive treatment. Ed.

Pyrogen, Crotalus Horridus and Rhus Toxicodendron

A different group of remedies is required to help an acute septic condition, such as a gangrenous appendix after surgery, and to talk about the complications of all surgical operations would cover the whole Materia Medica. As a routine, with no definite indications when dealing with a septic appendix, or even a fairly advanced peritonitis, there are certain remedies to consider. After a perforation of the appendix, with a sudden drop in temperature and increased pulse rate, the best prescription is several doses of Pyrogen, 15 minutes or half an hour apart. The results would probably be best if the Pyrogen is given before the abdomen is opened. If, when the abdomen is opened, there is a sloughing, haemorrhagic appendix which bleeds when it is handled and it is difficult to stop the bleeding, with a very offensive discharge, the best remedy is Crotalus Horr. Start this immediately after the operation.

There is only one other routine to give for these appendix cases. Where there has been a gangrenous appendix and next day there is a tendency to infection of the skin round the incision, this will very often clear up on some Rhus Tox.; it seems to have a strange affinity for that inflammatory reaction round such wounds. These remedies cover the majority of cases; the exceptional ones must be prescribed for on their individual symptoms.

INTESTINAL STASIS

There are several remedies to consider when dealing with a case of abdominal operation in which there are signs of stasis of the intestine.

Carbo Vegetabilis
The first and by far the commonest is Carbo Veg. There is the general Carbo Veg. picture but, in addition, the point that strongly indicates this remedy is that there are scattered areas of distension. There are loops of bowel which balloon out for a time and subside, and then it swells up in another place and subsides; it is not exactly a visible peristalsis, but rather an irregular distension in a Carbo Veg. patient.

Stannum
The next most common remedy for this condition is Stannum. The patients always feel deadly tired and exhausted. They have periods of complete quiescence when the abdomen is perfectly comfortable, although it remains distended. Then a slowly increasing abdominal discomfort begins, increasing to colicky pain that subsides suddenly. There is sudden relief and they are at peace again for a time. The symptoms indicating Stannum are the steadily increasing discomfort, and then the sudden relief of the pain.

Nux Vomica
Another type of case is one with acute colicky pains, first in one area of the abdomen and then another. Accompanying the attacks of pain are intense irritability, restlessness, a feeling of nausea, and usually vomiting – often a bitter, bilious vomit. Associated with these symptoms there is a certain amount of flatus being passed, and urging to stool, yet very little passing. These symptoms indicate Nux Vomica.

Opium
Patients who have generalised abdominal distension without colicky pain but with nausea, very often with vomiting, will be relieved by

Opium. The patient just feels nauseated and vomits a small quantity, which dribbles from the mouth. He is obviously very ill and no flatus is being passed at all. His appearance is congested, dark red or slightly cyanosed, not as in Carbo Veg.

Raphanus

This is one other remedy which is particularly useful in any case of resection of the bowel or a partial gastrectomy, in which there is a tendency either to an inactive stomach, or in which there is acute distension of the first or second part of the duodenum. There is an area of localised abdominal distension with colicky pain.

SPHINCTERS

Staphisagria

Another problem is the acutely painful after-effect of any interference with any of the circular fibres – any sphincters. If, after dilatation of any sphincter, there is residual pain, it is nearly always relieved by Staphisagria.

COLICS

Aconite

The only other conditions that can be treated as a routine are the colics – renal, gallstone and intestinal. They can be covered by three or four remedies.

The acute, typical colic, associated with agonising pain, often terror on the part of the patient, extreme restlessness, and a certainty that they are going to die, is relieved by Aconite.

Colocynth, Magnesia Phosphorica and Berberis

In addition, there are three remedies to consider – Colocynth, Mag. Phos. and Berberis. Colocynth and Mag. Phos. have similar indications. The patients feel as if the area is becoming increasingly constricted, with waves of pain coming to one definite painful spot, and a feeling as if the bowel is being twisted up almost to the state of bursting. Any movement aggravates the condition. They want to keep as still as possible, and obtain relief from both heat and pressure. In an intestinal colic, Colocynth is more likely to be indicated than Mag. Phos. Where it is a renal or hepatic colic, Mag. Phos. is more likely to be indicated than Colocynth.

The distinguishing point of Berberis is again the typical colicky pain, but instead of the pain gradually increasing in one spot, it starts in one spot and tends to radiate either down the canal, or through to the back, or out in all directions from the painful area. It has much the same modalities, with aggravation from movement and relief from heat, but the patients are much more sensitive to pressure than Mag. Phos. or Colocynth, and the pain is aggravated by it.

Chapter 10

The Kali Salts

The six common Kali salts are Kali Bichromicum, Kali Bromatum, Kali Carbonicum, Kali Iodatum, Kali Phosphoricum and Kali Sulphuricum. There are certain points of similarity running through them all, but their differences are very definite. In trying to compare them, it is impossible to consider them all together; the only way is to take the remedies one after the other, take the outstanding characteristics of each one, and mention the similarities and differences of the others.

Kali Bichromicum

The Kali Bich. patient is a fair, fat, somewhat sluggish individual, either male or female. Their faces are rather puffy, and they give the impression of having an unhealthy skin; the majority have a tendency to acne. Their eyes are rather dull, they may have a yellow tinge of the conjunctivae and there may also be a blepharitis. Suppose the patient is a man. He will be above the average height and look strong and muscular. He is easily tired, and when he is tired he wants to stretch out relaxed in a chair and do nothing ; he is definitely sluggish and almost lazy.

Their complaints fall into three definite classes. The common Kali Bich. patient is the typical catarrhal dyspeptic. Others tend to get bronchitis and attacks of asthma. Then there is a third group of Kali Bich. patients who are not so fat or so heavy, who have more colour in their cheeks and have darker hair. These are the people who come along with fibrositis. There is one other condition in which Kali Bich. may be needed, but that person does not correspond in appearance to the typical Kali Bich., and that is the patient with migraine. A certain type of migraine will not respond to any other remedy but Kali Bich. All these types are now considered here in greater detail.

Among the general reactions there are apparent contradictions in temperature reactions. Most Kali Bich. patients tend to be worse in summer and to get fibrositis in hot weather. At the same time they get skin irritation and their acne tends to develop. The respiratory conditions, bronchitis and asthma, tend to be worse in spring and autumn. When they are actually ill, Kali Bich. patients often complain of being chilly and feeling the cold, and they are worse from damp cold weather and from being in the open air.

They have one or two time reactions during the 24 hours. In all the Kali salts the patients have an early morning aggravation; it varies in time but it is round about 2 a.m. to 5 a.m. In Kali Bich. patients it tends to be earlier, in Kali Carb., later. Kali Bich. patients feel worse on waking in the morning and their respiratory troubles are worse. That is not the early aggravation, but an aggravation at the ordinary time of waking. One other characteristic is worth remembering. Kali Bich. patients have an aggravation after food; they feel more uncomfortable, heavier and have less energy.

One other useful point is that they tend to have definite alternations of symptoms, their fibrositis will clear up and be followed by digestive troubles or diarrhoea, or migraine clearing up may be followed by eye trouble. Pains may move from joint to joint.

In typical catarrhal dyspeptics, the patients complain of catarrh tending to be very troublesome in cold and wet weather. With their colds, their noses and all their nasal sinuses get blocked up with stringy yellow mucus. The mucus may be white if the complaint is chronic. The more chronic it is, the more the mucus tends to be white; the more acute it is, the more the mucus tends to be yellow. There may be involvement of any of the accessory sinuses, but all have a typical Kali Bich. pain – it is a boring pain, as if a blunt plug was being forced into the affected area. The most common area to be involved with a pain of this character is the frontal sinus, and it is often accompanied by a severe general headache. There may be similar pains over the antra or just over the eyes, depending on which of the sinuses are involved.

In between the attacks the appearance of the throat is very characteristic. There is very marked deep congestion of the whole of the back of the throat, often with strings of mucus hanging down from the posterior nares, an oedematous appearance of the tonsils, uvula and soft palate. It is a very typical throat requiring Kali Bich.

The catarrhal condition may extend right down into the lungs, leading to capillary bronchitis with a very troublesome cough. One point that often indicates Kali Bich. is the patients' marked tendency to choke. With the bronchial irritation they choke on solids; they can swallow liquids, but solids make them cough and they may vomit. Expectoration is worse in the morning. They have a 2 a.m. to 5 a.m.

aggravation, but also get a later aggravation on waking at their usual time. In the morning they cough and bring up very abundant stringy muco-purulent sputum with difficulty. They often feel better out in the open air as far as the respiratory condition is concerned, provided the air is not too cold and damp. They say that the most comfortable thing is to get into bed and get as warm as possible.

They often complain of a sensation of coldness in the chest. This cold sensation is common to both Kali Bich. and Kali Carb. patients, but in Kali Bich. it tends to be precordial, and in Kali Carb. it is a general coldness throughout the chest. One of the commonest complaints with the respiratory condition is a pain in the chest going from the sternum right through to the back. Kali Carb. have stabbing pains in the chest, but not this peculiar pain that extends right through to the back.

If the catarrhal state spreads down to the stomach instead of the lungs, Kali Bich. patients develop a typical acute gastritis or gastric ulcer. They complain of loss of appetite and flatulence, with attacks of nausea and vomiting coming on quite suddenly. They have severe distension of the stomach with eructations and a very distressing sense of weight in the stomach after taking food.

Their food likes and dislikes are very marked. They have a very marked dislike of meat; they have a bad taste, and water tastes particularly unpleasant. Usually they develop a dislike of fats during their attacks. They often crave sour things and have a marked longing for beer. The chronic beer drinker is fairly typical of Kali Bich. In spite of their longing for it, it gives them a definite aggravation; it makes them sick and often sets up acute gastritis. They also have an aggravation from coffee. Practically all vomited material is sour; it is a very watery, yellow stringy vomit. Occasionally they vomit up a meal and, after the stomach is empty, start bringing up a quantity of glairy white mucus, but this is not as common as the yellow glairy material. In gastric ulcer, there may be blood. It may be fresh or stale blood, but gastric ulcer is not so common as acute gastritis. The patients tend to get hepatic congestion, a feeling of weight, and a feeling of heaviness in the right subcostal region associated with diarrhoea, with clay-coloured stools.

Kali Bich. patients are liable to develop a catarrh of the bladder with strings of yellowish white mucus in the urine. Where this condition is present, a strong indication for Kali Bich. is a peculiar pain in the region of the coccyx coming on during micturition.

The next type of Kali Bich. patient is the fibrositic. The most frequent cases in which Kali Bich. is indicated have acute fibrositic pains and they all tend to sweat. The leading indications are the wandering characteristics of the pains. One joint gets inflamed and tender, then it clears up and another starts. The patient is lying quite comfortably and suddenly gets an acute pain that does not last long. Although the pain occurs in summer it is better from heat and worse from cold; it is aggravated by motion and relieved by rest. Sciatica in Kali Bich. patients is definitely relieved by motion, though fibrositis is aggravated by it. The sciatica occurs in hot weather and is better from applied heat, but not to the same extent as the fibrositis. It is also better from flexing the leg, and is particularly sensitive to weather changes.

A certain number of patients suffer from migraine. The type calling for Kali Bich. has visual aura; the vision is blurred, dim or hazy. This comes on quite suddenly some time before the headache, usually clears before the pain develops, but may continue throughout the headache. These migraine headaches are one-sided, sometimes right, sometimes left, and the pain is particularly violent. Often it is situated in a small area in one or other temporal region. It is relieved by firm pressure over the small area. It is helped by warmth, and definitely better from hot applications. Often these headaches tend to recur periodically; they are aggravated by stooping or by any violent motion. Often they develop during the night and are particularly severe on waking in the morning. They are often accompanied by violent sickness in which the patient brings up the typical, white, stringy, glairy mucus in the vomit. That is the typical migraine headache, and it is quite different from the catarrhal headache which begins at the bridge of the nose, extends up into the head, is quite different in its onset, and is connected with the nasal catarrh.

Kali Bromatum

There are one or two conditions in which Kali Brom. is particularly useful. The majority of Kali salts tend to be fat, and Kali Brom. patients are usually fat and fair, lethargic, rather depressed, heavy looking and dull. In spite of this apparent dullness there is a certain amount of local restlessness. They have fidgety hands and feet and there may be a definite tendency to twitch. They often complain of being unusually sleepy, and that they fall asleep in their chair if they sit down; they are thoroughly drowsy and heavy. They often complain of a tendency for their hands, feet or legs to go numb, and often also of a sensation as though the legs are trembling. Associated with this and their dullness they get a fear of insanity.

Patients I always found very difficult to prescribe for, before I came across Kali Brom., were children who were not getting on well at school. They are dull and apparently lacking in intelligence, rather like Pulsatilla children, but they have too coarse a skin for Pulsatilla. The first indication for Kali Brom. is a tendency to develop acne. Severe acne in a child with no other definite indications will often clear up on Kali Brom. It is the same with acne during menstruation in a woman; if there are no other indications it will often respond to Kali Brom. Occasionally a girl of that type who gets very long periods should also respond to Kali Brom.

General Reactions in Kali Brom.

Kali Brom. patients are hot-blooded, worse from heat, worse in summer, worse in hot rooms. They are better in cold weather and, like all the other Kali salts, they tend to have an early morning aggravation, round about 2 a.m.

Associated with their unhealthy skin there are three pathological conditions in which Kali Brom. may be indicated. The first is when definite choreiform movements have developed after a shock or fright – an adolescent of that type usually responds to Kali Brom. The next, in advanced nephritis, the patient seems heavy and sleepy with a slightly besotted appearance and threatened convulsions, and Kali Brom. will often help. Then there is another associated condition in which Kali Brom. is useful; in a bad case of infantile diarrhoea, where the child is beginning to develop signs of meningeal irritation, and there is the very peculiar liquid diarrhoea associated with the meningeal symptoms.

Kali Brom. used to be prescribed in conventional medicine for controlling epilepsy, and a certain number of epileptic cases respond to it in homoeopathic doses. In women, there is a definite relationship between the period and the onset of the fits. They occur either during or near the period, and without that relationship I have never seen any good result from using Kali Brom. In both the male and female it seems that there tends to be an aggravation at the new moon. In all these epileptics requiring Kali Brom., both male and female, the fit is followed by a severe headache.

They have a curious aura before the attack, as if their whole body was swelling, whereas there is no actual swelling at all.

Kali Carbonicum

Kali Carb. is the most difficult of the Kali salts to grasp, with the possible exception of Kali Phosphoricum, but on the other hand, though these are the most difficult, they are also the most valuable.

The first impression of Kali Carb. is that the patients are soft. That is not the impression given in Kent – the Kali Carb. patient he describes is irritable, highly strung and nervous, but that is not the usual type occurring in the UK. They are not taut at all, but pale, soft, flabby people, easily tired out by any exertion. When tired, they always have backache, which compels them to lie down. They tend to be fat and often have flat feet.

Their mental picture is very much the same. The slightest effort of thought or excitement tires them, and they get into a peculiar state of mental confusion. They get up in the morning knowing they have a fair amount of work to do. They start something, and immediately think that there is something else they ought to be doing, so they leave the first job and dash off to do the second. They have no sooner started it than they leave it for a third, and so they get into a thorough muddle and end up by completing nothing at all. They also say that they are constantly misplacing things. For instance a man will explain that he can never find his notes in his office; he puts them away carefully enough but cannot remember where he put them. With that mental state they get the fear that they are going insane. They get hurried, make mistakes in their speech, miss words out, put wrong ones in, forget to finish their sentences, and so on. They become annoyed with themselves and get scared; they get annoyed with their circumstances, and become jealous and suspicious of those who are working with them. When they are in this state they are very difficult to get on with and often show a strange vindictiveness. Another constant complaint is that they get absolutely worn out with the slightest physical or mental effort. If they have any excitement they are quite exhausted and have to go to bed, and it takes them two or three days to get over it.

Kali Carb. patients have many fears: fear of insanity, fear of poverty, fear of the future and fear of death. Associated with this fear they get a very marked hoarding instinct. Kali Carb. patients are essentially possessive. They tend to hold on to everything; they hold on to life and are afraid of dying, even though their life may appear hardly worth living. They hold on to their husbands, even when they appear to dislike them; they hold on to their children, even when their children appear to be nothing but a worry to them, and when they treat them none too well. They hold on to their money and may be positively miserly, though this is often the result of their fear of poverty. Another thing that very often crops up, associated with this mental dullness, is the feeling of failure. They become timid and cannot stand up for themselves; if anyone accuses them of a mistake, especially a mistake they have not made, they simply lie down under it. This does not conform at all to Kent's picture of Kali Carb. Another important point about Kali Carb. patients is a very peculiar dislike of being touched; they simply cannot bear it.

Their usual complaint is a feeling that they are heading for a breakdown. They have a general catarrhal condition, they are susceptible to colds and usually have some digestive disturbance.

General Reactions in Kali Carb.

Kali Carb. patients are generally chilly, in fact they are about as cold as any remedy in the pharmacopoeia. They are not only sensitive to draughts but also to any cold air. Their complaints are very much aggravated by any exertion, mental or physical, and they are very susceptible to damp. An apparent contradiction to this aggravation from cold, and amelioration from warmth, is that they get an aggravation from warm drinks. What really happens is that they get warmed up by the hot drink and then, immediately after, they get chilled, and the aggravation is due to the subsequent chilling more than to the actual warm drink.They are usually more uncomfortable and more aggravated after meals.

These are the main points about them, except the typical Kali time aggravation from 2 to 4 a.m., and Kali Carb. patients have also the later morning time aggravation on waking. They always feel particularly unwell and lacking in energy when it is time to get up. Another point in Kali Carb. is the character of the pains. Wherever they have a pain it is the same type, whether in the arms, the back, the chest or the joints, and whether due to respiratory, digestive or fibrositic troubles. The pains are always very sharp and cutting, and are constantly flitting about from place to place. They are almost always relieved by heat, incredibly sensitive to cold, and mostly aggravated by pressure. Occasionally the pain comes on during rest and is slightly better if the patients move about, but if they move fast they are definitely made worse.

An old lady with a typical trigeminal neuralgia was about the best example of Kali Carb. I have ever seen. She was not only sensitive to draughts, but also so acutely conscious of any movement of air in the neighbourhood, that if a handkerchief was waved in front of her all the branches of her trigeminal nerve were mapped out in pain. The slightest movement of any sort brought on the pain, eating, talking, laughing, smiling, in fact any movement whatsoever. She was so sensitive to touch that she could not bear to wash her face, and she was the typical worn out, tired out, backachy middle-aged woman of the Kali

Carb. type. This is very like the description of Mag. Phos.; they both have the incredible sensitivity to cold, but the Mag. Phos. patient is relieved by pressure, whereas the Kali Carb. patient is aggravated by pressure. Mag. Phos. may relieve this type of neuralgia, but will never clear it up completely where there is this sensitivity to pressure.

Kali Carb. is as catarrhal as any remedy in the Materia Medica. The patients are always catching cold, and get a certain amount of nasal discharge when over-heated, either by exertion or by being in a hot room and going out and getting chilled afterwards. Kali Carb. also tend to develop a violent headache from the same cause. It is usually a temporal headache, either on one or both sides, and it is so acute that it gives rise to nausea.

The nasal catarrh tends to spread quickly down into the throat, and the patients have very typical dry, painful, hot tonsils with a large quantity of white, or sometimes yellow, tenacious mucus. There is early enlargement of the tonsillar glands, which are painful, tender and markedly sensitive to cold – this is a valuable diagnostic point. If this condition is not checked immediately, they tend to develop bronchitis, with a paroxysmal, dry, hacking cough. There is not much mucus, and what there is is mostly swallowed rather than expectorated. The cough is so violent that it is liable to go on to vomiting, and with it there is the typical Kali Carb. violent stabbing pain in the chest. There is also the usual 2 to 4 a.m. time aggravation.

Kali Carb. is hardly ever required at the early stage in pneumonia; it is after actual consolidation of the lung that it is needed. The indications are the time aggravation in the early morning, the character of the pain, the character of the sputum, the character of the cough, and the fact that the patients get definite relief from sitting, propped up and leaning foward. They have an aggravation from lying on the affected side, which as a rule is the right lower lobe. Associated with the pneumonia there is often marked dyspnoea, and they can only sip fluids, as they cannot hold their breath long enough to take a long drink. They cannot take anything solid, as it starts them coughing, and the cough goes on until they vomit. They always tend to get a peculiar pallid, slightly cyanotic, puffy look about the face. The great danger in Kali Carb. pneumonias is from a failing heart.

The remedy most likely to be confused with Kali Carb. is Hepar Sulph. Hepar Sulph. patients have the same respiratory trouble, the same type of cough, the same sensitiveness to cold air, the same involvement of glands, but do not have the same 2 to 4 a.m. time aggravation. This is much later – 7, 8 or 9 a.m., and they do not have the same puffy face. They are always much thinner, more drawn, more anxious-looking.

Kali Carb. patients always complain of a tendency to digestive difficulties, and the main complaint in every one of them is the tendency to flatulence; they get acute abdominal distension after food. They also have the very greatest difficulty in getting rid of this distension, which involves the whole abdomen, and is not merely a gastric one. They have a feeling of emptiness in the abdomen; they feel hungry and want something to eat, but are no better after eating.

Another quite frequent Kali Carb. symptom is a sensation of internal coldness in the abdomen, and, in respiratory troubles, a feeling of coldness in the chest. Often these patients strongly object to being examined because of being so acutely sensitive to cold, not only internal cold but external cold also.

Kali Carb. patients are liable to get colic. It may be intestinal, or it may be hepatic; often it is just a feeling of fullness and tenderness over the liver. They may have gallstone colic, but are more likely to develop cholecystitis than actual gallstones. Most Kali Carb. patients are constipated, and they frequently develop piles, which are incredibly painful, protruding as large masses and tending to thrombose. Occasionally they bleed, but the characteristic symptom is their extreme painfulness and acute hyperaesthesia – the patients cannot bear them to be touched.

Most Kali Carb. patients are definitely thirsty, and have a desire for sour things. In acute illnesses they have a desire for sweets. It may be for chocolates or sweets, or it may be an actual craving for sugar, which is quite a natural desire when over-tired, and such people are in a constant state of over-tiredness. As a rule there is an aversion to meat. Although it is not in the textbooks, most Kali Carb. tend to eat an excessive quantity of starchy foods.

They all tend to get dental trouble; they hardly ever come with a sound set of teeth. They usually have inflamed gums, an unhealthy, offensive mouth, and a rather suggestive pale flabby tongue. The usual Kali tongue, thickly coated at the root, may be present; more commonly they have a flabby, pale, swollen-looking tongue.

One other point constant to every Kali salt – and Kali Carb. has it more marked than any other with the exception of Kali Phos. – the patients are all aggravated after sexual intercourse; it leaves them absolutely exhausted. In Kali Carb. there tends to be an unusual degree of sexual excitement, and yet there is this absolute prostration afterwards. In Kali Phos. there is not the same degree of excitability, but the prostration is even worse.

There is very marked haemorrhagic tendency in Kali Carb. In the female, the periods may be too frequent and they are always very profuse. There is often a history of periods where the patient is never free from an oozing of blood, at times there is almost flooding, and then it eases down again into this state of oozing, but never really stops. The pathological condition is most likely to be a polyp or a fibroid.

It is repeated in all the textbooks that Kali Carb. is a dangerous remedy. Kent warns against its use in acute gout, but this is seen less often today, and the few cases I have seen have never called for Kali Carb. Many say it is dangerous to give it in a patient with enlarged joints, but that is simply not true, at least for rheumatoid arthritis. Many patients in whom there were definite indications for Kali Carb. received it in high potencies, and they did well on it. In pneumonia it has been given many times without dangerous results. It is, however, very dangerous in tuberculosis and the potency must be carefully chosen, as these patients do not stand the reaction well. In stomach conditions it has also been used many times without any bad result. Do not give Kali Carb. for gallstone colic in a patient whose constitutional remedy is Kali Carb. (The same is true in Lycopodium, where there will tend to be a marked aggravation if you give Lycopodium for a hepatic colic in a Lycopodium patient.) But if there are indications in gallstones for Kali Carb. in a patient whose constitutional remedy is something else, say Phosphorus, then Kali Carb. may be given.

If you have a Kali Carb. patient with colic, and no indication can be found for any other remedy, then give Kali Carb. in a very low potency. Aconite is very often indicated in a Kali Carb. patient with gallstone colic. This will relieve the symptoms, and when the pain has gone, it may then be followed up by Kali Carb.

(*Note.* Dr Borland also presented the following material on Kali Carb., which overlaps to some extent with the section above. However, it is not a direct repetition, and is included here because it contains valuable additional information. Ed.)

Kent states that Kali Carb. is difficult to assess. The impression I have of Kali Carb. patients is of pale, very chilly, fat, flabby, sweaty, slow people. They are very slack. They have slack joints, tend to have a fairly broad pelvis, and often have swollen ankles. Their ankles swell over their shoes and look puffy, more oedematous than fat. The next point – one links it up with their puffy, thick ankles – is the appearance of their face, which is pale and puffy. There is no colour, the skin is moist and gives the impression it will pit on pressure. They are heavy about the eyes, with swelling particu larly of the upper eyelid – not the puckered condition of Causticum. In colouring they are dark more commonly than fair. Another complaint found almost constantly in Kali Carb., no matter what else they are suffering from, is backache. It is similar to the Sepia backache, but lower down, more sacral. It comes on very easily from any exertion, walking or standing, and starts as an ache over the sacrum. Quite unlike Sepia, it tends to spread down over the buttocks on to the upper part of the thigh. It is relieved from lying down on a hard surface, and does not get the Sepia relief from sitting in a chair and pressure. Kali Carb. have to lie down flat before they get any comfort.

In personality, they are a queer mixture. An outstanding characteristic of typical patients is the fact that they are muddled. Their story is always one of confusion. They start to do one thing, leave it half done and start something else. They take on three or four jobs and finish none of them, and then become worried and agitated about it. If it is a man in business, he may start giving instructions to one of his staff, stop to begin dictating letters, then feels he must telephone an appointment. When he has started half a dozen things, and is getting on with none of them, he gets into a panic and nothing gets done at all. In that state, instead of slowing down and trying to get one thing finished, he becomes more agitated, more and more occupied, and never finishes anything. Another peculiarity about them is that they have a surprising inability to stand up for themselves. They get very irritable, but if they themselves are attacked, particularly if they are unjustly accused, they tend to become quite silent and cannot make any reply. They feel miserable and hurt, but they cannot fight back. That is the dull state of Kali Carb.

They are very apt to become jealous of anyone who is more capable, or who is helping them out of a difficulty, and they are often malicious in the statements they make about them. Another strange peculiarity, more commonly found in older Kali Carb. patients, is a strong hoarding tendency – they never throw anything away. It is different from the miserly tendency of some of the remedies, just an inability to part with anything. Occasionally the same sort of reaction will come out in another way. They become very possessive of members of the family, yet are unpleasant to them and make life difficult for them.

Another point is that they are acutely hypersensitive. They are very sensitive to noise, which irritates them intensely. When they are getting muddled they become annoyed about it. Even the dull patients are hypersensitive to noise, touch and always to pain. They are terrified of noise, which makes them start and they complain of a sick, sinking feeling in their stomachs. Afterwards they throb all over, even right down to their finger tips. The dull types of Kali Carb. will often say that they become much more muddled mentally after food, or even while they are eating, and will often yawn during a meal. They are depressed, sleepy and heavy, and are troubled by flatulence after eating. Practically all Kali Carb. patients have a fear of being alone.

They have an aggravation in the early hours of the morning of whatever is their particular complaint. If it is digestive, which is the commonest complaint in Kali Carb., they will be worse in the early morning, about 2 to 4 a.m. Occasionally a surprising symptom occurs in these dull patients. They dream of some of their friends, very often friends they have not seen for a number of years, and after the dream they hear of an illness or unpleasant happening affecting the person they have dreamt about. This has been confirmed many times.

So far as placing Kali Carb., they seem to come midway between Calcarea and Sepia. They have the same kind of mental dullness and chilliness as Calcarea, the weakness of the ankles, and the same tendency to sprain muscles from over-lifting, but Kali Carb. is almost certainly indicated for backache from strain. On the other hand, there are the family disturbances similar to those associated with Sepia, for example dislike of their family, but Sepia has not the same possessive tendency. They both get dragging in the lower part of the abdomen, and both get menstrual headaches, but in Sepia the patients usually have scanty periods, and in Kali Carb. excessive ones.

Kali Iodatum
There are certain constant features in all patients who need Kali Iod. They are hot-blooded, and definitely better in the open air. As far as appearances are concerned, both the chronic and the acute condition need to be considered.

Chronic Conditions in Kali Iod.
The typical Kali Iod. patients tend to be pale and delicate looking, with an unstable vasomotor system. They flush easily. They are usually fair skinned, and very often fair haired. The acute type are mostly more obese than expected: more flushed and deeper red than the chronic type, heavier featured, rather cyanotic and heavy lipped. Both acute

and chronic patients are depressed, very easily discouraged, and often having a definite disgust for life. They are bad tempered, irritable, and if annoyed tend to be abusive. They are restless, and if at all agitated this becomes more marked. If any attempt is made to control them they are very liable to burst into tears. If they are trying to make themselves understood, and feel incapable of putting thoughts into words, they get so agitated that in despair they burst into tears, because they are so worried about themselves.

There are definite times of aggravation in the 24 hours. They have the ordinary Kali aggravation early in the morning from 2 to 5 a.m., and Kali Iod. patients also tend to feel worse on waking up in the morning. They tend to waken with a headache, dry throat and general depression. They are susceptible to damp weather, and in spite of their general feeling of heat, and their aggravation from heat, they are upset by cold food, particularly cold milk. Another useful point is that they tend to get urticaria, and some also get asthma, both of which tend to be worse at the seaside. All Kali Iod. patients have an increase of appetite; they are hungry people, usually they are thirsty too, and they tend to get flatulence – all Kali salts do.

Kali Iod. is a very useful remedy in fibrositis, arthritis and also in sciatica, and there is one characteristic feature. If it is sciatica there is a point of tenderness over the sciatic nerve, with a diffuse area of tenderness much wider than the nerve. If it is arthritis there is the tender joint, but also a diffuse tenderness both above and below the joint. There is a definite heat aggravation both in the arthritis and in the sciatica; the patient wants the affected part uncovered, or wants cold applications. There is amelioration from movement, increasing the more that they continue the motion. It may be painful to begin with, but the pain steadily improves as they keep on moving. There tends to be a nightly aggravation. With the sciatica they are worse from lying on the affected side, worse sitting, worse standing, but better when moving about.

Acute Conditions in Kali Iod.
Kali Iod. is particularly useful in acute conditions of the eye and nose. Of all the inflammatory eye conditions, acute conjunctivitis of intense violence with blepharospasm is the most usual in these patients. They have the typical flushed face, marked oedema of the eyelids, all the outside of the eyelids is inflamed, the face round about is red, and the redness and swelling spreads up on to the forehead, so that it looks swollen and puffy too. There is intense photophobia, marked headache,

and the conjunctivae are red and oedematous. The discharge is thick and greenish-yellow, and on opening the eyes they simply pour tears. The patient complains of an intense burning pain, and often there is a very early tendency to ulceration of the cornea. This condition, when associated with aggravation from warmth and amelioration from cold, almost always clears up on Kali Iod.

Acute inflammation of the accessory nasal sinuses is another condition where Kali Iod. is frequently indicated. They are severe cases, with swelling of the forehead spreading down into the eyes. They have a peculiar deep red colour with intense bursting pain and intense fullness about the root of the nose, extending right into the skull. Associated with that is a very acrid watery coryza, with burning in the eyes and intense lacrimation, a tendency for the nose to become sore and raw and for the upper lip to become swollen. With these nasal conditions there may be small ulcers in the mouth, usually situated on the tip of the tongue. There is one confirmatory symptom – an intense pain at the base of the tongue when protruding the tongue. That picture always indicates Kali Iod. It does not matter whether the condition is conjunctivitis, frontal sinus, antrum or ethmoid disease; provided there is the heat aggravation it should clear up on Kali Iod.

For a hot-blooded patient with singing in the ears and no other indication, give Kali Iod. The same symptom in a cold-blooded patient is very often cleared by a dose of China.

Kali Phosphoricum

There is an important difference between Kali Phos. and the other Kali salts. In all the others there is a tendency to excess fat deposit, whereas most Kali Phos. patients are thin with a typical pale, waxy skin, usually dark haired, very rarely fair, and they are irritable and nervously and physically exhausted. They usually walk with a slight stoop, their movements are uncertain and there is a tendency to stagger. Sometimes this is due to giddiness, but more often it is due to actual weakness of their limbs.

Their mental state is one of great despondency. They are anxious, and almost always of the neuraesthenic type. In Kali Phos. patients the irritability is the irritability of weakness, exasperation, and a conscious inability to cope with their situation. In the state of irritability they usually break down, weep and become exhausted, and then develop tremor and fears, and feel that they will lose control and scream. They want someone to hold them, either to save their reason, or to help them to keep control of themselves. There are various other mental characteristics. They are always shy and nervous of meeting either friends or strangers, and are particularly nervous of going away from home. This is said to be home-sickness, but it is actually a fear of strange surroundings. They are not only shy of strangers, but suspicious of them. Another symptom quite frequently found in Kali Phos. and which has occurred in provers, is a fear of open spaces – a symptom that is often difficult to find in the Materia Medica. In spite of their nervous and physical weakness, Kali Phos. patients often become restless. They are also very easily startled and unusually sensitive to noise. Another characteristic is that, in spite of their apparent weakness, fear and exhaustion, a curious obstinacy characterises them. This is especially noticeable when advising them to take a course of action which will benefit their health. With their extreme lassitude and tiredness there is a definite dislike of life. They are depressed and yet they have a fear of death, and are never the type of people who commit suicide. This state often occurs after a long and severe illness or chronic debilitating disease when the patients have little resistance.

They are always pale and obviously ill, but under stress or excitement the face becomes flushed. They are also troubled with flushing after meals; with that they have a tendency to perspire, particularly about the head and face. Kali Phos. and Phosphorus patients all have a tendency to flush and get hot, and yet otherwise there are many differences between them. Associated with the weariness of Kali Phos. they have a peculiar pain centering at the seventh cervical vertebra, and involving the whole of the dorsal area of the spine. This is one of the most common complaints in Kali Phos. and occurs whenever they are tired. The characteristics of this pain in the back are that it is worse if the patients are lying down or sitting, and a little better if they move about gently, and it is associated with a general feeling of weakness in the back.

General Reactions in Kali Phos.
Kali Phos. patients are extra sensitive to cold, in fact most of their reactions are aggravations – they have very few ameliorations at all. Warm weather makes them worse, they are aggravated by food, they are usually worse in the morning on rising, always worse from real exertion, but occasionally slightly better from moving about gently; they are always hypersensitive to noise. As a rule, female Kali Phos. patients have a pre-menstrual aggravation, with definite relief when the period starts. They all have the ordinary Kali salts time aggravation in the early morning. They are particularly sensitive to touch, and any

emotional excitement leaves them trembling and completely exhausted, for instance any bad or startling news. They are aggravated by the stress of talking to people, especially to several people at once and yet have a fear of solitude. They have a fear of crowds, and in a crowd become tremulous and frightened. The main complaint is a feeling of general weakness. Associated with various pains and disturbances in their arms and legs, there may be definite nerve degeneration. Patients with multiple sclerosis may be markedly helped by Kali Phos. All these patients with numbness, tremor and pain are aggravated by exertion, but gentle movement seems to keep their circulation going and they feel better for it.

Practically all suffer from digestive disturbances, and there are certain characteristic points. There is a peculiar apparent contradiction so far as their appetite is concerned. Very often they have a curious feeling of hunger, more a feeling of emptiness, which disappears at once on taking food. They feel satiated immediately and as if the whole abdomen were distended. Even after a small meal – and Kali Phos. patients are never able to take much – they have bad flatulence. Yet, within a few minutes after eating, they again have the feeling of hunger. They are the characteristic nervous dyspeptics who are always nibbling. They practically all dislike bread, so most resort to sweet biscuits or to chocolates. They often waken about 5 a.m. with an acute gnawing hungry pain and eat a biscuit in order to relieve it. They suffer from flatulence which is very difficult to move, and which gives rise to colic. Some Kali Phos. patients have longer periods between the taking of food and beginning of discomfort. They suffer from definite hunger pains, but not as a rule from an actual duodenal ulcer; they do not have the immediate relief from food found in a typical duodenal ulcer. It is a nervous dyspepsia, not a true duodenal ulcer. With the digestive disturbances they have an unhealthy mouth, with inflamed and tender gums which tend to bleed easily, and they may develop a definite dental neuralgia. The tongue of Kali Phos. patients, particularly in their digestive troubles, is flabby and has a very suggestive mustard-coloured coating.

One of the likes and dislikes for food of Kali Phos. is often a craving for ice-cold water. This is a peculiarity, as they often complain of a feeling of coldness in the abdomen. Like all the Kali salts they have a great liking for sweet things, and like most Kali salts they also like sour things, and sometimes have a craving for vinegar. In a tired-out woman with backache, who likes vinegar, the first two remedies to consider prescribing are Sepia and Kali Phos. Both are chilly, both tired and excitable, both pale, both rather better for motion. In Kali Phos. the pain is mainly in the dorsal region of the back, in Sepia in the sacral region. Kali Phos. patients are rather worse lying down, while Sepia are better. Kali Phos. tend to be pale and often have rings which are nearly black round the eyes; Sepia are sallow with brown rings round the eyes. Like all the Kali salts, Kali Phos. have an aversion to bread and to meat.

Practically all these nervous, debilitated patients suffer from headaches, particularly those requiring Kali Phos. There is also another type of patient who develops headaches in which there are definite indications for Kali Phos., and that is the student who has been doing intensive study. The headache comes on during the night, is very acute on waking in the morning, often slightly better after getting up and moving about, and increases again in the evening. The headache is generally worse from cold, and greatly aggravated by noise. The pain is intense and seems to involve the whole head; the scalp and even the hair become tender to touch. Eating a little food eases the headache for a short time but it returns when the patient gets hungry. Wrapping up the head and keeping it warm gives relief, but any excitement or mental effort causes a severe aggravation.

Associated with the general tremulous weakness in Kali Phos. patients, they may have attacks of palpitation, with myocardial inefficiency and low blood pressure, and occasionally they have true anginal attacks. In these attacks, they complain that after the acute radiating pain has subsided, a sensation of numbness persists in the area of the pain.

Kali Phos. patients tend to present with recurring attacks of acute cystitis. In an elderly person, tired out and debilitated, and with a tendency to incontinence, Kali Phos. will often clear up the cystitis and re-establish the sphincter control. The patients complain of a burning pain during micturition, starting with the flow of urine and continuing after the flow is over, and the pain is usually situated in the bladder, not in the urethra. Considering the sugar-loving, tremulous, worn out, hungry, emaciated, debilitated patient, it is not surprising that Kali Phos. is frequently indicated in diabetic patients.

Female patients tend to have a scanty menstrual flow. If they have any leucorrhoea it tends to be excoriating and highly coloured. Quite frequently this occurs with a very acute ovarian pain. Two other points to mention are that, apart from the tendency to perspire on the face and head after meals or from excitement, the sweat glands are generally rather inactive and these patients do not perspire easily. Also, their sleep tends to be disturbed and they get violent dreams and nightmares.

Kali Sulphuricum

Kali Sulph. has similarities to both Sulphur and Pulsatilla. The typical appearance is one of heaviness, weariness and sluggishness. The patients are usually highly coloured and tend to have rather a coarse skin. They are usually rather fat and slow in their movements. They always complain of feeling tired, and the feeling of tiredness is often due to laziness rather than physical exhaustion. They have a definite aversion to work of any kind, either physical or mental, and are usually depressed and sorry for themselves. They often lack confidence and may be actually timid and, associated with their depression, complain of a feeling of confusion and that their brains will not work very well. In spite of their apparent timidity, Kali Sulph. patients are very often impatient and liable to changeable moods – lively one moment and depressed the next. They tend to become anxious about themselves, think they are very ill, especially in the evening and during the night, and take a gloomy view of life when waking up in the morning. Encouraging them to a less serious view of their illness makes them angry, and they are always obstinate. Associated with their mental confusion they complain of giddiness and that their heads feel full and their faces hot.

Another characteristic is their skin irritation; Kali Sulph. patients are always troubled by itching – they itch practically all over the body, eyes, nose, scalp and skin in general. They are also always catarrhal. They tend to get catarrhal conjunctivitis; the eyelids are gummed up and itchy, and there are yellow crusts on the margins. The discharge also is yellow, as are all the body discharges, and they always tend to be irritating and to itch, whether from eyes, nose, chest, throat or vagina. There is an intense irritation of the nose and often some degree of ulceration of the nose, which is aggravated in a hot room and in hot weather. Kali Sulph. is one of the most frequently indicated drugs in chronic otitis media, with the typical Kali Sulph. yellow irritating discharge.

Kali Sulph. patients also tend to get haemorrhoids with the same intense itching – perianal itching.

Warmth in general aggravates Kali Sulph. and they are always better in the open air. They tend to be worse in the evening, and definitely worse from exertion, as it makes them hot, and they perspire and catch cold. They tend to stagnate when at rest, so they are better when moving about gently. They are worse on waking in the morning, then they are sluggish and usually have a headache, and they are worse after food. One peculiarity, unexpected in such sluggish patients, is the intense aggravation that they have from noise. They tend to catch cold after a bath, whether it is hot or cold.

They are always liable to congestive headaches, with a feeling of intense heat and heaviness in the head. As a rule, the headaches start over the eyes and spread to the forehead. From there the pain spreads over the whole head, more marked on the right side. The modalities are practically the same as in Kali Phos. The headaches are bad on waking in the morning, worse in the evening, aggravated by warmth, worse after food, and worse during the menstrual period in women. The patients are sensitive to sudden movements or jarring, which aggravate the headache. They are better in the open air and from cold applications. Unlike most congestive headaches, they are better from pressure and better lying down.

Practically all Kali Sulph. patients are catarrhal, usually in the upper respiratory tract. When indicated, Kali Sulph. is one of the most useful remedies in respiratory catarrh. The typical cases in respiratory conditions look flushed and, with chest catarrh, have a very profuse secretion of mucus and râles all over the lungs. The cough is aggravated by eating and is eased by cold drinks and cold air, and the patient has a feeling of irritation low down in the trachea. The sputum is yellow and difficult to bring up. The state of the mouth is also typical, with yellow mucus on the fauces and a yellow coating on the tongue. They always complain of an unpleasant insipid taste, and especially complain of water tasting bad. In addition they may have the ordinary Kali Sulph. desires, the desire for sweet things, for sour things and for cold food.

Another condition in which Kali Sulph. may be required is arthritis, with general aggravation from heat, amelioration of pains from moving about and being in the fresh air. Associated is the dry skin, usually scaly in character and itching, and there may be an urticaria. The pains wander about, start in one joint, go to another and then go to a third. Associated with these pains, Kali Sulph. patients often complain of very cold hands and feet – this immediately excludes Sulphur, with which Kali Sulph. might easily be confused. Sulphur patients always have hot extremities, whereas Kali Sulph. have cold ones.

One other point is in connection with their sleep, particularly in febrile conditions, when Kali Sulph. patients have terrifying dreams of ghosts, death, robbers or murder, with violent struggling in their sleep. They wake up terrified. Sleep in Kali Sulph. is never restful. In some respects, Kali Sulph. and Rhus Tox. have similar symptoms, but Kali Sulph. are always worse for heat and Rhus. Tox. for cold.

Chapter 11

The Natrum Salts

Natrum Muriaticum
Not all Natrum Mur. patients fit the textbook description of having a
pale, waxy skin. The majority tend to have an oily skin, not the waxy
pallor which Kent stresses. They are much more likely to be people with
a good colour in their cheeks, which increases during conversation or
when they are embarrassed. Natrum Mur. patients are tense, they
quickly become embarrassed, the pulse rate increases very quickly, and
it is then that the skin becomes oily. They tend to develop small
herpetic vesicles at the corners of their lips, along the margin of the hair
and on the ears.

The textbook description of Natrum Mur. stresses the extreme
emaciation, but it is the exception to see extreme emaciation. Natrum
Mur. often have thin necks, but need not be thin otherwise. As far as
colouring is concerned, they may be dark or fair. There is a yellow tinge
of the skin, not very noticeable when they are flushed, but obvious when
the flush recedes.

At a consultation, Natrum Mur. are often slightly embarrassed and
self-conscious. They are apprehensive and yet they do not want to
appear to be finding the consultation a strain. They have an appearance
of self-assurance, almost of opposition. They are not the most friendly
of patients and seem to be definitely on their guard. They will answer
questions, usually fairly shortly, often abruptly, and do not give
anything away at the beginning of the interview. After their confidence
is gained they often pour out their troubles, but this defensive mechanism must be broken first.

Natrum Arsenicatum
Natrum Ars. are definitely pale and look slightly cyanotic, not sallow
like Natrum Mur. They have blue rings round the eyes and the lips are
pale. Instead of the herpetic eruptions that Natrum Mur. develop round
the mouth, Natrum Ars. tend to get dry, cracked lips. They are much

more nervous, much more frightened, but much less resentful than Natrum Mur. The nervousness of Natrum Ars. is revealed by their general physical restlessness. Their hands are restless, their fingers are restless, and often there is a slight twitch of their shoulder, arm or the muscles of their face during conversation. A certain amount of perspiration develops, but not the same greasy appearance of Natrum Mur. They are obviously tired. Observing these patients walking across the room, Natrum Mur. plant their feet firmly down on the floor, Natrum Ars. come in rather shyly and quietly.

Natrum Carbonicum
There is a general Natrum similarity with all patients needing a Natrum salt. The appearance of the typical Natrum Carb. patient, instead of the taut Natrum Mur., is much more fleshy. They are pale, with rather indefinite features. They tend to be more plump than Natrum Mur. and may be definitely fat. Natrum Mur. may be quite neat and trim, but Natrum Carb. will almost always have thick ankles. In conversation they tend to flush up, somewhat like Natrum Mur., but it is a much more blotchy redness.

The general impression given by Natrum Carb. is that they are less positive. They are tired, and waddle across the floor rather than stamp across it as Natrum Mur. do. While sitting in a chair they tend to slouch, whereas Natrum Mur. sit up and look people in the eye. One confirmatory symptom in Natrum Carb. is their reaction to sudden noise – it startles them and makes them acutely irritable.

Natrum Phosphoricum
Of all the Natrum salts, Natrum Phos. are the thinnest. They are generally underweight and often tall. The colour of Natrum Phos. is almost always pale, but they flush under stress, both cheeks becoming bright red.

The skin tends to be greasy, but not to such a degree as in Natrum Mur. Most Natrum Phos. patients tend to be over middle life, and are not so trim and tidy as would be expected from their general outlook and from the way they talk; they have rather lost their vitality. It is a great effort for them to remember details of their complaints. They are quite willing to help, but either cannot remember or cannot express themselves. Natrum Phos. are very hopeless about their condition. They do not think that much can be done for them, and usually come for consultation under some compulsion – someone has been urging them and they have had to come eventually.

Natrum Sulphuricum

Natrum Sulph. patients are definite characters. Practically all are fat and often rather under-sized. They usually have a high colour and may be florid, but with their high colour there is an underlying yellowness. In acute conditions they often develop a congested liver and may become jaundiced. They tend to get skin eruptions, similar to the Natrum Mur. eruptions, and they have a slightly greasy skin. The main impression that they give is of being rather miserable and discontented, and some are bad-tempered, although many just seem depressed and hopeless.

PERSONALITY

The main characteristic of all Natrum patients is that they are, without exception, hypersensitive. Take Natrum Mur. They are sensitive to noise, to surroundings, to music, to thunder and to people. That is constant throughout all the Natrum salts – there is a degree of lack of balance in them all, and in Natrum Mur. it may become extreme. They may either be over-conscientious, or may lose all interest in what they ought to be doing. They may either be over-affectionate or have no interest in people around them. They may either be full of fears – afraid of all sorts of things – or else they may get into the state when, they say, they are afraid of nothing. The same patient may change from one state to the other. One day he will tackle anything, the next day he will want someone to back him up in everything he does. One day he weeps from the slightest cause, next day nothing would make him weep. Natrum Mur. are said to have absolute intolerance of consolation; as a matter of fact they crave for consolation from the right people. They crave for understanding and appreciation, they dislike being touched, their pains are aggravated by touch.

They are always rather tense, and tend to be restless and fidgety. They move their feet, fidget with their bag, and complain that they are liable to get sudden muscular jerks. Comparing Natrum Mur. with Natrum Ars., Natrum Ars. are very much more nervous and have all sorts of fears, fear of disease, fear of impending evil, fear of something about to happen. Typical of the Natrum personality is that they are over-conscientious and complete what they have begun, though it is a great effort. If they undertake anything and meet with any opposition it makes them very angry, which exhausts them. Any mental effort is very trying for them. When occupied, they always have the feeling of being hurried and working against time, which brings on a great sense of mental and physical weariness. This is so marked that they will say that after any mental effort they are compelled to go and lie down. Becoming angry affects them so much that they tremble.

Natrum Carb. more nearly corresponds to Natrum Mur. than any other Natrum salt, but the hypersensitiveness, particularly to noise, music, thunder and people, is even more marked in Natrum Carb. than in Natrum Mur. The reaction to any of these is either a reaction of irritability, or else they have a severe attack of palpitation. The reaction to music in Natrum Mur. and Natrum Carb. is sometimes rather different. Music sometimes upsets Natrum Mur. emotionally; they weep from it. The common Natrum Carb. reaction is the same. Occasionally a Natrum Carb. patient cannot stand any loud noise, and for this reason cannot stand a full orchestra, but they can tolerate quiet music although they always get a certain amount of emotional disturbance from it. There is a degree of difference in their reaction to sympathy and social relations. Natrum Mur. want to be looked up to and thought well of. Natrum Carb. feel rather cut off from their friends. They feel that their friends do not quite understand them, and the feeling of being cut off often starts a dislike and criticism of friends or relatives. Of the two, Natrum Carb. are much more sensitive to people than Natrum Mur., and they take an unreasonable dislike to certain people, particularly to strangers. Natrum Mur. on the other hand are much more likely to develop a sudden passion for somebody.

The Natrum Phos. personality is one of being tired, discouraged and rather hopeless, and a little discontented. That is their normal state; but with interference Natrum Phos. become irritable and often very impatient of advice, not of criticism as some of the Natrum salts are, but of friendly advice. In spite of their weariness they often delay seeking medical advice, and this is often due to a fear of illness. As a rule they are rather restless and fidgety in spite of their weariness, and they feel tense. Any mental effort, or effort of concentration, produces this state of tension more than anything else. Natrum Phos. have the critical side that is present in most Natrums, but it is much more liable to be a criticism of somebody who is absent rather than the sudden unpleasant reaction of the other Sodium salts to somebody who is present. They usually have a grievance of some kind.

Natrum Sulph. patients are definitely depressed, and the depression may go on to thoughts of suicide. During their depression they dislike people; they do not want to talk to anybody or see them. They resent questions and are suspicious of the questioner's motive. They may appear sullen and yet, underneath this sullen exterior, they are apprehensive, fearful and anxious. Their discomfort and their apprehension appears to be more marked amongst people, and they are afraid of crowds. They often shun people even if they do not actually fear them. They often have a fear of evil. What form it is going to take they do not know; it is just a fear of something hostile to them.

TEMPERATURE REACTIONS

Temperature reactions are of definite help in distinguishing the Natrum salts. Natrum Mur. are typically hot-blooded. They are intolerant of heat in general, but are much more intolerant of any stuffiness than warmth; a stuffy room crowded with people really upsets them. They are also quite sensitive to cold and to draughts in spite of the general intolerance of heat. They are always better mentally out in the open air, but if they do any violent exercise and get heated up they perspire and the skin of the face becomes greasy, which upsets them.

By contrast, Natrum Ars. are sensitive to the cold. They like as much warmth as they can possibly get, yet if they have had an emotional upset, if they have lost their temper and are shaky, they are better in the open air. They are always worse in winter and are very sensitive to damp.

Damp cold upsets them intensely. They are aggravated by any exertion either mental or physical, and are usually definitely worse after food.

Natrum Mur. tend to get an aggravation of all symptoms round about mid-morning, 10.30 to 11.30 a.m., and they may get a sun aggravation, worse at noon and improving at sunset. Natrum Ars. have a definite aggravation on waking in the morning and another round about midnight.

Natrum Carb. are very much aggravated by cold, and very much better from heat, with one exception – they cannot stand hot sun on their head, it will always cause a headache. With that one exception, Natrum Carb. are worse from cold.

All the Natrum salts have thunder aggravation, but in Natrum Carb. it is more marked than any of the others. Natrum Carb. and Natrum Mur. have most marked times of aggravation, which are definite and typical. Natrum Carb. with gastric complaints tend to have an aggravation about 5 a.m. They often wake feeling very hungry, with definite gastric pain, and their only relief is to have something to eat. They are ameliorated by warmth but do not like great heat. They have a general aggravation at 5 p.m. Natrum Phos. are much more sensitive to draughts than any other Natrum patients. They are very sensitive to cold; they are miserable in winter and much aggravated by any change in weather. They are aggravated by damp weather or a damp atmosphere, and say that if they have a cold or a cough the symptoms are aggravated after having a bath. They get a good deal of digestive trouble too, and that is worse after a bath. They feel better after a meal. One other point is constant and very marked; they are always prostrated by sexual intercourse, and it is the only Natrum salt to have that symptom.

Natrum Sulph. are essentially hot-blooded, much aggravated in warm weather, and extremely sensitive to lack of air, a warm room, a stuffy room or a room full of people. They are very sensitive to damp, wet weather, and hot damp days exhaust them completely. In spite of their aggravation from heat, they are very susceptible to night air, particularly if there is a little mist about. Natrum Sulph. is a common chest and asthmatic remedy and people who get wheezy at night frequently need it. They have a tendency to an aggravation of most of their complaints in the spring due to the soft, damp weather. They are better when moving about and tend to be worse when keeping still. Natrum Sulph. tend to feel at their worst in the morning on waking. They are singularly irritable before breakfast, and feel better tempered after they have eaten.

They often say they feel better, brighter and more cheerful after they have had an action of the bowels.

FOOD REACTIONS

One outstanding factor in Natrum patients is their aggravation from milk. This is present in them all, in some more than in others. Natrum Carb. are the most sensitive to milk. All Natrums have an aggravation from rich foods, particularly fatty foods. Also an aggravation from starch, which is very much less marked in Natrum Carb. than in any of the others. Most Natrum Carb. are starch eaters, and they do not get the same degree of aggravation from it as the other Natrum patients do. In addition to these generalities that apply to all the Natrums, certain of them have aggravations peculiar to themselves. For instance, Natrum Ars. have an absolute intolerance for fruit; Natrum Mur. have not. Natrum Carb., Natrum Phos. and Natrum Sulph. all have an aggravation from fruit. This intolerance is most marked in Natrum Ars. and, after that, in Natrum Sulph.

There is a very marked aggravation in Natrum Phos. from sour things, and particularly acid things. They have the fruit aggravation, but only from acid fruit. A certain number of them have aggravation from alcohol, particularly Natrum Ars. and Natrum Phos.

Natrum Carb. have an aggravation from sweets, not found in the other Natrum salts. Natrum Sulph. have a very definite aggravation from vegetables, particularly green vegetables and potatoes.

Natrum Sulph. have an aggravation from coffee, which the others do not have. There is a good deal of apparent contradiction between their desires for food and their aggravations. In spite of all Natrum patients having an aggravation from bread, many of them like it. This is quite marked in Natrum Mur., less so in the others, but it is present in Natrum Carb. and Natrum Ars. Most of the Natrum patients have an aggravation from alcohol, more marked in some than in others, yet they all have a definite desire for beer and acid drinks. They all have an aggravation from milk, yet occasionally a Natrum Mur. patient will have a desire for it. They all have a desire for salt in varying degrees.

Sometimes there are apparently contradictory indications in the Materia Medica, which indicate a desire and an aversion for the same item of food in the same remedy. The desire and the aversion do not occur in the same patient, but in different patients requiring the same remedy. For instance, a Natrum Mur. patient may have a definite desire for sweets or a definite aversion to sweets. And again, some Natrum Mur. have a definite desire for meat, while the majority of them have an aversion to it. A certain number of Natrum Mur. have a craving for salt; others have an aversion to salt. If the patient has an aversion to salt, Natrum Mur. cannot be excluded.

Some Natrum Mur. have a real desire for wine or beer, yet some have a definite aversion to it. This is more marked for wine than for beer.

One peculiarity that is not recorded under many remedies, is that Natrum Mur. have a desire for soup. There are not many remedies that have a record of it, and Natrum Mur. is one.

Another constant feature of all Natrum patients is that they tend to be thirsty, especially for cold drinks, though a certain number of them have an aggravation from cold food. Natrum Ars. and Natrum Phos. have an aggravation from cold food, though they have a desire for it. Natrum Ars. have more desire for sweets than most of the others, with the exception of Natrum Carb. which also have this desire. Some Natrum Mur. have a moderate desire for sweets, but not any of the others.

Natrum Ars. patients often have a craving for bread, and almost always a desire for juicy fruits – an exception to the general Natrum reaction – and an aversion to fat. Natrum Carb. have similar desires to Natrum Mur., as well as a strong desire for sweets, and they have a desire for all sorts of stodgy, heavy, farinaceous foods. Usually they dislike coffee and have a very strong aversion to milk. Natrum Phos. often have a desire for eggs, which is not found in the other Natrum patients, and a desire for fish, particularly fried fish, and for all types of highly-seasoned food. The only exception sometimes found in Natrum Sulph. is that, in spite of their strong dislike for milk, they like boiled milk and often have a craving for ice cream. Natrum Mur. have a definite aversion to tobacco, but not so the other Natrum patients. The aversion to salt is more commonly met with in Natrum Mur. than in the other Natrums. The aversion to coffee is common to both Natrum Carb. and Natrum Mur. There is no record of it for the others.

DISCHARGES

The discharges of Natrum Mur. patients look very much like white of egg, and may come from any mucous surface. Natrum Mur. complain that the affected mucous membranes feel dry. With pharyngitis, on examination of the throat, there is discharge all over the back of the throat. But the patient feels it is dry, so that they have difficulty in speaking, and yet there is this sticky mucus all over. There is not the same complaint of dryness in the other Natrum patients with the exception of Natrum Ars., who complain of the same dryness. Other patients may have a burning sensation, but they do not complain of it being dry. The typical discharge of Natrum Ars. is usually rather watery, sticky and yellow, and it is practically always offensive. The offensiveness is not present in the discharges of Natrum Mur.

Quite commonly Natrum Carb. have an offensive discharge and so sometimes do Natrum Sulph. Natrum Ars. have the most offensive discharge. It is rather thin, sticky, yellow and offensive. Natrum Carb. have two types of discharge, one which is similar to that of Natrum Mur. It is white in colour, but not so thin; it tends to be lumpy and more ropey and stringy than the Natrum Mur. discharge. The other type of discharge in Natrum Carb. is rather thick, yellow and offensive.

In Natrum Phos. the discharge tends to be yellow, but is much more like pus than in any of the others. It varies between creamy colour and definite yellow, and the distinguishing feature is that it is an acrid excoriating discharge, and often has a peculiar sour smell. The discharges in Natrum Sulph. are usually thicker. They are yellowish-green, definitely purulent and usually fairly profuse. It does not matter which of the mucous membranes one is considering – eye, ear, nose, throat, rectum, vagina – the same type of discharge occurs in each of the individual patients.

TONGUE

The tongues in the five Natrum salts are fairly characteristic as a rule. Natrum Mur. tend to complain of the whole mouth feeling dry, and the tongue is either shiny and red, or else the shiny red surface is broken up by patches of white exudate. That is the typical Natrum Mur. 'mapped' tongue. In Natrum Ars. the tongue is rather flabby and toneless, with a quantity of viscid mucus in the mouth. The tongue resembles the typical Merc. tongue – large, flabby and pale, but without the typical ulcers in the Merc. mouth. In Natrum Carb. the tongue is very sensitive, slightly inflamed with a tendency to develop small blisters along the margins. It may be moderately coated, but it usually has a bright red tip, which is very sensitive to touch.

The Natrum Phos. patient has a thickly coated tongue, tending to be white or yellow at the root.

The Natrum Sulph. tongue tends to be very dirty. It is thickly coated, either dirty yellow or dirty brown. There is always a good deal of mucus and occasionally blisters, but the blisters are on the cheek or on the inside of the lips rather than on the tongue itself.

Natrum Mur. often complain of a salty taste, and Natrum Ars. of a bitter taste. Natrum Carb. complain much more of the burning sensitiveness of the mouth than of the actual taste, though if they have a definite stomach upset there is a degree of acidity. Natrum Phos. complain of sourness in the mouth, and Natrum Sulph. commonly complain of loss of taste and a feeling of disgust at the sliminess of their mouths.

DIGESTIVE TRACT

Natrum Mur. tend to have a sluggish digestion and high acidity, and complain of discomfort and a burning feeling in the stomach after meals. Associated with that, the majority of them suffer from obstinate constipation. Occasionally Natrum Mur. will be required for a patient with very chronic, persistent diarrhoea, particularly if they have a red, shiny tongue. But the typical Natrum Mur. patient is a constipated person. All the digestive disturbances in Natrum Mur. tend to be aggravated by eating. That is one of the points that distinguishes it from Natrum Carb. If they are suffering from an acid stomach they are very liable to become extremely thirsty. With the thirst they have a desire for cold drinks, which often relieve the stomach disturbances for a time. In abdominal disturbances there is a good deal of flatulence, and the patients are intolerant of any pressure on the abdomen. Both Natrum Mur. and Natrum Carb. tend to get a feeling of hunger. Natrum Mur. feel hungry between 11 a.m. and 12 noon, Natrum Carb. tend to waken feeling hungry about 5 a.m., and again have an empty feeling between 10 and 11 a.m. However, with a mid-morning hunger period the patients are more likely to need Natrum Carb. than Natrum Mur.

Natrum Ars. are much more liable to acute digestive upsets with burning pain in the stomach and vomiting, either an acute gastritis or a gastric ulcer. There is one peculiarity present in Natrum Ars. patients: they get a feeling of emptiness without a feeling of hunger, particularly in their stomach conditions. Associated with that, if they take any food, it immediately produces a sensation of nausea. With most of their gastric pain they develop thirst and want frequent small drinks. Even when the pain is not present they are hypersensitive to hot drinks, which always produce a burning sensation in the epigastrium. They have sour eructations and may have attacks of diarrhoea. These are usually fairly painful, accompanied by tenesmus. The attacks often start after the evening meal and may be precipitated by catching cold. The characteristic stool is bright yellow.

The outstanding characteristic of the Natrum Carb. digestive system is flatulence. All Natrum Carb. patients get a certain amount of flatulence and they all tend to have a lot of loud eructations. Also, very often, they suffer from troublesome waterbrash and heartburn. Most of the abdominal symptoms are relieved by eating. All Natrum Carb. tend to be hungry. They want food every two hours, and get a special hunger period about 5 a.m. and between 10 and 11 a.m. Another characteristic is their extreme susceptibility to milk. If they have an acute gastric upset and are put on a milk diet they will vomit, and if the diet is continued they will develop acute diarrhoea.

Most Natrum Carb. patients are thirsty and desire cold (but not iced) fluids. Apart from their acute attacks of diarrhoea they are constipated, but considering the type of food they like to eat, their flatulence and constipation are not surprising.

Natrum Phos. have one or two unusual symptoms. They get the Natrum sensation of hunger, but the circumstances are peculiar. They get a feeling of emptiness that is aggravated after meals and which is not relieved by eating. They also get this aggravation after a bowel motion. Apart from that, they get a sense of fullness after meals with eructations, which are definitely sour, more sour than any of the other Natrum salts.

There is a good deal of general bowel irritability in Natrum Phos. and a marked tendency to diarrhoea. The stool is usually greenish, watery diarrhoea accompanied by flatus. There is always marked urging before stool and a feeling of weakness in the rectum. There may be incontinence of stool.

Natrum Sulph. complain of fullness and weight under the right costal margin, as if the liver is heavy and congested, and as if it drags over the abdomen when the patients lie on the left side. Associated with that there is a good deal of nausea that develops after breakfast. It is not present first thing in the morning, but immediately they take food it develops, and with it they get the slimy feeling in the mouth.

Further down the digestive tract they get a tendency to a very congested, stagnant colon. They often complain of a feeling of weight in the region of the caecum and on examination there is a tender, full caecum. They have a slimy mouth and a tendency to jaundice.

Natrum Sulph. complain of frequent urging to stool. It feels as if they were going to have an action, but they only pass a quantity of flatus. Their aggravation time is 4 to 8 a.m. for abdominal conditions.

They tend to get morning diarrhoea and are not unlike Sulphur. It is useful to remember that in Sulphur diarrhoea comes on before the patient gets out of bed. In Natrum Sulph. the diarrhoea does not come on till after the patient gets up in the morning.

Another point is that Natrum Sulph. are very liable to develop piles, which are not very painful but which bleed profusely.

Chapter 12

Seventeen Important Remedies

Sulphur

The average Sulphur patient does not necessarily give the impression of the 'ragged philosopher'. Kent's description – and it is the same in Nash and Clark – is of an emaciated, scrawny, irritable, nervy, excitable patient. This type of patient is seen and does occasionally require Sulphur, but the more common type of Sulphur is a well-nourished person. They have usually rather more than the average amount of fat, a big figure, above the average height, and they give the impression of being very well satisfied with themselves. That self-satisfaction keys in with Kent's description and is, in fact, a lesser, slightly different form of it. They think their clothes are marvellous, and sometimes they think rags are beautiful. They are not very sure of themselves, yet they put up a good bluff and give the impression of being hale and hearty and self-confident; yet when cross-questioned their self-confidence goes. They are not really very sure of themselves and are resentful if found out. Then they are apt to become stubborn and rather obstinate, and to stick to what they have already said, even if it is not accurate. That tallies with the description in the books – 'taking up definite beliefs, and sticking to them'. Associated with that they tend to be untruthful. If a lie will serve their purpose they will lie without any hesitation, and sometimes it is difficult to decide whether they are deliberately lying or whether they are deceiving themselves. It appears that they can convince themselves of anything they want to believe, and they use that to serve their immediate purpose. These are all different shades of the typical Kent description.

As regards appearances, there is one thing pretty constant about Sulphur – one sees them very well turned out, often perfectly tidy, and often definitely proud of their appearance and not always without reason. This is a fairly common picture. In spite of this, they have always just missed being completely right, either their jacket does not sit well, or they have the wrong coloured tie, or their finger nails are dirty or something of the sort just gives the show away. Another constant characteristic is that they always have a high colour of the face and particularly of their mucous membranes. Their lips are red and they tend to have blepharitis and a mild congestion of the conjunctivae. That is the general appearance of individuals who may need Sulphur.

One thing constant in Sulphur is that they all have increased appetites. It is much more bulk than quality that they want. They enjoy their food irrespective of its taste, and tend to take large mouthfuls. They are definitely greedy.

A point which occasionally appears contradictory is the question of heat reactions. The Sulphur patient is aggravated by heat, there is no question about that. Yet some are apparently perfectly comfortable in a hot stuffy room with no air at all. In these conditions, they always look far too hot, their face is congested and sweaty, even if they do not complain of the room being hot. One thing they do dislike is a draught.

Calcarea Carbonica

The impression given by Calcarea is that they are soft. The outline of their faces is usually smooth. Very often in the adult Calcarea the patient is not overfat, and yet they give the impression of having a large head and a rather large face. Calcarea are always slow mentally and physically. They walk across the room in a very slow, deliberate manner. Another striking thing is the feel of their hand. It is a soft hand, very often slightly cold, not necessarily clammy, but it is boneless, soft and yielding, and they do not grip.

Then there is their slow mentality. They are slow in their speech, and pause to take in what is asked before they reply. They tend to get rather depressed. It is not an acute depression, rather a sort of condition where everything is in a minor key. If they talk about themselves, their difficulties or ailments, they are apt to weep. It is not a violent weeping, they just gently shed tears and are very sorry for themselves, and very hopeless.

They tend to go over and over their difficulties. Their friends complain that they are always referring to the same things, the same old difficulties, the same old worries, and they are always referring to them in the same old way. If it is the question of health, they repeat the fear that they are sure they are going to die, till the people who live with them become exasperated. It is this spinelessness that is noticeable. They have intense anxiety during the night, but this is due to a fear of the dark. They always have a feeling that they are mentally below the average. They are scared of things, and also have the fear that they are going to have a cerebral haemorrhage. This is a very common fear in Calcarea. They have particularly poor memories. They get confused and cannot remember the dates of their various illnesses, and they cannot remember any details of what they have read as soon as they put the book down.

Another fairly constant point is that they have quite a good appetite, though it is nothing like as good as might be expected from their appearance of fatness and flabbiness. They always have a good appetite for breakfast. If they miss breakfast, they develop a violent headache within 10 or 15 minutes, whereas if they have had some food they are quite all right. One other rather surprising characteristic, from their appearance, is that in spite of the fact that they are always complaining and making a nuisance of themselves, they are extremely sensitive. If they are told to pull themselves together and get on with things, they are very much upset by it. They are very sensitive to adverse criticism, also to any injustice or cruelty to others, which makes them go to pieces.

Calcarea people are always chilly and wear far too many clothes. If the room is hot, the skin is moist to the touch, yet their lower extremities are cold. It is said that Calcarea types have a fear of heart disease – it is wise to take this fear seriously as in many instances they are correct.

Graphites

This remedy has a very similar symptomatology to Calcarea, but there are differences to be noted in order to distinguish it. Graphites patients have rather large heads and faces, and tend to be fat, particularly about the face. Their features are heavy. Both remedy types tend to have rather pale mucous membranes. Their lips are pale and also their hands, but although a Calcarea occasionally has bluish extremities, Graphites is never blue.

Another difference is that Calcarea are definitely nervous when they come for consultation and have rather dilated pupils, which is not present in Graphites. Also in Graphites there is a droop about the eyelids as if they have been awake for several nights. It is a drooping and heaviness of the upper lids, not a narrowing of the eye.

Calcarea get tired out with any effort, particularly any mental work; Graphites get distressed, excited and worried. The Calcarea type gives up, whereas the Graphites type frets about it.

The typical Graphites patient finds it very difficult to make up his mind. He vacillates and hesitates over every decision. The Calcarea type usually sheds the whole thing and just does not bother. They both have a degree of depression. The depression in Calcarea is much more gentle and weeping than it is in Graphites. In the Graphites type there is a definite foreboding of trouble ahead.

Another thing that distinguishes the two is that Graphites tend to be fatter than Calcarea; patients needing Graphites are heavier in build throughout. The skin of the typical Graphites is not the very soft, moist skin of the typical Calcarea; it is much more rough, harsh and dry. In practically all their complaints the two remedies have a symptom which from the textbook is very alike – a feeling of a rush of blood to the head. In Graphites the sensation is a feeling of blood flowing up from the feet, as if the head would burst, and there is often epistaxis. In Calcarea it starts in the abdomen and, from there, surges up into the neck, not so much into the head as in Graphites.

Another distinguishing point is that Graphites have a peculiar sensitiveness to music, not present in Calcarea. Calcarea are often musical, but they do not have that same liability to weep when listening to music which is noticeable in Graphites. A further point to look for in Graphites, either at a consultation or in their history, is a skin disease with a honey-like discharge, yellow, slightly sticky, and most commonly found at the back of the ears, round the side of the nose or at the back of the neck round the hair. Another point that sometimes distinguishes Graphites from Calcarea is that many of these Graphites patients are singularly critical. Calcarea, provided they have had a good breakfast, are alert in the mornings. Graphites are slow and dull in the mornings, and tend to wake up in the evenings. This is a definite contrast.

In both of these remedies the patients tend to be constipated. Calcarea usually feel at their best while constipated; they do not get headaches or feel heavy. Graphites are disturbed by constipation; they feel uncomfortable, and are better when their bowels are acting regularly.

Thuja

Without exception, the Thuja patients I have seen have been fair-haired and with a fine skin, very much the sort of appearance seen in a pre-tuberculosis patient, fair fine hair, fine skin and rather delicate, with variable colour.

The classical description of Thuja is one of intense irritability and bad temper, depression and a definite loathing of life. That is not the Thuja familiar to me. Thuja patients are singularly well mannered;

they are sensitive, polite and grateful. They do get depressed, the depression usually arising from a consciousness that they are not doing everything that they ought to be doing, or they are not progressing as fast as they ought to be with the attention they are getting; or else they feel they are a trouble to their relatives because they require attention.

They are definitely impatient people. They like things done fairly fast and get impatient with those who are slow. In the Thuja patients I have seen there has always been a tendency to muddled thinking. When talking to them they are very polite, and want to do all they can to help. They hunt for the exact word to tell their symptoms. If they cannot find the exact word at first, they come back to it later and say that is the word they wanted. When writing letters they often complain that they miss words out or misspell them, and it worries them. This may become more marked and they begin to leave things undone. An even more marked symptom in children is that they stop in the middle of something because their attention wanders, and they have to be constantly reminded to go on with what they are doing.

A fairly constant symptom is that, in spite of being affectionate, they have a definite dislike of any contact with strangers. They often shrink when anyone comes near, and do not want to be touched. This is accentuated if there is any mental breakdown; they feel brittle, but even in the normal state they have this dislike of people touching them. They are very individualistic, but are not likely to make a mark in the world, and they do not like to have their privacy imposed upon.

All Thuja patients are truthful and scrupulous in everything they do. They are conscientious in the way they carry out anything they undertake, even to the last detail, unless their attention wanders. If it does and they omit something, they get very upset about it. They are very sensitive and they also become angry. Ordinarily big things which anyone would be justified in being angry about do not aggravate them, yet some quite minor thing makes them strangely angry. That is my impression of the typical Thuja patient.

Psorinum

Practically all Psorinum patients feel at their best immediately before they are going to be ill – one of the best key-notes for this remedy. Suppose they have a racking headache: they say that the day before they felt exceptionally well and so knew that they were going to have a headache. This is similarly true if they are going to have a cold or any other illness.

The appearance is characteristic. They are usually thin or on the thin side. They always have a very harsh, dry, cold skin, which gives the impression of being dirty. They are particularly susceptible to cold east winds or working in water. The skin cracks and peels, with deep fissures in the fingers and small cracks across the cheeks, which may actually bleed. They always tend to have very sensitive eyes that get red and inflamed in any irritant atmosphere, dust, wind or smoke. They often have a history of recurring styes and chronic blepharitis.

Causticum

Two other remedies, almost as similar as Calcarea and Graphites, are Causticum and Phosphorus. Yet from the point of view of prescribing, they are very different. The best way of considering them is to take their points of similarity first, and then to take up their differences.

Patients who may need either Causticum or Phosphorus have one thing in common: they are liable to develop colds and to lose their voice. Both have a twilight aggravation; they tend to get nervous and apprehensive in the evening just when the light is beginning to fail. Both have a tendency to tremble and also a tendency to stiffness, particularly when they start to move. These are the most common points.

There are certain other similarities. Consider Causticum first.

Typical Causticum patients have rather fine delicate features and extremities, and are usually pale. It is that pallor that gives the first distinguishing point. It is a peculiar greyish pallor, rather like the kind of greyness seen if a piece of porcelain breaks and this greyness is under the porcelain glaze. Another indication is a certain amount of pigmentation over the temples, a yellowish tinge. Often there are small warty growths near the eyes. These are the visible indications for Causticum.

They are definitely anxious individuals, particularly about their friends. For instance, if friends are late they get worried about them in case something has happened to them. They are also rather shy and timid. They try to conceal their anxiety, either about their affairs or their health, by a slightly nervous laugh. Their memory is weak. They find difficulty in telling their story, and the effort of concentration produces a very unpleasant feeling of tension in their heads. They frequently have disturbed nights, with a general feeling of restlessness and discomfort. Their eyes look heavy. The lids are usually thin and wrinkled; they are not puffy at all and yet there is a definite droop about them and there may be an actual ptosis.

Causticum give the impression of being thin, but it is much more a thinness of the face and neck than of the extremities, and most of them have peculiarly flabby, toneless abdominal muscles. They are definitely irritable people, and often slightly difficult to deal with. They have a fairly good opinion of themselves – if their wishes are not carried out accurately and rapidly they are apt to become irritable and fly into violent passions. It is always an aggravation of their present complaint. These bursts of temper always aggravate their complaint.

Associated with the lax conditions of the abdominal wall is their liability to sphincter weakness, particularly of the bladder. Most Causticum patients with a cough complain of some urinary incontinence. They are always worse in fresh, clear, bright weather. They are sensitive to cold, sensitive to draught, and better in a soft, moist atmosphere.

Phosphorus
Phosphorus patients typically have a physical appearance similar to Causticum, with delicate features, rather thin faces, fine skin, and slender hands and feet. They may be pale, but the pallor is a different colour from that in Causticum. It is a strange, waxy, transparent pallor. To contrast it – one is the porcelain with the broken glaze, the other is the porcelain with the glaze still on it, which is transparent. That is the type in a Phosphorus who has been ill for years and comes for consultation when acutely ill – either a haemorrhagic patient or one with tuberculosis. But the average Phosphorus patient is absolutely full of vitality. They are alert, very much alive, quick in their movements, bright and intelligent and definitely sensitive; sensitive to their surroundings, to people, to noise, to the atmosphere of the room.

They are tense and restless, quick, impatient and liable to fidget if they are kept waiting. They move their hands or walk about the room – showing the Phosphorus irritability. They have the same explosive anger of Causticum patients, although it is less violent and the after-effects are very different. In Causticum there is an aggravation of their illness; Phosphorus are exhausted and rather ashamed of themselves. Causticum always justify themselves, e.g. people had annoyed them and they were quite right to be angry. Phosphorus are anxious, but it is not the same kind of anxiety as in Causticum, who anticipate trouble particularly for themselves or their relatives. In Phosphorus the anxiety is more a feeling of general dread. They are anxious, nervous and worried, often without being able to say why they are worried. They are tense, and the tension increases in the late afternoon – the twilight aggravation that is mentioned in the Materia Medica. It tends to continue right through the night. Phosphorus patients are afraid of the dark, and all their anxieties tend to persist through the hours of darkness. Almost all Phosphorus are very susceptible to what is called atmosphere, to a sudden drop of the barometer, a thunderstorm or any condition that alters the atmospheric pressure; it may affect their aches and pains, but it always affects them personally.

One helpful point in recognising Phosphorus is that they always have a very variable circulation. During conversation with a Phosphorus patient who is pale, if a sudden idea occurs to him, he colours up at once. Any strong idea makes him colour and he often says that under any excitement he feels his face becoming hot. Any hot or stimulating meal, hot tea or highly seasoned food produces the same effect.

Another point is that, in spite of the fact that they have all this nervous energy and vitality, Phosphorus do become very exhausted. When they are tired they want to keep quiet, their restlessness disappears, they prefer to lie down, and then they like company. Causticum do not mind whether they have anyone near them or not; Phosphorus do. They like sympathy, they are very affectionate, and they are particularly sensitive to certain people. Sometimes Phosphorus have either waking or dreaming premonitions of what is going to happen, which are very often accurate. They say that they have strange feelings on meeting new people – that they have known them before, they know what they are going to say. This type of sensitiveness seems unique to Phosphorus. Another point is that they have almost as much stiffness as Causticum; Causticum patients may develop an acute fibrositis in neck muscles after being out in the cold. Phosphorus have almost the same, but they have a very different reaction. Causticum are not relieved by movement, but Phosphorus can gradually ease the stiffness by movement – massage will help them. Phosphorus patients enjoy being massaged.

Phosphorus have a strong desire for salt. A patient who otherwise appears to need Phosphorus but has no desire for salt should not be given Phosphorus; he might need some Phosphorus compound, but not Phosphorus itself. Phosphorus are worse in damp weather, and much better in a fresh dry atmosphere, as a distinction from Causticum. Phosphorus are aggravated by working in a hot steamy atmosphere.

Phosphorus may be fair or dark and have very lovely hair. There is always a surprising amount of colour and life in their hair, which is fine, whatever the colour. They are never coarse skinned or coarse haired.

Nitric Acid
In appearance, typical Nitric Acid patients are always sallow. They have quite a good colour in their red cheeks, but they look sallow round the eyes. They have dark hair, well-marked eyebrows and soft lips. They are very alive and definite, but have a gloomy outlook. They get intense irritation of the skin, and wounds are slow to heal. They always take a very bad view of the future, and often a very bad view of their attendants too.

They are very obstinate. They are difficult to reason with if they have an idea of their own. Another interesting point is that they have strange appetites. All Nitric Acid patients want pungent-tasting food to stimulate their appetite. They are easily annoyed and get very angry, and will rarely accept an apology. They tend to think people are being unfair to them. They get great amelioration of almost all their symptoms and also of their temper from riding in a car. There is only one exception – a certain number of them tend to get headaches from vibration, which may be brought on in a car that is driven over rough ground. They are always very sensitive to cold.

They are hypersensitive in every way – sensitive to noise, to touch and to pain, and they feel things very acutely.

Normally, Nitric Acid have a strong liking for fats and fatty foods, yet in their digestive disturbances they have an aggravation from taking fats, and this is a point to remember. The only other constant feature is that in any illness they develop a strong odour in the urine.

Medorrhinum
It is not easy to distinguish between Medorrhinum and Thuja patients; their personality, their reactions and their symptoms are so similar. A person who does not respond to Thuja, yet has all the indications for it, will probably be helped with Medorrhinum.

The distinguishing modalities for Medorrhinum are amelioration from lying on the abdomen, amelioration from sea air and a 5 a.m. aggravation.

Lachesis
(The following description is of a person who Dr Borland felt was 'the very essence of Lachesis', Ed.) The patient was a middle-aged woman with reddish-brown hair. She had a very high colour, and the particular point about her colour was the venous engorgement, little veins standing out on her cheeks, little veins standing out on her nose, and a definite bluish appearance of her nose and ears. Her eyes were bright

and clear and she was very much alert. Her hands were also rather congested, red, a little swollen and tremulous. She was very restless. In conversation she demonstrated the typical manner in which the Lachesis patient talks – it is very difficult to keep them to the point. It is not that they withhold information, but they do not pay attention to the question. Often they have not got the drift of it, and something else appeals to them and they start off on what they want to say, not on what has been asked. They are at no loss for words, which always stream out of them. She was perfectly frank in telling her tale, and her symptoms were quite well given. On asking about her life and conditions, the outstanding thing was the definite jealousy she had of those members of the family who were well. Her husband was a strong, healthy man who went to business every day and played golf at the weekend, and she was definitely jealous that he was fit and she had to stay in bed. Her daughter was married and had four healthy children. This lady was jealous that her grandchildren were healthy, whereas her own daughters had always been seedy and a worry to her when they were children.

Another typical symptom is that Lachesis are always mixing up the time of day; they think it is evening when it is morning, and morning when it is evening. Another fairly definite characteristic is a very obvious self-consciousness and a weird conceit. In this patient it was mixed up with another typical Lachesis symptom, a very narrow religious outlook. She belonged to some small sect, but she was perfectly certain it was the only sect on the earth; her whole day was spent talking about her religion to those around her, and trying to make them join her own sect. At times she would speak of the amount of money she gave away to keep it going, and it was interesting to note the self-gratification she was getting about it all. At other times she would say that she was a very poor member of the sect and no use to them, and in the next breath, if only she had good health like her husband, she would be able to do so much more. One thing she mentioned was that she had a rather unpleasant experience with her protégés, who had rather done her down. Her husband said that for the past two years his wife had been very suspicious and would give nothing to anyone, even to people she had known for years. He said life was very difficult. He said, 'I don't want to offend my wife because she is not well at present, and one of the things she dislikes is that I should take any alcohol. I am not narrowly religious, but she wants me to keep to her standards. I go out to golf and I want a drink occasionally, and almost the first question I get asked when I come in is, "Have you had a drink?" And she is always wanting to know where I have been and whether I have done anything contrary to her own religious beliefs.'

Another patient has the typical Lachesis suspicion to an even greater degree. She lives in a small village in the country, and is always in trouble because of her suspicion of her neighbours. She is constantly looking for offence and slights, and thinks that people are doing her down – a typical Lachesis reaction.

That is only one type of Lachesis patient. There is another, the chronic alcoholic. They have a more congested appearance than the one that is typical. There is the same tendency to the venous stasis, dilated veins on the face and nose, but not the brightness or the same mental sharpness – the edge of things is a little blunted. There is the same tendency to wander, to half finish one subject and move to the next one. They have the tremor that is frequently present in Lachesis. They are more irritable and much more malicious in their statements about other people than most Lachesis. Lachesis patients are sometimes pale, but the skin is not clear, there are always freckles or congested veins on the face and hands.

Another point about Lachesis alcoholics is that they get a very marked aggravation from food. After food they are more drowsy, more heavy, more muddled, and very liable to get a congested face. They are difficult to treat. Another common reaction in alcoholics is that they are very conscious that they themselves have been responsible for the state they are in, and are very melancholic about it. They are hopeless about anything being done for them, and are very suspicious about any medicine they are given. They think that either it will poison them, or that they are being drugged.

All Lachesis patients have the typical sleep aggravation, i.e. symptoms increase during sleep, so that the patient is worse on waking. They are all very sensitive to heat, and with such congested characteristics they are intolerant of any tightness round them, tight collars, tight belts or anything similar. With any cardiac embarrassment they get very short of breath, want to push the bedclothes down and open the windows.

Ferrum Metallicum

The outstanding feature of Ferrum patients is a very clear skin and, as a rule, a very unstable circulation. They are liable to become pale or to flush on any emotional excitement, exertion, or stimulus of any kind. With the fair skin they have a good colour, particularly over the cheek bones, but very pale mucous membranes. They are definitely anaemic.

They are very easily tired and, without exception, say that if they attempt to hurry they get out of breath, feel absolutely exhausted, and are often faint and giddy. The faintness and giddiness occur with all their complaints, as well as with any over-exertion, talking too much, having to entertain people, or anything similar.

Ferrum patients are very chilly. They feel the cold intensely, usually have very cold extremities, and tend to get very troublesome cramp in their feet. This tends to come on either when they are sitting still or after over-exertion. Another symptom is that they are perfectly all right while going about in the house, but immediately they go out of doors and have to go a little faster, or a little further, they become exhausted.

Mentally, the typical Ferrum condition is a state of depression, despondency and weepiness. In the depression they tend to become confused and anxious, but are unable to give a clear explanation of what is worrying them. Usually they are irritable, particularly from noise, and especially from loud noise.

They are extremely sensitive to pain, may faint if given an injection – yet cannot tolerate any dental work without a local anaesthetic. It is true hyperaesthesia. They appear to be very gentle, pleasant people, a little under the weather, a little depressed, with a pessimistic outlook on life. Yet they simply will not tolerate any opposition, and get into a rage immediately if it is offered. That is one of the main characteristics of Ferrum. They feel exhausted, hot-headed and faint amongst a number of people, and dislike talking to more than one person at a time.

Ferrum and Pulsatilla are rather similar in appearance and temperament, but there is never the intense opposition from Pulsatilla that comes from Ferrum, and their temperature reactions are different. Another symptom often present in Ferrum is constipation. They are always worried by it, and their depression is much more marked when they are constipated.

Ferrum will often clear enuresis in children and may also clear incontinence in the adult.

One other point in connection with Ferrum, a symptom sometimes but not always present, is that they cannot tolerate any dry wine at all, and yet are perfectly all right on a sweet wine. The dry wine gives them a stomach upset and diarrhoea. Chronic diarrhoea that comes on while the patient is actually eating, not after the meal, is a symptom of Ferrum and no other drug. The urging occurs immediately they put anything into their mouths. Ferrum will clear up summer diarrhoea of babies which occurs immediately they begin to feed. A number of remedies have diarrhoea immediately after eating – that is quite common – but only in Ferrum does the diarrhoea occur while eating.

Lycopodium

The typical appearance of Lycopodium patients is that of rather spare, sallow, somewhat wrinkled people. They tend to be dark-haired and, as a rule, are rather above the average height. Usually there is a slight tendency to stoop, and they give the impression of having a long, narrow chest. Sometimes the stoop is more marked in a decidedly thin patient with an almost scaphoid abdomen. They tend to have a worried expression and are a little difficult to get symptoms from. They are rather reticent, and the reticence may become distrust and suspicion, or the reticence may arise from a feeling of diffidence and insecurity. It can happen both ways in Lycopodium. I have never yet met a Lycopodium who was at all expansive. With their very intimate friends they may relax and express their feelings, but they always do it with a certain amount of reservation; they always keep something back and do not give themselves away entirely. As patients this reticence is even more marked, and often gives the impression that they are haughty.

Practically all Lycopodium patients have digestive difficulties. As a rule, they have either jaundiced or muddy conjunctivae, and are lean and livery. They are irritable, peevish and fretful. They want to sit about and be quiet, and dislike being disturbed. They get anxious and apprehensive and dislike being entirely alone, but resent interference. They do not have much stamina and are easily exhausted from either mental or physical exertion. Practically all of them, particularly businessmen, complain that they are exhausted by the end of the afternoon. Their digestion is impaired; they complain of painful flatulence and abdominal distension. After getting home in the evening, if they have an hour's rest and a small meal – they cannot take a big meal because it makes them uncomfortable – they feel much better. That late afternoon aggravation is very constant and agrees with the 4 to 8 p.m. aggravation in all Lycopodium complaints. They are always very slow in the morning. They feel ill and depressed, as if the day's work is going to be too much for them. This occurs at the time they are getting up. After they have had breakfast they feel better, and are confident that they can tackle the day ahead of them.

Associated with the feeling of inability to tackle things is the feeling that their business will not succeed; and, arising out of that, they may become very careful in regard to money matters. They are afraid that they will not have enough to live on, and may become real misers. They are never out-going, are careful with their money, narrow in their outlook, and may become rather intolerant. They have unusual beliefs and ideas, and will not listen to any argument on the subject.

One peculiarity about them is sometimes a little misleading. Although they get a good deal of digestive upset, and practically always get flatulence, and with their flatulence are unable to take a large meal, practically all of them say they cannot manage without food. If they are late for a meal it upsets them. A businessman will say that if he is late for his lunch it upsets him, and yet when he has a meal it has to be a small one.

Lycopodium are very much aggravated by taking any cold food. They have an aggravation from tightness of any kind, particularly around the abdomen, but also a tight hat on the head gives them a headache. They are better from having the head uncovered and from getting out into the fresh air.

One other characteristic point is that they are definitely sensitive to noise, and have a marked hyperaesthesia to any smells, particularly unpleasant smells. A further point is that typical Lycopodium patients do not perspire easily. After strenuous exertion, they may perspire a little and feel better. They tend to have a dry skin, particularly the palms of the hands, which become very hot, burning and uncomfortable. It also occurs on the soles of their feet, particularly from walking about.

Another distinctive feature is that they tend to get a very yellow discolouration of the teeth. It is not due to neglect of the teeth, because many of them are very particular about it. The textbooks say that Lycopodium have a hunger for sweet things, but this is not always present.

Arsenicum Album

One point of contact between Arsenic and Lycopodium is that the typical Arsenicum Alb. patient may occasionally have a miserly tendency. This is the only point of contact between the two remedies – otherwise they are in no way similar. In Arsenicum Alb. the miserliness arises from an entirely different cause. Occasionally it is from a fear of failure, or fear of losing their money, and the over-careful Arsenicum Alb. becomes miserly. The typical cause, however, is covetousness. They appreciate anything beautiful and want to have it. It is more the desire of possession than the fear of poverty. As far as appearance is concerned, typical chronic Arsenicum Alb. people are always very quick, restless, active, intelligent, and alive. They are usually rather finely made. In complexion they tend to be pale, often with dark rings round their eyes, and are usually spare. They have far too much nervous energy, and are too active ever to become really fat.

They are definitely nervous and fussy. They fuss about themselves, they fuss about their health, imagine they have all kinds of diseases, go from one doctor to another, and take up new crazes. They fuss about the family, and are never happy unless they are constantly seeing a doctor. If there is definite opposition to their fussiness, if the members of the family will not go to the doctor, or will not take the latest medicine, then the Arsenicum Alb. patient is very angry with them and is quite sure they will be seriously ill.

They are also fastidious about themselves. They keep themselves neat and tidy, and they like their rooms, bedrooms and their houses very orderly, and are often unduly fussy about it.

Arsenicum Alb. are over-sensitive in every way, to smell, to touch, to light. They are acutely sensitive to cold, and they are liable to get scared and apprehensive if the room gets dark. If there is a noise in the neighbourhood they are afraid it may be burglars. They are always anticipating trouble. They are hypersensitive to tobacco, which makes them very unwell. Many of them suffer from troublesome constipation, and as they are upset almost without exception by fruit and vegetables, it is very difficult to deal with this condition.

I have seen two distinctive types of skin in Arsenicum Alb. patients. In one they have a very fine, smooth skin and very fine hair, and that type usually tends to perspire fairly easily. But there is another Arsenicum Alb. who has a very rough skin, which gets scaly, coarse and unhealthy, and tends to crack. Such people tend to have great difficulty in perspiring; with exertion they get hot and flushed in the face and often develop an acute congestive headache.

Arsenicum Alb. patients sleep badly. They are light sleepers and any noise wakens them about 1 and 2 a.m., and they have a bad nervous spell about that time. Occasionally they will say they never get off to sleep again unless they get up and move about, make some tea or eat something, which often helps them to go to sleep again.

Arsenicum Alb. is frequently indicated in children. They are usually nervy, precocious children who have developed too rapidly and been pushed at school, and if not carefully handled are liable to develop nervous tics. They have nightmares and scream out in the night, they have a terror of the dark and hate to be left alone. Practically always they are very fine-skinned children with fair hair and variable complexion, inclined to be pale yet flushing easily on exertion. They are very restless, the kind of children to whom to sit still is absolute torture. Their skin tends to feel hot and burning rather than itching.

They get definite burning pains, and the surprising thing about the burning pain is that it is relieved by heat, which is exceptional. Lycopodium gets similar burning pains relieved by heat, and it and Arsenicum Alb. are the two remedies that have these pains more than any other. There is one apparent contradiction in Arsenicum Alb. to remember. In connection with their symptoms, they get neuralgic pains. There is intense burning pain in the nerve involved, often the trigeminal, which is relieved by hot applications. They also get congestive headaches accompanied by persistent vomiting. The head feels uncomfortably hot and is relieved by cold applications, or a current of cool air, yet the rest of the body is icy cold. They want the bedclothes up to the neck, they want many blankets and hot bottles, but need their head right by an open window. That is quite different from their neuralgias, where they want hot applications.

Silica

In the textbooks it appears difficult to distinguish Silica and Lycopodium from the mental point of view, and yet Silica and Lycopodium are very different. Typical Silica patients are much more commonly fair-haired. They have a clear skin, never a sallow skin; they usually have a good colour in the cheeks. Very often the skin of the cheeks is a little rough. They tend to have dry lips which crack easily, and they get cracks about the corners of the mouth. If they have nasal catarrh they are liable to get cracks at the corner of the nose. Their hair is fine and they almost always have small bones.

As far as their mentality is concerned, haughtiness never characterises the Silica patient. The typical impression given by Silica is of rather gentle, yielding persons; people who seem as if they would give up very easily. But it is an entirely false impression. They are gentle and polite up to a point, but beyond that they are obstinate, irritable, peevish and most persistent. Silica people are difficult to persuade to take on a job but, if they do take it up, they carry it through to the limit of their ability. They are very conscientious in what they do, and would rather somebody else did it.

Silica children are rather amusing. If handled properly they are very easy to manage. But, if mismanaged, they are just about the most obstinate children it is possible to have, and will often scream and kick.

Both Silica and Lycopodium have a poor memory and from the Materia Medica it is difficult to distinguish them, although in fact they are quite different. In Lycopodium, the tendency to forget is a tendency to forget particular things, like names or something similar. In Silica it is more a question of the patients having had too much to do and the brain being tired and refusing to respond. Thus it is not a lack of memory for individual things, but a tired brain which can take in no more, and cannot remember what it has already learned. Both Lycopodium and Silica are reported as disliking interference. Lycopodium patients want to be left alone, not interfered with or disturbed. In Silica it is much more a matter of disliking personal interference. They do not like to be touched or handled unexpectedly. It makes them jump, and they become annoyed and irritated. If they are depressed and an attempt is made to soothe them, their depression is usually aggravated. They tend to weep, but it does not do them any good. The Lycopodium patient, when depressed, is definitely better from sympathy and understanding. In both remedies the patients are sensitive to cold, but in Lycopodium that sensitiveness to cold is linked up with a definite air hunger, which is not found in Silica.

In both there is an anticipatory dread of undertaking anything. The main distinguishing point about them is that, unless Silica patients are absolutely broken down, although they have a dread of undertaking things, they are capable of doing them well once they start. Lycopodium have a dread of undertaking things and probably make a mess of them.

One thing constant to practically all Silica patients is that under any stress, mental stress or physical exertion they are almost certain to develop a headache, usually a one-sided frontal headache. They may also suffer from recurring headaches which start rather differently. These tend to start in the back of the head, to extend forward and settle in one eye. The stress headache starts over the eye and it may be either eye.

Not only do Silica dislike being touched unexpectedly, even when well, but also they hate jarring of any kind, and commonly get train sick, or develop an acute travel headache, or become generally exhausted by any rough motion.

One other point indicating the possibility of Silica for a patient is that the skin of the finger-tips gets rough, so that it is unpleasant to touch anything. It is a very common Silica symptom; associated with it are cracks round the nails and a tendency to septic fingers. More commonly it is just that roughness of finger-tips which makes it unpleasant to do fine work. It is present even in warm weather, but is more definite if the patient has to have the hands in water frequently.

There is very little to be seen, yet it causes great annoyance. They get deep fissures too, on the tips of the fingers and thumb. If these occur at the sides of the nails they tend to go septic. This is strange, as the typical Silica hand is moist and yet they have this dryness of the finger-tips.

Tuberculinum

It is difficult to get a typical clear-cut picture of Tuberculinum because it may be indicated, at least temporarily, in all sorts of patients. So far as physical make-up is concerned, Tuberculinum is not indicated as a recurring constitutional remedy. Patients may need it occasionally but, as a rule, after it has been given they go on to some other remedy, which they are much more likely to stay on than to revert to Tuberculinum.

However, there is a type of patient that does require a dose of it sometimes. There is one outstanding physical sign which indicates the possibility of Tuberculinum, and this is the peculiar blue colour of the sclera. Apart from that, all sorts of complexions may occur in patients requiring a dose of Tuberculinum.

In children, it has been more commonly indicated in fair children, but in adults all sorts of people may require it. There are certain constant characteristics of Tuberculinum, one of the main indications being a peculiar state of mental restlessness, which is not at all like the Arsenicum Alb. restlessness. It is much more a state of dissatisfaction with their present surroundings and condition, a desire to move about, a desire for change, a desire to go for a holiday, or a desire for travel, anything to alter the present conditions. They are always relieved by motion, whatever their complaint.

Another thing to look for is a change of temperament, from being very good-tempered to being an individual who has become disagreeable, angry or weeping easily. It is a definite change from a previously pleasant disposition. In most Tuberculinum patients, although they have this desire to move about, to see new places and new things, they have a very definite dislike of any mental work. They do physical work quite well, because motion relieves them. This hatred of mental work is linked up with their restlessness; they cannot settle to it.

Another fairly constant symptom in the Tuberculinum state is that they are apt to have acute personal aversions, which have developed recently. A person who has changed, becomes irritable and is developing very definite aversions to individual people, indicates Tuberculinum. Patients with fibrositis which is better from motion, and worse from the cold, require Rhus Tox., whereas if it is better from motion, and worse from heat, they require Tuberculinum. Tuberculinum patients are certainly worse in the heat, but are also aggravated by any sudden change of temperature, whether from cold to hot, or hot to cold, and also any change from dry to damp. Tuberculinum is definitely aggravated in damp cold and in damp hot weather. Rhus Tox is better in warm weather.

Tuberculinum is sometimes very useful in adolescent children. Schoolgirl headaches should respond very well to a dose of Tuberculinum, particularly when dealing with a child who is advanced for her years, bright, intelligent and becoming more irritable than before, becoming nervous of thunderstorms and disliking damp weather, who develops headaches whenever she begins to work, and begins to lose interest in her studies. Tuberculinum is certainly indicated if the child also has a definite fear of dogs.

They are sensitive to music, which often makes them weep, even non-gloomy music. Even though they are so restless, they find standing very exhausting and need to sit down frequently.

Sarsaparilla

There are two, possibly three, types of case with definite indications for Sarsaparilla. The commonest is the one with a definite infection of the urinary tract, in which there is an offensive turbid urine. Clinically the indications for it are either in an infected kidney or cystitis, and there is always a tendency to the formation of calculi, either in the kidney or in the bladder. Associated with the calculus formation are the typical Sarsaparilla modalities. The patient has a certain amount of pain and discomfort on micturition. The pain becomes particularly acute at the end of micturition when the bladder wall contracts either on itself – an inflamed wall – or on a quantity of gritty material in the bladder. The patient feels as if the trouble was actually at the urinary meatus, although it is the bladder contracting down on the calculus that causes the pain. The patient has difficulty in passing urine, which is increased if he or she is lying down. The urine is offensive and there is often a dirty, greyish-greenish deposit.

That is the acute picture. Indications for Sarsaparilla occur occasionally in children with nocturnal enuresis, provided there is a high-smelling urine with a deposit of phosphates and if they tend to get pain on micturition during the day. They have irritating moist eruptions about the genitals where the urine comes in contact with the skin.

Sarsaparilla may also be indicated in skin eruptions. The patients have a marked tendency to skin eruptions of all kinds, but particularly moist excoriating eruptions about the buttocks or the genitals. These are intensely irritating, become raw on scratching and are very much aggravated by washing. Sarsaparilla is the indicated remedy if in addition to the local conditions there is a history of any urinary irritation, particularly if the irritation is most marked at the end of urination, in patients who are sensitive to cold (which distinguishes them from Sulphur) and if the skin irritation is aggravated by any hot stimulating food, such as hot soup.

Sarsaparilla may also be indicated in elderly people with skin eruptions – old patients who look worn and tired and who have an unhealthy wrinkled skin. Very often they have a tendency to varicose veins, their veins stand out on their hands, and they give a history that the skin is difficult to heal after any injury. If they get varicose ulcers they are very slow to heal. They tend to have bluish-coloured stains on the backs of the hands. They are sensitive to cold, particularly cold and damp. They tend to be constipated and are liable to urinary infections. They look rather faded and dirty and they often have a sinking feeling in the abdomen, not associated with hunger, just an uncomfortable empty feeling. They are the kind of people that seem to need Sulphur. Yet mentally and physically they improve on Sarsaparilla.

Occasionally, younger patients with very severe dysmenorrhoea will be helped by Sarsaparilla. They have extreme pain in the back and the lower abdomen, extending down the thighs, which completely incapacitates them and which is associated with faintness, perspiring, vomiting and diarrhoea. With the dysmenorrhoea they tend to have very acute mammary sensitiveness, often one-sided; the left side is more commonly involved than the right. They also get a very distinctive headache. They have a sensation as if they had a tight band right round the head, from the occiput to the forehead. The headache is much worse from any pressure and is often associated with a feeling of fullness and possibly actual swelling of the bridge of the nose. These cases respond very well to Sarsaparilla.

That description will indicate the relationships of Sarsaparilla. Patients who need Sarsaparilla for acute conditions frequently have indications for Sulphur or Sepia. Patients with skin conditions need the Sulphur-Sarsaparilla follow-on. Dysmenorrhoea patients have their acute Sarsaparilla symptoms and very often, once the acute stage is over, there are indications for Sepia, which is the Sarsaparilla-Sepia follow-on.

The Psorinum picture is almost identical with that of Sarsaparilla, particularly in old people.

Sanicula

Sanicula is one of the most valuable remedies in the Materia Medica, and in a very large number of cases Silica is prescribed where Sanicula should be given. There are certain clear distinguishing points between Silica and Sanicula, and Sanicula seems to be rather wider in its action than Silica. Sanicula is more often needed for patients with skin eruptions than Silica.

The picture of Sanicula in children and in adults is rather different. In children the typical Sanicula make-up is one of intense irritability. They are very restless and active. They are intensely irritable, extremely obstinate, and they hate being handled. Patients requiring Sanicula are very similar in character to those who benefit from Chamomilla. Sanicula children have a very marked aggravation from downward motion. Chamomilla children enjoy being rocked and tossed about. Sanicula children shriek immediately they are moved downward. Chamomilla children hate to be left alone because they want attention; Sanicula children hate to be touched and resist it, and are also terrified in the dark. As a rule, Sanicula children want to be fed all the time, and yet they cannot digest what they eat. After being fed, they vomit almost immediately, no matter what food they have been given – milk, water, barley water – and immediately want to be fed again. They have a marked time of aggravation from about 9 p.m. until some time after midnight. Sanicula children are almost always constipated. They sometimes have an attack of diarrhoea, with the variation in the colour and consistency of the stool that is characteristic of Sanicula. Whether they are constipated or whether suffering from diarrhoea, there is always intense straining to stool.

With acute digestive upsets, Sanicula children tend to have a very dry mouth with painful, hot, ulcerated patches on the tongue, particularly on the under surface. This tendency to ulceration of the mouth may also occur in adults, and these ulcerated patches are acutely sensitive.

Sanicula children tend to perspire freely. The typical textbook description is that the children perspire about the back of their head, but actually they perspire on the part of the body they are lying on. If they are lying on their back, the back of their head perspires, but they also perspire all down the back. In adults, if they are lying in bed with their hands on the chest, the under surface of the arm where it is in contact with the chest is damp, or the side of the head and body that is lain on.

Sanicula patients tend to have unhealthy skins. The hands and feet perspire, the perspiration is often offensive, and yet in spite of the moisture they tend to have cracks on the backs of the hands, which bleed and are sensitive. They get eczema on the fingers, and tend to develop eczematous eruptions round the backs of the ears. All these eruptions have a similar discharge to that found in Graphites or Petroleum – a sticky, yellowish discharge which is offensive.

The perspiration of Sanicula is both offensive and excoriating. It makes their feet raw and rots their socks and sometimes even their shoes.

Although the extremities feel cold and clammy to touch, these children constantly put their feet out of bed at night. Their feet get very hot and burning, perspire and are extremely offensive.

As far as likes and dislikes are concerned, one thing that helps to distinguish between Sanicula and Silica children is that Sanicula children like ice-cold milk, and Silica children mostly dislike milk in any form. Sanicula also have a definite craving for salty things, bacon particularly, or actual salt.

These children often have sticky eye discharges and they have a very marked photophobia, often without any obvious eye lesion at all or with very little inflammatory disturbance in the eye. Linking up with the sticky eye discharge, they very often have a troublesome nasal discharge, a crusty nasal discharge, with a scabby, scaly eruption on the upper lip. They are very frightened of the dark.

Usually these children are under-nourished, underweight, very thin about the neck, and often have a distended abdomen. They tend to have enuresis. In other words, the 'pot-bellied' marasmic child is often a Sanicula child and not a Silica.

Adult Sanicula patients are more interesting. They are very like Silica. Their main complaint is of a feeling of complete exhaustion. They say that they feel so exhausted that the mere thought of work is impossible, they feel all they want to do is to lie down and go to sleep. With that feeling of exhaustion they are usually depressed, they have a sense of dread, a feeling of impending trouble, although it is not usually very definite. Another characteristic is that they have a marvellous faculty for misinterpreting what is being done for them.

They practically always suffer from headaches, and the Sanicula headaches are very typical. The pain usually starts in the back of the neck just below the occiput, and spreads right up over the head and settles in the forehead. The patients are acutely sensitive to any cold or draught; going out into the cold air will very often bring on the headache or, if already present, will make it very much worse. During the headache the pain is aggravated by any exertion, any motion, light or noise, and is usually associated with a certain amount of photophobia. Associated with the tiredness, one of the marked Sanicula characteristics is a pain in the lumbosacral region. It is a completely crippling pain and it has definite modalities. Patients are usually fairly free of pain in the morning after a night's rest, and it gradually develops during the day. While it is bad they feel completely exhausted and want to lie down. The pain is relieved by pressure and lying on the back. As the day advances, the pain tends to ease up and has usually disappeared by evening round about 6, 7 or 8 p.m.

Sanicula also have an arthritic condition of the shoulder joints, particularly marked on the right side. It is worthwhile linking this with the back condition, because while their back is bad any attempt to use their arms increases the pain; and while the shoulder region is involved it is completely impossible for the patient to put the arm behind his back. They are unable to put on their coat, and find it almost impossible to raise the arm up to the head. The pain is usually situated just in the top of the shoulder. Patients with shoulder pain who need Ferrum have practically the same modalities, except that they are eased by moving the arm gently, although they have the same limitation of movement. In Ferrum the pain is relieved by gentle motion; Sanicula are not relieved by motion at all.

These tired out patients have a very slow digestion. After a meal they do not want any more food for six or eight hours. If they eat anything sooner, they may vomit. Associated with their slow digestion is the most obstinate constipation. They are uncomfortable with it and feel that their bowels want to act, and there is intense straining. The stools are very small in size and usually hard. Alumina and Silica patients have a similar type of constipation – a great effort and very little result. The stool is usually in hard lumps.

Another useful point about Sanicula is that they tend to have a dry scaly eruption on the eyebrows. A similar condition is seen in Phosphorus. Remember that Sanicula are sensitive to cold and have a desire for salt. They have this general weariness and this scaly eruption on the eyebrows. All these symptoms are also found in Phosphorus, so that it is important to distinguish between them.

There are two other points. One is that Sanicula are very sensitive to motion. They get violent headaches and become sick from any journey, and they are particularly sensitive to the motion of going down in a lift.

The other point is that they tend to sleep very badly, with most distressing dreams. The dreams are of two types. One is a dream of burglars in the house. It is so vivid and real that they sometimes must get out of bed and go round the house to make sure that there is no one there before they can settle down and go to sleep again. The other is a dream of murder; either they themselves are being murdered, or they are committing murder.

One other mental characteristic Sanicula patients have, which is the same as in children, is a marked dislike of the dark, particularly of going out and walking in the dark. They are thoroughly scared, and have a feeling that there is someone behind them. They do not get this feeling during the day; only in the dark. Sepia have the same feeling, but in the daytime as well. Medorrhinum have it during the dark too, and also the dreams of robbers. But Sanicula only have it when out in the dark.

Chapter 13

Comparison of Lilium Tigrinum, Natrum Muriaticum and Sepia

In comparing Lilium Tig., Natrum Mur. and Sepia patients one notes various impressions as they come into the consulting room. It is a little difficult to place Lilium Tig. in appearance. The first thing to realise is that they are fairly compact and full-blooded, and the majority of them fair rather than dark. They are determined personalities, not soft and yielding, yet not taut like Natrum Mur., and different from the resentful attitude often present in Sepia. They tend to be fat rather than thin, and definitely hot-blooded. If they enter a hot room they loosen their coat immediately and prefer to keep away from any source of heat. They tend to be slightly cyanotic. Their lips are often quite dark in colour and usually pretty full.

The Natrum Mur. patient always strikes one as being a very definite character. The description in textbooks as being a thin patient is not true in many cases. Children are thin but adults are well-covered; women especially tend to be broad, but they are usually thin-necked, surprisingly so for their build. Their hair may be any colour from sandy to dark brown, not usually black. Their skin is always sallow, but very often when they come into the consulting room they are excited and flushed. This rather high colour masks the sallowness and may cause them to be confused with Phosphorus, who have a malar flush. Looking at them they appear quite intelligent, quite alive.

Their movements are fairly short, rapid and definite. It is an effort for them to consult a doctor. Their carotid pulsation will show that their pulse rate is accelerated, and their hands tremble. With this excitement there is a tendency for their skin to become rather oily – it only occurs under excitement or if the room is hot. If the patient has recently had a cold, almost certainly there will be a herpes about the lips. The textbooks state that Natrum Mur. patients are anaemic but quite a number have very red lips, and there is very often a crack in the lower or upper lip, about the centre.

Consider Sepia patients as a contrast. They may be fair or dark-haired, and are more often women than men. They come resentfully. There are two types – either the patient comes because she has been sent and resents it, or she resents being ill and having to talk about it. Usually she gives no pleasant word of greeting and as a rule enters with a sullen expression.

The next impression is the rather stupid expression, which may be caused by stupidity, tiredness or a slow-acting brain. It may be any of them. In contrast with Natrum Mur., the Sepia patient's face is often fatter than expected – quite often the person is thin in body, above average height, yet in spite of their thinness elsewhere, the face is fat. Their colour is a quite distinct sallow not seen in any other remedy. It is especially noticeable round the eyes and is a peculiar brownish pigmentation spreading out on to the nose and cheek bones. Possibly she will have a wart somewhere and almost always it is brownish in colour, especially after 40 years of age. The Sepia patient is generally pale and almost always has pale lips. The next thing to notice is the way they sit down in the chair. They sink into it. They are tired. Natrum Mur. sit on the edge of the chair and get annoyed if asked questions. The one is taut, the other relaxed. There is one point that suggests Natrum Mur. – the first appearance is of a very tidy and neat, trim patient, but on looking closer they are not nearly as tidy as they seem to be. Phosphorus is always scrupulously tidy and so is Arsenicum Alb., but not Natrum Mur.

MENTALITIES

Lilium Tig., Natrum Mur. and Sepia patients are all aggravated by consolation, but there are differences. The Lilium Tig. reaction to consolation is definitely bad-tempered. They have all sorts of strange ideas, that people are annoying them deliberately, and any sympathy or attempted explanation only increases their annoyance. The Natrum Mur. reaction to consolation is quite different, particularly when depressed. When they are ill and depressed and anyone consoles them they break down and weep. They do not display the same irritability as Lilium Tig. The Sepia aggravation from consolation is again quite distinct. They have a general resentment against their fate, think that they have had a poor deal in life and are tired out, and if consolation is given they will turn on the giver. They are physically worn out, depressed and weak, they develop a headache and if consoled start weeping. It is, however, different from Natrum Mur.; Natrum Mur. gets relief from weeping but Sepia is always worse if she has wept.

There are other differences. The main characteristic of Lilium Tig. is their irritability – it is almost impossible to please them. They are most exacting; they want everything to centre round themselves, and if it does not they fly into a rage. There is often a certain amount of fear associated with their complaints, and they are very likely to develop fear of insanity. They also have the idea that they have some undiagnosed disease, which they feel is always undiagnosed through lack of knowledge on the part of the physician who is looking after them, and they have a dread of it. With these bad tempers, after a spell where everyone has tried to please them, they go on to a religious phase of remorse. They become tearful, depressed and generally indifferent to their surroundings. With Lilium Tig. patients, the phrasing of the questions and the wording of the advice given must be carefully chosen, as they will take it as criticism of what they have done previously rather than as advice for the future. If there is a possibility of taking anything the wrong way they will always do so.

Contrast this with Natrum Mur. and there is a great difference. Natrum Mur. are either depressed or excited, never anything for long at a time, a weird mixture. There is an absolute lack of a sense of humour; they are often laughing and often weeping, but a pure sense of fun is simply lacking. They are also very difficult to get on with. They crave attention yet, if it is given, they are just about as disagreeable as they can be. They resent it if they do not get it, and are dissatisfied if they do. Impatience is a very marked characteristic. They want a thing done at once or not at all. They are very much upset by excitement and extraordinarily sensitive to noise, particularly to sudden noises. If anyone is in a room when a Natrum Mur. patient is reading, and fidgets or moves about, it makes them extremely irritable. They have a strange susceptibility to music. All Natrum salts have it, but especially Natrum Mur. They are sensitive to some types of music only, as they are not really musical, but are especially sensitive to sentimental music which they really enjoy, while serious music causes no reaction. They remember every slight they have ever had. If an explanation is given they forget the explanation and remember the original idea. They are excellent haters. They are most difficult people to live with, though often very pleasant to meet.

Almost the same terms are used in the textbooks with regard to Sepia, yet they are as different as night from day. Sepia has about as much excitement and intolerance to noise, yet the whole mentality is different. Sepia is a tired-out patient, nervously, mentally and physically. They do a good deal of weeping, but it is a sort of despairing weeping. They feel defeated and that they cannot go on, and sit down and weep. As a rule, any attempt to encourage them puts them into an obstinate and resentful mood, thinking they are martyrs and that people have not been fair to them. In this exhausted state they tend to become melancholy. They dislike to be spoken to or interfered with; they do not want anyone to help them out or to make them well. That is the characteristic Sepia mentality, but occasionally they may become more excitable if under stress, becoming apprehensive and developing illogical fears. Worries become exaggerated, and they fear that something dreadful is going to happen, or that they are becoming insane. If their husband is ill they dread disaster. They say that they have always been independent and now they are heading for charity. This is more the dread of dependency than of poverty. When they are tired out they become envious of people who are not having such a bad time, and they are very spiteful in their remarks about them.

GENERAL REACTIONS

In the general temperature reactions of these three remedies there is apparent similarity and a real difference. All three have intolerance of warm, stuffy rooms, but there the similarity ceases. Lilium Tig. have definite aggravation in heat, are much worse in a stuffy room and develop headaches and breathlessness from it. They are always better from moving about, particularly from moving about out of doors. The one exception to this amelioration from movement is when they are suffering from actual uterine prolapse. In all three remedies there is a marked tendency to symptoms of prolapse, even without actual uterine displacement. Natrum Mur. have aggravation in a warm room but are aggravated by both heat and cold. They do not stand heat well and are intolerant of the sun. On the other hand, they cannot stand draughts and are sensitive to extreme cold, and often suffer from cold and numb extremities.

Incidentally, Lilium Tig. patients have warm extremities and might be confused with Sulphur patients, especially as they also have the early morning 'Sulphur diarrhoea'. Sepia has a definite aggravation in a warm room, which causes faintness. They are liable to faint if standing or kneeling for too long. They do not stand cold well in any form, yet stuffiness upsets them. They often have cold damp extremities and often have an offensive foot sweat. They are very sensitive to weather, cold damp weather, or a change from cold to warm or from dry to wet. Natrum Mur. and Sepia have a definite aggravation from thunder, but Sepia have a desperate fear, much more marked than Natrum Mur. Lilium Tig. are better from walking about in the open air. Sepia are better if they exert themselves enough to warm them up. Natrum Mur., on the other hand, are aggravated by exercise which is strenuous enough to make them hot. There is one point which is very often a useful differentiating one – the mid-morning aggravation of Natrum Mur., which the other two remedies do not have. It is round about 10 to 11 a.m., when all their symptoms tend to be worse. Lilium Tig. patients have early morning aggravation; Sepia have a general morning aggravation. If Sepia have a good night's sleep they feel better, but after only a short sleep they almost certainly waken with a severe headache and feel as if they are going to die.

HEADACHE

Headaches are quite different in the three remedies. A typical Lilium Tig. headache is a frontal one with mental confusion. The patients say they feel half crazy. There is ocular disturbance, and if the headache is very severe they may develop an internal strabismus. The headache may extend down the back of the neck. One interesting point is that they often develop abdominal disturbance, especially pain in the right iliac fossa, associated with their headaches. Natrum Mur. headaches are very different. There are two types. In the first, the patient wakes up with slight headache in the morning and it increases all day. It is a very severe headache and is usually associated with the menstrual period, coming just before or just after. In the second type, the headache comes on during mid-morning, 10 to 11 a.m., and eases off about 4 p.m. This is a sun headache increasing and decreasing with the heat of the sun, at its maximum when the sun is strongest and disappearing about sunset. There is a certain amount of ocular disturbance associated with the Natrum Mur. headaches. The patients are exceedingly sensitive to light, their eyes become hot and tired, and smart with pain which increases from any attempt to use the eyes for close work, like reading or sewing.

The Sepia headache on the other hand usually starts in morning. If severe it tends to get worse till early in the evening, when the patient is likely to vomit. There is a feeling of intense congestion all over the head. One distinguishing feature between Natrum Mur. and Sepia headaches is that Sepia tend to be relieved by applied heat; not so Natrum Mur. Both are bad in a stuffy room. Also in Sepia the headache is relieved by hard pressure, and they often tie the head up tight. Both Natrum Mur. and Sepia are aggravated by jarring or any movement.

FOOD

Patients requiring any of these three remedies tend to be hungry. Lilium Tig. probably have the biggest appetites. Occasionally, there is complete loss of appetite in any of the remedies, but usually the patients have big appetites. Lilium Tig. remain hungry in spite of having had a good meal. Natrum Mur. are hungry but have no capacity, and are very soon satiated. Sepia have a feeling of emptiness which is not relieved by food; it is an artificial feeling of hunger. Lilium Tig. dislike coffee and sometimes bread, although by no means constantly, but they do have a very strong dislike for meat. Natrum Mur. have quite marked food idiosyncrasies. They like salt, often in excess, like all Natrums. They like bitter foods, such as beer, and often like fish very much, but have a definite aversion to fat food. Natrum Mur. often have an aggravation from sour wine, and dislike tobacco. Sepia have a definite intolerance for tobacco, it makes them sick; the smell of cooking also makes them feel sick. They have a definite dislike for meat and milk, and a liking for spicy foods. They have also a peculiar desire for vinegar and stimulants, possibly in order to stimulate a jaded appetite.

ABDOMINAL

Lilium Tig. is typical of the fat well-nourished abdominal neurasthenic, like a woman with a sensation as if everything in the abdomen were dragging down. This is so marked that she will very often apply support to the perineum because she feels everything is coming out. She feels as if the whole abdominal contents were dropping down. In spite of her relief from supporting the abdomen she has a peculiar sensitiveness to any pressure in the epigastrium, which makes her feel sick. The most common displacement in Lilium Tig. is an anteversion of the uterus;

associated with this there is a sensation of something pressing into the rectum and an urgent desire for the bowels to act. With the displacement there is a good deal of pelvic congestion and marked sexual excitement. The periods are scanty, commonly the flow stops when in bed and only starts again on getting up in the morning and moving about. Natrum Mur. patients do not have the severe dragging sensation. They have irregular periods which may last a day or may last a week, may be excessive or may be scanty, but are extremely variable. All complaints are aggravated at the period time, it may be during or after, but occasionally may be before. The most common form of disturbance is backache, especially in the morning, and getting better when the patient is up and moving about. They tend to develop general backache. This is generally aggravated by moving about and better from pressure, especially from lying down on something hard. Sepia patients have almost as much drag as Lilium Tig., but not so widely spread. They feel all their pelvic contents coming down, but not the whole abdominal contents. The typical Sepia patient is the kind of woman who has had half a dozen children, all close together, possibly with some pelvic infection. They may have any displacement, but the common one is a retroversion, though they may have a prolapse. Lilium Tig. patients feel as if there is a lump in the rectum, with tenesmus. In Sepia patients there is not much tenesmus, but they feel the bowel is full and they have a moist oozing from the anus. During the menstrual period they have a very acute sacral pain and they may get a certain amount of backache, but not so marked as in Natrum Mur. The ache is relieved by movement, and immediately they rest it recurs. It is relieved by pressure, but never by lying down on something hard, as in Natrum Mur. This is a differentiating point.

SEXUAL

There is one final point in which the three remedies show strongly marked differences, namely in their sexual relationships.

In Lilium Tig. there is marked sexual over-excitability, sometimes even to a pathological degree. In the other two remedies there is a definite aversion to sexual relationships. In Natrum Mur. this is commonly because sexual intercourse is often extremely painful, owing to the dry state of the vaginal mucous membranes, this dryness of the mucous membranes being a very general symptom in Natrum Mur. In Sepia there is a sexual coldness; they are tired out physically, they often have a dread of further pregnancy, and in many cases there is an aversion to the husband.

Chapter 14

The Use of Four Nosodes

Consider using a nosode in any illness, whether acute or chronic, where there are definite clear indications for a remedy, and where it does not produce the effect that is justifiably expected. Dealing with an acute case, in the normal way, if the improvement lasts a few hours the chosen remedy is repeated and is again effective. It is purely a question of spacing the doses. There are a certain number of cases in which repeated doses of the apparently indicated remedy do not give the expected effect – these are the ones which call for a nosode.

If the condition is sub-acute, and the clearly indicated remedy helps the patient for only ten days or so rather than the expected four to five weeks, that is nevertheless within the normal range of reaction. The remedy should be repeated either in the same or a higher potency. If instead of improving the symptoms for ten days it holds for a fortnight or a little longer, that is a perfectly satisfactory response. But if, on repeating in a higher potency, the effect of the remedy again only lasts a week or ten days and the patient's symptoms are returning, or becoming worse, a nosode is indicated. Similarly in a chronic case, if the effect of the remedy lasts two or three weeks, with the same sort of response to the repeated or higher potency, a nosode is required.

There are one or two other conditions which interfere with the action of the remedies and which shorten the effective length of action of the dose. In both acute and chronic cases the commonest cause is a hidden septic focus of some kind. In acute cases after an operation, where there may be the beginning of a stitch abscess or a deep-seated infected blood clot, the infection may interfere with the action of the remedy. This may occur in chest conditions where the patient is developing a small empyema, occasionally in ear infections where there is mastoid involvement or in a dental abscess.

It is necessary to eliminate the presence of a septic focus before prescribing a nosode, because a septic focus in either an acute or chronic case does interfere with the action of the remedy. In a chronic case there is also a possibility that the patient has been put on a remedy which is antidoted by one of the common foods. Quite a number of drugs are antidoted by coffee. These food aggravations are listed in the Repertory – if the indicated remedy is not in that list it can be ignored. If it is present in first or second type, the patient should be warned against taking the particular article of diet as long as he is on that remedy. (*Note.* First type in the Repertory is heavy black type and indicates a well proved reaction – second type is italic and indicates a less well proved reaction. Ed.)

The most difficult decision to make is which of the nosodes is required, and this depends to a large extent on the actual symptoms given by the patient. Unfortunately, there is a percentage of cases which do not give clear indications for any particular nosode.

If there are indications for one particular nosode, then there is no difficulty. Without clear indications, the choice lies between Psorinum, Tuberculinum, Medorrhinum and Syphilinum. That was entirely true until the bowel nosodes were introduced into homoeopathic practice. The kind of case likely to need a bowel nosode is one where there is a low grade toxaemia, chronic mild headaches, chronic mild digestive upsets, chronic fibrositis and occasionally disturbance of thyroid secretion. If such a case does not respond to treatment, it is advisable to have a series of stool examinations. An isolated stool examination is useless – the seat of maximum growth of these bowel organisms is in the small intestine, not the large intestine. It is necessary to use liquid material from the small intestine, or the culture will be negative. If there is no access to a laboratory, a polyvalent bowel nosode can be used.

In the majority of cases requiring a bowel nosode, indications for Sulphur have usually been present. Kali Carb. is the next most commonly indicated remedy where the expected reaction has not occurred and where a nosode may be needed. A bowel nosode may be required when indications for any Potassium salt have been present. The next most common remedies are the Silver salts, either Argentum Nit. or Argentum Met. After these, the cases in which bowel nosodes may be required are digestive ones giving indications for Lycopodium, Graphites, Anacardium or Chelidonium. In each case the expected improvement has not taken place and a nosode may be required.

Of the four nosodes first mentioned – Psorinum, Tuberculinum, Medorrhinum and Syphilinum – the commonest is Psorinum.

Psorinum

The main indication for Psorinum is the state of general sluggishness of the whole body. The patients have a very poor resistance to acute disease, and there has been a progressive decrease of vitality in the chronic case. They are always tired, have no energy, have a poor circulation, and are sensitive to cold. They have a poor skin reaction that is shown either in the form of a very unhealthy looking skin with a greasy surface, or a tendency to pimples, boils and skin eruptions of all kinds. Practically all Psorinum patients have what they describe either as hunger or emptiness. With some of them it is actual hunger, and with others it is just a feeling of emptiness and sinking in the abdomen. This describes the case where there are no characteristic Psorinum indications. These are the indefinite indications which are present in a patient who is giving no clear prescribing symptoms at all, and that is the kind of case for Psorinum. Naturally, the remedy which has already been prescribed in such cases is one indicated for patients with a lowered vitality, and the commonest is probably Sepia. Think of all the chilly drugs in which the patient has a lowered vitality – Sepia, Silica, Phosphorus, Phosphoric Acid, Lycopodium, Calcarea. Those are the types in which an intercurrent dose of Psorinum may be required.

Tuberculinum Bovinum

Probably the next most common nosode to be required is Tuberculinum. It is imperative to remember that the Tuberculinum temperature reaction is very definite. Tuberculinum patients are sensitive to extreme heat and particularly sensitive to any lack of oxygen in the atmosphere. They may be chilly in themselves.

Constant in all Tuberculinum patients is the fact that they are better from moving about. They may be very tired, but if they move about gently it does help them. They may get more tired after exertion, and any violent exertion that heats them up will certainly exhaust them, but gently moving about – no matter what their complaint – does ease them.

They also tend to lose weight, are mostly thin or at least underweight, and are over-sensitive to atmospheric changes.

Considering these indications, it is quite easy to see the type of remedy in which an intercurrent dose of Tuberculinum might be required. Any of the hot-blooded drugs might require it. For instance an acute Apis case very often needs a dose of Tuberculinum during convalescence; Argentum Nit. also quite frequently need intercurrent doses of Tuberculinum; the Baryta Mur. patient with repeated sore throats is another case. Often these throat infections can be stopped altogether with an intercurrent dose of Tuberculinum – it does not have the same effect on the Baryta Carb. who is a chilly patient. A certain number of patients who are Arsenicum Alb. but who do not have the Arsenicum Alb. chilliness, if given Arsenicum Iodide do very well indeed, up to a point; these Arsenicum Iodide patients mostly need a dose of Tuberculinum sooner or later. A Calcarea Carb. child, who has responded to the remedy and becomes less sensitive to cold, is very often improved by an intercurrent dose of Tuberculinum when he is not making any further progress. It is much more common in the Calc. Phos. child, who is thinner, and commoner still in the Calc. Sulph. child or adult, that an intercurrent dose of Tuberculinum is required. Not infrequently it is indicated in Lycopodium types and also in those requiring the Natrum salts, with the possible exception of Natrum Carb. Very frequently, indications for an intercurrent dose of Tuberculinum may occur in Sulphur and in Pulsatilla types.

There is one exception to the normal Tuberculinum temperature reaction. With a history of tuberculosis in the family – not in the individual patient – and where the patient is chilly, despite the chilliness they respond very well to an intercurrent dose of Tuberculinum, particularly in the Phosphorus or Silica type of patient.

In cases where Tuberculinum is used as an intercurrent remedy, after a single dose, prescribe the original remedy after an interval and the patient should progress for months. Tuberculinum has to be repeated more frequently than other remedies when prescribed as an indicated remedy on its particular indications. It has to be repeated in about three weeks. A certain number of patients with symptoms similar to those of Rhus Tox., but with temperature reactions altered, need Tuberculinum. However, the effect rarely lasts more than three weeks without a repetition.

Medorrhinum

There are two types of case in which to look for Medorrhinum indications. The first and commonest is the patient with a chronic catarrhal chest, whether with or without asthmatic attacks. The next commonest is the patient with fibrositis. In the majority of catarrhal chest conditions with Medorrhinum indications, the patients complain of chronic laryngeal irritation, either a laryngeal cough or a tendency to hoarseness or sensitiveness of the voice. In patients with indications for remedies like Natrum Sulph., Argentum Nit., Kali Sulph., Causticum or Sepia, in a chest condition – chronic bronchitis or bronchitis with asthma – a dose of Medorrhinum is almost always required sometime during the course of treatment. When dealing with a fibrositic or an arthritic condition in patients with indications for Apis, Calcarea, Ferrum, Fluoric Acid, Manganese, Phytolacca or Thuja, again look for Medorrhinum indications.

Syphilinum (Lueticum)

The last of the common nosodes is Syphilinum. There are certain types of cases with indications for Syphilinum, apart from a definite syphilitic history. But where there is a syphilitic history, particularly in the parents of the patient, it is more than probable that a dose of Syphilinum will be needed in the course of treatment. Where there is a syphilitic history in the patient himself, with the story that the syphilis has been effectively treated and he now has a negative Wassermann, Syphilinum is also very likely to be required.

In some patients there may be indications for Syphilinum apart from an actual history of syphilis. The commonest is a catarrhal condition of the upper respiratory passages, chronic nasal catarrh, particularly where the catarrh tends to produce an atrophic condition of the mucous membrane, with a certain amount of bleeding – the patient who says he gets a crusty condition of the nose. It is a case which is very obstinate to treat, but there is a response to a dose of Syphilinum quite apart from a syphilitic history. Occasionally a dose of Syphilinum sets up a reaction and improvement in a granular pharyngitis which is not responding to treatment.

The next most common case is recurring iritis, not necessarily syphilitic, which often responds well to Syphilinum.

Indications for Syphilinum may occur in arthritic cases, such as rheumatoid arthritis. In these rheumatic cases there is a guide to prescribing from the remedy which the patient has been on previously. Syphilinum often helps in an arthritic patient who has been requiring Arsenicum Alb. and any of the Aurum salts, Aurum Met., Aurum Chlor. or Aurum Sulphide; any of these patients may give indications for Syphilinum. All the Kali salts – Kali Bich., Kali Ars. and, more than any other possibly, Kali Sulph. – in rheumatic conditions often give indications for Syphilinum. There may also be indications for Syphilinum where any of the Mercurius preparations have been used. It may be needed in a case that has had benefit from Nitric Acid. Rheumatic cases that have responded to Phytolacca very often progress to Mercurius and then on to Syphilinum. Sometimes it may benefit typical Silica patients – Silica arthritics – who have had some improvement which has not persisted, and after an intercurrent dose of Syphilinum they will continue to make progress.

Some ulcers of the legs that have the typical appearance of Carbo Veg., the sluggish, atrophic ulcers, respond to Syphilinum although there is no syphilitic history. A certain number of these ulcers also respond to Tuberculinum or Psorinum.

The improvement following a nosode usually lasts for 2–3 weeks. If there are definite indications for one particular nosode, it may be given in a high potency, otherwise it is best to use a 30c.

Remedy Index

THE TRUE HEALING ART

List of Pharmacies and Companies in the United States and Canada that Can Supply Homeopathic Remedies

(Courtesy of the National Center for Homeopathy, Falls Church, Virginia 22042)

CALIFORNIA

City Pharmacy
1435 State Street
Santa Barbara, CA 93101

College Pharmacy
90 N. Ashwood Avenue
Ventura, CA 93003

Horton and Converse
621 West Pico Boulevard
Los Angeles, CA 90015

Mylans Homeopathic Pharmacy
222 O'Farrell Street
San Francisco, CA 94102

Nutri-Dyn
717 S. Bristol Ave.
Los Angeles, CA 90049

Santa Monica Drug
1513 Fourth Street
Santa Monica, CA 90401

Standard Homeopathic
Company
436 West 8th Avenue
Los Angeles, CA 90014

Village Drug Store
Ojai, CA 93023

ILLINOIS

Ehrhart and Karl
17 N. Wabash Ave.
Chicago, IL 60602

MARYLAND

Washington Homeopathic
Pharmacy
4914 Delray Avenue
Bethesda, MD 20014

MISSOURI

Luyties Pharmacal Company
4200 Laclede Avenue
St. Louis, MO 63108

NEW JERSEY

Humphreys Pharmacal Company
63 Meadow Road
Rutherford, NJ 07070

NEW YORK

Keihl Pharmacy, Inc.
109 Third Avenue
New York, NY 10003

Weleda, Inc.
841 South Main Street
Spring Valley, NY 10977

PENNSYLVANIA

Boericke and Tafel, Inc.
1011 Arch Street
Philadelphia, PA 19107

John A. Borneman and Sons
1208 Amosland Road
Norwood, PA 19074

VIRGINIA

Annandale Apothecary
7023 Little River Turnpike
Annandale, VA 22003

CANADA

D. L. Thompson Homeopathic
    Supplies
844 Yonge Street
Toronto 5, Ontario
Canada M4W 2H1